Adolescents

Second Edition

ADOLESCENTS

DEVELOPMENT
AND RELATIONSHIPS

Mollie S. Smart, Russell C. Smart,
and Laura S. Smart

Macmillan Publishing Co., Inc.
NEW YORK

Collier Macmillan Publishers
LONDON

Macmillan Publishing Co., Inc.
866 Third Avenue, New York, New York 10022

Collier Macmillan Canada, Ltd.

Library of Congress Cataloging in Publication Data

Smart, Mollie Stevens, comp.
  Adolescents.

  Based on Children: development and relation-
ships, 3d ed., 1977, by M. S. Smart and R. C. Smart,
and Readings in child development and relationships,
1977, by R. C. Smart and M. S. Smart.
  Includes bibliographies and indexes.
  1. Adolescence — Addresses, essays, lectures.
I. Smart, Russell Cook, joint comp. II. Smart,
Laura S., joint comp. III. Title.
HQ796.S52 1978   301.43'15   77–5504
ISBN 0–02–412120–7

Printing: 1 2 3 4 5 6 7 8   Year: 8 9 0 1 2 3 4

Contents

Introduction

Key concepts in understanding development during adolescence are "identity" and "formal thinking." In Erikson's description of healthy personality development, the establishment of a sense of identity is the crucial task of adolescence. Piaget says that most adolescents achieve the adult form of cognition, formal thought. Both men point out that the development during the teen years is built on development that has occurred previously, and is in turn the base for further growth.

The changes in physical structure that occur during puberty are great. Size increases rapidly while proportions change. Sexual organs take on adult size and function. These physical changes are described in Chapter 1, as are developments in motor skills and special health problems of adolescence. An adolescent has to come to terms with bodily changes, realizing that although he looks and feels different, he is still the same person and will continue to have an identity that will stay the same even as it changes. Readings by other authors included in Chapter 1 include a description of changes in human posture, a report of a study of the effect of endurance training by male adolescents on their self-concepts, and a discussion of the effects of early and late puberty on adolescents' personalities. The text part of this chapter (and of all five chapters in this book) is from the third edition of our book *Children: Development and Relationships;* the readings are from the second edition of our *Readings in Child Development and Relationships.*

Chapter 2 describes and discusses intellectual development during adolescence, particularly the attainment of formal thought, and the ramifications of formal thought on other aspects of intellectual behavior. Formal thinking operates at a more abstract level than school-age concrete operations, but even those individuals who have acquired formal thinking do not use it all the time. Even adults use concrete operations in their thinking under some circumstances. Some adolescents and adults operate at the concrete level most of the time. But to the extent that formal thinking is achieved, adolescents think about their thinking, think about how things might be, and struggle with the problems of identity that follow from this more powerful kind of cognition. As thinking becomes more complex, so does language because the two processes are intimately connected. The family, the school, the culture in which the adolescent lives all effect both kinds of development. The greater flexibility of thinking leads to greater expressions of creativity. The articles by other authors in Chapter 2 include: a study of the relationship of family size and sibling position on achievement test results; a study of age changes in self-description that reflect differences in thinking between the stage of concrete operations and the stage of formal thought; and a study of the factors that influence individual differences in the attainment of the concept of horizontality.

During the school years children's peers become increasingly important influences on their behavior and attitudes. To the extent that the parents' values are different from the peers', adolescents have to choose between the two sets of values. Friendship with peers of both sexes provides the area in which adolescents move toward establishing bonds of varying strength and varying permanence with members of their own generation. The adolescent's growing sense of identity influences this bonding, which is a kind of intimacy. Because of changing cultural standards, intimacy may include sexual intimacy before marriage, or marriage between adolescents. These topics are discussed in Chapter 3. One of the readings in this chapter is an excerpt from Erikson on the development of the sense of identity in adolescence. The second reading describes the social structure of a high school and the individuals to whom males in the four observed groups go for help and counsel. The third article deals with adolescent rebellion in relation to certain characteristics of the parental marriage.

As an adolescent achieves a sense of identity and a concept of herself with a past, present, and future, involved in a variety of groups and institutions, she becomes committed to the continuation of certain values and ideals that she shares with other people. She accepts responsibility for herself, she cares for other people, she strives for achievement in one field or many. She prepares herself to take her place among workers and may begin to do so part time or for short periods of time. Part of the identification with groups and institutions is the adoption of a set of moral and ethical codes, but moral development is also influenced by the increasing flexibility of thinking. Chapter 4 contains this subject matter, dealing with the adolescent's growing control of her own life. There are two readings by other authors in this chapter. The first deals with the development of behavior and attitudes toward law. The second reports a study that replicated in Israel a United States study dealing with the predictors of achievement and intelligence in high school students.

Chapter 5 is philosophical and theoretical. It is concerned with life and development of human beings and deals with topics that apply to all age levels. We urge the teacher to consider assigning the last chapter first. Some teachers prefer to start the course with the adolescent, while others like to lay a theoretical groundwork first. One of the readings in this chapter is by Erikson and one is by Piaget. The one by Erikson in this chapter is more general than the one in Chapter 3. Because the theories of these two men form the basic framework of the text, we include these short excerpts so that students of child development will have read at least a little of these great men's writings.

Suggestions to the Student

The first part of each chapter, which is from our textbook *Children,* Third Edition, gives basic subject matter. We show you by means of the headings what we think most important. When you are taking notes, we suggest that you use our headings as a framework. Put under them, in your own words, what the section says to you.

The articles in each chapter elaborate on something mentioned much more briefly in the chapter, or they may lay a background for the chapter. You will need to adapt your note taking to the style of the article. Reviews of research and statements of theoretical positions require about the same kinds of notes. There are usually not a great many main points, although some of them may have subsidiary points made in connection with them. Often these points are reiterated in a summary that may come at the beginning or the end of the selection. If there is no summary, the author may have omitted it because he thought he made his points so clearly that they would not be missed. In any case, assume the author had a message and ask yourself, "What does the author want me to learn? Why does he think it important? What evidence does he present for accepting the truth of his statements?"

The selections that are research reports are more specialized kinds of writing and therefore require a different kind or form of note taking. Here is an outline that we have developed over our years of teaching. Students have found it helpful.

HOW TO MAKE AN ABSTRACT OF RESEARCH ARTICLES

Author, Name of. The complete title of the article, as stated in the journal. Name of journal, year, volume, inclusive pages. (Month). For the selections in this book add the bibliographic reference for this book also, in the same form. Note that so far you have been copying, exercising your writing muscles. You should not do much more copying.

Purpose. State the purpose in the author's words if he has not been too verbose. Do you see why copying may be a good idea here? But make an active decision to copy. Do not just keep on writing.

Subjects. Name, ages, sex, socioeconomic status, hereditary factors, environmental factors, all the important identifying material that the author gives. Put it in tabular form if possible.

Apparatus and Procedure. A brief description of any special apparatus, tests, or techniques. If a standard test is used, be sure to mention any deviations from the usual method of presentation or scoring. If the length of time the test continued or the number of determinations is important, be sure to include these facts.

Results. What the investigator found, in terms of scores, and so on. Put these in tabular form also if you can. Keep in mind that you are writing a summary, but do not leave out any important items. Also remember that you usually make abstracts for use over a long period of time, and that later you may want to know the results of this study for a purpose different from your present one.

Conclusions. How the author interprets his findings. Does he think his hypothesis is substantiated? What does he think is the "next step?" Does he tie his results into the main body of knowledge in his field?

Remarks. This is the place, and the *only* place, for you to say what you think. Is it a good study? Are there any points on which you disagree? Can you offer any interpretations other than those given by the author? What are the theoretical implications? Are there implications for practice? What further studies does this one suggest to you?

The following questions are some of the points you should investigate under each of the major headings. All of them, of course, are not applicable to any one study, and there may be others in some instances. A beginning student will not have the background for answering all of them.

Purpose. Does the author state the purpose clearly? Allowing for personal enthusiasms, was the purpose worthwhile?

Subjects. Is the number adequate? Is the sample clearly described as to age, sex, SE status, education, race, and so on? Remember that in different studies different things are important. The two criteria here are whether the sampling is good and whether the sample is reproducible. That is, if you wanted to check the experiment, has the author given you enough information so that you could reproduce the group in all important characteristics?

Apparatus and Procedure. As far as you can tell, did the investigator set up his procedure so that his results are not biased by it? Are factors controlled that might invalidate the results? Is there a better way of testing the same hypothesis? If statistics were used, are they adequate? Why did the investigator use the ones he did? If statistics were not used, why did he handle the data as he did? Do you approve of his methods? Why?

Results. Are the results clearly stated? Are sufficient raw data given so that someone else could rework them? Would the results be different if better methods of handling the data had been used? What effect does the sampling have on the results? Do you know of any other studies that bear on this one, either substantiating it or contradicting it?

Conclusions. Do the author's conclusions follow from the results he has stated? Do they bear any relation to his stated purpose? Do the conclusions as stated take into account any limitations in the sampling or method?

This is not the only way of keeping track of research articles. This outline, however, is as exhaustive as most people will need for ordinary purposes. Only occasionally, when you are engaged in writing a minute analysis of the literature on one topic, will you want to keep a more inclusive record of the details in an article. More often you will want to record less material than this outline requires. It is a lot of work to make a complete abstract, but when you have done it, your thinking becomes clearer and your files are that much more well stocked. Complete abstracts should not be neglected.

A VERY SHORT COURSE IN STATISTICS

Many students who read this book will not have had a course in statistics. Usually the authors of research articles interpret the statistics they use and state the conclusions that follow from them. But because you should not get into the lazy habit of skipping over them, we include this section in order to help you to understand some of the important kinds of statistics. When you come across a statistic (correlation, for instance), refer back to this section. Some that are used only occasionally, like the sign test and the Mann-Whitney test, are not described here. A text on statistics will explain these.

Averages or Measures of Central Tendency. What a nonstatistician calls the average, a statistician calls the *mean* or the *arithmetic mean*. The average (mean) cost of your textbooks for this semester is the sum of what you paid for all the books divided by the number of books. A mean is a number that, mathematically, is most representative of a series of similar numbers.

Another kind of average is the *median*. A median is the middle number when a series of numbers is arranged from small to large. There are two conditions under which it is used. The median is used when some of the numbers are much larger or smaller than the others. If you were able to get four used textbooks for $4, $4.75, $5, and $7, but had to spend $15 for a new edition, the mean cost would be $7.15. The median cost of $5 is more representative of the series of numbers. The median is also used when the unit of measurement is not divisible into smaller units. The mean number of children per family is an incorrect use of the mean, although it is sometimes reported, because there can be no such thing as a fractional child, and means rarely come out as integers. Since a median can be an integer, the average number of children per family should always be stated as a median.

The *mode* and the *harmonic mean* are occasionally used as a measure of central tendency. A statistics textbook will explain them.

Tests of Significance. In most research two or more groups are compared with each other. The important question is, "Are the differences due to chance, or to a real difference in condition or treatment of the groups?" The researcher sets up the hypothesis (called the null hypothesis) that there is no true difference. He applies an appropriate statistical test, on the basis of which he decides to accept or reject the null hypothesis. He would accept the null hypothesis that there is no significant difference if the test showed that a difference as large as the one discovered could have arisen by chance. If the test showed that the difference could have arisen by chance less than five times out of 100 repetitions of the study, he rejects the null hypothesis and concludes there *is* a true, or significant, difference. The statistical notation for such a statement is $p < .05$, which is read, "the probability is less than five in 100." Occasionally a more stringent test of significance is used, which is written $p < .01$. This means that the result could be obtained by chance less than 1 per cent of the time. Note that a statistician does not say a difference could *never* occur by chance, but the probability of its occurring by chance is so many in 100.

There are many different kinds of tests of significance, depending on the kind of data being used. Some of the more usual are χ^2 (chi-squared), the *t* test, and the F test of analysis of variance. Always a test of significance gives the basis for deciding whether the difference could have arisen by chance.

The *t* test and analysis of variance (ANOVA) are statistical tests that are similar: In the *t* test two conditions or situations can be compared; in a one-way ANOVA more than two (high, moderate, and no nutritional supplement, for instance) can be compared. A two-way ANOVA makes it possible to compare the effects of two variables (nutritional supplement and sex of subject) and also determine the effect of the interaction between the variables. In such a study, there would be boys and girls in the three nutritional supplement groups. All of them would be measured for height at the beginning of the period of nutritional supplement and again at the end. The gains of all the children, both boys and girls, in each of the nutritional supplement groups would be compared; this would be a one-way ANOVA. Similarly, the gains of all the girls, regardless of level of supplement, would be compared with all the boys' gains, another one-way. The analysis of variance is two-way, because it is possible, also, to find out if there is an interaction between nutritional supplement and sex of subject—do high-level boys react differently from high-level girls *and* from moderate-level and no-level boys. Because there are computers to do the immense number of calculations, there are three-variable and even four-variable ANOVAs reported in the literature, although they are rare, for very large numbers of subjects are necessary in order to make the subgroups big enough.

Correlation. A coefficient of correlation measures the degree to which two measures (height and weight, for instance) vary together — positive correlation if one measure gets bigger as the second one does, and negative correlation if one gets smaller as the other one gets bigger. Zero correlation means that there is no relationship between the two. Note carefully that correlation coefficients do not say anything about causation. Heights and weights are positively correlated, but a person's weight does not cause her height, nor does her height cause her weight.

Coefficients of correlation range in size between +1.00 and −1.00. If the coefficient is .00, there is no relationship between the two measures. The closer it is to 1.00, either positive or negative, the closer is the relationship. If there was discovered to be a correlation of +1.00 between height and weight in a group of children, the tallest child would be the heaviest, the second tallest would be second heaviest, and so on to the shortest, the lightest. If you knew the height of one of these children in relation to the others, you could place him exactly in weight in relation to the others. If a correlation coefficient is −1.00, the relationship is perfectly inverse. Suppose the coefficient between reading and arithmetic scores is .00 or not significantly different from .00. The best prediction of any child's reading test score, knowing what his arithmetic test score is, would be the mean reading score of the group of children. Such a prediction would not be very helpful, unless the score in arithmetic (the independent variable) is itself close to the mean.

Most often the correlation coefficient reported is the Pearson product-moment coefficient (r). Another one often used is the rank-order coefficient (rho, or ρ).

Factor Analysis. As noted above, correlation coefficients are measures of the degree to which pairs of scores vary together. Therefore a set of coefficients can be used to obtain an indication of the *factors* underlying the co-variation of the scores. The method is called *factor analysis*. Although factor analysis was invented before there were computers, the number of calculations involved in the method prevented its wide use. If there are 50 variables to be correlated with each other, 1225 correlation coefficients are necessary, and each coefficient involves several arithmetic calculations. Then many more calculations must be made on those coefficients in order to measure the factors. These kinds of repetitive calculations are what a modern computer does very well. More factor analyses are reported in the research journals now than were reported even five years ago.

A factor analysis yields from two up to nine or ten factors. Each variable (test) in the analysis has a loading on each factor. Loadings range from .00 up to .99. A loading not significantly different from zero means that that factor does not contribute anything to that test. The bigger the loading, the more important is that factor in influencing the variability of the test scores. When several tests or measures all have large loadings on a factor, there is evidence that all of them share something in common. The investigator then sets about naming the factor, by considering what it is that all members of the group have in common, and that the rest of the tests have not at all or in only small amounts. Unlike the calculation of correlation coefficients and factor loadings, the naming of the factors is not precise, since judgments have to be made about what the members of each subset share. Often, perhaps usually, the naming of the factors is obvious when the reader of the research considers what the original measures are. But sometimes an investigator has not considered all the possibilities of the meanings of the factors the computer has extracted from his data.

Chapter 1
Physical Growth, Health, and Coordination

A child changes into an adult during *adolescence,* a period lasting from about 11 to about 18 years of age. The changes that take place during adolescence include not only physical events but also psychological and social ones.

Growth

The child's body is transformed into an adult's through an almost invariable sequence of events. A person familiar with pubescent growth could tell from a physical examination what change could be expected next and how far the youngster had progressed toward maturity.

BODILY CHANGES DURING PUBERTY

Puberty is the period of time during which a child becomes a person capable of producing offspring. During puberty there is a series of physical changes under the control of endocrine substances whose production is triggered in the first place by changes in the hypothalamus. *Adolescence* is a period of time that begins when puberty begins, but adolescence continues longer in most cultures, certainly in the North American culture. Adolescence includes puberty, but also has to do with changes in the roles and attitudes that are part of the culture in which the individual lives. The normal range for the length of puberty is between 18 months and six years.

The following list of changes in boys and girls shows the normal sequences for development during puberty [28, 29]. Note that the age of most rapid growth comes not at the very end of puberty but before *menarche* (first menstruation) for girls and toward the end of the period for boys.

Because of its position in the sequences of changes during puberty, the peak of height velocity, or the maximum yearly increment in height, is often used as a criterion of sexual maturity. It is difficult to pinpoint the achievement of sexual maturity, the capacity for reproduction. Menarche is often assumed to be the time when a girl becomes able to have babies, but a sterile period of a year or more probably occurs in most girls after their first menstruation. Menarche is usually considered the point of sexual maturity, however, since it is a definite event that is easy to remember. There is no corresponding definite event for boys, although a criterion sometimes used is the production of spermatozoa. In research studies on growth in adolescence, the growth events in the sequence of puberty are often used, rather than one point such as menarche.

The range of median ages for menarche in a variety of populations throughout the world is large, from 12.4 to 18.8 years [20]. There is no evidence that menarche is directly affected by warmth of climate; both early maturers and late maturers live in hot climates. Five African groups' medians were reported in this study; they were all late in reaching menarche, with Afro-Cubans being the earliest. The three earliest median menarches were those of a black, a white, and a Chinese group. Genetic influences on menarche can be seen, however, by noting the degrees of similarity in menarcheal age between women of varying degrees of relationship. The average difference in menarcheal age between identical twins is 2.8 months,

Girls	Boys
Initial enlargement of breasts.	Beginning growth of scrotum and testes.
Straight, pigmented pubic hair.	Beginning growth of penis.
	Straight, pigmented pubic hair.
	Pubic hair darker, coarser, more curled.
Peak height velocity.	Peak height velocity.
Further enlargement of breasts.	Pubic hair adult in type, but limited in area.
Pubic hair darker, coarse, more curled.	Genitalia adult in size and shape.
Pubic hair adult in type, but limited in area.	Pubic hair adult in quantity and type, but no hair above base of inverse triangle.
Projection of areolae and papillae beyond level of breasts.	
Menarche.	Voice change.
Axillary hair.	
Pubic hair adult in quantity and type.	

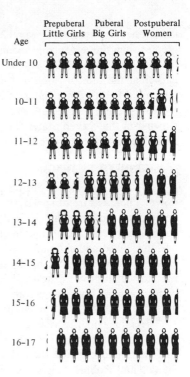

Figure 1-1. Pictogram showing proportion of girls at each age in each stage of sexual development.

SOURCE: B. MacMahon. *Age at menarche.* National Center for Health Statistics. Data from the National Health Survey. Series 11. No. 133. DHEW Publication No. (HRA) 74–1615. Washington, D.C.: U.S. Government Printing Office, 1973.

between fraternal twins it is 12.0, between sisters 12.9 months, and between un-related women it is 18.6 months. Socioeconomic status, expressed through nutrition and other influences on growth, is definitely related to menarche, as is shown in connection with nutrition (see page 18).

The National Health Survey studies of children 6 through 11, and of youths 12 through 17 were done between 1963 and 1965 and 1966 to 1970. Questionaires filled out by the parents gave information as to whether the girl had begun to menstruate. From the percentages of girls at each age from 11 to 14 who had reached menarche, MacMahon [27] has calculated the median age of menarche for girls in the United States. The figure is 12.80 years for white girls and 12.52 years for blacks. The earlier menarche for blacks holds true for all categories of family income, size of place of residence, and in all geographic regions except the South. Figure 1-1 shows the progression from girlhood to womanhood of American girls between 10 and 16 during the late 1960s.

Secular Trend in Puberty. Size increases over time were discussed on pages 348–349. Not only are children growing bigger, but they are maturing earlier in the more prosperous parts of the world [45]. Around 1900, men reached their full height at about 26 years of age, but now Europeans and Americans are full grown at 18 or 19 [45]. Puberty is occurring earlier in children living in the most favorable circumstances, as can be seen in records of age of menarche from several countries. In a recent American sample of white mothers and daughters, the mean age at menarche for daughters was 12.88, for mothers 14.38 [13]. This difference is greater than the advance in menarcheal age usually seen in one generation. During the past century, girls in Western European countries have been reaching menarche earlier at the rate of three to four months per decade. Thus, puberty takes place two and a half to three and a half years earlier today than it did a century ago [45]. However, there is some evidence that the rate of decline in the age of menarche is slowing in the United States for girls with histories of good nutrition and pediatric care. There appears to be a limit to the amount that maturing can be speeded up.

GROWTH IN HEIGHT

Growth speeds up during puberty, reaching a maximum and then slowing down. The measure of speed is *velocity,* the distance covered per unit of time. The velocity of growth in height is the number of centimeters grown during a year, or some other period. During late childhood the velocity of growth is steady for three or four, or sometimes more, years, having declined from a very high velocity in infancy. Then, triggered by changes in endocrine secretions to be described later, the individual grows faster and faster for a few years to a maximum velocity, after which growth slows down rather abruptly. When the velocity reaches zero in late adolescence, the individual stops growing. Adult height has been reached.

Height gain per year can be charted against age, as has been done in Figure 1-2 for two hypothetical individuals, Dana and Robin, both of whom were 117 centimeters tall on their sixth birthdays. The upper part of Figure 1-2 shows Dana's and Robin's heights on their birthdays each year. Starting out at six years they were equal in height. Although both of them grew taller each year, by their twelfth birthdays Dana was 7.8 centimeters taller than Robin; the next year Dana was 6.7 centimeters taller; when they had both reached their adult height, Dana was 11.6 centimeters shorter. The lower part of Figure 1-2 shows the amounts each child grew during each year; the points are placed midway between the birthdays. (Note that the vertical scale of the lower chart is ten times bigger than the upper height scale.) Each year between 6 and 10 Dana grew only slightly more than Robin, the biggest difference in gain being .5 centimeter. But between 11 and 12 Dana grew 8.4 centimeters while Robin grew only 4.6 centimeters. From their twelfth birthdays on Robin grew more than Dana, the biggest difference being between their fifteenth and sixteenth birthdays, when Robin grew 5.2 centimeters and Dana had stopped growing.

Although everybody expects a youngster to spurt in height, the spurt is still an amazing and often mysterious phenomenon to family, friends, and most of all the person experiencing it. It is amazing because the middle years of childhood are so stable and uneventful from the standpoint of growth. Then suddenly, velocity picks up and the child seems to grow overnight. (The average white boy grows 16.4 centimeters between ages 13 and 15½; the average white girl, 7.1 centimeters between 11 and 13½.) Families often discuss and wonder about the spurting child's eventual height, how long he will grow so fast and when he will stop. The factors behind each child's peculiar style of growth are so complex and interwoven that parents have little success in this prediction.

The taller the child, the taller he can expect to be as an adult. At each age from infancy to the onset of puberty, height correlates increasingly with adult

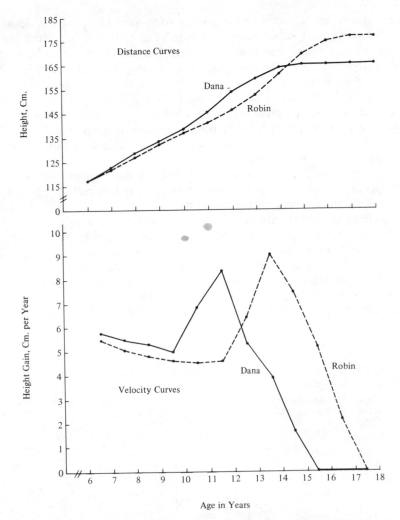

Figure 1-2. Two hypothetical growth records. The upper curve shows Dana's and Robin's height on successive birthdays (distance curves). The lower curves show the amounts Dana and Robin grew in the year between their birthdays (velocity curves).

height. Mary Jane, at age 7, is tall for her age, while Felecia, at 7, is short. The chances are that Mary Jane will grow to above average height for women, but Felecia will be petite; however, it is not a certainty.

The wide normal range in the age at which puberty is reached means that children vary widely in when they begin the growth spurt, when they reach the peak, and when they finish. Josh and Bill, the same height at age 13, will be inches apart as adults because Josh has been rapidly increasing in height for the past year, while Bill has not grown noticeably. Josh will soon shoot ahead of Bill, but Bill will eventually overtake him.

The velocity and duration of the growth spurt vary from one individual to another. When the spurt occurs early, it tends to be more intense but to last over a shorter period than when it occurs at a later age. Early maturers tend to be shorter than late maturers because the longer duration of the growth period in late maturers more than makes up for the brief advantage that more intense velocity gives to the early maturers. This factor accounts for most of the difference in height between men and women. Men have a longer time in which to grow.

Linear people, as contrasted with people of rounded shape, tend to be late maturers. Only a small part of their linearity is a result of their late maturing, which allows a greater time for growth of the legs than the early maturer has. From the age of 2, people who will mature late weigh less for their height than do those who will mature early. Figure 1-3 shows the weight per centimeter of height for early-, average-, and late-maturing boys and girls.

Because of the wide variation in both height and weight during adolescence, percentile tables are not so useful at this time as they are earlier for assessing an individual child's status. However, for their value in showing how height and weight are distributed during the teen years, height and weight percentiles (Tables 1-1 and 1-2) are included here. These figures were calculated from the data of the National Health Survey conducted between 1966 and 1970. The data are for a carefully chosen sample representing all United States adolescents.

Figure 1-3. Weight per centimeter of height for boys and girls who mature early, late, and at the average time.

SOURCE: Reprinted by permission from J. M. Tanner. *Growth at adolescence,* 2nd ed. Oxford: Blackwell Scientific Publications Ltd., 1962. Copyright © 1962, Blackwell Scientific Publications Ltd.

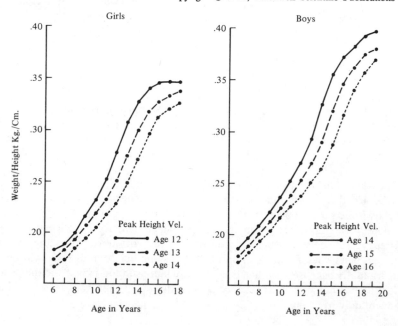

Table 1-1. Percentile Distribution of Heights of Males and Females From Age 12 Through Age 17, by Race: United States 1966–70.

Race, Sex, and Age	Percentile in Centimeters						
	5	10	25	50	75	90	95
Black							
Female							
12 years	145.6	149.0	153.1	150.0	159.8	167.7	170.0
13 years	149.2	150.1	153.8	158.8	163.2	168.4	169.7
14 years	148.1	148.7	154.5	159.6	165.1	168.3	169.1
15 years	150.6	153.4	157.5	162.3	165.4	170.2	173.4
16 years	153.4	155.4	158.7	163.1	166.1	170.1	170.6
17 years	154.1	155.0	159.2	163.1	168.2	174.0	174.6
Male							
12 years	141.3	142.8	146.2	150.3	153.9	159.8	161.8
13 years	138.5	144.2	150.5	156.5	163.4	167.4	170.6
14 years	150.4	151.4	153.7	163.8	167.5	174.8	178.4
15 years	155.2	156.4	163.0	168.1	173.4	179.4	190.0
16 years	157.4	162.1	166.4	174.2	178.3	180.2	181.6
17 years	163.2	165.3	169.2	173.6	177.6	182.6	183.6
White							
Female							
12 years	140.8	145.3	149.5	152.8	156.2	159.4	167.2
13 years	144.5	147.0	152.1	156.9	161.5	166.4	167.9
14 years	149.3	151.8	156.5	160.7	164.5	167.8	170.1
15 years	152.3	154.5	157.4	161.6	166.8	169.6	171.8
16 years	150.8	153.5	157.7	162.5	166.8	170.1	172.5
17 years	151.6	155.0	158.8	163.7	166.8	171.5	173.5
Male							
12 years	138.1	138.7	144.6	150.2	156.4	161.7	165.5
13 years	142.0	145.5	149.8	155.5	160.7	166.5	170.1
14 years	148.6	152.2	157.6	163.5	170.2	174.3	177.4
15 years	156.1	159.3	164.1	170.3	175.3	179.2	181.8
16 years	162.1	169.8	169.7	173.8	177.7	181.1	184.2
17 years	163.3	166.4	170.6	176.1	180.0	184.2	186.6

SOURCE: P. V. V. Hamill, F. E. Johnston, and S. E. Lemeshow. Body weight, stature, and sitting height: White and Negro youths 12–17 years. Vital and Health Statistics. Data from the National Health Survey. Series 11. No. 126. Washington, D.C.: U.S. Government Printing Office, 1973.

We suggest that the reader use the height measurements on Dana and Robin in Figure 1-2 in conjunction with the percentiles of Table 1-1. Suppose first that Dana is a girl either white or black. What are her approximate percentiles for height at each birthday? Suppose Robin is a boy. How does he rank with other boys each year? Next compare Dana's measurements with the boys' percentiles. If Dana is a boy, how does he compare at each birthday to his age mates? Similarly, consider Robin as a girl. Only for Dana as an adult male, and Robin as an adult female, are their heights in the extreme percentile ranks; and note how each year

Table 1-2.   Percentile Distribution of Weights of Males and Females From Age
12 Through Age 17, by Race: United States 1966–70.

Race, Sex, and Age	Percentile in Kilograms						
	5	10	25	50	75	90	95
Black							
Female							
12 years	35.55	36.97	41.59	44.46	57.21	62.57	66.91
13 years	34.64	37.30	42.80	48.46	62.22	67.37	69.63
14 years	35.37	37.33	45.68	50.92	59.02	68.39	75.25
15 years	42.63	47.08	49.12	53.84	60.53	71.30	84.17
16 years	45.30	46.26	50.92	56.14	59.86	66.57	73.67
17 years	45.18	46.66	48.79	58.26	63.91	74.63	79.98
Male							
12 years	31.29	31.95	36.24	38.45	46.64	52.92	54.89
13 years	31.06	33.48	36.75	42.21	50.83	61.23	66.24
14 years	36.93	37.86	42.73	49.29	57.18	68.05	88.32
15 years	42.02	42.47	46.25	51.54	56.79	65.34	73.09
16 years	46.39	48.41	51.64	60.24	68.41	71.91	86.08
17 years	46.32	50.26	59.66	64.82	68.81	84.16	85.49
White							
Female							
12 years	32.38	33.79	37.24	42.87	49.22	58.04	62.08
13 years	35.01	37.10	41.52	47.03	53.17	60.93	66.34
14 years	38.66	40.47	46.22	51.10	57.43	63.58	67.37
15 years	41.16	43.96	47.96	54.13	59.73	65.20	69.54
16 years	44.33	46.47	50.75	54.58	60.71	69.28	77.71
17 years	44.34	47.09	50.43	56.69	61.94	72.02	76.65
Male							
12 years	28.07	30.29	35.51	39.75	45.41	55.64	59.93
13 years	31.41	34.68	39.10	44.66	50.81	59.04	62.13
14 years	39.00	40.72	45.54	51.83	59.98	68.86	76.72
15 years	44.38	46.90	51.55	59.48	67.03	74.53	76.87
16 years	46.82	51.56	56.91	62.27	68.61	78.14	86.03
17 years	50.42	53.09	59.17	64.78	73.51	80.52	85.90

SOURCE: P. V. V. Hamill, F. E. Johnston, and S. E. Lemeshow. Body weight, stature, and sitting height:
White and Negro youths 12 to 17 years. Vital and Health Statistics. Data from the National Health
Survey. Series 11. No. 126. Washington, D.C.: U.S. Government Printing Office, 1973.

after age 14 or 15, when they are average, do a male Dana and a female Robin
move further away from the average.

Actually, the figures for Dana were chosen to be typical of height measurements for females, and those for Robin were chosen as being typical for males.
The differences between the distance curves for Dana and Robin at ages 12 and 13
are the differences that show up in fifth and sixth grades in school, where many of
the girls are taller than many of the boys.

ACCOUNT NO.	DEPT.	FACULTY	SERIAL NO.	DATE	DEPT. CODE	SALESMAN CODE	WAREHOUSE CODE
550470	080	999	017797	12/04/78	300	330	RIVRSD

BIN LOC.	ISBN 0-02	✓	QTY.	AUTHOR	TITLE	SERIAL NO.
1476	347300-2	✓	1	GRINDER	STUDIES IN ADOLESCENCE 3ED PPR	017797
1517	360610-X	✓	1	JERSILD	PSYCHOLOGY OF ADOLESCENCE 3ED	017797
1653	412120-7		1	SMART	ADOLESCENTS 2ED PPR	017797

PICKER

CHECKER

PACKER

PACKING SLIP FROM: MACMILLAN PUBLISHING CO., INC., RIVERSIDE, NEW JERSEY 08075

PRESENTATION ORDER

GROWTH IN WEIGHT

The curve of increments of weight begins to rise earlier than does the curve of increments of height. This difference can be accounted for in part by the earlier increase in the width and depth measurements of the chest and hips. The preadolescent increase of subcutaneous fat and muscle also contributes to the earlier increase in weight.

Unlike muscle and bone, *fat* has periods of decreasing as well as of increasing during the growth span. The amount of subcutaneous fat is measured in several ways, but skinfold thickness is the way that is most often used. The clinician grasps a fold of the skin at one or more sites on the body and measures the thickness of the fold. The site most often used because of its accessibility and the agreement between its measurement and other measures of subcutaneous fat is just below the lower point of the right scapula (shoulder blade).

Fat thickness increases during the last three months of pregnancy and until nine months after birth, decreases until the child is about 6 years old, and then increases slowly until just before or at the time of greatest increase in height. The median measurement of fat thickness for girls is at all times ahead of the median for boys. From puberty on, the subcutaneous fat of females is always thicker than that of males, not only in the well-noticed places (hips and breasts), but everywhere. The increase in subcutaneous fat continues for both sexes until the fifth or sixth decades [21].

Fat thickness throughout childhood is closely related to weight at maturity [17]. By measuring fat thickness semiannually, it was shown that between 1.5 and 12.5 years of age, children in the top 14 per cent in fat were advanced by about half a year's growth. Fat thickness was associated with skeletal maturity. The authors suggest that overnutrition or supernutrition results in speeded maturation, and general dimensional growth, in addition to subcutaneous fat. A series of studies on obesity in adolescents [7] revealed activity level as a crucial difference between obese adolescents and normal ones who ate about the same number of calories. The level of activity affects metabolic rate and hence the rate at which calories are used. These results raise the question of whether inactivity is related to early maturity, as well as to fat.

ENDOCRINOLOGY OF GROWTH

In addition to stature and weight, other dimensions of the human body have been studied in similar ways. These include sitting height and dimensions of the chest and head. Even diameters of the head show increments that follow the same kind of pattern of increments, although the curve for each dimension is unique in some way. The spurt in growth that occurs around pubescence is the result of the complicated but interrelated ebb and flow of endocrine substances in the bloodstream.

Because every cell extracts materials from the bloodstream and gives up substances to it, every cell is *endocrine,* that is, it secretes internally. But the endocrine glands have specialized functions in relation to growth. The most important of these is the anterior portion of the *pituitary* gland, which is located in the center of the head, near the *hypothalamus,* a part of the central nervous system. The hypothalamus and the pituitary are interconnected so that some stimuli coming to the former activate messages sent to the latter.

Growth Influencers. Five hormones originating in the anterior pituitary have been identified as regulators of growth (Figure 1-4); four of these hormones stimulate other endocrine glands to function. The fifth, or perhaps first in order of importance, is called *growth hormone.*

1. Growth hormone (GH) affects all body tissues [26], except the central nervous system and possibly the adrenal glands and the gonads. It operates at the cellular level, influencing DNA synthesis and cell multiplication. GH has been found in the blood of fetuses as young as 15 weeks. It is produced throughout life, with bursts and pauses [37].

2. Thyroid stimulating hormone (TSH) stimulates the production of *thyroglobulin* directly into the blood. The thyroid hormone is related to the growth of

Figure 1-4. Endocrine influences on postnatal growth and development.

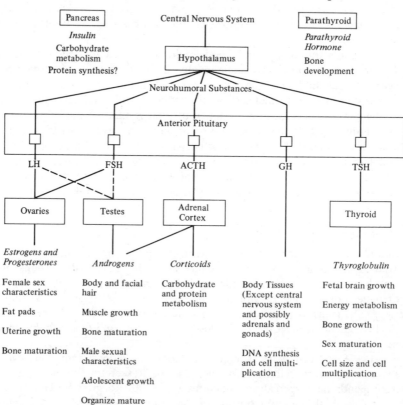

the fetal brain, to bone growth, sexual maturation, and to energy metabolism through its effects on cell multiplication and cell size.

3. Adrenocorticotropic hormone (ACTH), as its name implies, stimulates the production in the *adrenal cortex* of three groups of hormones, the water electrolyte hormones, the corticoids, and the androgens. The first influence water, sodium, and potassium balance in the body. The corticoids control the carbohydrate-protein balance. The androgens are produced in the adrenal glands of both sexes. They influence muscle growth, bone maturation, and adolescent growth.

4. and 5. Luteinizing hormone (LH) and follicle stimulating hormone (FSH) are the other two tropic hormones from the anterior pituitary. They stimulate the production of hormones in the gonads. In the ovary, FSH brings about the secretion of *estrogens,* which produce the female sex characteristics and growth of the uterus; in the male it stimulates the tubular cells to produce sperm. The ovary responds to LH by producing *progesterones,* which bring about changes in the lining of the uterus; the testes produce androgens. These are similar to the androgens produced by the adrenal cortex. In the postpubescent male there are, therefore, higher concentrations of androgens than in the postpubescent female. This higher concentration brings about the male sexual characteristics, body and facial hair typical of males, the greater male muscle growth, and the longer duration of growth in size.

6. Parathyroid hormone affects bone development. It is, therefore, related to growth, but is not controlled by a hormone from the anterior pituitary.

7. Insulin, also not controlled by the anterior pituitary, has to do with carbohydrate metabolism and possibly with protein synthesis. It is produced in the pancreas.

The maximum effect of GH occurs when there is some thyroglobulin present. Both of these hormones influence the growth and duplication of cells. GH and insulin have opposing and balancing effects within the body. With the possible exception of GH, there are feedback mechanisms so that the presence of growth-influencing hormones in the blood depress the secretion of the pituitary tropic hormones. Stress on the individual stimulates the production of ACTH. This is one of the results of the close linkage of the hypothalamus and the anterior pituitary.

GH was so named because its growth-promoting activity was its first discovered function. Its influence at the cellular level, and its continued presence throughout life are more recent discoveries. Still to come is the discovery of what process or mechanism dampens its effect after puberty. Of course, new cells are formed throughout life, but obviously at a replacement, not a growth, rate.

The different timings of the adolescent growth spurts of the various organs and tissues can be explained by differential sensitivity to the androgens. For instance, the sequence of appearance of pubic, axillary, and facial hair is probably caused by different thresholds of stimulation and reactivity to either adrenal or testicular androgens [44]. The skin of the pubis thus responds to the smallest increase of androgen, and grows hair in early puberty. The skin of the axilla requires a larger amount of androgen before it produces hair, and the skin of the face requires an even larger amount.

The differences between early and late maturers are in part differences in the timing of the beginning of the adolescent growth spurt. These differences are probably genetic in origin since the spurt is related to the age of sexual maturity, which is known to be strongly hereditary. Environmental factors also influence pubertal growth, as is shown in the section on nutrition at adolescence.

CHANGES IN PROPORTIONS

In addition to changes in the distribution and thickness of fat, the human body changes in the ratios of linear measures to each other. The ratios change because the various bones grow at different rates, some growing longer slowly while others are growing relatively fast. One example is the Sitting Height/Stature ratio, the proportion of sitting height to standing height. The changes in average ratios for black and white boys and girls are depicted in Figure 1-5. From 6 to 12 the average ratios decrease, showing that the legs are growing faster than the upper parts of the body. There is not much difference, on the average, between boys and girls, but as is true throughout the age range shown, the trunks of black children contribute slightly less than those of white children to total stature. But from 12 to 14 for girls and 13 to 15 for boys, the ratios become slowly larger, as the upper part of the body grows faster than the legs.

The ratio of hip width, the distance between the crests of the pelvis, to shoulder width, the distance between the outer ends of the acromium at the ends of the clavicle, changes little from 6 to 12 years [5], although the average ratio for girls increases slightly faster than for boys. After puberty, the girls' average ratio

Figure 1-5. Changes in proportions from 6 to 18 years of age, as shown by the ratio of sitting height to standing height.

SOURCE: R. M. Malina, P. V. V. Hamill, and S. Lemeshow. *Body dimensions and proportions: White and Negro children 6 to 11 years.* Data from the National Health Survey. Series 11. No. 143. DHEW publication No. (HRA) 75–1625. Washington, D.C.: U.S. Government Printing Office, 1974. P. V. V. Hamill, F. E. Johnston, and S. Lemeshow. *Body weight, stature, and sitting height: White and Negro youths 12 to 17 years.* Data from the National Health Survey. Series 11. No. 143. DHEW Publication No. (HRA) 74–1608. Washington, D.C.: U.S. Government Printing Office, 1973.

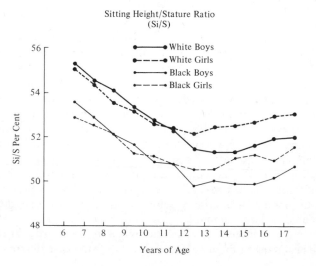

continues to go up as the hips grow broader faster than the shoulders, but in boys the growth of the hips slows down in the width dimension while the growth of the shoulders speeds up, thereby reducing the boys' average hip/shoulder ratio.

Pubertal changes can be seen in almost every part of the body. The growth spurts of the various parts of the body do not coincide exactly with one another but are spread throughout the pubertal period [44]. For instance, the peaks for growth in weight and head circumference come after the peaks for growth in height and hand length.

If a child grew in the way that a balloon blows up, he would keep the same proportions all the way along, but he does not. Spurting now in one measurement, now in another, he often looks different from the way he looked just a short time before. Spurts in head length and breadth makes the eyes look smaller. The nose and lower jaw grow more than other parts of the face, changing its proportions from childish toward adult. The ways in which a boy grows out of his suits are predictable, since the spurts of the various parts of the body follow a sequence. First the trouser legs become too short. If his mother can lengthen them, they will last for another four months until his hip growth makes the trousers too tight. Since chest breadth increases at the same time as hip width, a new suit is in order. It is a good idea to buy it wide in the shoulders, since the spurt in shoulder breadth comes just a few months after the spurts in chest and hip width. This suit will become too short in the jacket with the peak of growth in trunk length that comes about a year after the peak of growth in leg length. A filling-out process will make the jacket too tight just after it becomes too short, since the peak in muscle growth comes soon after the peak in trunk length. (Although boys' suits illustrate these changes better than girls' clothing, the same sequence of changes takes place in girls.)

Both boys and girls tend to worry as their feet spurt in growth. This spurt happens when the height spurt gets under way or before it [34]. The earlier it happens, of course, the larger the youngster's feet seem to him and to his family, who tend to be concerned about the frequent need for new shoes as well as about what looks like awkwardness.

CHANGES IN ORGANS

The *viscera* undergo pubescent growth spurts [44, p. 18]. Most data on visceral growth are cross-sectional, and, therefore, the nature of their spurts has not been so clearly demonstrated as with outer body measurements. The cardiovascular system has been studied in terms of blood pressure, pulse rate, capacity for athletic and work effort, and recovery from work. Blood pressure rises gradually and continuously throughout childhood, adolescence, and, indeed, through the seventh decade [26]. The small sex difference, with the girls having higher median pressure, found in childhood [48] is reversed during adolescence so that thereafter males have higher blood pressure, both systolic and diastolic. Pulse rate decreases during pubescence [26]. Chest cavity and lungs increase, while rate of breathing decreases. Along with the increase in the size of the body, however, puberty brings a steady decrease in the volume of air taken in. The sex difference grows in favor of boys, who develop a much larger lung capacity than girls.

The *nervous system* matures during the adolescent period, but the exact nature of the changes has not been mapped in much detail. The intellectual changes at adolescence must have their counterparts in the nervous system. There is evidence for a small growth spurt in the brain at adolescence [44]. Physical measurements of heads indicate that there may be some brain growth along with growth in bone and membranes. An adult type of brain wave pattern becomes established during adolescence [47]. Sex differences in the timing of brain lateralization have already been established for school-age children, showing that boys' right hemispheres become specialized for spatial processing earlier than girls' [51]. Canadian studies of tactual perception indicate that girls are much slower than boys in developing right-hemisphere superiority for spatial processing. Not until age 13 did girls show the left-hand superiority that boys began to show at age 5. The task used involves simultaneously presenting a different nonsense shape to each hand, not visible to the subject. The subject selects from a visual display the stimuli he touched. The left presentation is perceived in the right hemisphere, and vice versa. Superiority of either hemisphere is shown by more accurate choice of stimuli.

Physical Care and Health

Because any period of rapid growth is a time of vulnerability to certain deprivations or noxious influences, the period of puberty deserves high priority in meeting physical needs. Extra food and rest for fast growth stand out as important. Because the adolescent is declaring his independence, *how to* meet his physical needs is often as problematic as knowing what he needs.

ILLNESSES

Compared with other times of life, adolescence is less vulnerable to illness and death. About 1 per cent of persons between 15 and 19 are likely to die during one year [19]. Death rate of adolescents are lower for girls than for boys (1:2.5) and

Figure 1-6. Abnormal findings on health examination at ages 12 to 17, by parental health ratings, United States, 1966–1970.

SOURCE: J. Roberts. *Examination and health history findings among children and youths, 6–17 years. United States.* Data from the National Health Survey, Series 11, No. 129. DHEW Publication No. (HRA) 74–1611. Washington, D.C.: U.S. Government Printing Office, 1973. Figure 4, p. 7.

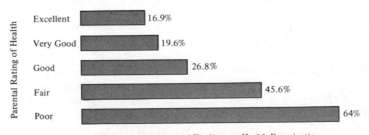

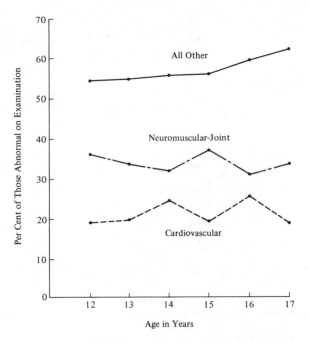

Figure 1-7. Per cent of significantly abnormal findings on health examinations, by type of condition, at ages 12 to 17, United States, 1966–1970.

SOURCE: J. Roberts. *Examination and health history findings among children and youths 6–17 years. United States.* Data from the National Health Survey. Series 11, No. 129. DHEW Publication No. (HRA) 74–1611. Washington, D.C.: U.S. Government Printing Office, 1973. Table 3, p. 3.

for whites than for nonwhites (1:1.5). The leading causes of death among adolescents, by rank, are accidents, homicide, malignant neoplasms, and suicide.

United States adolescents between 12 and 17 tend to see themselves as having good health [41]. Only four in 1,000 rated their health as poor. Parents also rated only 4 per cent of this age group as having poor health [39]. Physical examinations showed more than 20 per cent of adolescents to have an illness, deformity, or handicap. Apparently neither parents nor children consider all of these conditions as indicating poor health. Figure 1-6 shows the percentages of individuals with abnormal conditions who were rated very good, good, fair, and poor by parents. The figure indicates that the poorer the results of the examination, the more likely parents are to realize that something is wrong, but that they do not recognize all symptoms of poor physical condition in their children. Figure 1-7 shows the percentage of types of abnormalities found in the health examination for each year from ages 12 to 17.

According to parents' reports, 72 per cent of the adolescents had had a serious illness. Although the severity of illness was the same for girls and boys, fewer girls (70 per cent) than boys (74 per cent) had had a serious illness.

Infectious Diseases. Infectious childhood diseases, especially measles, were most often reported as serious. The next most frequent type of serious illness was respiratory infection. Figure 1-8 indicates how many persons at each age had had the common infectious childhood diseases. Since these curves are almost flat, they suggest that most of those who will ever have the diseases have already had them by age 17.

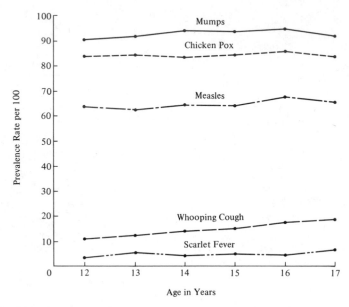

Figure 1-8. Prevalence rates for history of selected childhood diseases at ages 12 to 17, United States, 1966–1970.

SOURCE: J. Roberts. *Examination and health history findings among children and youths, 6–17 years. United States.* Data from the National Health Survey. Series 11. No. 129. DHEW Publication No. (HRA) 74–1611. Washington, D.C.: U.S. Government Printing Office, 1973. Table 4, pp. 34–35.

Venereal disease is a serious health problem in the adolescent and adult years. Gonorrhea is the most prevalent reportable communicable disease in the United States, and syphilis ranks third. The most recent government figures for the 15 to 19 age group show that per 100,000 population 20 girls and 19 boys had syphilis, and 1,235 girls and 1,075 boys had gonorrhea [9]. These rates do not represent all the cases existing, because many are undiagnosed. The Venereal Disease Control Division estimated that although 874,161 cases of gonorrhea were reported to health departments in 1974, actually at least 2.7 million cases occurred. The rates of venereal disease, especially of gonorrhea, have increased faster in girls than in boys. The situation requires better strategies of both prevention and treatment, through education before teenagers become sexually active, continuing education and information, and treatment available in ways that will not be frightening, threatening, or disruptive to parent-adolescent relationships.

Chronic and Other Conditions. Over 10 per cent of 16- and 17-year-olds have had hay fever and 6 per cent have had asthma. Other allergies were reported by 11 per cent of those between 12 and 17. About 4 per cent of the subjects had had kidney trouble, girls being twice as likely as boys to have such problems. Heart conditions were reported by almost 5 per cent. Frequencies of reported respiratory difficulties were 12 per cent with frequent bad sore throats; 21 per cent with more than three colds in the previous year; 11 per cent with persistent coughs; 16 per cent with bronchitis; 6 per cent with colds that went to the chest [39].

SENSORY AND NEUROLOGICAL CONDITIONS

Figure 1-9 shows the frequencies of various sensory-neurological problems. The eye troubles shown in this graph refer to problems such as strabismus (crossed eyes), which is caused by eye muscle imbalance. About 12 per cent of children between 12 and 17 have eye muscle imbalance at a distance, and 16.5 per cent have this problem in near vision [40]. About 43 per cent of this age group (48 per cent of girls, 39 per cent of boys) need corrective lenses for seeing clearly at a distance. Medical histories showed that 34 per cent or 7.7 million adolescents were wearing glasses or contact lenses. About 934,000 or 4.1 per cent of the population from 12 to 17 have deficient color vision, 12 boys to one girl showing some defect. Red-green deficiencies were more common than blue-yellow deficiencies affecting 6.6 per cent of boys and 0.4 per cent of girls. The affected girls were likely to have milder deficiencies than were the boys [42].

ACCIDENTS

The survey of 12- to 17-year-olds found that 21.1 per cent of boys and 13.1 per cent of girls had had broken bones, 10 per cent of boys and 7.8 per cent of girls had been knocked unconscious, and 15.9 per cent of boys and 8.6 per cent of girls had had other accidents. For every 10,000 15- to 19-year-olds, during one year, accidents caused the death of ten boys and three girls. The totals represent 64

Figure 1-9. Prevalence rates for history of sensory-neurological conditions at ages 12 to 17.

SOURCE: J. Roberts. *Examination and health history findings among children and youths 6–17 years. United States.* Data from the National Health Survey. Series 11. No. 129. DHEW Publication No (HRA) 74–1611. Washington, D.C.: U.S. Government Printing Office, 1973. Table 4, pp. 34–35.

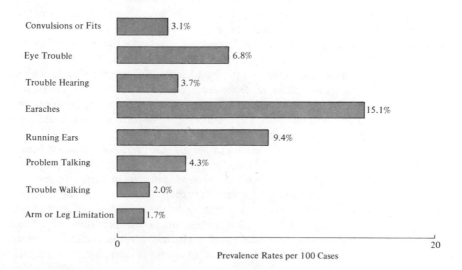

Prevalence Rates per 100 Cases

per cent of all male teenage deaths and 48 per cent of female [36]. A comparison of accidental deaths in Canada and the United States showed more fatal accidents in Canadians under 15 years of age (3.9 to 2.9 per 10,000) but more in American youths from ages 15 to 24 (10.9 to 11.5 per 10,000) [36a]. As in childhood, males had many more accidents than females, probably reflecting greater activity and aggression in the male, as well as the greater restrictions placed upon the activities of females. Motor vehicle accidents were much more frequent for males than for females, 8.8 to 2.8 in the United States and 7.4 to 2.2 in Canada.

NUTRITION

Childhood nutrition affects the timing of the onset of puberty. During the growth spurt, of course, the body needs more nutrients than during the previous period of slow growth. For present growth and health it is important for adolescents to have sufficient quantities of high-quality food. For the health and growth of the next generation, it is important that girls eat the nutrients that will prepare their bodies for excellent reproductive performance. When pregnancy occurs, it is too late to repair nutritional deficiencies in the woman.

As Appendix A indicates, the recommended number of calories for girls between 12 and 18 is from 2,300 to 2,400 and for boys, 2,700 to 3,000. These figures do not indicate the enormously increased caloric needs during the peak of the growth spurt, since they are derived from groups. A fast-growing boy may feel hungry most of the time, because his stomach is probably too small to hold all the calories he needs unless he eats at frequent intervals. To his mother, he seems to be eating all the time. Many teenagers do not get enough calories, according to these standards. The United States national survey gives the average calorie intake for this age group as 2,423 for whites above the poverty line and 2,164 for blacks above the poverty line. For those below the poverty line, whites received 2,076 calories and blacks 1,877. Iron deficiency has been found in a small percentage of the population between ages 12 and 17, with black children showing low values in iron measurements about seven times as frequently as white children [1].

Deficiencies in any of the elements required for growth—vitamins, minerals, and proteins—can have adverse effects on energy level, resistance to disease, behavior, emotions, and appearance. Adolescents are all too likely to eat empty calories, foods that contain mostly sugar, starch, and flavorings, and perhaps fats, such as soft drinks, pastries, potato chips, and candy. School vending machines may make it too easy to buy these foods instead of milk, whole grains, fruits, and other nutritious foods. If the empty-calorie foods are added to the wholesome diet, the result is too many calories and a fat adolescent. If they are substituted for wholesome foods, the result is dietary deficiency.

Although the reported U.S. Government survey does not give separate figures for boys and girls, a nutritionist [33] maintains that adolescent boys are much better nourished than girls and that of all groups, adolescent girls are most in need of nutritional help. In view of the fact that many teenage girls soon will be mothers, it is disturbing to realize the deprivation to the next generation that will result from their impoverished bodies. Nutrition education, important at all age levels, has special significance for adolescent girls and for the society in which they will bear children. An example of an effective course is the minicourse recently developed at M.I.T. [38]. Subject matter includes food composition, health, and labeling of nutrients. Using a table of recommended dietary allowances, students analyze various diets. They study outcomes of different types of meals, macrobiotic, drive-in, and basic-four food group meals.

Vegetarianism. Although vegetarian diets can be adequate, it takes careful planning to provide adequate protein and other nutrients. Certain vegetarian cults expose their followers to physical dangers. The Vegan diet does not supply enough vitamin B 12, but its effects may be masked by folic acid until irreparable damage has been done to the spinal cord [16]. The Zen macrobiotic diet may lead to scurvy, anemia, starvation, and kidney failure. Some of the adolescents who have been damaged by these diets have accepted nutritional counseling. Few people know enough about nutrition to provide an adequate diet within severe restrictions, but nutritionists can help them to do so.

Obesity. Being overweight is likely to be a psychological hazard as well as a serious physical liability to the adolescent. A recent conference on childhood obesity emphasized the complexity of the causes and treatment of excess fat [50]. The fat adolescent may be expressing a genetic potential, since the child of two obese parents has an 80 per cent chance of being too fat. With one obese parent, the child's chances of being fat drop to 40 per cent. Of course, environmental factors are probably at work here, also. Some fat adolescents have been destined for obesity since infancy, when they grew more than the normal number of fat cells. The peak periods for the onset of obesity are late infancy, early childhood, and adolescence. There is evidence from animal studies to suggest that later onset arises from the enlarging of fat cells, rather than from growing new fat cells. The effects of poverty have been observed to differ between the sexes. In males, poverty is likely to result in thin children and thin adults but in females, the result tends to be thin children and fat adults. Affluence is more likely to produce heavy girls and slim women.

Weight reduction is as complex as are the reasons for obesity. Often obese adolescents eat no more than their normal peers, but they exercise less and are more likely to eat when they are bored rather than when hungry. Although the attention of a specialist may be required by some fat adolescents, others have been helped to achieve normal weight by diet control, increased exercise, and psychological support. Clubs, camps, and other groups are often successful in providing the right combination of guidance and support. Since fat children are likely to be rejected and to suffer discrimination, it is important to give them adequate help.

REST

For many youngsters, pubescence ushers in the desire to sleep on Saturday mornings and on other mornings, as well. Their rapid growth requires more rest than did the quiescent growth of the elementary school years. Adolescents tend to stay up later at night than they did as children. They are busy with schoolwork, visiting with friends, especially over the telephone, and paying attention to appearance. Parental control is resisted. When growth slows down, they can and do get along with less sleep than they needed as children.

DRUGS

A World Health Organization study group concluded that drugs are being taken earlier at all ages and that more and more people are trying dependency-producing drugs [52]. Physical and mental health problems arise from this world-wide tendency of youth to use chemical substances to induce changes in body and mind. A United States survey revealed 10,957 narcotics addicts under 21 years of age [46].

Alcohol. A study in Metropolitan Toronto showed alcohol to be the most popular drug among high school students. Over half the students in grade 7 and 92.6 per cent of those in grade 13 said they had used alcohol [8]. Among over 7,000 New York State high school students in grades 10, 11, and 12, 85 per cent said they used alcohol [53]. In Massachusetts, officials noted "a recent dramatic and alarming rise in the incidence of alcoholism among teenagers" [14]. They attributed it partly to the lowered legal age for drinking.

Tobacco. It is common knowledge that smoking damages the heart and lungs. Many people also know that when pregnant women smoke, their babies are likely to be born prematurely and with low birth weights. A few people are also aware that when a baby lives in a household where people smoke, she is likely to have more

Figure 1-10. Per cent of United States youths who report smoking cigarettes regularly.

SOURCE: J. V. Scanlon. *Self-reported health behavior and attitudes of youths, 12 to 17 years. United States.* Data from the National Health Survey. Series 11. No. 147. DHEW Publication No. (HRA) 75–1629. Washington, D.C.: U.S. Government Printing Office, 1973. Table 3, p. 27.

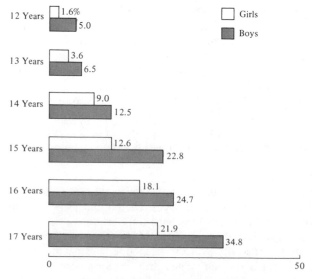

Per Cent Reporting Smoking Cigarettes Regularly

respiratory troubles than in a smoke-free home. The habit of smoking is difficult to break. In spite of all these reasons against smoking, the number of regular smokers increases with age, as shown in Figure 1-10. More than 3 out of 4 12-year-olds have never smoked, but only one out of three 17-year-olds had not done so [41]. For teenagers' present health, and for the health of their future children, it is important to find out why children start to smoke and how to prevent it. Knowledge of the dangers of smoking does not seem to influence smoking behavior.

Youngsters may start to smoke because of peer pressure and/or because smoking represents adult status and independence to them. Over 5,000 British boys between 11 and 15 were questioned as to how they perceived smoking in regard to themselves, their ideals, and peers [32]. The boys associated toughness and precocity with smoking. Smokers were influenced by these perceptions to continue smoking. Nonsmokers were attracted by the notion of toughness which gave them some incentive to start smoking. Both groups associated educational success with nonsmoking and both valued educational success. Evidence from another study [43] shows that smokers are more rebellious than nonsmokers during the elementary and junior high school years. Furthermore, adult smokers showed more

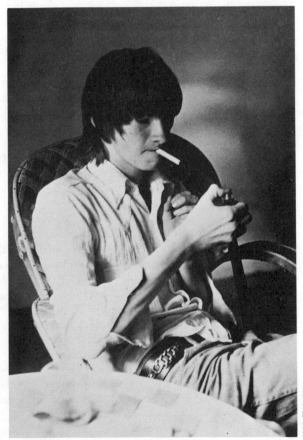

SAM HODGKIN

rebelliousness than nonsmokers. The authors of this study point out the futility of trying to prevent adolescents from beginning and continuing smoking by making authoritative pronouncements.

Hallucinogens. Drugs that cause sensory distortions without greatly disturbing consciousness are called *hallucinogens* [22, p. 50]. Marijuana and LSD are probably best known. The *cannabis* plant produces a chemical used in several different forms and called by many different names throughout the world. North Americans smoke the leaves, as "pot" or "grass." Or they smoke the much stronger resin, as "hash" (hasheesh). Physical reactions include rapid heartbeat, twitching of muscles, pupil dilation, reddish eyes, lowered body temperature, lowered blood sugar, and dehydration. Hunger and drowsiness are likely. The mind-altering effects, showing action on the brain, are, of course, the reason for using the drug. Most young users of marijuana are looking for new experiences and these they find in the form of mood changes, perceptual distortions, and changes in conceptualizing. Driving while high on marijuana is, therefore, dangerous. The psychological reactions are very variable, depending on the social environment, the mood the user is already in, the strength of the drug, and past experience with the drug. Marijuana is thought not to be physically addicting, which means that withdrawal does not cause physical symptoms such as cramps and vomiting. Users can and often do become psychologically addicted or dependent on marijuana, however. Because adolescents hear that it is not physically addicting, they often think that it cannot become a habit. False reassurance also comes from the mildness of the drug and the ease of taking a small amount at a time.

Light use of cannabis is thought to have no serious results. However, a review of five years of research on cannabis concludes that there is evidence that *prolonged, heavy* use of marijuana and/or hasheesh is associated with at least six types of hazard [30]. Cannabis *may* cause chromosome damage; disrupt cellular metabolism including synthesis of DNA; interfere with the immune system; disrupt hormone regulation so as to induce impotence, sterility, and male breast development; harm the bronchial tract and lungs; cause personality changes; and damage the brain.

Among the Toronto students surveyed, about one third of those in grades 11, 12, and 13 had used cannabis [8]. In a representative sample of public secondary schools in New York State, the heaviest users were those whose best friends and parents were also drug users [22a]. The influence of peers was greater than that of parents. Other hallucinogens are LSD, LTP, peyote, mescaline, and morning glory seeds. The physical side effects of LSD include nausea, vomiting, aches and pains, and possible chromosomal damage and damage to unborn children [22]. The action of LSD upon the brain is indicated by dilated pupils, increased blood pressure, and stronger reflexes. Sensory areas of the brain are stimulated, and inhibiting mechanisms are blocked. Thus, visual hallucinations are produced and the senses of hearing, touch, temperature, and pain are often either intensified or diminished. Senses may become fused or scrambled and the individual hears colors or smells music. He may be euphoric and feel that he has great mental clarity or comprehension, possibly the result of the combination of brain arousal and disturbed sensory activity leading to a heightened awareness of previously stored information

[22, p. 51]. This information becomes available as preconscious material. (An aspect of the normal creative process is the receiving and using of preconscious material.) A shared LSD trip often makes bonds between members of the group. Teenagers' use of LSD seems to be decreasing [2].

Amphetamines. Providing stimulation to the brain and sympathetic nervous system, these psychic energizers produce an increased heart rate, increased blood pressure, constriction of certain blood vessels, pupil dilation, faster breathing, sweating, and a dry mouth [22]. Bodily activity increases and the user feels more confident, happy, fearless, and less tired. He becomes more talkative and impulsive. Appetite decreases. Amphetamines are taken in pills for reducing and for staying awake and alert for working, playing, or studying longer than the person normally could. They are used for kicks, sometimes combined with alcohol or barbiturates. *Speeding,* injecting a huge amount of amphetamine into a vein, gives a euphoric high called a *rush.* Repeated injections keep the speed freak awake and active for days until he is completely exhausted.

Excessive and prolonged use of amphetamines causes physical and mental damage. The student who uses it to stay awake for long periods becomes exhausted. He may become dependent, feeling depressed and sluggish without the drug. Liver damage may result. Prolonged use and increasing doses can cause sleeplessness for long times, mood changes, and severe mental disorder, with feelings of superiority, suspiciousness, hallucinations, and excitement [22]. Speeding may transmit hepatitis, since contaminated needles are often used. Drivers under the influence of amphetamines are extremely dangerous.

Cocaine. Expensive, but fast gaining in popularity, cocaine stimulates the nervous system, relieving depression and anxiety. Like marijuana, small amounts are probably not harmful and are not physically addicting. Like amphetamines, cocaine is a psychic energizer, increasing alertness and motor control when a person is tired. Users often think that cocaine improves potency and creativity, but studies show that it does not. Massive doses cause death by paralyzing the respiratory center in the brain [9a].

Volatile Solvents. Glue sniffing is done by younger adolescents and even by grade school children, probably because airplane glue is easily available. Solvents are depressants but the first psychological effect is a feeling of pleasantness, cheerfulness, euphoria, and excitement, very similar to the first stages of drinking alcohol [22]. Then the glue sniffer acts drunk and disoriented. His speech is slurred. Next comes drowsiness, stupor, and unconsciousness, which may last for an hour. Toxic effects include irritation of the skin, mucous membranes, and respiratory tract and injury to heart, liver, kidneys, blood, bones, and brain. Insomnia, nausea, increased salivation, and weight loss occur. Solvents produce strong psychological dependence and strong tolerance, which means that the dosage has to be increased in order to get the desired effects. Repeated daily use of solvents has caused many deaths.

Heroin. Teenage heroin addicts have become a serious medical problem. Heroin is a depressant, blocking out experience of the world. Addiction occurs rapidly and often irreversibly. An overdose is likely to kill. The use of heroin often leads to tetanus, hepatitis, skin ulcers, damaged veins, heart disease, and allergic reactions. Addicts come from a wide variety of family backgrounds and socio-economic levels. They tend to be passive, avoiding conflicts instead of trying to solve them. The childhood histories of 100 addicts showed that drug addicts were less likely than nonusers to have had happy childhoods and more likely to have been punished severely [4]. Addicts had lacked parental guidance in areas of school, sex, friends, and career.

SUPERVISION OF ADOLESCENT HEALTH

It takes the combined efforts of home, school, and community to see that adolescents get even a minimum of health protection. Schools and other community agencies usually offer something in the way of screening for sensory defects and certain gross physical defects. Immunizations may be given on a community basis. The school lunch program is effective in raising the nutritional level of some youngsters, but is not generally appreciated for its potentially great contribution. A good physical education program can contribute enormously to sound health and growth. Many responsibilities are left to the home—providing regular medical and dental care, giving an adequate diet, planning for rest, seeing that clothing is not only warm enough but that it protects growth, such as bras and shoes that fit. Here, as in other areas, the adolescent's search for independence often collides with parents' duties as protectors.

Motor Development

Spectator sports are very popular in the United States. Few people can be professional athletes; many sit and watch games and televised games. A counter-trend is intended to promote individual development. In such a program, instead of training all high school students as though they were headed for the Super Bowl, many teachers now teach enjoyable, enduring games, sports, and skills, with the aim of lifelong pleasure and fitness.

Body build and rates of growth, factors that are strongly dependent on he-redity, are important factors in determining who become outstanding athletes. Boy athletes on interscholastic teams in both elementary and high schools are definitely superior to other boys in maturity, body size, muscular strength, endurance, and power [10]. College athletes have larger vision fields than nonathletes [49]. In the United States, there are many outstanding black athletes, and black children are likely to excel white children on tests of motor performance [24].

Social, cultural, and climatic conditions also play a part in the degree and type of motor coordinations that are developed. Polynesians, living on islands surrounded by warm water, are good at swimming and other rhythmic movements. New Zealanders, with a British heritage for sports and living in a cool climate, play many vigorous outdoor games. They watch others playing, too, but spectator sports do not crowd out neighborhood and class teams, as well as individual sports such as hiking, swimming, and mountain climbing.

PHOTO BY DANIEL DUNN

FUNDAMENTAL MOTOR TASKS

Motor development has been studied by measuring performances at different age levels on basic skills such as running, jumping, balancing, footwork, and throwing [24]. Averages for boys usually improve until 17 or 18 years, but girls' average performances tend to reach a plateau at 12 to 14. Even when the average levels of development are higher for both sexes, as they were in a comparison of British and United States children, the shapes of the curves were the same, with girls reaching plateaus early in adolescence, boys later [12]. Individuals may increase their performances beyond the ages when group plateaus are reached. Improvement is achieved through training and practice.

The averages for jumping and throwing follow closely the course described. Boys throw much better than girls. Improvement in throwing results not only from more power but also from better coordination. Young men do better than young women in throwing, catching, striking, and kicking. Sex differences are neither great nor consistent in running, although boys usually run faster. In sequencing footwork, as shown by hopping, girls usually do better than boys. Balancing or maintaining control in different positions is a part of all motor skills. Therefore, balancing is tested through many different tests, some of which show age differences, and some of which favor girls, while others favor boys [24].

FITNESS

Exercise can be used to promote health and excellent physical development. Fitness is measured by performance tests and by physiological measures, such as heart rate and oxygen intake [11]. Health-related aspects of fitness include endurance, flexibility, strength, and muscular endurance. Skill-related aspects are agility, reaction time, balance, coordination, and speed. When adolescents improve in fitness, their self-concepts also improve [31].

Endurance. Stamina or endurance refers to being able to keep up an activity for a considerable length of time. Endurance is developed by muscles and also by the circulatory system. For example, hopping tests the endurance of feet and leg muscles, whereas running a mile requires considerable endurance from the circulatory and respiratory systems, as well as from feet and leg muscles and other muscles [12, p. 90]. Analysis of cardiovascular endurance has shown that at least eight measurable factors are involved, including such conditions as velocity and force of heart ejection stroke, vagus tone, pulse rate in the quiet state and after moderate exercise, and blood pressure adjustment to hard work. Thus, stamina and its improvement can be measured not only by noting how long a boy can keep at a given activity but also by making a large number of laboratory measurements.

The following methods of developing endurance have been proved successful at the University of Illinois Sports-Fitness School [12, pp. 92–93]:

1. Adjustment to the full program is expected to take several weeks, even up to eight.
2. Activities are cycled and paced to permit continuous activity over a long period, such as by alternating walking and running, by cross-country running,

long cycling trips, canoe trips, long hikes, and by gradually working at a faster pace.

3. Rest intervals are planned also, with provision for a midday rest and for a longer night sleep than boys usually take.
4. Deep breathing is taught and emphasized.
5. Careful attention to motivation includes participation and demonstration by instructors, use of standards and records, and inspirational stories of athletes.
6. Nutrition is planned and supervised and moderation required. Emphasis is placed on the use of vegetables, fruits, lean meats, and whole grain cereals. Skim milk is preferred to whole milk and real fruit juices to imitation. Animal fats, chocolate, soda, and fried foods are curtailed.
7. The best activities for developing circulatory-respiratory endurance include steeplechase running, continuous muscular exercise for 30 minutes, interval training (cycles of fast and slow) in running, skating, swimming, cycling, rowing, and taking tests in endurance runs.

Influence of Training on Physical Fitness and Physique. Youngsters who have had good physical education show up consistently as superior to those who have had poor programs or none [12, pp. 142–145]. Improvements after training have been demonstrated in many different motor activities, including balancing, flexibility tests, agility tests, strength, power and endurance tests, and also in such specific performances as hopping, dipping, rope skipping, and chinning [12].

Fat, muscles, and even bones change during the course of a good fitness program. A special program for boys with underdeveloped upper bodies resulted in significant increases in biceps, chest, abdomen, and shoulders [3]. Both structural and functional improvement occurred in the feet of boys who had foot defects [12]. Well-functioning feet, of course, are basic to good posture.

Girls and Fitness. Until recently, boys have received more acclaim for athletic performance than have girls, at least in the United States. Opportunities have been unequal, with boys' sports financed much more generously than girls'. The result has been greater male participation and fitness. Although it is at present unlikely that female teams will receive the equivalent of money spent on male football and basketball performances, the day-to-day programs for boys and girls are becoming more alike in scope and social approval. Some teams include both sexes, especially when games are played primarily for fun. The Women's Movement has wrought changes in the athletic scene, not only by demanding that girls have the same opportunities for athletic participation that boys have, but by influencing woman's role in society. Some women are now pictured on television as daring detectives who can jump over fences, throw a man over their shoulders, and win a running race.

Girls may fear injury to their reproductive systems, because of a myth that heavy exercise will damage the uterus [11]. Actually the reverse is true. Physical fitness improves reproductive performance. Some girls are frightened by another myth, the notion that exercising will make them have masculine muscles. We expect that increasing gender-role equality will help girls to achieve more self-esteem, more pride in their own bodies, more efforts to control their bodies, and, hence, pursuit of physical fitness. Girls also need physical education that will help them to achieve and maintain fitness.

Physical-Psychological Relationships

Growth and health affect the adolescent's concept of herself. She must come to terms with her new body, updating the body image, its boundaries and powers, its beauty or ugliness, its continuity with the childish body that it used to be. In the process of adjusting body image, face image, and feelings about them, the teenager compares herself with peers and with ideals. She looks into mirrors and measures herself, sometimes unhappily. Attempts to improve her appearance include diets, cosmetics, beauty treatments, and peer-approved clothing.

STEREOTYPES OF BODY BUILD

Boys between 10 and 20 years showed certain expectations of various male physical types, in their ratings of photographs [25]. On a list of desirable characteristics, such as leadership, popularity, not smoking, and enduring pain, strong, athletic-looking boys were rated highest. Stereotypes associated with other physical types, such as skinny or fat, are generally negative. Thus, the nonpreferred type of boy (and girl, too) has the destructive experience of low expectations from peers.

EFFECTS OF ILLNESS ON BODY IMAGE

The body image includes internal, as well as external structures. Even if a person has never seen a liver or a lung, he may have some notion of how it looks. In a children's hospital, teenagers discussed their illnesses and drew pictures of them [23]. Their explanations and descriptions bore some relation to reality and also revealed their feelings and imaginings. A 15-year-old diabetic boy drew a normal pancreas as an oval and then drew his own, as an oval with half deleted. He believed that a portion of his pancreas was missing, that it had been violently broken away from him. The painting shown in Figure 1-11 is the work of a 13-year-old boy who was being treated for eye lacerations. In some cases, the drawings

Figure 1-11. While in the hospital for treatment of eye lacerations, a 13-year-old boy painted this picture.
SOURCE: Kristine W. Angoff.

showed the patient's ideas of how his health could be restored and with it, his self-esteem. Studies such as this give clues as to how to help adolescents deal with the psychological trauma of illness.

EARLY AND LATE MATURITY

A generation ago, several California studies indicated that early maturing boys and girls were healthier in personality development and had greater prestige among peers [15]. More recently, among 600 Australian girls, no relationship was found between physical maturity and esteem of peers [18]. Perhaps the cultural setting makes a difference in the evaluation of sexual maturity. Another probable factor is the extent of the earliness and lateness of puberty. Errors in pubertal onset and development and associated psychological problems were studied at Johns Hopkins University [35]. Problems grew out of people having inappropriate expectations of children, based on physiques that did not match their chronological age. Peers, as well as adults, respond to the physical appearance of a child or adolescent, boy or girl, expecting the late maturer to act like a child and the early maturer to act like a teenager. Delayed onset of pubertal physique is more common in boys than girls, since late menarche is not accompanied quite so much by childish appearance. Late maturers often play with younger children and thus delay their own social development. Early maturers are often advanced socially, especially if they are advanced intellectually, which they fairly often are.

Summary

A predictable sequence of physical events constitutes pubertal growth. Adolescence includes the physical changes of puberty and also has psychological and social aspects. The age of reaching sexual maturity, indicated in females by menarche, varies between individuals, between populations, and over time.

The growth spurt that occurs during puberty varies as does menarche, since both are part of the same process that is under endocrine control. Variations in velocity and duration of growth spurts result in variation in size at maturity, time of reaching maturity, and type of physique.

Five growth hormones originating in the anterior pituitary regulate growth. The first of them, GH (growth hormone), is present throughout life but promotes growth in size only until maturity is reached. Others stimulate production of hormones by the gonads which, in turn, control the maturation of the reproductive system and secondary sexual characteristics. Different organs and systems spurt in growth at different times, causing changes in proportions, contours, and functioning. Vital capacity increases, especially in boys. There is evidence for continuing brain maturation.

Good health in adolescents is generally perceived by adolescents and their parents, although more than 20 per cent actually have an illness or handicap. The infectious diseases of childhood are rarely contracted during adolescence, but venereal disease is a serious problem. Visual deficiencies occur frequently. Accidents are the leading cause of death, occurring more frequently with males than with females.

Nutritional needs increase greatly during the pubertal growth spurt. Nutritional deficiencies in adolescent girls are of special concern because the demands of pregnancy can be met only with a well-nourished body. In adolescent pregnancy a new set of growth needs is added to a still growing body. Some cult diets pose threats to health and growth. Obesity is a complex physical and psychological problem. Rapid growth requires extra sleep and rest.

The use of drugs is a problem for increasing numbers of adolescents and at earlier ages. Effects of various drugs include physical damage, dependency, addiction, and disruption of education, achievement, and life-style.

Motor development and behavior are influenced by culture, climate, and geography. United States adolescents, especially girls, have been less active in sports and games than adolescents in other Western cultures. Fitness programs have produced physical improvements in those exposed to them. Self-concept is affected by adequacy of health, growth, and motor coordination. Appearance and type of physique affect the expectations and evaluations of others.

Body image includes internal as well as external features. When suffering illness or damage, an individual must deal with feelings aroused by changes in the body image, in addition to pain and loss of function.

Problems may arise when a child reaches puberty earlier or later than most children of his age, since social demands and opportunities are often consistent with physical maturity rather than age. Social development may thus be delayed in late maturers.

References

1. Abraham, S., F. W. Lowenstein, and C. L. Johnson, *Preliminary findings of the first health and nutrition examination survey, United States, 1971–1972.* DHEW Publication No. (HRA) 74-1219-1. Washington, D.C.: U.S. Government Printing Office, 1974.
2. Andrews, M. *The parents' guide to drugs.* Garden City, N.Y.: Doubleday & Company, Inc., 1972.
3. Araki, C. T. The effects of medicine ball activity on the upper body development of young boys. Unpublished Master's thesis, University of Illinois, 1960. Cited in Cureton [12].
4. Baer, D. J., and S. J. Corrado. Heroin addict relationships with parents during childhood and early adolescent years. *Journal of Genetic Psychology,* 1974, **124,** 99–103.
5. Bayer, L. M., and N. Bayley. *Growth diagnosis.* Chicago: University of Chicago Press, 1959.
7. Bullen, B. A., L. F. Monello, H. Cohen, and J. Mayer. Attitudes toward physical activity, food and family in obese and nonobese adolescent girls. *American Journal of Clinical Nutrition,* 1963, **12,** 1–11.
8. Cannabis increasing in popularity, new studies in Metro say. *Globe & Mail,* Toronto, December 5, 1974.
9. Center for Disease Control. *VD fact sheet 1974.* 31st ed. DHEW Publication No. (CDC) 75-i195. Atlanta, Ga.: Center for Disease Control, 1975.
9a. Clark, M. and D. Shapiro. What the doctors say. Newsweek, May 30, 1977, 25.

10. Clarke, H. H. Contributions and implications of the Medford, Oregon, Boys' Growth Study. Unpublished manuscript. Eugene: University of Oregon, 1968.
11. Corbin, C. B. (ed.). *A textbook of motor development*. Dubuque, Iowa: William C. Brown Company, Publishers, 1973.
12. Cureton, T. K. Improving the physical fitness of youth. *Monographs of the Society for Research in Child Development*, 1964, **29**:4.
13. Damon, A., S. T. Damon, R. B. Reed, and I. Valadian. Age at menarche of mothers and daughters, with a note on accuracy of recall. *Human Biology*, 1969, **41**, 161–175.
14. "Dramatic" increase in teen alcoholism. *Evening Bulletin*, Providence, May 10, 1974.
15. Eichorn, D. Biological correlates of behavior. In J. Kagan and C. Spiker (eds.). *Child psychology*. The Sixty-second Yearbook of the National Society for the Study of Education, Part I. Chicago: University of Chicago Press, 1963, pp. 4–61.
16. Erhard, D. The new vegetarians. *Nutrition Today*, 1973, **8**:6, 4–12.
17. Garn, S. M., and J. A. Haskell. Fat thickness and developmental status in childhood and adolescence. *American Journal of Diseases of Children*, 1960, **99**, 746–751.
18. Harper, J., and J. K. Collins. The effects of early or late maturation on the prestige of the adolescent girl. *Australian and New Zealand Journal of Sociology*, 1972, **8**:2, 83–88.
19. Hetzel, A. M., and M. Cappetta. *Teenagers: Marriages, divorces, parenthood and mortality*. Data from the National Vital Statistics Survey Series 21. No. 23. DHEW Publication No. (HRA) 74-1901. Washington, D.C.: U.S. Government Printing Office, 1973.
20. Hiernaux, J. Ethnic differences in growth and development. *Eugenics Quarterly*, 1968, **15**, 12–21.
21. Johnston, F. E., P. V. V. Hamill, and S. Lemeshow. *Skinfold thickness of youths 12–17 years, United States*. Data from the National Health Survey. Series 11. No. 132. DHEW Publication No. (HRS) 74-1614. Washington, D.C.: U.S. Government Printing Office, 1971.
22. Jones, K. L., L. W. Shainberg, and C. O. Beyer. *Drugs and alcohol*. New York: Harper & Row, Publishers, Inc., 1969.
22a. Kandel, D. Inter- and intragenerational influences on adolescent marijuana use. *Journal of Social Issues*, 1974, **30**, 107–135.
23. Kaufman, R. V. Body-image changes in physically ill teen-agers. *Journal of the American Academy of Child Psychiatry*, 1972, **11**, 57–70.
24. Keogh, J. Development in fundamental motor tasks. In C. B. Corbin (ed.). *A textbook of motor development*. Dubuque, Iowa: William C. Brown Company, Publishers, 1973.
25. Lerner, R. M. The development of steriotyped expectancies of body-build-behavior relations. *Child Development*, 1969, **40**, 137–141.
26. Lowrey, G. H. *Growth and development of children*. 6th ed. Chicago: Year Book Medical Publishers, Inc., 1973.
27. MacMahon, B. *Age at Menarche. United States*. Data from the National Health Survey, Series 11, No. 133. DHEW Publication No. (HRA) 74-1615. Washington, D.C.: U.S. Government Printing Office, 1973.
28. Marshall, W. A., and J. M. Tanner. Variations in the pattern of pubertal changes in girls. *Archives of Disease in Childhood*, 1969, **44**, 291–303.
29. Marshall, W. A., and J. M. Tanner. Variations in the pattern of pubertal changes in boys. *Archives of Disease in Childhood*, 1970, **45**, 13–23.

30. Maugh, T. H., II. Marihuana: The grass may no longer be greener. *Science,* 1974, **185,** August 23, 683–684.

31. McGowan, R. W., B. O. Jarman, and D. M. Pedersen. Effects of a competitive endurance training program on self-concept and peer approval. *Journal of Psychology,* 1974, **86,** 57–60.

32. McKennell, A. C., and J. M. Bynner. Self images and smoking behavior among school boys. *British Journal of Educational Psychology,* 1969, **39,** 27–39.

33. McWilliams, M. *Nutrition for the growing years.* 2nd ed. New York: John Wiley & Sons, Inc., 1974.

34. Meredith, H. V. Human foot length from embryo to adult. *Human Biology,* 1944, **16,** 207–282.

35. Money, J., and R. R. Clopper. Psychosocial and psychosexual aspects of errors of pubertal onset and development. *Human Biology,* 1974, **46,** 173–181.

36. Mortality from accidents by age and sex. *Statistical Bulletin,* 1971, **52:**5, 6–9.

36a. Mortality from accidents in Canada and the United States. *Statistical Bulletin,* 1973, **54:**6, 9–11.

37. National Institutes of Health. *How children grow.* DHEW Publication No. (NIH) 72-166. Washington, D.C.: U.S. Government Printing Office, 1972.

38. Picardi, S. M., and E. R. Pariser. Food and nutrition minicourse for 11th and 12th grades. *Journal of Nutrition Education,* 1975, **7:**1, 25–29.

39. Roberts, J. *Examination and health history findings among children and youths, 6–17 years. United States.* Data from the National Health Survey, Series 11, No. 129. DHEW Publication No. (HRA) 74-1611. Washington, D.C.: U.S. Government Printing Office, 1973.

40. Roberts, J. *Refraction status of youths, 12–17 years. United States.* Data from the National Health Survey, Series 11, No. 148. DHEW Publication No. 75-1630. Washington, D.C.: U.S. Government Printing Office, 1974.

41. Scanlon, J. V. *Self-reported health behavior and attitudes of youths.* Data from the National Health Survey, Series 11, No. 147. DHEW Publication No. (HRA) 75-1629. Washington, D.C.: U.S. Government Printing Office, 1975.

42. Slaby, D., and J. Roberts. *Color vision deficiencies in youths.* Data from the National Health Survey, Series 11, No. 134. DHEW Publication No. (HRA) 74-1616. Washington, D.C.: U.S. Government Printing Office, 1974.

43. Stewart, L., and N. Livson. Smoking and rebelliousness: A longitudinal study from childhood to maturity. *Journal of Consulting Psychology,* 1966, **30,** 225–229.

44. Tanner, J. M. *Growth at adolescence.* 2nd ed. Oxford: Blackwell, 1962.

45. Tanner, J. M. Earlier maturation in man. *Scientific American,* 1968, **218,** 21–27.

46. United States Department of Commerce. *Statistical Abstract of the United States.* 95th ed. Washington, D.C.: U.S. Government Printing Office, 1974.

47. Walter, W. G. Electroencephalographic development of children. In J. M. Tanner and B. Inhelder (eds.). *Discussions on child development.* vol. I. New York: International Universities Press, 1953.

48. Weiss, N. S., P. V. V. Hamill, and T. Drizd. *Blood pressure levels of children 6–11 years: Relationship to age, sex, race, and socioeconomic status. United States.* Data from the National Health Survey, Series 11, No. 135. DHEW Publication No. (HRA) 74-1617. Washington, D.C.: U.S. Government Printing Office, 1973.

49. Williams, J. M., and J. Thirer. Vertical and peripheral vision in male and female athletes and nonathletes. *Research Quarterly,* 1975, **46,** 200–205.

50. Winick, M. Childhood obesity. *Nutrition Today,* 1974, **9:**3, 6–12.

51. Witelson, S. F. Age and sex differences in the development of right-hemisphere specialization for spatial processing as reflected in a dichotomous tactual stimula-

tion task. Paper presented at meetings of the Society for Research in Child Development, Denver, 1975.

52. World Health Organization. *Youth and drugs.* Technical Report Series, No. 516, 1973.

53. Yancy, W. S., P. R. Nader, and K. L. Burnham. Drug use and attitudes of high school students. *Pediatrics,* 1972, **50,** 739–745.

Readings in
Physical Growth, Health, and Coordination

The puberal growth spurt brings bodily changes that require new physical and psychological responses. New motor coordinations are both possible and necessary. Food intake has to adjust to growth demands. A fast developing body calls for frequent changes in body image, as well as continual re-evaluation of one's own body and self in relation to others'. Newly acquired sexual powers have to be understood and integrated into living. In reworking and elaborating his sense of identity, the young person has to deal with all these aspects of his bodily development.

Because fast growth involves postural changes, the subject of posture is discussed here. David Sinclair traces postural changes with growth, basing it on a description of mechanics in the human body. Postural deformities and the drawbacks of erect posture are discussed.

Physical educators know how to conduct endurance training programs that increase children's physical fitness. The research reported here by Robert W. McGowan, Boyd O. Jarman, and Darhl M. Pedersen demonstrates positive psychological effects of improvement in fitness and endurance. The effects were in self-concept, not in peer attitudes.

The timing of puberty determines the age when the child grows fast and when secondary sex characteristics are established. If the timing is fast or slow, the individual is out of phase with his age mates. Problems faced by children with early and late puberty and incongruous puberal development are discussed by John Money and Richard R. Clopper, Jr. The problems, both social and personal, can be minimized by appropriate education and sometimes helped by endocrine treatment.

One of the most unfortunate teenage physical problems is pregnancy. Teenage pregnancy is not only a physical problem but a psychological and social one as well. Not only does pregnancy affect the body of the girl who has not completed her own growth but it handicaps the baby she bears. Treatments for teenage pregnancy, both preventive and ameliorative, involve social and cultural factors, as well as physical factors. Cynthia P. Green and Susan J. Lowe discussed this topic.

Changes in Posture with Growth; Drawbacks of the Erect Posture

David Sinclair

PERTH MEDICAL CENTRE

CHANGES IN POSTURE WITH GROWTH

The vertebral column of the new-born infant has two primary curvatures which depend largely on the shape of the component bones [Figure 1]. Both are concave forwards, one being in the thoracic region, and the other being formed by the curve of the sacrum, which at this stage consists of separate sacral vertebrae. Later on the sacral curvature becomes permanently fixed by the fusing together of its vertebral components; the thoracic curve allows a certain limited amount of movement, but the intervertebral discs in this region are thin, and this restricts the scope of movement of one vertebra on another; movement is also limited by the oblique set of the spines of the vertebrae and the fact that their laminae overlap each other.

At about 3 months of age the baby begins to hold its head up, and in association with this a secondary curvature appears in the cervical region of the column. This curvature, unlike the two primary ones, is convex forwards, and remains mobile, for its radius depends on the tension of the muscles which stretch across its concavity. The mobility of the cervical curvature is largely due to the thick intervertebral discs, which allow a considerable "play" between one vertebra and its neighbours.

On top of this secondary curvature the skull has to be held balanced. At birth the position on the skull of the facets which articulate with the atlas vertebra is similar in all anthropoids. In apes the portion of the base of the skull in front of the joint grows more than the portion behind, so that the joint shifts backwards and the centre of gravity of the skull and brain falls well forward.

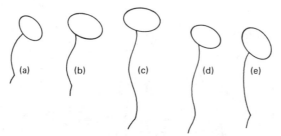

FIGURE 1.   *Changes in the spinal curvatures with growth.* (a) Infant. Two primary curvatures. (b) Six months. The secondary cervical curvature has appeared. (c) Adult. Two primary and two secondary curvatures. (d) Old age. The two secondary curvatures, dependent on the discs and the postural muscles, are becoming obliterated. (e) Final stage, corresponding to condition in infant.

From *Human Growth After Birth.* 2nd ed. London: Oxford University Press, 1973. Pp. 113–121. Reprinted by permission.

35

In man there is much less discrepancy between the growth of the skull in front of the joint and behind it. The result is that the joint comes to lie relatively much further forwards than in the apes, although the centre of gravity of the head is still in front of it. The skull therefore balances reasonably well on top of the vertebral column, but it still requires some muscular effort to keep the gaze horizontal.

When the baby begins to sit up, the lumbar curvature appears. This secondary curvature, like the cervical one, is mobile, depends largely on the discs rather than on the shape of the bones, is controlled by the great postural muscles of the vertebral column, and is convex forwards [Figure 1]. Both the secondary curvatures may fail to develop at the expected time should there be any delay in the development of the postures of sitting and holding the head up.

At the creeping stage the baby is essentially a four-footed animal, albeit with exceptionally mobile forelimbs, and his centre of gravity is supported in a very stable manner by his quadrupedal posture. When this quadruped rears himself up on end in his first efforts to walk, he has an awkward and unstable stance. Since his centre of gravity is high, he must stand with his legs widely apart in order to balance himself securely, and since it lies well forward, partly because of the large liver, there is a compensatory exaggeration of the lumbar curvature in order to bring the upper part of the body into the vertical position; this usually ceases to be necessary about the age of 4 years. In the early stages of walking the baby is often bow-legged [Figure 2]; this corrects itself gradually, and may even be followed by a knock-kneed period. As the baby stands up, so the weight of the body pressing down on the lumbosacral joint forces the upper part of the sacrum forwards and downwards; the posterior part of the sacrum and the coccyx are restrained by the sacrotuberous and sacrospinous ligaments from rotating upwards in consequence of this, with the result that the sacrum sinks more deeply in between the two innominate bones. As the legs straighten and the weight is transmitted through the pelvis to the heads of the

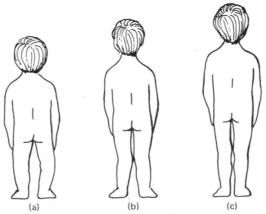

(a)   (b)   (c)

FIGURE 2.   *Development of stance.* (a) *18 months old: bow legs.* (b) *3 years old: knock knees.* (c) *6 years old: legs straight.*

femora, the pelvis becomes steadily remodelled; the force applied to the sacrum tends to lever outwards the lower part of the pelvis, thus broadening the region of the symphysis and increasing the subpubic angle. The acetabula become deeper and the hip joints more stable as the child becomes more active in his newly acquired two-legged freedom.

In the new-born the legs are flexed and the feet inverted; as walking begins the lower limbs straighten out and the feet evert, and at the same time the angle made by the neck of the femur with the shaft decreases gradually from about 160 degrees to the adult value of about 125 degrees.

In the adult the center of gravity is approximately 55 per cent of the total height from the floor, being higher in men than in women. The line of gravity naturally alters constantly according to posture. When standing at rest it falls through the external auditory meatus, behind the hip, in front of the ankle, and half-way between the heel and the balls of the toes [Figure 3]. It passes through the dens of the axis vertebra, the front of the body of the second thoracic vertebra, and the back of the body of the twelfth thoracic vertebra, and the back of the body of the fifth lumbar vertebra [Figure 4]. If the centre of gravity is

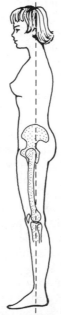

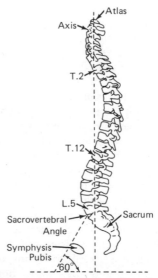

FIGURE 3.   Position of line of gravity in erect posture. The line passes through the external auditory meatus, the tip of the acromion process of the scapula, and the mid-point between the heel and the balls of the toes. It falls behind the hip joint, through the middle of the knee joint, and in front of the ankle joint.

FIGURE 4.   The line of gravity. The line passes through the dens of the axis vertebra, the front of the body of the second thoracic vertebra, the middle of the body of the twelfth thoracic vertebra, and the back of the body of the fifth lumbar vertebra. The angle made with the horizontal by a line passing through the sacral promontory and the upper border of the symphysis pubis is known as the pelvic tilt, and is usually about 60°.

allowed to fall too far backwards or forwards, muscular effort is needed to prevent falling.

The most important single factor in faulty posture is the tilt of the pelvis in relation to the horizontal. This is defined as the angle with the horizontal made by a line through the sacral promontory and the upper border of the symphysis pubis [Figure 4], which is normally about 60 degrees. The pelvic tilt is determined by the postural pull of the muscles of the back, abdomen, and thighs, and these pulls are in turn influenced by the way the individual habitually stands. A "tense" habit of standing increases the tilt, so that the pelvis rotates forwards on the thighs, carrying the lumbar spine forwards, and with it the centre of gravity. In compensation, the upper part of the body is thrust backwards, so increasing the lumbar curvature. The neck is held stiffly, with the chin tucked in, in order to maintain the horizontal gaze of the eyes. If this posture is held as a routine, the muscles which have pulled the pelvis out of position may shorten and their opponents lengthen, so that after a time the individual is unable to stand in any other way.

The converse of the "tense" posture is the "slack" posture. The pelvic tilt decreases, the center of gravity passes backwards, and the head and thorax are thrust forwards to compensate. There is thus a mild increase in the thoracic curvature, and the neck is extended, the chin being poked forwards. The joints of the lower limb tend to flex, and become mechanically unstable.

Poor posture results from many causes, which are not always as easy to determine as might be thought. The damage may originate in any part of the body, for posture is an integral whole, and anything that tends to upset one part of the mechanism will throw the rest of it out of gear. A good example is the very common defect known as "round shoulders." By this is meant a failure of the muscles of the shoulder girdle to hold the scapulae back towards the spine, so that the whole shoulder girdle drifts round the side of the chest towards the front of the body. This in turn upsets the gravitational equilibrium of the upper part of the body, for arm weight in front of the gravity line must be compensated for by alterations in the curvatures of the spine, and this in turn causes a movement of the pelvis which has repercussions on the posture of the joints of the lower limb and on the distribution of weight in the foot.

Conversely, the wearing of high-heeled shoes, which tip the body weight forwards, can lead to disturbances of the posture of the whole body working upwards through the pelvis to the spine; a complaint of aching pain in the neck can sometimes be cured by wearing a lower heel.

Postural deformities can obviously be caused by injury or disease, but there is also a hereditary factor, and mental attitudes are also of importance in determining how the child "holds himself." Deformities commonly develop in adolescence, when the weight increase at the time of the adolescent spurt may not be accompanied for some time by a corresponding increase in the strength of the postural muscles, especially in girls. Those people who have six lumbar vertebrae instead of five have a greater part of their spinal column unprotected by the leverage of the rib cage, and tend to have trouble in this region. One of the most difficult conditions to explain is scoliosis, which is a twisting deformity affecting the whole column. It is often attributed to faulty working postures in poorly designed school seats and desks, but there are certainly other factors concerned.

DRAWBACKS OF THE ERECT POSTURE

The erect posture brings with it certain advantages. The hands are freed, allowing manipulation of objects and co-ordination between the hands and brain. This in turn is responsible for an increase in the size of the brain, and thus for our capacity to make and use tools. A second advantage is that the eyes are brought further from the ground and made more mobile, since the skull can now be poised more freely on the top of the vertebral column.

But the erect posture also brings with it many disabilities, some of which are apparent quite early in life, while others tend to appear later, when the pull of gravity and the effects of tissue degeneration have been operating for a long time.

In the first place, it is a precarious equilibrium, and consequently a great part of the large central nervous system has to be devoted to maintaining this equilibrium by a complex system of reflexes and controls. These are easily lost as a result of illness, or in old age. Secondly, there is an increased strain on the bones and joints of the lower limb, particularly on the foot, and this is shown by the incidence of flat feet, sprained ankles, etc. These are much in evidence following the adolescent spurt, when violent exercise may throw an intolerable strain on the ankle region, and when periods of prolonged standing at work may place too much gravitational load on the arches of the feet.

There is also a considerable strain on the cantilever structure of the vertebral column, which is not yet fully adapted by evolution to being tipped up on end [Figure 5]. Aches and pains, degenerating joints, and damage to intervertebral discs are all common in the lower part of the column.

The pelvis is also not yet properly adapted, and remains essentially the pelvis of a four-footed animal. Nevertheless, it has to continue to allow the passage of the fetal skull, which in the course of evolution has grown bigger, while at the same time coping with a very large gravitational strain. This mechanical problem is aggravated by the postural burden which a heavy pregnant uterus lying in front of the line of gravity imposes on the vertebral column, and women who have borne several children may have troublesome pain in the lower part of the back resulting from the stress laid upon their lumbosacral and sacro-iliac joints.

In the upright position the forelimbs hang down at the side of the trunk, at right angles to their former "neutral" position. The resulting extensive anatomical alterations in the shoulder region have made some of the nerves and vessels entering the limb liable to compression and injury.

Breathing is hampered, since the whole weight of the chest wall must be raised against the pull of gravity instead of swinging at right angles to it as in the four-footed animal. The rib cage therefore tends to fall in old age, when the muscles are no longer equal to the heavy task of raising it in inspiration; this is responsible for respiratory difficulties due to deficient ventilation. At the same time the thoracic and abdominal viscera descend, and the anterior abdominal wall becomes weakened because of increased pressure on the lower portion of it; this in turn is a factor in the frequency of hernia. Similarly, there is an increased gravitational load on the pelvic floor, and this shows itself in the frequency of the condition of prolapse, in which the uterus and bladder descend through a pelvic diaphragm, weakened or damaged by childbirth.

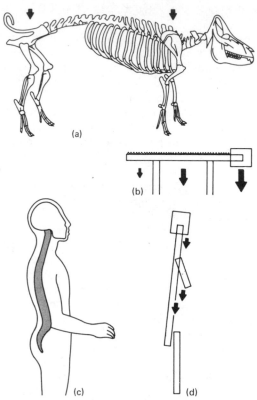

FIGURE 5.   *Stresses in the vertebral column. (a) Skeleton of a pig: the arrows indicate the points at which weight is transferred to the limbs. (b) Compare with the plan of a two-armed cantilever. The solid line indicates compression forces taken by the bones, the dotted line indicates tension forces. The spines of the vertebrae in (a) are long and powerful in order to afford attachment to muscles and ligaments resisting tension forces. (c) and (d) When this structure is stood on end, the stresses which it has to withstand are quite different.*

Finally, the elevation of the brain above the heart means that gravity interferes with its blood supply. The return of blood to the heart from the lower limbs is also impeded by the long vertical haul against gravity. For this reason the autonomic nervous system has had to develop a complicated system of vasomotor controls, and these are not always adequate to the occasion, as is seen in the condition of postural fainting, in which the blood supply to the brain is interrupted when the patient suddenly stands up. The common condition of varicose veins also testifies to the incomplete adaptation of the vascular system.

The erect posture is therefore not an unmixed blessing, and the gradual achievement of it during the first part of childhood carries with it liabilities as well as advantages. In old age many of these liabilities come home to roost, and posture undergoes regressive changes.

Effects of a Competitive Endurance Training Program on Self-Concept and Peer Approval *

Robert W. McGowan, Boyd O. Jarman, and
Darhl M. Pedersen
BRIGHAM YOUNG UNIVERSITY

Summary

The purpose of this study was to investigate the effects of a cardiovascular fitness program on the self-concept and peer approval of seventh grade boys. Thirty-seven low self-esteem Ss were randomly divided into a control group (participated in no formal physical education activity) and an experimental group (participated in a special running training program).

At the end of an 18 week training program the two groups were significantly different in cardiovascular endurance, indicating the efficacy of the experimental treatment. There was an increase in self-concept from pretest to posttest for the experimental group only. Neither group had a significant change in peer approval.

A. INTRODUCTION

Physical educators tend to promote physical education on the premise that physical fitness leads to the development of the whole person. It is believed that physical conditioning enhances a number of personal variables including the self-concept and the ability to relate to others. Empirical studies have substantiated these beliefs in part. Tillman (7) found that personality changes occurred for males in a training program if they achieved a high degree of physical fitness. In a similar study Reed (5) showed that winning in competitive activities produced a significantly improved self-concept. Stein (6) and Jones (4) both found positive relationships between physical strength and peer approval. Stronger Ss were rated higher in prowess and social popularity, whereas weaker Ss were less popular, experienced feelings of inferiority, and reported difficulty in social relations.

These studies suggest that by significantly increasing physical fitness through a program of contrived and actual success a person's self-concept and peer relationships should be significantly improved. The purpose of this study was to examine the effects of a success-oriented endurance training program on self-concept and peer approval of seventh grade boys.

B. METHOD

1. SUBJECTS Ss were male seventh grade students enrolled at Farrer Junior High School in Provo, Utah.

2. MEASURING INSTRUMENTS *a. Tennessee Self Concept Scale* The Tennessee Self Concept Scale was developed by Fitts (2) and has a reliability

Reprinted from *The Journal of Psychology*, 1974, **86**, 57–60. By permission.

* This experiment was supported in part by a Faculty Research Fellowship granted to Boyd O. Jarman and Darhl M. Pedersen by Brigham Young University.

41

of .92. Ss rated items describing relationships to peers, family, and self as to how descriptive they were of themselves on a five-point scale from strongly agree to strongly disagree.

  b. Cooper's Twelve Minute Run   This is a measure of cardiovascular fitness which was developed by Cooper (1). The task requires Ss to cover the maximum distance they can by running and walking during a 12 minute time limit. The score is the distance traveled. This score is highly correlated (.90) with the physiological measure of oxygen uptake (VO_2). It is easy to administer and has a high test-retest reliability (.91).

  c. Sociogram   The Sociogram consisted of a list of all seventh grade males. The Ss indicated their five best friends and circled their own name. It was scored by obtaining the frequency with which each S was selected as a best friend. This was the measure of peer approval utilized in the study.

3. PROCEDURE   During registration in September, 1972, all seventh grade males were given the Tennessee Self Concept Test and the Sociogram in that order. Those who scored 47 or below on the Positive Total Score (a general indicator of self-image) of the Tennessee Self Concept Scale and were chosen by three or fewer peers as "best friend" were retained as subjects. During the first two weeks of school all Ss completed Cooper's Twelve Minute Run.

  The students who were selected to participate in the experiment were randomly assigned to one of two groups—an experimental group and a control group. The experimental group was an endurance training group. They followed a training schedule similar to a running training program outlined by Gardner and Purdy (3). However, their program was adapted to a three or four day per week program instead of a seven day per week program. On nonrunning days Ss participated in various competitive activities: viz., floor hockey, basketball, football, and volleyball. Every three to four weeks the experimental group competed against the regular physical education class in a variety of activities including Cooper's Twelve Minute Run.

  The endurance training group was positively reinforced for each activity. They were told that they won on each occasion. Sometimes the win was actual and sometimes it was contrived. For the team sports, players were assigned by the experimenter to the teams in such a way as to assure victory for the experimental group. For Cooper's task, average distances were reported to the Ss in favor of the experimental group whether or not they actually had a better mean distance. They also ran mile and two mile races with experimental and physical education groups mixed. Again the mean time for the experimental group was always reported as superior.

  The endurance group was divided into three teams. Average times for the one mile, two miles, one-half mile runs were recorded every third week for each team, as well as for each individual. They ran one mile the first week, two miles the second week, and one-half mile the third week. The winning team was rewarded with sweat suits, golf caps, instructor's praise, and free time during the week. The same rewards were given for outstanding individual efforts. It was arranged so that each team won an equal number of times; i.e., success was administered with a variable ratio of 1/3.

The control group attended regular classes with no participation in physical education classes.

At the end of the 18 week semester the experimental group and the control group were retested on the Sociogram and the Tennessee Self Concept Scale.

4. ANALYSIS   The experimental and control groups were compared on each of the three measures by means of a t test to insure equality between the groups on the pretest. A t test for paired data was used to determine whether or not there were significant within-group differences from pretest to posttest over each measure.

C. RESULTS AND DISCUSSION

The t test between groups for the three measures given in the pretest revealed no significant differences, substantiating the randomness of the assignment of Ss to groups. Following the 18 week program the experimental group experienced a positive within-group change in cardiovascular fitness ($t = 8.71$, $p < .005$), indicating the efficacy of the experimental treatment. There was also a significant increase in self-concept ($t = 1.79$, $p < .05$); however, there was no significant difference in peer approval. No significant difference from the pre- to posttesting was found for the control group. This last finding indicates that the scores of the control group Ss on the posttest measures were unaffected by any intervening experiences or by the fact that they had previously taken the measures during the pretest. Thus, it may be concluded that the competitive endurance training program increased self-concept.

References

1. COOPER, K. H. The New Aerobics. New York: Bantam Books, 1972.
2. FITTS, W. H. Tennessee Self Concept Scale. Nashville, Tenn.: Counsel. Recordings & Tests, 1965.
3. GARDNER, J. B., & PURDY, J. G. Computerized Running Training Programs. Los Altos, Calif.: Tafnews Press, 1970.
4. JONES, H. E. Motor Performance and Growth, Berkeley: Univ. California Press, 1949.
5. REED, D. A. The influence of competitive and non-competitive programs of physical education on body image and self-concept. Diss. Abst. Internat., 1969, 19, 4312–4313.
6. STEIN, J. U. Physical fitness in relation to IQ, social distance, and physique of intermediate school mentally retarded boys. Diss. Abst. Internat., 1966, 27, 1253.
7. TILLMAN, K. Relationship between physical fitness and selected personality traits. Res. Quart., 1965, 36, 485–489.

Psychosocial and Psychosexual Aspects of Errors of Pubertal Onset and Development *

John Money and Richard R. Clopper, Jr.
THE JOHNS HOPKINS UNIVERSITY SCHOOL OF MEDICINE

Abstract

Pubertal anomalies fall into two major groups: errors of timing (delayed puberty and precocious puberty) and errors of congruence (for example, adolescent gynecomastia in boys, and hirsutism in girls). In cases of timing errors, the disparity between physique age and chronologic age creates a problem in social age which cannot correspond precisely with either. Social age includes academic age, recreational age, and pyschosexual age. Physique age dictates, in an almost automatic fashion, the expectancies of other people, who, therefore, overestimate the social age in precocious puberty, and underestimate it in delayed puberty. In consequence, the patient receives negative reinforcement when behaving concordantly with chronologic age.

The patient with precocious puberty, for example, is expected by others to behave in a more adult manner than his chronologic age permits. From the patient's point of view, it is a challenge to close the gap between social age and physique age, without the benefit of the usual period in which to learn more mature behavior. When I.Q. and school performance permit, school acceleration has been successfully used to foster precocious social maturation. This, in turn, assists to ameliorate the feeling of being a misfit. Psychosexual maturation is concordant with social age rather than physique age, for the most part. Masturbation may or may not be increased in frequency, relative to chronologic age. Masturbation imagery is dependent upon erotic knowledge. Dating and romance follow the usual chronologic age patterns and do not parallel the precocious maturation of physique. Early and straightforward sex education is imperative and successful in guiding sexual behavior. To date, treatment with antagonistic hormone therapy has been unsuccessful. Consequently, psychologic help is primary to the successful management of cases of precocious puberty.

For the teenager with delayed puberty, the discrepancy between physique age and chronological age induces others to infantilize or juvenilize the delayed boy or girl. In consequence, the patient may react accordingly. Also he may become a social isolate or loner. Psychosexual maturation is typically delayed and may be associated with long-term sexual inertia. Amelioration of problems of age-physique discrepancy in delayed puberty usually requires psychologic counseling and appropriate exogenous sex hormone therapy.

The major problem for people with incongruous pubertal development is to reconcile the self-concept of body image with actual physique. Typically their major concern is the matching of physique and gender identity, by means of appropriate hormonal and/or surgical therapy. Teenagers with incongruous pubertal development tend to withdraw from social relationships—particularly those that may risk their revealing their medical problem to others. Dating and romantic relationships may be disrupted. While psychologic counseling is often helpful it is not always readily available.

From *Human Biology*, 1974, **46**, No. 1, 173–181. Copyright © 1974 by Wayne State University Press. Reprinted by permission.

* This research was supported by Grant HD-00325 (USPHS) and by the Erickson Educational Foundation.

Statistically, pubertal development begins around age 11 in girls and age 13 in boys (Marshall and Tanner, 1969, 1970). Normally, this physical development is congruent with the child's gender identity, which differentiates much earlier in life (Money and Ehrhardt, 1972). When puberty occurs on schedule and is congruous with gender identity, psychosocial and psychosexual development proceed with minimal difficulty. However, when pubertal onset occurs too early or too late, or, when pubertal development is unexpectedly incongruous with respect to gender identity, normal psychosocial and psychosexual development become more difficult.

The purpose of this paper is to present the psychologic problems associated with anomalies of pubertal timing and incongruous pubertal development. Most of the information reported below was gathered in the Psychohormonal Research Unit at the Johns Hopkins Hospital and has been summarized recently in Money and Ehrhardt (1972). It is our intention to outline the nature of these adjustment problems, and the therapeutic methods that these researchers have found successful in the amelioration of these problems.

AGE DISPARITY IN INCORRECT PUBERTAL TIMING

The paradigm for understanding the psychologic problems posed by errors of pubertal timing is based on the concepts of chronologic age, psychosocial age, and physique age. The term chronologic age is self-defining while physique age and psychosocial age are not. Physique age refers to the stage of development in physique normally associated with a particular chronologic age. Psychosocial age refers to the stage of development in social behavior normally associated with a particular chronologic age. Psychosocial age includes academic, recreational, and psychosexual age.

In normal individuals chronologic age, physique age, and psychosocial age coincide. For example, a boy 13 years of age looks and behaves like a 13 year old. His physical maturation and psychosocial behavior are appropriate for his chronologic age.

Owing to the usual correspondence between these three ages, the behavioral expectations for conventionally appropriate and inappropriate behavior can readily be made with reasonable accuracy. The most available age, from the point of view of an observer's first impression, is physique age, conveyed through the visual sense. Normally, physique supplies all the information required for an accurate estimate of chronologic age. Thus one's almost automatic response is to expect a person to behave consistently with the chronologic age impression inferred from the physique age. Rewards and punishments for age-appropriate and age-inappropriate behavior can then be administered accordingly.

When physical maturation is grossly disparate from chronologic age, as is the case in atypical pubertal timing, it is virtually certain that all newcomers, meeting the patient for the first time, will erroneously estimate the patient's chronologic age. When the observer's error is not corrected by behavioral feedback appropriate to either the physique age or chronologic age his error is further compounded: his reactions and expectancies are based on either an underestimation or overestimation of chronologic age and also of the reservoir of experience that age normally implies. Herein lies the psychologic problem central to errors of pubertal timing.

ERRORS OF PUBERTAL TIMING

Errors of timing in pubertal physical development are classified as either precocious or delayed. Both occur in males and females. In precocious puberty, the abnormally early onset of pubertal development can appear as early as birth, but more typically occurs around the ages of 4 to 6 years. It is marked by the early onset of the secondary sexual signs of maturation and of the adolescent growth spurt and epiphysial closure. It is related directly to early pituitary stimulation and the release of gonadal sex hormones into the blood stream. Adult height in affected individuals is often around 5 feet, owing to premature epiphysial closure. Reproductive fertility is established as much as six to ten years before the usual age.

Delayed puberty is, with respect to timing, the converse of precocious puberty in that sexual maturation is delayed beyond the normal age of pubertal onset. Delayed pubertal onset is more common in males than females. In females, the more common problem is delay of onset of menstruation rather than delay of onset of pubertal physique. Delayed puberty is related directly to a lack of sex hormones in the blood stream and may be either temporary or chronic in duration. Hormonal lack may itself be secondary to gonadal failure or to hypothalamo-pituitary failure; the latter may be idiopathic or consequent upon a brain lesion. Dependent on diagnosis, the problems of delayed puberty may be transient or chronic. Only the chronic form is referred to in this paper.

PRECOCIOUS PUBERTY

In cases of precocious puberty, physique age rapidly accelerates beyond chronologic age. Social age remains somewhere in between. As a consequence of physique and chronologic age disparity, precocious children automatically and routinely are expected by others, parents and other adults included, to behave in a more adult manner than their chronologic age permits (Money and Alexander, 1969).

The same age discrepancy that creates problems in adult behavioral expectancies also may present problems for the precocious child, himself or herself, in forming friendship and play relationships. Though precocious children prefer to play and make friends with children who resemble them in size and strength, they have difficulty being accepted by older and bigger children (Money and Alexander, 1969). They lack the social expertise, if not the greater physical maturation, of older children. At the same time, however, age mates may have difficulty accepting the precocious child, because of his or her larger physique and greater strength and energy. As a result, precocious children tend to view themselves as freaks or misfits, rather than feeling superior because of their size. They need to close the gap between social age and physical age. School acceleration is one way of helping to close this gap.

Psychosexual development need be no more difficult for precocious children than for pubertally normal children. In boys who are physically precocious (Money and Alexander, 1969), the capacity for erection, ejaculation, and erotic fantasy are precocious in their appearance. The content of erotic fantasy, however, seems to be contingent upon the boy's knowledge of sex and, developmentally, to closely parallel the imagery reported by normal boys. In girls who are physically precocious, Money and Walker (1971) reported that no persistent progression of erotic fantasies was found, and no evidence, including observed or reported masturbation, indicated an early interest in genitopelvic sexual behavior. Romantic and sexual involvements typically did not occur until middle teenage, or later, in precocious boys and girls, and were sometimes complicated by feelings of inferiority and being undesirably different. Precocious sexual development did not lead automatically to sexual promiscuity. Paraphilias were conspicuous by their absence in both males and females.

The successful management of sexually precocious children is, to date, primarily psychologic in nature, since antagonistic sex hormone therapy has not proved entirely successful. School acceleration by 1 to 2 years has been shown to be helpful in fostering an acceleration of social age, but is dependent on I.Q. and prior school achievement (Money and Neill, 1967). Fortunately, I.Q. frequently allows school acceleration (Money and Lewis, 1966; Money and Meredith, 1967; Money and Walker, 1971). Complete and accurate sex education, close to the time of pubertal onset, has proved valuable in guiding sexual behavior. Such education should include the physiology of sex and reproduction, including intercourse, and the social facts of sex such as privacy (Money, 1968), and love education, graded according to social age.

DELAYED PUBERTY

The age discrepancy in cases of delayed puberty is one in which physique age lags behind chronological age, with social age somewhere in between. The psychologic difficulty facing teenagers with delayed puberty is the problem of keeping the social age congruent with chronological age. The almost automatic reaction of both peers and adults is to treat a pubertally delayed teenager according to his physique age rather than his chronologic age. This infantilization makes it easy for the individual to be delayed in social development, since he is too often rewarded for behaving younger than his age, and held back from behaving in a manner appropriate for his age. The tendency toward marking time socially is seen most frequently as a preference for playing with chronologically younger children. Another reaction to disparity between physique and chronologic age may be that of being a loner—often as a consequence of peer rejection. Owing to delayed physical maturation, delayed teenagers often have difficulty competing successfully with their age mates, especially in sports (Money and Alexander, 1967).

Psychosexual development is typically delayed until the time of physical pubertal onset. Sexual inertia, after the induction of puberty with appropriate sex hormone therapy is common, though dependent on the diagnosis and etiology (Bobrow, Lewis, and Money, 1972; Ehrhardt, Greenberg, and Money, 1970; Money and Alexander, 1967; Money and Mittenthal, 1970). Masturbation, which is less frequent in females than in males, is variable in frequency prior to sex hormone treatment and generally increases following such therapy. Its post-treatment frequency, however, is usually lower than for normal individuals.

The frequency of erection and ejaculation is increased by the institution of appropriate sex hormone therapy, and may or may not reach normal levels. Libido or interest in sex is usually low even after exogenous sex hormone treatment. Erotic fantasies are infrequent prior to hormone therapy but they tend to increase following the induction of puberty. Dating and romantic involvements, as well as sexual experience including intercourse, are, with very few exceptions, delayed chronologically until after the onset of puberty. Marriage frequency varies according to the diagnosis. Paraphilias, that is sexual behavior disorders associated with an unusual object stimulus as in fetishism, are rare or non-occurrent. So also is homosexuality.

The endocrine treatment for delayed puberty depends on the diagnosis and, specifically, on whether the delay is temporary or chronic. Exogenous sex hormone therapy to induce and/or maintain pubertal development must be timed individually, since the administration of sex hormone is accompanied by epiphysial closure and the cessation of linear growth. In cases of statural dwarfism with pubertal delay, the timing of treatment is particularly important because ultimate height is typically of prime concern to the patient.

The psychologic aspects of case management in late puberty include counselling to aid in the maintenance of a social age congruent with chronological age, as well as complete and factual sex education.

BODY IMAGE AND GENDER IDENTITY IN INCONGRUOUS PUBERTAL DEVELOPMENT

The psychologic problems associated with incongruous pubertal development primarily involve the reconciliation of gender identity with a sexually incongruous body image. Usually, gender identity is differentiated as male or female by puberty, though it may be ambivalent. It is not determined exclusively by chromosomal sex, prenatal hormonal sex, or pubertal hormonal sex, but is heavily dependent on postnatal socialization (Money and Ehrhardt, 1972). The male faced with a feminizing puberty, or the female faced with a masculinizing puberty, usually experiences fears of further incongruous development and its unknown consequences. Usually gender identity *per se* is not affected, except in unusual cases in which the pubertal child's gender identity is ambiguous, or when incongruous development is so precocious in its onset as to interfere with gender identity differentiation.

Persistent adolescent gynecomastia or breast growth in the male, may be idiopathic or associated with another endocrinologic and/or cytogenic anomaly. The degree of breast development varies. A mild degree of gynecomastia, in the sense that there is some non-fatty, glandular, or ductal tissue palpable, has been estimated to occur transiently in as many as 70% of pubertal boys (Gallagher, 1968). Because it is self-regressing and creates no visible problem, this minimal degree of gynecomastia needs to be distinguished from the more persistent degree in which the proliferation of breast tissue can approximate the amount normally found in an adolescent girl. The size and persistence of gynecomastia is related directly to the magnitude of the psychologic problem that ensues.

In girls, incongruous pubertal development usually takes the form of abnormal body hair growth (hirsutism), which may be associated with menstrual irregularity or failure. In some untreated syndromes, for example, the adrenogenital syndrome, the development of a masculine skeletal and muscular physique occurs also. Like gynecomastia in males, the origins of hirsutism are only partially understood, but are related to an elevated level of androgen.

PERSISTENT ADOLESCENT GYNECOMASTIA IN THE MALE

Upon reaching puberty and being confronted with the development of breasts in contradiction to gender identity, a boy may fear continued incongruous anatomical development and sex change. Since gender identity disturbances are seldom involved, the primary concern of such a boy is to have his breasts surgically removed. Hormones that feminize the chest do not feminize the mind. The sense of shame experienced by a boy with breasts may lead to self-sabotaging modesty. Such modesty can even delay his seeking medical help. The boy may tend toward social isolation and reclusiveness, to avoid ridicule and teasing from age mates.

Psychosexually, there is no correlation between incongruous pubertal development and either bisexuality or homosexuality. Erotic behavior follows gender identity differentiation. Dating and romantic involvements, however, may be delayed until medical treatment restores an appropriate body appearance.

When breast enlargement does not regress, surgical treatment of adolescent gynecomastia is indicated. Parallel psychologic counseling is desirable also. In rare cases, sex appropriate hormone therapy may be prescribed in addition.

HIRSUTISM IN THE FEMALE

The psychologic problems for a girl with hirsutism closely parallel those of a boy with gynecomastia. Since gender identity is already well differentiated, in the majority of cases, the primary concern of such a girl is the restoration of a female appearance. Hirsutism may breed a sense of shame or freakishness, social reclusiveness, and fear of exposure. Dating and romantic interests are frequently disrupted, though bisexuality and lesbianism are not in general a problem, since sexual behavior and gender identity are typically consistent with sex of assignment and rearing.

The management of these cases usually includes appropriate sex hormone therapy and psychologic counseling.

PROBLEMS OF SECURING PROFESSIONAL GUIDANCE

One difficulty, not yet mentioned, for patients with pubertal anomalies, is the problem of securing adequate professional help. Professional counseling is required when problems reach severe psychologic proportions. Often physicians are hard pressed for time to provide the psychologic help required, even if adequately trained to do so. Psychologists and psychiatrists seldom have an adequate endocrine background on which to base their counseling. Ideally, both the psychologic and medical services should be coordinated. This ideal requires the development of new programs in medical psychology for medical students and graduate students.

References

BOBROW, N. A., J. MONEY AND V. G. LEWIS, 1971. Delayed puberty, eroticism, and sense of smell: A psychological study of hypogonadotropinism, osmatic and anosmatic (Kallmann's syndrome). Archs. Sexual Behavior 1: 329–344.

EHRHARDT, A. A., N. GREENBERG AND J. MONEY, 1970. Female gender identity and absence of fetal hormones: Turner's syndrome. Johns Hopkins Med. J. 126: 237–248.

GALLAGHER, J. R., 1968. Adolescents and their disorders. In The Biologic Basis of Pediatric Practice, Edited by R. E. Cooke, McGraw-Hill, New York.

MARSHALL, W. A. AND J. M. TANNER, 1969. Variations in pattern of pubertal changes in girls. Archs. Dis. Childh. 44: 291–303.

—— 1970. Variations in the pattern of pubertal changes in boys. Archs. Dis. Childh. 45: 13–23.

MONEY, J., 1968. Sex errors of the body. Johns Hopkins Press, Baltimore.

MONEY, J. AND D. ALEXANDER, 1967. Eroticism and sexual function in developmental anorchia and hyporchia with pubertal failure. J. Sex Res. 3: 31–47.

—— 1969. Psychosexual development and absence of homosexuality in males with precocious puberty: Review of 18 cases. J. Nerv. Ment. Dis. 148: 111–123.

MONEY, J. AND A. A. EHRHARDT, 1972. Man & woman, boy & girl: Differentiation and dimorphism of gender identity from conception to maturity. Johns Hopkins Press, Baltimore.

MONEY, J. AND V. LEWIS, 1966. I.Q., genetics and accelerated growth: Adrenogenital syndrome. Bull. Johns Hopkins Hosp. 118: 365–373.

MONEY, J. AND T. MEREDITH, 1967. Elevated verbal I.Q. and idiopathic precocious sexual maturation. Ped. Res. 1: 59–65.

MONEY, J. AND S. MITTENTHAL, 1970. Lack of personality pathology in Turner's syndrome: Relation to cytogenetics, hormones, and physique. Behav. Genet. 1: 43–56.

MONEY, J. AND J. NEILL, 1967. Precocious puberty, I.Q., and school acceleration. Clin. Ped. 6: 277–280.

MONEY, J. AND P. A. WALKER, 1971. Psychosexual development, maternalism, non-promiscuity, and body image in 15 females with precocious puberty. Archs. Sexual Behavior 1: 45–60.

Teenage Pregnancy : A Major Problem for Minors

Cynthia P. Green and Susan J. Lowe

Teenagers account for one out of every five births in the U.S., nearly 617,000 births in 1973. A large proportion of these births (70–85%) are unplanned. One in ten teenagers has a child in her teen years. About four in ten teenage mothers are married; three in ten are unmarried, and three in ten marry before giving birth or soon after. In addition, one out of every three abortions is performed on a teenager; teenagers had an estimated 275,000 abortions in 1974.

Teenage pregnancy is a long-standing social problem which has only recently received public attention. Contrary to popular belief, the incidence of teenage

From *Zero Population Growth National Reporter*, 1975, 7:6, 4–5. Reprinted by permission of Zero Population Growth.

pregnancy is not increasing, except for women under the age of 15. From 1972–1973 the birth rate for women under 15 increased eight percent. While women aged 15–19 experienced a four percent decline in fertility during the same period, this was the lowest decline for all age groups from 15–49.

Increased public concern over teenage pregnancy may be attributed to the increasing proportion of teenage births in relation to total births and to the rising proportion of out-of-wedlock births among teenagers.

In the past, pregnant teenagers were pressured to get married or have their babies secretly and put them up for adoption. Previously, pregnant teenagers were routinely expelled from school; today teen mothers are asserting their right to an education, and special classes and programs have been started in many communities. There is growing recognition that social sanctions to punish the teenager neither prevent pregnancy nor solve the problems teen mothers encounter.

In addition to facing higher health risks both for themselves and their children, teenage mothers are often forced to leave school and to forego job training and other opportunities for economic advancement. Unmarried mothers face social disapproval, financial hardship, and difficulty in finding work and child care facilities. If they marry, teenage mothers are more likely to have unstable marriages and financial problems than others of the same age and socioeconomic status. Women who have their first child in their teen years tend to have more children in quicker succession than their peers.

Planned Parenthood officials predict an epidemic of teenage pregnancies due to increased sexual activity, non-use or ineffective use of contraceptives, and lack of contraceptive information and services for teenagers. Nearly three in ten teenage women are sexually experienced; only one in five of those who are sexually experienced consistently uses contraceptives. Moreover, only one-fifth to one-third of the teenagers in need of family planning are being served in organized programs.

DEMOGRAPHIC PROFILE

The Census Bureau estimates that in mid-1974, there were approximately 10.3 million females aged 15–19 and 10.2 million females aged 10–14. With about one million fewer women aged 20–24, the emergence of this large group of young people into their childbearing years will have major significance for future population trends.

The 1970 Census found that school enrollment dropped off rapidly after the age of 16, with 86% of 17-year-old females and 61% of 18-year-old females in school. In the 16–17-year-old age category, 37% of the females were employed full or part-time, as were 56% of those aged 18–19. Over one-quarter (28%) of those 19-year-old females surveyed were married, compared with 12% of the males. Half of all married teenage women had had at least one child at the time of the 1970 Census. Six out of ten females aged 14–19 had an annual income of less than $1,000.

TEEN SEXUAL ACTIVITY RISING

Surveys confirm that a large number of teenage females are sexually active, and there are signs that the age of initiation is decreasing. A 1971 study

TABLE 1
Out-of-Wedlock Births

| | NUMBER | | PERCENT OF LIVE BIRTHS WHICH ARE OUT-OF-WEDLOCK | |
YEAR	Under 15	15–19	Under 15	15–19
1973	10,900	204,900	85	34
1971	9,500	194,100	82	31
1968	approx. 168,600		81	27

AGE-SPECIFIC FERTILITY RATES (number of births per 1,000 women in each age group)

	1973	1970	1960
Under 15	1.3	1.2	.8
Ages 15–19	59.7	68.3	89.1

SOURCE: U.S. Dept. of Health, Education, and Welfare, National Center for Health Statistics, *Monthly Vital Statistics Report Final Natality Statistics, 1968, 1971, and 1974,* Vol. 23, No. 3, 11, June 7, 1974 and Jan. 30, 1975.

of women aged 15–19 found that 28% had some coital experience, and the experience increased with age. The researchers estimated that about three percent of those aged 19 in 1971 had had sexual intercourse by age 15, compared with nine percent of those aged 15 in 1971. The number of unmarried black females aged 15–19 who had had intercourse was twice that of whites—54% compared with 23%.[1]

More than two million unmarried women age 15–19 are sexually active and at risk of unintended pregnancy.[2]

TEEN CONTRACEPTIVE USE IRREGULAR

Teenage pregnancy is largely the result of non-use or sporadic use of contraception. A 1971 nationwide study found that 53% of the sexually active 15–19-year-olds failed to use any kind of contraception the last time they had intercourse. Teenagers tend to believe that they cannot become pregnant easily. Of those who did not use contraception at last intercourse, 56% stated that they were too young to get pregnant, that they had sex too infrequently to get pregnant, or that they had intercourse at the wrong time of the month.[3]

A recent study of contraception and pregnancy among American teenage women showed that 71% of sexually active teenagers do not use contraception because of ignorance of pregnancy risk and 31% because of inaccessibility of contraceptive services. Eight out of ten (84%) of the non-users of contraceptives did not wish to become pregnant; seven percent of the teenagers wanted to have a baby, and nine percent said that they didn't mind if they became pregnant.

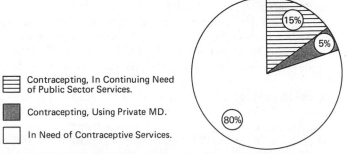

Contracepting, In Continuing Need of Public Sector Services.

Contracepting, Using Private MD.

In Need of Contraceptive Services.

FIGURE 1.   *Percent distribution of currently sexually active never-married women aged 15–19 not desiring pregnancy, by contraceptive use status, United States, 1973 (minimum estimate).*

The study found that teenagers from poor families, those with limited educational backgrounds, and those with low educational aspirations were less likely to use contraceptives. Fewer black teenagers than whites used contraceptives, though this difference in largely related to their poverty status. Catholics reported higher levels of contraceptive use than either Protestants or those with no religious affiliation.[4]

Researchers found no evidence that the availability of abortion would weaken the motivation to use contraception. When asked what they thought a young unmarried girl should do if she finds herself pregnant by a boy she does not love, only one-fifth of the sexually experienced teenagers chose the option of ending the pregnancy.[5]

According to a 1971 study, the condom, withdrawal, and the Pill account for almost three-quarters of all contraceptive use among teenagers. The condom was named the "most recently used" method by 27% of the sexually experienced teenagers, while 24% used withdrawal, 21% used the Pill, six percent used foam, cream, diaphragm, or rhythm, five percent used a douche, and one percent had an IUD. As age increases, non-use of contraception decreases, use of withdrawal decreases, and use of the Pill increases.[6]

PREGNANCY AMONG TEENAGERS

Nearly three in ten teenage women who have premarital intercourse become pregnant, according to a 1971 study. Of these, 35% marry before the outcome of the pregnancy (birth or abortion) and an additional 10% marry after the outcome of the pregnancy. Of the 55% who do not marry, 60% have live births, 19% obtain abortions, and eight percent miscarry.

The study found that whites were more likely to marry as a result of pregnancy; 51% of the whites and nine percent of the blacks married before the outcome of the pregnancy. White teenagers are also more likely to opt for abortion, with 36% of the whites and five percent of the blacks choosing abortion in the 1971 survey.[7]

TEENS HAVE ONE-THIRD OF U.S. ABORTIONS

Single teenagers accounted for at least one-quarter of the abortions performed in the U.S., according to Planned Parenthood Federation of

America. In 1974, some 275,000 abortions were performed on unmarried women under the age of 20.[8]

H. E. W.'s Center for Disease Control found that in 1973 one-third of the legal abortions reported by states were to women under the age of 20. Data from 23 states showed that women under 15 had 1.2 abortions for every live birth, while women aged 15–19 had about two live births for every abortion.[9]

There is evidence that the legalization of abortion has influenced the nationwide decline in out-of-wedlock teenage births between 1970–1971, though it has not substantially reduced out-of-wedlock births. States with liberal abortion laws in 1970–1971 experienced declines in out-of-wedlock births of 14% for white teenagers and eight percent for non-whites. In states prohibiting abortion, out-of-wedlock births declined six percent for white teenagers and rose three percent for non-whites.[10]

Teenagers appear to have somewhat more conservative attitudes toward abortion than adults. In a national survey, a majority supported a woman's right to have an abortion in cases of danger to the woman's health, rape, and possible deformity. Although more than two in five teenagers believed that abortion should be available to a very young unmarried woman, a majority did not believe that this was a strong enough reason for abortion.[11]

CHILDBEARING AMONG TEENAGERS

In 1973, nearly one out of five (19%) of all live births in the U.S. were to teenagers—13,000 to women under 15 and 604,000 to women aged 15–19. Between 1972 and 1973, the number of births to women under 15 increased by six percent, and the birth rate for this group increased by eight percent. In the same period, births to women 15–19 decreased by two percent and the birth rate by four percent.[12]

The proportion of births rises rapidly with age. The National Center for Health Statistics calculated that in 1968, one percent of the 15-year-old females gave birth, three percent of the 16-year-olds, six percent of the 17-year-olds, ten percent of the 18-year-olds, and 13% of the 19-year-olds. Teenagers tend to have their children in quick succession. In 1968, one-quarter of all teenage mothers had more than one child before the age of 20, and 23% of the births to teenagers were second or higher order.[13]

Three out of ten teenage births are out-of-wedlock, and the proportion of births to unmarried teenagers compared with married teens is increasing. With the decline in marital fertility there has been a shift to child bearing outside of marriage for both black and white teenagers. It is estimated that in 1973, more than one-fourth of the babies born to white teenagers and almost three-fourths of the babies born to black teenagers were out-of-wedlock. Increased availability of abortion has slowed the rise in out-of-wedlock births which occurred in the late 1960's, but it has not reversed the trend.

Over half (53%) of the out-of-wedlock births in 1973 were to teenagers—10,900 to women under 15 and 204,000 to women 15–19. Between 1972 and 1973, there was a 19% increase in out-of-wedlock births to white women under 15.

PREGNANCY-RELATED MARRIAGES LIKELY TO FAIL

Early marriage as a result of a premarital pregnancy is fairly common. The National Center for Health Statistics estimates that six out of ten infants born to teenage mothers in 1968 were conceived out-of-wedlock. Studies show that nearly half of all teenage marriages break up within five years and that teenage marriages resulting from pregnancy are three times more likely to dissolve.[14]

Teenage marriages which involve a pregnancy are economically disadvantaged in terms of occupation, income, and assets when compared with couples of similar socio-economic status.[15] Many pregnant teenagers drop out of school, which contributes not only to social and economic difficulties but also leads to repeat pregnancies and larger than average families.[16]

TEEN MOTHERS RUN HEALTH RISK

With improved medical techniques, deaths related to childbearing have been dramatically reduced in the past two decades. Mortality risk for teenagers has declined considerably, although teenagers are more likely to have complications related to pregnancy. For whites, the risk of mortality associated with pregnancy is higher for teenagers than for women aged 20–29, but lower than the rate for women 30 and over. The maternal mortality rate for nonwhites is four times that of whites and increases gradually until the age of 30 when it rises sharply.[17] The most common complications of teenage pregnancy are toxemia, prolonged labor, and iron-deficiency anemia. Poor nutrition, inadequate prenatal care, and physical immaturity contribute to the risk of complications.

Children born to teenage mothers face substantial health risks. Infant mortality for both white and nonwhite mothers under 15 is more than twice as high as for mothers in their early 20's. Children born to both white and nonwhite women aged 19 or younger have higher mortality rates than for mothers in their 20's and 30's.[18] The incidence of prematurity and low birth weight is higher among teenage pregnancies, increasing the risk of such conditions as epilepsy, cerebral palsy, and mental retardation.

CLINIC SERVICES FOR TEEENS INADEQUATE

Until recent years, teenagers had difficulty obtaining contraceptive services unless they had married or produced an out-of-wedlock child. Today, unmarried teenagers are legally entitled to contraceptive services on their own consent in 22 states (47 states for women 18 and over). Despite the more liberal laws, unmarried teenagers in many communities still have trouble locating contraceptive services.

National studies indicate that some two million unmarried women aged 15–19 are in need of contraceptive services and that only one-fifth to one-third of them are being served by organized family planning programs.[19] In 1973, nearly three in ten (28%) of the 3.2 million patients seen in organized family planning programs were teenagers; a large proportion of these 896,000 teenage patients may have been married.[20] Planned Parenthood clinics have seen an eightfold increase in the number of new teenage patients in the past six years (828% between 1968 and 1973).[21]

Studies show that most teenagers seek contraceptive services after they have become sexually active; many of them come to clinics initially for pregnancy tests. Traditional sanctions against premarital sex have not kept teenagers celibate but rather appear to have contributed to the non-use and sporadic use of contraceptives as well as the tendency to select unreliable contraceptive methods. Ironically, moral codes intended to prevent out-of-wedlock pregnancy appear to have had the opposite effect.

LAWS REGARDING MINORS

The last five years have seen expanded rights for teenagers as most states lowered the age of majority to eighteen. At present, an unmarried 18-year-old woman can legally consent to all aspects of medical care including contraception in 47 states and the District of Columbia. In all states but Nebraska and Wyoming she can obtain most pregnancy-related services, abortion, and treatment for venereal disease on her own consent.

Although it is still difficult for young people under age 18 to obtain contraceptive services, 22 states and the District of Columbia now allow minors contraceptive care on their own consent; 17 states and the District of Columbia permit persons under 18 to consent to abortion. The doctrine of the "mature" or "emancipated" minor is gaining acceptance. It holds that a minor intelligent enough to understand the nature and consequences of a particular medical treatment may consent to it. Five states (Ark., Id., Miss., Mont., N.H.) have "mature minor" statutes, and several other states have recognized the doctrine through court decisions.

Although 18-year-old women may obtain abortions on their own initiative in all states except Nebraska and Wyoming, minors face complicated obstacles in obtaining abortions without parental consent. Many states have laws specifically requiring parental consent, and other states which permit contraceptive services to minors on their own consent specifically exclude abortion. A minor's right to privacy has been recognized in court decisions in Colorado, Florida, Kentucky, Massachusetts, Utah, and Washington, where parental consent requirements for abortion were declared unconstitutional.[22]

Much more work needs to be done to educate teenagers and their parents on the problems related to teenage pregnancy and the availability of contraceptive information, counseling, and services. In addition, school authorities, social workers, and health personnel, especially physicians, must be made aware of the special needs of teenagers.

Teenage pregnancy is a complicated problem which will be with us for some time to come. Failing to act today only compounds the high human, social, and economic costs to be borne by teenage mothers, their children, and society in general.

Reference Notes

1. JOHN F. KANTNER and MELVIN ZELNIK, "Sexual Experience of Young Unmarried Women in the United States," *Family Planning Perspectives*, IV:4 — (Oct. 1972), p. 10.

2. Joy G. Dryfoos, "A Formula for the 1970's Estimating Need for Subsidized Family Planning Services in the U.S.", *Family Planning Perspectives*, V:3 (Summer 1973), p. 145–172.
3. John F. Kantner and Melvin Zelnik, "Contraception and Pregnancy: Experience of Young Unmarried Women in the United States," *Perspectives*, V:1 (Winter 1973), p. 22.
4. Kantner and Zelnik (1973), *Ibid*, p. 26.
5. Kantner and Zelnik (1973), *Ibid*, p. 26.
6. Kantner and Zelnik (1973), *Ibid*, p. 26.
7. Melvin Zelnik and John F. Kantner, "The Resolution of Teenage First Pregnancies," *Perspectives*, VI:2, (Spring 1974), p. 74–80.
8. Gene Vadies and Richard Pomeroy, "Pregnancy Among Single American Teenagers," unpublished paper delivered at meeting of the Association of Planned Parenthood Physicians, Los Angeles, 1975.
9. U.S. Dept. of Health, Education, and Welfare, Center for Disease Control, *Abortion Surveillance: Annual Summary 1973* (May 1975), p. 1, 16.
10. June Sklar and Beth Berkov, "Teenage Family Formation in Postwar America." *Perspectives* VI:2 (Spring 1974), p. 85–86.
11. Melvin Zelnik and John F. Kantner, "Attitudes of American Teenagers Toward Abortion," *Perspectives* VII:2 (Mar./Apr. 1975), p. 89.
12. U.S. Dept. of Health, Education, and Welfare, National Center for Health Statistics, Monthly Vital Statistics Report: *Summary Report, Final Natality Statistics, 1973*, Vol. 23, No. 11, Jan. 30, 1975.
13. U.S. Dept. of Health, Education, and Welfare, National Center for Health Statistics, *Vital Statistics of the U.S.*, Natality, Vol. 1.
14. Lolagene C. Coombs et al., "Premarital Pregnancy and Status before and after Marriage," *American Journal of Sociology*, 75:5 (March 1970), p. 800–820.
    John G. Claudy and James M. Richards, Jr. "Psychological and Social Factors in Fertility in the Early Years of Marriage: An Exploratory Study," paper presented at the annual convention of the American Psychological Association, Washington, D.C., Sept. 3–7, 1971.
15. Lolagene C. Coombs et al. *Ibid*.
16. Linda Ambrose, "Discrimination Persists Against Pregnant Students Remaining in School," *Perspectives*, IV:1 (Feb. 1975).
    Elizabeth Whelan and George Higgins, *Teenage Childbearing: Extent and Consequences* (Washington, D.C.: Child Welfare League of America Inc./Consortium on Early Childbearing and Childrearing, 1973).
17. Jane Menken, "The Health and Social Consequences of Teenage Childbearing," *Family Planning Perspectives*, IV:3 (July 1972), p. 49.
18. Menken, *Ibid*, p. 47–48.
19. Leo Morris, "Estimating the Need for Family Planning Services Among Unwed Teenagers," *Perspectives*, VI:2 (Spring 1972); F. S. Jaffe et al., "Who Needs Organized Family Planning Services?: A Preliminary Projection, 1971–75," *Perspectives*, III:3 (1971).
20. Farida Shah, Melvin Zelnik and John F. Kantner, "Unprotected Intercourse Among Unwed Teenagers," *Prespectives*, VII:1 (Jan./Feb. 1975), p. 39–43.
21. Vadies and Pomeroy (1975), *Ibid*.
22. Eve W. Paul, Harriet F. Pilpel and Nancy F. Wechsler, "Pregnancy, Teenagers and the Law, 1974," *Perspectives*, VI:3 (Summer 1974).
23. Commission on Population Growth and the American Future, *Population and the American Future* (Washington, D.C.: U.S. Government Printing Office, 1972), p. 42.

Chapter 2
Intellectual Development

Psychological growth is just as dramatic as physical growth at the beginning of adolescence. Between 12 and 14 years, on the average, thought processes are reorganized on a higher level, making the adolescent different from the school-age child just as the school-age child is different from the preschool child. The new level of thinking, formal thought, is not the automatic result of accumulated years any more than the transition from sensorimotor to preoperational intelligence is automatic. New schemas result from the child's using what he has already to interact with the environment. His achievements depend upon his own resources and what the environment offers. Some adolescents, therefore, go further than others in building and using the structures of formal thought. Some individuals never achieve formal thought.

Even though an individual, either adolescent or adult, is capable of formal thinking, she uses it only sometimes, not always [13]. In fact, most adult reasoning incorporates concrete information from the present situation instead of confining itself to the premises given. Whether a person uses formal thought in a particular

59

instance seems to be influenced by familiarity with the task, credibility of the situation, and attitude toward the subject matter [27].

The Stage of Formal Thought or Logical Operations

Each new stage in thinking brings greater freedom and stronger control in intellectual operations. The stage of formal thinking carries the greatest mobility of all the stages. The infant is confined to her own sensory perceptions and motor acts of the immediate present. The preschool child uses words and symbols to represent actions and perceptions, thus speeding up her dealings with the world, but she is still confined largely to individual objects and events. Egocentric in that she is tied to one perception or another, her thought is not free and mobile enough to weigh and balance various aspects of an experience with each other and with other knowledge. The school-age child's thought is free in that she can delay response while considering and judging much information. She can also think an act and then think it undone, since thought is reversible at this age. The adolescent excels her, however, in freedom, control, elaboration, and completeness of thought.

When children are in the process of moving from the stage of concrete operations into the stage of formal thought, their achievements differ from one area to another. Transition into the higher level is not a sudden, all-or-none event, but a gradual working through, in the various subject matter areas. Seventh-grade and tenth-grade students were tested on acquisition and application of concepts from science, social studies, and literature [41]. The two grades were similar on acquisition, which represents a lower level type of understanding, probably including rote learning. The tenth grade was definitely superior on application, which requires more abstract understanding. Intercorrelations between tests of application in the three areas were significantly higher for tenth-grade students. That is, seventh graders were unevenly developed across subject matter areas, in regard to formal thinking, but tenth graders had achieved some consistency as to formal thinking in the three areas. This finding has educational implications for the junior high school, where a student is likely to be able to do abstract thinking in one area but not in another.

CHARACTERISTICS OF ADOLESCENT THINKING

The distinctive characteristics of thinking in the stage of formal operations, as compared with previous stages, can be summarized under the following headings:

Freedom, Mobility, and Flexibility. The adolescent can think in terms of abstract symbols, instead of having to base his thought on concrete things and events. He is thus freed from restraints of time and space, able to range throughout the universe, entertaining concepts with which he has had no real experience, such as the notion of infinity. Thus he is free to move in his thoughts and he is flexible, free to move in any direction. He does not get stuck with his perceptions, as does the preschool child, or stuck with his conclusions, as does the school-age child. A child–adolescent difference in flexibility of thought is demonstrated by a concept–production task [10]. Fourth-grade and ninth-grade subjects were asked to tell how a shoehorn, a table knife, and a pair of scissors were alike. Half of each group saw real objects and half were given the names verbally. The older group produced significantly more concepts than the younger (4.71 versus 2.88). For the adolescents, it made little difference whether the stimuli were given in concrete or verbal form but for the fourth-grade children it made a large difference. The younger subjects gave over twice as many similarities when the objects were presented as they did when the verbal labels were given. Thus, the younger children's thinking was more dependent upon perception than was the adolescents'. Further study [11] showed that adolescents could shift more readily than could children in their mode of conceptualizing.

Control. Formal thinking requires strict control of thought. Similar to the child's achievement of considering more than one perception before acting, but much more complex, the adolescent's achievement includes keeping herself from being distracted by irrelevant thoughts, taking account of all premises or pertinent information, holding all aspects in mind while considering one, organizing information, relating it and reflecting on all aspects of the situation before concluding.

One particular facet of the abstract attitude that distinguishes the stage of concrete operations from formal operations is this: the adolescent can think about her own thinking; the child cannot. Here, then, is another step away from egocentrism and toward mobility of thought, to be able to stand off and reflect upon one's own intellectual activity. This is to be truly self-conscious, a complex, differentiated being.

Logical thought involves starting with the premises or what is given, neither adding to it nor subtracting from it, and reasoning with that information. For example:

Blonde hair turns green on St. Patrick's Day.
Bertha has colored her hair blonde.
It will turn green on St. Patrick's Day.

When asked if the last statement is true, the person employing formal thought would say *yes*. The person not thinking formally would probably say, "Blonde hair does not turn green on St. Patrick's Day. I've never seen it happen," or perhaps, "Bertha's wouldn't turn green, anyway, because it isn't really blonde." Piaget [34] places the change to formal thinking at around 11 or 12. Below 12, he says, children rarely solve this problem:

Edith is fairer than Susan.
Edith is darker than Lily.
Who is the darkest of the three?

Until then, they give such answers as, "Edith and Susan are fair, Edith and Lily are dark; therefore Lily is darkest, Susan is fairest and Edith in between."

In her study of children's thinking, Donaldson [8] found that between 12 and 14, children increased sharply in being able and willing to accept the given conditions and to reason within them, but even the sharp increase did not mean that a child *always* reasoned formally. She tells of Robin, when faced with this problem:

Five boys, Jack, Dick, James, Bob and Tom go to five different schools in the same town. The schools are called North School, South School, East School, West School and Central School.
Jack does not go to North, South or Central School.
Dick goes to West School.
Bob does not go to North or Central School.
Tom has never been inside Central School.
What school does Jack go to? What school does Bob go to?
What school does James go to?
What school does Tom go to?

Robin eliminated North, South, and Central to deduce that Jack went to East or West. He then apparently could not see how to combine the negative information about Jack with the positive statement about Dick. "You would have to find out the district he was in," Robin suggested. Unable to deal with the problem as stated, he added his own experience. He knew that children usually went to schools near their own homes and so pulled in this information with disregard for the premises as given. Difficulty in solving a problem increases the tendency to ignore premises.

Flexibility and control of intellectual operations increased between ages 12 and 14 in an experiment on concept formation [47]. Each problem, consisting of a series of slides, required an answer of a single attribute, such as *black* or *cross*. It was possible to get the right answer after the first four slides. Each successive cycle of three slides gave enough information for solution. Results showed significant differences between the 12-year-olds and 14-year-olds, but not between the 14-year-olds and 16-year-olds. The 12-year-olds gave answers not in accord with the immediately previous slide, showing that they were less efficient than the older subjects in dealing with information given directly. The younger subjects were less able to remember their previous guesses in order to check them with current information. They were less able to maintain their guesses when current information confirmed them and less able to change their guesses when current information did not confirm them. The older subjects, both 14-year-olds and 16-year-olds, more readily held or changed their guesses in the light of all previous information.

Explanation of Phenomena. Although the school-age child feels satisfied after he has *described* something, an adolescent explains it [33]. *Description* means relating the parts of a phenomenon with each other; *explanation* means relating the phenomenon and its parts to other phenomena. For example, take the physics experiment of boiling water in a tin, sealing, and cooling the tin. The child will describe the collapse of the tin. The adolescent is more likely to try to explain what he saw, relating it to a vacuum being produced and atmospheric pressure acting on the tin. He will attempt to make as complete an explanation as he can, possibly invoking concepts of boiling, gaseous state, condensation, vacuum, pressure, and strength.

Consideration of What Is Possible. "The adolescent is the person who commits himself to possibilities . . . who begins to build 'systems' or 'theories' in the largest sense of the term" [20, p. 339]. The child is concerned with *what is,* the adolescent with *what is* plus *what could be.* The relationship between the real and the possible is new in adolescent thinking, as compared with childish thinking. In formal thinking, the individual uses a system to discover all possible combinations or relationships and to make sure that he *has* found them all. He uses a system to establish a rule, from which he can make predictions. By 14 or 15, according to Inhelder and Piaget, the adolescent can use the combinational system. That is, he varies one factor at a time, keeping all other things equal, and determines the effect of one factor. This method, of course, is the essence of research.

The acquisition of the combinatorial system has been studied in children 10 and 13 years old, who could be expected to be in a transition between concrete and formal operations [39]. Subjects were given different degrees of help in learning to plan and execute factorial experiments. The task was to learn the proper combination of four switches to run an electric train, requiring that the child generate 16 combinations. The first and second groups were given a conceptual framework that included teaching about factors, levels, and tree diagrams. The first group in addition was given training in solving analogous problems but the second group was not. The control group was given neither conceptual framework nor examples. Figure 2-1 shows the success (measured in number of combinations made) by younger and older children under the three conditions. Thus, the more help that was given, the better both ages did at using the combinatorial system, but the older children did better than the younger. Another significant difference between the age levels was that the older children made more use of written records in problem solving, even though all children had equal opportunities to make such records.

Figure 2-1. Performances of 10- and 13-year-olds on combinatorial problems: Percentages making all combinations and percentages keeping records.

Source: Data from R. S. Siegler and R. M. Liebert. Acquisition of formal scientific reasoning by 10- and 13-year-olds: Designing a factorial experiment. *Developmental Psychology,* 1975, **11,** 401–402.

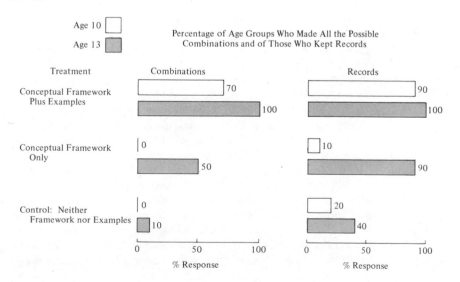

Probably the 10-year-olds had less foresight in regard to the difficulty of remembering and therefore did not see the need to write down what they did as they went along.

In addition to being able to try out all possible combinations systematically, the formal thinker realizes that hypotheses are arbitrary. He can think of a possible explanation and then think of another, discarding one as it is found wanting. The child, in contrast, is likely to get trapped by his own hypotheses because when he thinks of an explanation, he tends to think that he has settled the matter. Thinking the explanation has made it a reality to him. The adolescent hangs onto the fact that it was a thought and, therefore, reversible and replaceable. He can entertain the idea that a hypothesis is possibly right or probably right, seek new evidence, weigh it and change the degree of probability of correctness, hang on again, and look for further information. Because he can control his thought processes, he can delay conclusions while considering possibilities. Because he is mobile and flexible in thought, he can discover the possibilities to weigh.

Conservation. At each Piagetian stage, the child becomes convinced of certain permanencies in the world. As an infant, she comes to know that objects continue to exist even when she cannot perceive them. During the stage of concrete operations, she acquires conservation of substance, coming to realize that when the shape of an object is changed, it still contains the same amount of material. Questions of conservation of substance can be made more or less difficult by the familiarity of the material under discussion or by whether the change is in shape or in state. Thus, although most children achieve conservation of substance in the elementary school, a few do not do so until later.

Adolescents' concepts of physical quantity were assessed in grades 7 through 12 [19]. Conservation of weight was achieved by 10 to 20 per cent of the students in grades 7, 8, and 9. Among subjects in all grades, 96 per cent conserved substance when a ball of clay was transformed into a different shape, but only 61 per cent conserved for heating a metal bar and 51 per cent conserved for melting of ice. A sex difference was found in conservation of volume. Among all subjects, 40 to 50 per cent of the boys and 20 to 30 per cent of the girls acquired volume conservation. In grade 12, the law of displacement was understood by nearly all the boys but by only half the girls.

Male superiority also shows up in tests of conservation of horizontality. When a container of water is tilted and the subject is asked to choose a picture [17] that shows the orientation of the water level, boys are right more often than girls. Choosing the horizontal shows that the subject conserves. When college students and sixth-grade children were tested, the men answered 84 per cent of the questions correctly and the women 59 per cent. Boys' scores were 58, girls' 37. Success in the horizontality test and conservation of volume tests probably depends upon visual-spatial skills, in which boys generally do better than girls.

Sex differences in visuo-spatial abilities *may* be the result of experiences, of different upbringing and education of girls and boys, as many radical members of the women's movement believe. There is evidence to suggest, however, the existence of a sex-linked gene for excellence in spatial-mathematical abilities that is dominant in males and recessive in females [16]. If such is the case, a group of males would outnumber a group of females in successes on visual-spatial-mathematical tests, but some females would do just as well as some males. Furthermore, as in the previous chapter, a sex difference in brain lateralization was reported. The average girl at 13 began to show right hemisphere specialization for tactual perception, whereas the average boy began at age 5. Perhaps actual physical-based ability differences form the foundation upon which boys and girls are allowed different experiences, the boys getting more opportunities for dealing with spatial problems and, therefore, growing better and better at it.

TIME ORIENTATION

The ability to delay before responding to a problem is correlated with success in solving certain kinds of problems. Being able to delay immediate gratification in order to achieve more gain and pleasure in the future is an aspect of *future orientation*. Whereas different cultures vary in time orientation, North Americans generally esteem future orientation as an attitude necessary for achievement. North American children become more future-oriented as they mature, as shown by an analysis of stories written in response to pictures [26]. Subjects included five age groups: school children, adolescents, college students, businessmen, and senior citizens. There was an age trend up to college age, adolescents being more future-oriented than children, and college students more than adolescents. The adults were less future-oriented than the adolescents and college students.

Future-time orientation is functional for adolescents who can realistically look forward to a future in which they are rewarded for delaying gratification. Studies on economically depressed groups, such as American Indians and Mexicans, have found them to be more present-oriented than middle-class Americans [38]. The author suggests that present orientation is not a cause of poverty but a mentally healthy adjustment to it. He notes that future-oriented American Indians have been found to have more personality disturbances than their present-oriented peers.

Disturbances in Time Orientation. During adolescence a mild diffusion of time perspective is common, according to Erikson [12, p. 169]. The young person feels a sense of urgency and yet acts as though time were of no importance. She finds it hard to start and stop activities, to go to bed, to get up, to get her work done. Eventual coming to terms with time is essential for the development of a sense of integrity, which means accepting one's place in time and space, one's own particular life cycle [12, p. 139]. Perhaps problems of time are more significant today than they ever have been before, because of the ever-present possibility of annihilation of mankind. Enabled by her cognitive growth to consider a new time perspective, the adolescent may become intrigued with the overwhelming importance of the present moment or the mysterious joys of merging with an eternal entity.

CORRELATES OF FORMAL THOUGHT

The use of formal thinking is related to various personal and environmental characteristics.

Measured Intelligence. Both chronological age and mental age are related to the acquisition of abstract thinking. Boys of average intelligence made significant gains in formal thinking between 12 and 14 years, while those below average made their greatest gains between 14 and 16 [46]. The group that was superior in intelligence was already using logical operations at age 12 and made increases between 12 and 16. At ages 11 and 13 bright (as measured by Raven's test) boys used formal operations much more often than average boys the same age [21].

Conceptual Style. The development of concept usage was explored in children and adolescents, using a series of classifying tasks [6]. Each choice was from five categories: color, shape, relational function (for example, bat and ball), homogeneous function (for example, bat and hammer), and abstract function (for example, bat and deck of cards). The first two represent perceptual bases of classifying; the last three, logical. Adolescents used all five categories of concepts. The use of relational concepts increased steadily up to age 11 and then leveled off. Use of homogeneous and abstract concepts increased throughout childhood and adolescence.

As a child is growing up, he builds his cognitive structures in response to the demands and opportunities offered by his culture. A peasant village and an industrialized setting in Mexico were the sites of an investigation in which rural and urban children were compared in cognitive style [28]. In order to see what type of concepts 12- and 13-year-olds would form, this array of items was used: banana, orange, bean, meat, milk, air, fire, and stone. The first two items were presented and the child was asked, "How are a banana and an orange similar?" Then, "How is a bean different from an orange and a banana?" Next, "How are a bean, a banana, and an orange alike?" Then another item was added and the two questions asked and so on to the last item, the stone, where only the difference was asked. The response style most typical of the village children was one concerned with concrete reality. This peasant type tells differences accurately but is likely to fail at explaining similarities, not because he cannot do so but because he does not choose to do so. Similarity to him means almost exact likeness, such as between two oranges. An example of the *concrete* style of thinking is this response to the first four times, "All of them can be eaten but they are not alike because meat is not round nor is it like a banana or a bean." This type of child is not interested in similiarities but in the uniqueness of things. The type most characteristic of urban children, although it by no means included all of them, was called *abstract*. In telling how things were similar, they classified them abstractly, either by name or by function. An intermediate type, *concrete–abstract,* included both village and city children but more of the latter. This type was likely to use functions and names for telling similarities, moving from concrete to abstract as the tasks became more difficult. They tended to use concrete, perceptual terms when the problem could be answered adequately by such methods.

The conceptual style of children is thus consistent with the demands of the culture. Peasant children, like peasant societies, are concerned with concrete reality and perceptible attributes and with differentiation and not equivalence. Urban children, like industrialized societies, can easily move away from their perceptions to organize their experiences into abstract classifications. The differences noted here are probably significant in understanding the difficulties peasants have in moving into an industrialized society.

Cognitive Style. Field independence and reflectivity were measured along with children's transition from concrete to formal operations [31]. Field independence was assessed by finding out how quickly and accurately a child could identify figures embedded in pictures. Reflectivity, as opposed to impulsivity, was measured by the child's matching one of six pictures with a standard after delaying his choice. Both field independence and reflectivity were associated with cognitive development. There was some suggestion that reflectivity was more influential in concrete operations and that field independence was more influential in formal operations. Field independence or dependence and reflectivity-impulsivity seem to be quite enduring characteristics of individuals. There are some training procedures known to promote reflectivity, but little has been done to show how to increase field independence.

Locus of Control. Individuals vary in how much they feel themselves to be in charge of what happens to them. When a person believes strongly that he controls many significant events, he is said to have an internal locus of control. A person with an external locus of control believes that what happens is the result of luck, fate, or the actions of other people and things. When 14- and 15-year-olds were tested for degree of formal thinking and locus of control, the internal-control subjects scored higher in formal thought than the externals [35].

THINKING ABOUT THINKING

The adolescent develops the ability to think about her own thinking and about the thinking of other people.

The Thoughts of Others. "I wonder what he is thinking of me. I wonder what he thinks I am thinking about him. I wonder what he thinks I think he is thinking about me." This kind of thinking develops in adolescence, with slight beginnings in childhood and an upswing around 11 and 12 years of age [30]. More of the children tested were capable of the first thought than the second. The third statement implies even more complex thinking.

The ability to think about the thoughts of others enables the adolescent to construct an imaginary audience for himself [9]. He gets the feeling of being the focus of attention, being on-stage. When he is critical of himself, he imagines his audience as critical, also. When he is self-admiring, his audience admires him. He often imagines other people as having thoughts that they do not have and that are, in reality, his own. Herein lies the basis of egocentrism in adolescence: failing to distinguish between his own thoughts, feelings, and wishes and those of others. The loud, show-off, faddish behavior of an adolescent group is easier to understand when one realizes that every member is both actor and audience. The ability to imagine the thoughts of others is also the basis for the sense of intimacy, which develops in late adolescence. As the adolescent differentiates more and more between other people's thoughts and his own, he interprets theirs more realistically.

Another result of confusing her own thoughts with those of other people is that she develops magnificent ideas about how society can and should be improved. She assumes that her fellow citizens want these improvements and makes vague plans for her own future that encompass the changes. Thus, she does not distinguish between her own point of view as a person organizing her future and the point of view of the social group to which she belongs [20, pp. 343–345].

The mobility of thought achieved in the formal period is what empowers the adolescent to think of many possibilities for his own future and for transforming society. Instead of being tied to the concrete aspects of reality, to what *is,* he can soar out into the realm of the possible. Thus, an adolescent is able to fuse (or confuse) two viewpoints *because* a new level of thinking has been achieved. This kind of egocentrism disappears gradually as the young person assumes adult roles, especially the work role in a real job. When he meets the realities of dealing with the society that he has considered reforming, he learns the difference between what he can actually do, what he wishes could happen, and what society wants.

This special kind of adolescent thinking is very enduring in Western culture. Adults expect young people to be idealistic and impractical in their dreams of remaking the world. There is general belief that this type of thought has value for both the adolescent and society, in opening up possibilities for his future development and for social innovations.

His Own Thoughts. The young adolescent, in early stages of awareness of himself as a thinking being, often regards himself, particularly his feelings, as very

EDWARD C. DEVEREUX

special and unique [9]. His imaginary audience probably contributes to this notion. Sometimes the conviction of personal uniqueness results in a "personal fable," expressed in a very private diary, a personal relationship with God, a belief that one cannot die or that one cannot become pregnant. The personal fable, along with grandiose schemes for improving society, is gradually transformed into more manageable proportions. As the adolescent differentiates the thoughts of others from his own, he also becomes able to regard his own thinking more objectively. As thought grows more mobile and flexible, he can stand off and look at himself as a person. He can consider himself as a physical specimen, as a person-among-persons, as an intellectual being or as a person in any one of the numerous roles he plays—son, friend, sweetheart, student, and so on. He sees himself as a person-in-relation.

Self-cognition makes it possible for the adolescent to see himself as continuous with the child he once was, how he differs and how he is the same. He can see his continuity with the adult that he is becoming. He can look at himself in the ways in which other people and the community see him. Integrating all of this information and all of these points of view, he strengthens his sense of identity. At the same time, he begins to grow beyond the limits of adolescent thinking as he differentiates between his own plans and hopes and those of his social group.

Language Development

Increasing sophistication of thought is intimately bound up with the growing understanding and use of language. Along with the development of formal operations, adolescents continue to learn new words, new structures, new concepts, and the symbolic organization presented by the culture in which they live.

RELATION OF LANGUAGE TO THOUGHT

Through language, experience is put into symbolic form in which it can be manipulated and processed by methods that other people use. The individual gets from his social group these methods of dealing with his experience. He gets them through the use of language, and he uses language to check back on his experiences, their results and their meanings. Cultures differ in how they use language to organize thought, and in the degree of abstraction and complexity of organization attained. Rigorous training in language and thought provides opportunities for attaining formal thought. The adolescent who lacks such training is likely to think on a concrete level [5, p. 390]. Such a difference is marked between children who go to school and those who do not. Although most people are capable of taking methods of thinking from their culture, few contribute new methods to their fellow men. For example, many students are capable of understanding and using calculus, but few will invent a comparable method of organizing data.

The relationship between thought and speech that adolescents achieve includes three functions: external speech, inner speech, and thought, according to Vygotsky, the Russian authority on thought and language. External speech is usually interwoven with thought, although it can occur without thought. Inner speech, derived from both external speech and thought, can be simply silent reciting, but rarely is it just that. It can be largely thinking in pure meanings, but it is not just that. "It is a dynamic, shifting, unstable thing, fluttering between word and thought . . ." [43, p. 149].

Thought itself does not have to be put into words. Sometimes a thought cannot be put into words. There are no units of thought, unlike speech, which has words as units. A thought is global, present at one time, but to be expressed in speech, it has to be developed in a succession of words. Vygotsky has likened a thought to a cloud shedding words. Words rarely express the whole thought, since a thought has a feeling and willing part to it. These subtle aspects are communicated somewhat through words, but largely through gesture, intonation, and context.

ELABORATION OF CONCEPTS

Many words have fuller and more abstract meanings for adolescents than for younger children. When asked to define words, the more complete definitions of adolescents indicate the more complex thought processes at work. Formal thought tries to take account of all possibilities inherent in the situation. Hence a word definition must encompass all meanings of the word. A child might say "Poverty means you're hungry"; an adolescent might say, "Poverty is a state of being without desirable goods and/or qualities." Interpretations of pictures, like definitions of words, show a progression from concrete to abstract and from limited to complete as the child progresses through the stages of thinking. The preschool child names objects ("Dog, mommy, basket"), the school-age child describes the picture by relating some of the elements ("The lady is chasing the dog. The dog has a shirt in his mouth.") The adolescent interprets the picture ("It's washday. The lady's cross at the dog for running off with the clean clothes. The dog is only playing.")

Use of More Difficult Structures. Certain complex, infrequently used structures are acquired rather late in life or, by some people, not at all. One such situation involves certain uses of the words *ask* or *tell*. An exception to the regular use of such words provided the basis of research on the age of its acquisition [24]. An example of regular use is "Tanya asked Yvette to play." Here *Yvette,* the subject of the complement verb phrase, is placed next to the complement, *to play.* The irregular use occurs in "Tanya asked Yvette what to play." Here the subject of the complement is *Tanya.* A test of use and understanding of this irregular structure was given to 122 subjects between 8 and 19 years of age, all of average or superior IQ. Even at the college-age level, some subjects failed. More successes occurred in children over 12 than in children under 12. When told "Ask Ben which book to read," the subject who failed would say, "Ben, which book do you want to read?" Another response, more frequent among younger children, was telling instead of asking, as in "Read this one." When retested two years later, some but not all of the unsuccessful subjects were able to use the exceptional structure. It thus seems that some adolescents and some adults do not achieve full use of complex language structures.

Increase in Vocabulary. Although averages tell little about an individual and nothing about the mechanisms by which words are acquired, the size of average

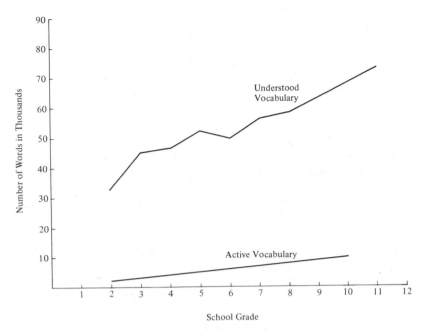

Figure 2-2. Average sizes of understood vocabulary and active vocabulary (estimated) at various ages.

SOURCES: M. K. Smith and A. F. Watts. *The language and mental development of children*. London: George G. Harrap & Co., Ltd., 1944. Measurement of the size of general English vocabulary through the elementary grades and high school. *Genetic Psychology Monographs*, 1941, **24**, 131–345.

vocabulary at various ages gives an indication of the course of mental development. And for a quick estimate of IQ, there is nothing better than a vocabulary test.

The number of words understood far exceeds the number used in speech. When children were given a recognition vocabulary test, the average number of words understood in grade 1 was 23,700, with a range from 6,000 to 48,000, and in grade 12, the average was 80,300, with a range from 36,700 to 136,500. Figure 14-2 shows the results of this study for grades 2 through 11, indicating the steady rise in number of words understood. In a study that dealt with university students, their recognition vocabulary was estimated at an average of 156,000 words [40]. An individual's vocabulary continues to grow throughout his life span [36].

To figure out how many words an adolescent actually uses is an almost impossible task. An estimate of the average English child's vocabulary at age 14 is between 8,000 and 10,000 words, a number similar to estimates made for American children [44]. Between 7 and 14, the English child is judged to increase his vocabulary by about 700 words a year. The increase from 14 to 20 averages about 10,000 words, resulting in an adult vocabulary of 18,000 to 20,000 words.

A particular kind of vocabulary develops during adolescence, especially in subcultures of crime and delinquency. *Argot* is the term for the special words devised and used by participants in these cultures and, to a certain extent, by other adolescents as well. Knowledge of argot increases during adolescence.

WRITTEN LANGUAGE

Style of writing is in part a product of choice of language. It is also an expression of personality characteristics. An analysis of stories written by high school junior girls and girls of 19 and 20 years of age shows definite age-level differences [42]. The high school girls were more flamboyant in their writing, showing melodramatic, personal self-expression. "She seems to enjoy letting herself go, using many 'exclamation point' statements and naïve clichés." The older girls wrote much more objectively, in a controlled or constricted style. "She tends to an Olympian or dispassionate stance and often sounds like a rather condescending bluestocking." The age-level difference held across social class and education. The more abstract thinking of the older adolescent is thus reflected in her writing.

FAMILY INFLUENCES ON LANGUAGE DEVELOPMENT

Because of considerable evidence that early born children and children from small families score higher in intelligence than later borns and children from large families, the family structures of almost a million National Merit Scholarship participants were examined [4]. The summed sub-test scores of firstborns from small families were highest and scores from lastborns of large families were lowest. Further analysis, however, showed that these results were due to verbal sub–tests and not from the mathematical sub–tests. Eldest siblings scored higher than only children. When children were spaced far apart, both (or all, in three-child families) did better than when children who were spaced closely. The authors suggest that the first child benefits in the beginning from talking with parents and having their full attention. Then when a sibling is born and the first child is already a good talker, the elder child benefits from her own efforts in explaining and teaching, adapting her language use to the younger child and children.

Creativity

Just as inner speech flutters between word and thought, so does thought itself shift between controlled thinking and fantasy or imaginative thinking. Adolescence sees a resurgence of imagination in many forms. Having greater control over her intellectual processes, the adolescent can move more rapidly and easily between purposeful thinking and fantasy. Unlike the preschool child who loses herself in a dramatic role, the adolescent can imagine herself into a role and then stand off to observe herself in it.

Whereas creativity is the breath of life to the preschool child, the school-age child is concerned with industry, duty, and accomplishment, with matters of fact, with learning what reality is and how to cope with it. The adolescent, thinking about what is possible, not just what is, creates new situations and original solutions in her imagination. Some teenagers are exploring different modes of thinking and feeling in order to integrate themselves with the universe and eternity. Creativity is thought to be involved not only in artistic expression but also in meditation and peak experiences [14].

ASSESSING CREATIVITY

Genius is a term applied by a social group to a person who has been extremely creative over a long period of time, and whose products are highly valued by the group [2]. Individuals are judged to be more or less creative according to the novelty and usefulness of their products, whether they be works of art, scientific theories, new problems, or solutions to problems.

Because a child has not lived long enough to build a reputation as a genius, and because a child's products cannot be judged against an adult's, other ways of assessing children's creativity have been developed. Much of creative thinking is, in Guilford's [15] terms, *divergent,* the kind that produces many different answers. *Convergent* thinking finds the one right answer. In creating a solution, convergent thinking may be used to select the best answer from the many possibilities produced by divergent thought. Factors in divergent verbal thinking include fluency, flexibility, and elaboration. Tests for *fluency* focus on easy recall of information, words that fit certain classes, words or phrases that make certain relationships, and connected discourse in phrases or sentences. An example of a *flexibility* test is thinking up clever titles that give new interpretations, such as "snake and sidney pie" for "steak and kidney pie." *Elaboration* means building up or rounding out what is given. The fluency, flexibility, and elaboration factors just mentioned had to do with verbal information. Other parallel factors pertain to visual and symbolic information. Some people are creative verbally, others artistically, and still others are creative mathematically. Tests based on these concepts have been used to study creativity in children, adolescents, college students, and adults. Everyone is creative to a certain extent, but some people are more so than others. The tests give quantitative comparisons.

RELATION OF CREATIVITY TO OTHER MEASURES

Many kinds of social and personal characteristics have been investigated in efforts to find out what makes for creativity.

IQ. Many studies have been concerned with the relationship between creativity and tested intelligence. Results generally substantiate the commonsense point of view, that the two have something in common but are not exactly the same. Intelligence of a certain level is necessary for creativity, but does not guarantee it. In a large, unselected sample of high school students, divergent thinking tests showed a moderate positive correlation with IQ [32]. The most gifted people and, of course, geniuses typically are high in both IQ and creativity, but it is possible to have a high IQ without being highly creative.

Socioeconomic Status. When measured by fathers' education and occupation, socioeconomic status of high school students showed a low but significant correlation with measures of divergent thinking [32].

Personality Characteristics. Research on creative people indicates that they are high in flexibility, fluency, drive, involvement, openness, curiosity, autonomy, independence of judgment, self-confidence, self-acceptance, humor, empathy, desire for complexity, and easy tolerance of ambiguity. Characteristics related to low creativity include rigidity, premature judging, defensiveness, contentedness, gentleness, conservatism, patience, virtuousness, and concern for others [3].

Self-concepts of adolescents, as shown by responses on an adjective checklist, showed a distinctive picture of creative adolescents [37]. Chosen for creativity through testing and rating of productions, these high school students showed awareness and acceptance of opposing forces in their personalities. More often than controls, they saw themselves as imaginative, original, uninhibited, outspoken, rebellious, complex, reflective, cynical, idealistic, and aloof. The control group more often described themselves as dependable, cooperative, conventional, quiet, and silent.

A study of creative artists points out that these people often see what other people do not observe, in addition to what people ordinarily see. They often call attention vividly to unnoticed phenomena, using their powers of accurate observation not only for their own satisfaction but also for the benefit of mankind. With their greater mental capacity, creative people can hold many ideas at once, compare more ideas and hence synthesize more than the ordinary person. Often extremely vigorous, both mentally and physically, they lead complex lives, in touch with a complex universe. They contact and use the unconscious life liberally, with broad and flexible self-awareness. They can easily regress to primitive fantasies, naïve ideas, and tabooed impulses and then return to rationality and self-criticism. "The creative person is both more primitive and more cultured, more destructive and more constructive, crazier and saner, than the average person" [3, p. 159].

Brain Waves. Highly creative people differ from average people in the patterning of their brain waves [29]. *Alpha waves* are slow, high-amplitude waves that are characteristic of states of relaxation and drowsiness in the average person. Rational work requires medium arousal levels, with faster, lower-amplitude brain waves. When male college students were tested for alpha waves in a resting state, low-creatives produced alpha waves about 55 per cent of the time, whereas high-creatives produced alpha waves about 40 per cent of the time. When a creativity test was given, the former reduced alpha wave output by about one half, but the latter increased their output of alpha waves. This result suggests that the high-creatives were more able to get in touch with unconscious memories and primitive ways of thinking. In addition, the high-creatives were more able to block out alpha waves, suggesting that they could focus their attention more rigorously. Thus, it seems that the brain wave patterning fits with studies of the behavior of highly creative people, in which they use both primitive thought and highly rational thought. The unconscious nature of some available material is consistent with experiences reported by composers who wrote down symphonies they heard in their heads, by mathematicians who suddenly became aware of new formulas, and by the more frequent creative person who sleeps on a problem and wakens with the solution.

FAMILY BACKGROUNDS AND EXPERIENCES OF CREATIVE PERSONS

Family experiences are different from the average among persons of high creativity and of high measured intelligence. A review of studies concluded that such individuals were likely to have been born when their parents were older (in the early thirties) and to have been given respect, freedom, and autonomy [1]. Their parents were nonpossessive, emotionally open, unconcerned with status, involved in their work, and ready to deal with tensions verbally. Mothers were likely to have careers and fathers tended to be involved and confident in their occupations. Among the most eminent, including geniuses, parental death during childhood was three times as likely as among creative college students. Thus, the children probably often felt a sense of aloneness, because of parents who were busy with work, or even dead, and because the values and standards of their families differed from those of other families. Being on their own, and trusted, they had plenty of opportunities to think, to imagine, and to make their own decisions. Values were more important than specific pieces of behavior.

When male college students were questioned about their parents and the results related to creativity scores, findings were consistent with those already mentioned [18]. Subjects whose mothers were seen as highly controlling and low in nurturance were lower in creativity than the subjects whose mothers controlled less and nurtured more. Highly creative high school students, in contrast to their less creative classmates, said that their parents provided consistent discipline, that fathers engaged in many activities and hobbies with daughters and that mothers were very involved in activities with sons, showing much interest in the boys' achievement [7].

GENDER ROLE AND CREATIVITY

On tests of divergent thinking and other creativity tests, there are no consistent differences between males and females [22]. How can this be, when many more men than women are known for their creative achievements in science and the arts? Opportunities and restrictions are, of course, very different for men and women, boys and girls. A narrow, rigid gender role requires a person to limit all sorts of behavior, including creativity. It seems that females have been more restricted than males, but actually, both have had limitations on where, when, and how they were permitted to create. A loosening of gender stereotypes means that males are free to be sensitive and tender in addition to the traditional masculine modes of aggressive achievement, while females are allowed to assert themselves, to compete, and to relish success frankly, in addition to being sensitive and nurturant.

Adolescents carry with them their childhood experiences in gender-role training. Although they benefit from the freedoms recently won by women and the consequent freedoms for them, adolescents continue to be influenced by the old stereotypes. There must be many girls who believe, for example, that men do not like women and boys do not like girls who are creative, competent, and successful. When creativity tests are correlated with other tests, results suggest that although males and females may have equal potential, the patterning of their creativity may take different courses of expression and development. Girls were more affected than boys by the external situation in which a creativity test was given [23]. Retested five years after tests given in grade 5, girls showed stability of creative performance when they were tested by one nonevaluative female examiner, but not when they were tested in a group. Boys showed more stability when they were tested in a group. Further analysis suggested that the girls' creativity was depressed by anxiety, but not the boys'. Apparently, girls' creativity was related more to emotion than was boys', and boys' creativity was related more to cognition than was that of girls [22].

Some insight into feminine role and creativity is provided by a study of children and adolescents. Gifted, creative boys, as defined by both IQ measures and measures of creative behavior, were high in dominance, venturesomeness, individualism, self-assurance, self-discipline, and independence of group opinion [45]. Gifted, creative adolescent girls were more enthusiastic, individualistic, and non-conforming than their peers. However, they differed less from peers than did gifted, creative girls in middle childhood, and they also differed less from peers than their male counterparts did. In contrast to the boys, the gifted girls differed from peers in sociability, dominance, self-assurance, self-discipline, and self-sufficiency. Also, they were less accepted by classmates [25]. Most likely, the girls were caught in society's ambiguous attitudes toward gifted women. Although they themselves and their parents and teachers wanted them to achieve and realize their potentialities, they feared for their feminine image and popularity with boys. As they grew from childhood into adolescence, they became more aware of the problem of conflicting roles. Hence the gap widened between gifted boys and girls in freedom to express creative potentiality.

APPLICATION OF KNOWLEDGE ABOUT CREATIVITY

It seems likely that there is a genetic influence on the patterning of alpha waves, giving some persons more creative potential than others. The stability of creative performance from grades 5 to 10 [23] supports the notion that there is a physical base on which such behavior is built. But how much can creative potential be enhanced or depressed by experience? Persons of average endowment seem to produce more new ideas in relaxed social settings, such as in brainstorming, where individuals are respected and encouraged, and criticism is withheld.

Both parents and teachers may wonder if they can purposefully promote creativity in children. Research on family background and relationships has shown that the parents' personalities and background are significant. The likelihood of producing a creative child is increased when parents are active in intellectual, cultural matters; when parents guide the child while recognizing him as an active, able, trustworthy person; if parents do not mind being unconventional and different from their neighbors. This is hardly a blueprint for parental procedure, since nobody can turn on such global conditions at will.

Many authorities have given advice to teachers on nurturing creativity in their students. There is a question as to how great a factor is the teacher's own personality. How creative must a teacher be in order to perceive and promote creativity in students? Research indicates that highly creative teachers stimulate more originality in their students than do less creative teachers. Since teachers are less globally involved with their pupils than are parents with offspring, the former can often control their interactions more objectively and hence use "methods" more effectively than can parents.

Consider the findings on creativity together with what is known about adolescence. Intellectually, adolescents are able to think more freely and flexibly than are children. Although originality is related to firmness in sticking to one's judgments, adolescents often need the support of their peers in order to feel a sense of identity. Being different from the group involves some disapproval from both peers and teachers. The most creative adolescents, however, seem to care relatively little about approval. Their values differ from those of more ordinary peers and teachers. Inner satisfaction seems to matter more than marks, prizes, money, and praise. Perhaps adults can do some deliberate promotion of creativity by encouraging youngsters to think and act independently. If unusual ideas and products are valued, then perhaps approval-dependent adolescents will feel freer to create.

Much remains to be done in the way of recognizing the creative achievements of women and girls, encouraging them, strengthening their abilities, and structuring their social roles flexibly. At the same time, men and boys also need an environment that is conducive to their creativity. Unless boys grow up with broadened concepts of masculine behavior, they may be threatened by assertive, achieving, creative, self-confident women.

Summary

Psychological growth at adolescence restructures cognitive processes on a new level of thought that is more abstract than the preceding period. Formal thought is not used all the time by anyone, or even part of the time by some individuals.

Formal thought deals with abstractions and uses increased freedom, control, mobility, and flexibility. The combinatorial system is the method by which it explores all possibilities in a given situation. During the teen years, improvements are made in use of the combinatorial system and in conservation. Sex differences in visual-spatial abilities give some boys an advantage in certain conservation problems.

North American adolescents tend to be future-oriented. Among poor and depressed groups, however, present-orientation is more functional.

Conceptual style, consistent with the demands of a particular culture, may limit the extent to which abstract thinking is used. Rapid cognitive development is associated with the cognitive-style dimensions of field independence and reflectivity. An internal locus of control is more typical than an external locus of control in abstract thinkers.

The adolescent's newly developed complexity of thought permits him to view himself as a person-among-persons, a thinker-among-thinkers. He think about what is and what could be, for society and for the special, unique person he considers himself to be.

Language becomes increasingly complex, with words, structures, and concepts added. Since language and thought are intimately connected, training in language and thought is important for attaining the cognitive level of formal thought. Culture, school, and family contribute to language education. Family position and structure make a difference, the most favorable spot being the eldest of two or three children.

Creativity is expressed in various modes of which divergent thinking is the easiest to measure. Most studies on adolescent creativity relate test results to various personal and background characteristics and to other types of achievement. Physiological, psychological, and social factors are all implicated. Rigid gender-role stereotypes restrict not only females but males as well.

References

1. Albert, R. S. Cognitive development and parental loss among the gifted and exceptionally gifted, and the creative. *Psychological Reports,* 1971, **29,** 19–26.
2. Albert, R. S. Toward a behavioral definition of genius. *American Psychologist,* 1975, **30,** 140–151.
3. Barron, F. The needs for order and for disorder as motives in creative activity. In C. W. Tyler and F. Barron (eds.). *Scientific curiosity: Its recognition and development.* New York: John Wiley & Sons, Inc., 1963.
4. Breland, H. M. Birth order, family configuration, and verbal achievement. *Child Development,* 1974, **45,** 1011–119.
5. Bruner, J. S., and J. M. Anglin. *Beyond the information given.* New York: W. W. Norton & Company, 1973.
6. Crager, R. L., and A. J. Spriggs. Development of concept utilization. *Developmental Psychology,* 1969, **32,** 433–440.
7. Dauw, D. C. Life experiences of original thinkers and good elaborators. *Exceptional Children,* 1966, **32,** 433–440.
8. Donaldson, M. *A study of children's thinking.* London: Tavistock Publications, Ltd. 1963.
9. Elkind, D. Egocentrism in adolescence. *Child Development,* 1967, **38,** 1025–1034.
10. Elkind, D., R. Barocas, and P. Johnsen. Concept production in children and adolescents. *Human Development,* 1969, **12,** 10–21.
11. Elkind, D., L. Medvene, and A. S. Rockway. Representational level and concept production in children and adolescents. *Developmental Psychology,* 1970, **2,** 85–89.
12. Erikson, E. H. *Identity, youth and crisis.* New York: W. W. Norton & Company, 1968.
13. Falmange, R. J. The development of propositional reasoning: Conceptual issues and suggestion of a perspective for empirical research. Paper presented at meetings of the Society for Research in Child Development, Denver, 1975.
14. Gowan, J. C. Trance, art and creativity. *Journal of Creative Behavior,* 1975, **9,** 1–11.
15. Guilford, J. P. *The nature of human intelligence.* New York: McGraw-Hill, Inc., 1967.
16. Harris, L. J. Sex differences in spatial ability: Possible environmental, genetic, and neurological factors. In M. Kinsbourne (ed.). *Hemispheric asymmetries of function.* Cambridge: Cambridge University Press, 1975 (in press).
17. Harris, L. J., C. Hanley, and C. T. Best. Conservation of horizontality: Sex differences in sixth-graders and college students. In R. C. Smart and M. S. Smart (eds.) *Readings in child development and relationships.* New York: The Macmillan Company, 1977, pp. 375–387.
18. Heilbrun, A. B. Maternal child rearing and creativity in sons. *Journal of Genetic Psychology,* 1971, **119,** 175–179.
19. Hobbs, E. D. Adolescents' concepts of physical quantity. *Developmental Psychology,* 1973, **9,** 431.

20. Inhelder, B., and J. Piaget. *The growth of logical thinking.* New York: Basic Books, Inc., 1958.
21. Keating, D. P. Precocious cognitive development at the level of formal operations. *Child Development,* 1975, **46,** 276–280.
22. Kogan, N. Creativity and sex differences. Paper presented at meetings of the Eastern Psychological Association, Boston, 1972.
23. Kogan, N., and E. Pankove. Creative ability over a five-year span. *Child Development,* 1972, **42,** 427–442.
24. Kramer, P. E., E. Koff, and Z. Luria. The development of competence in an exceptional language structure in older children and young adults. *Child Development,* 1972, **43,** 121–130.
25. Kurtzman, K. A. A study of school attitudes, peer acceptance and personality of creative adolescents. *Exceptional Children,* 1967, **34,** 157–162.
26. LeBlanc, A. F. Time orientation and time estimation: A function of age. *Journal of Genetic Psychology,* 1969, **115,** 187–194.
27. Lovell, K. Some problems associated with formal thought and its assessment. In D. R. Green, M. P. Ford, and G. B. Flamer (eds.). *Measurement and Piaget.* New York: McGraw-Hill Inc., 1971.
28. Maccoby, M., and N. Modiano. Cognitive style in rural and urban Mexico. *Human Development,* 1969, **12,** 22–23.
29. Martindale, C., and J. Armstrong. The relationship of creativity to cortical activation and its operant control. *Journal of Genetic Psychology,* 1974, **124,** 311–320.
30. Miller, P. H., F. S. Kessel, and J. H. Flavell. Thinking about people thinking about thinking people thinking about. . . : A study of social-cognitive development. *Child Development,* 1970, **41,** 613–623.
31. Neimark, E. D. Longitudinal development of formal operations thought. *Genetic Psychology Monographs,* 1975, **91,** 171–225.
32. Olive, H. The relationship of divergent thinking to intelligence, social class and achievement in high-school students. *Journal of Genetic Psychology,* 1972, **121,** 179–186.
33. Peel, E. A. Intellectual growth during adolescence. *Educational Review,* 1965, **17,** 169–180.
34. Piaget, J. *The psychology of intelligence.* London: Routledge and Kegan Paul, 1950.
35. Reiling, A. M., and D. J. Massari. Internal versus external control and formal thought. Paper presented at meeting of the Society for Research in Child Development, Philadelphia, 1973.
36. Riegel, K. F. Speed of verbal performance as a function of age and set: A review of issues and data. In A. T. Welford and J. E. Birren (eds.). *Behavior, aging and the nervous system.* Springfield, Ill.: Charles C Thomas, Publisher, 1965, pp. 150–190.
37. Schaefer, C. E. The self-concept of creative adolescents. *Journal of Psychology,* 1969, **72,** 233–242.
38. Shannon, L. Development of time perspective in three cultural groups: A cultural difference or an expectancy interpretation. *Developmental Psychology,* 1975, **11,** 114–115.
39. Siegler, R. S., and R. M. Liebert. Acquisition of formal scientific reasoning by 10- and 13-year-olds: Designing a factorial experiment. *Developmental Psychology,* 1975, **11,** 401–402.
40. Smith, M. K. Measurement of the size of general English vocabulary through the

elementary grades and high school. *Genetic Psychology Monographs,* 1941, **24,** 311–345.

41. Stone, M. A., and D. P. Ausubel. The intersituational generality of formal thought. *Journal of Genetic Psychology,* 1969, **115,** 169–180.

42. Tooley, K. Expressive style as a developmental index in late adolescence. *Journal of Projective Techniques and Personality Assessment,* 1967, **31:6,** 51–59.

43. Vygotsky, L. S. *Thought and language.* Cambridge, Mass.: M. I. T. Press, 1962.

44. Watts, A. F. *The language and mental development of children.* London: George G. Harrap & Co., Ltd., 1944.

45. Werner, E. E., and L. M. Bachtold. Personality factors of gifted boys and girls in middle childhood and adolescence. *Psychology and Schools,* 1969, **6,** 177–182.

46. Yudin, L. W. Formal thought in adolescence as a function of intelligence. *Child Development,* 1966, **37,** 697–708.

47. Yudin, L. W., and S. L. Kates. Concept attainment and adolescent development. *Journal of Educational Psychology,* 1963, **54,** 177–182.

Readings in
Intellectual Development

The following articles contribute to understanding the nature of intelligence and intellectual development in adolescence. They also give information about the processes of intellectual behavior.

Certain families produce children of higher intelligence than do other families. Families provide both heredity and environment for children. Of what does a family's influence on intelligence consist? Some differences in intellectual behavior appear to be hereditary, especially those that seem to be sex-linked. What, if any, environmental factors influence the expression of hereditary control?

Many researchers have been curious about the relationship between birth order and family size to children's cognitive functioning. Hunter M. Breland's study is an effort to provide answers to some of these questions. He obtained a very large number of subjects, nearly 800,000 high school juniors, who took tests for the National Merit Scholarships. Therefore, it was possible to control for socioeconomic variables and for mother's age. Breland's findings were similar to other studies in showing the favorable effects of small family size and wide spacing of children on verbal achievement. Several hypotheses are considered for explaining the results. This article has implications not only for children's verbal learning but also for family planning.

The way in which a child sees herself is the product of her cognitive structure. Contrasts between self-perceptions of children and adolescents are also contrasts between cognition on the level of concrete operations and cognition in formal operations. The paper by Raymond Montemayor and Marvin Eisen compares categories of self-description and gives examples in the subjects' own words, making it easy to get a feeling for the essence of each level of thought. One especially interesting part of the article is a discussion and illustration of the changeover from childhood to adolescence in the mode of self-perception.

Subjects of two cognitive levels are again compared in a cognitive performance, by Lauren J. Harris, Charles Hanley, and Catherine T. Best. The task here is to show understanding of the principle of horizontality by predicting where the water level will be when a bottle is tilted. As well as the expected age-level difference, Harris and his associates found a significant sex difference. Through a series of ingenious tests, developed from cues given by subjects in each previous test, reasons for success and failure were analyzed. The authors concluded that success requires visuo-spatial abilities primarily, rather than logical reasoning. A sex difference in visuo-spatial abilities has already been established by other investigators.

Birth Order, Family Configuration, and Verbal Achievement

Hunter M. Breland

EDUCATIONAL TESTING SERVICE

Two samples of National Merit Scholarship participants tested in 1962 and the entire population of almost 800,000 participants tested in 1965 were examined. Consistent effects in all 3 groups were observed with respect to both birth order and family size (firstborn and those of smaller families scored higher). Control of both socioeconomic variables and mother's age, by analysis of variance as well as by analysis of covariance, failed to alter the relationships. Step-down analyses suggested that the effects were due to a verbal component and that no differences were attributable to nonverbal factors. Mean test scores were computed for detailed sibship configurations based on birth order, family size, sibling spacing, and sibling sex.

The long history of research on relationships between birth position and achievement variables is well documented by numerous reviews (e.g., Altus, 1966; Bayer & Folger, 1967; Bradley, 1968; Hsiao, 1931; Jones, 1933, pp. 204–241, 1954, pp. 667–668; Murphy, Murphy, & Newcomb, 1937, pp. 349–363; Sampson, 1965, pp. 175–222; Schachter, 1963; Schooler, 1972; Sutton-Smith & Rosenberg, 1970). Only those reviews by Altus and by Schachter argued strongly for the existence of a relationship (that early-born, and especially firstborn, have higher achievement). Altus (1965) suggested that the observed relationship was due to a verbal factor. Most of the other reviewers indicate that little evidence exists for a relationship between birth order and intelligence or other achievement indicators.

Recent studies of large samples, however, clearly suggest that highly significant and consistent relationships do exist. Belmont and Marolla (1973), Eysenck and Cookson (1969), and Record, McKeown, and Edwards (1969) all obtained similar patterns of results (firstborn and early-born tended to score higher on various achievement and intelligence measures). The causes of those observed differences have been debated extensively (e.g., Breland, 1973; Schooler, 1973).

The analyses of the present study represented an attempt at verification of such birth-order effects, but with suspected confounding factors controlled. A second objective was to explore the possibility that any observed relationship is due to a verbal factor, as Altus had indicated. Finally, the question of the effects of specific family configurations formed by sibling spacing and sex differences was investigated. It was hypothesized that closely spaced siblings experience sociological influences similar to those of twins.

METHOD

Samples   Two samples of National Merit Scholarship participants tested in 1962 and almost the entire population of participants tested in 1965 were

From *Child Development*, 1974, **45**, 1011–1019. Copyright © 1974 by The Society for Research in Child Development, Inc. Reprinted by permission.

examined. The first sample of 670 subjects consisted of a random selection of the 1962 participants and was termed the "normative sample," The second sample of 1,147 subjects consisted of a random selection of high-scoring 1962 participants; this sample was called the "commended group." The third sample, essentially all participants tested in 1965, was termed the "1965 sample." In the spring of 1965, the National Merit Scholarship Qualification Test (NMSQT) was administered to 794,589 eleventh-grade students from a total of 17,608 different high schools.

Further details of these samples are given in Breland (1972a, 1972b).

Data All subjects involved were administered the National Merit Scholarship Qualification Test (NMSQT) in the spring of their junior year of high school. In addition, selected subjects tested in 1962 were requested to complete a student questionnaire. Questionnaires were also requested from parents and teachers of these selected participants. From the questionnaire information, a very large number of variables were available for examination. In the present study, particular attention was directed to mother's education, father's education, family income, and mother's age. The second major source of information involved in the present study consisted of NMSQT scores for 1965 participants. For the 1965 administration, all subjects were requested to complete an information grid immediately prior to taking the test. This information grid included an item concerning the position of the subject in his family, whether he or she was a twin, and the sexes and spacing of siblings. Using the ordinal position data collected from this grid, it was possible to categorize subjects into 82 different sibling configurations.

Instruments The NMSQT consists of five tests: English usage, Mathematics Usage, Social Studies Reading, Natural Science Reading, and Word Usage. The unweighted sum of the five tests, known as the Selection Score, has both Kuder-Richardson 20 and odd-even reliabilities of .97. For the 1962 participants (normative sample and commended group), four additional measures of father's education, mother's education, family income, and mother's age at birth were used. The three socioeconomic variables were obtained from questionnaire items. For the 1965 sample, information on socioeconomic status and mother's age was not available. On the other hand, very detailed information was available concerning the subjects' family structures.

Analyses The data for the two 1962 samples were analyzed by means of an exact least-squares multivariate analysis of variance and covariance as described by Bock (1963). Computations were performed using the multivariance program of Finn (1972). The design involved two factors, family size and birth order—each having five levels of observation—and four covariates—mother's education, father's education, family income, and mother's age. For the very large 1965 sample, practicalities of data reduction dictated a different approach. No analyses of variance or covariance were performed; however, mean scores were computed for each of the 82 sibship configurations, and these were then combined to test birth-order effects, spacing effects, and sibling-sex effects by means of t tests.

RESULTS

In all three samples, the relationships obtained between birth order and NMSQT Selection Score were similar. Firstborns from small families had the highest scores, and lastborns from large families the lowest. The analyses of variance and covariance of the two 1962 samples showed the effects were statistically significant and that these effects were not appreciably influenced by the covariates. Step-down analyses of the birth-order effects in the 1962 samples suggested that they were verbal in nature, since the more verbal of the NMSQT subtests (such as Word Usage) showed highly significant birth-order differences regardless of step-down orderings, and the least verbal subtests (Math Usage) showed no significant differences for any step-down ordering of subtest scores.

The nature of the relationships among the variables of birth order, family size, and NMSQT Selection Score is most vividly described by the plot of Figure 1, based on the large 1965 sample. Almost all the mean differences represented in Figure 1 are significant beyond the .01 level. But what is perhaps of more interest is the close consistency between the male and female subsamples. Although males score slightly higher overall than females, the pattern of relationships is the same. The plots of Figure 1 are remarkably similar to the one presented in Belmont and Marolla (1973), a study of 400,000 19-year-old men in the Netherlands.

Sibling spacing effects are indicated in Figures 2 and 3 for two-child and three-child families, respectively (larger families were not analyzed with respect to spacing because of the large number of categories involved). Again, the patterns of spacing effects are consistent for both males and females. Combinations of sibling configurations were examined so as to compare categories having different numbers of siblings of a given sex. None of these differences was statistically significant (despite the large number of cases), and no consistent patterns were noted.

Some intriguing results were obtained when each of the 82 sibship configurations were rank ordered by NMSQT Selection Score separately for males and females. The rank-order correlations between sexes, as indicated, is .96. The sibling configurations occupying ranks 1, 6, 10, 14, 20, 62, and 68 are identical for both males and females. Twins occupy rank 72 for males and rank 70 for females, indicating agreement with most twin research (that twins average low on achievement tests, especially tests having large verbal components). That the high correlation of ranks for males and females is not merely an artifact of increasing family size was demonstrated by a similar rank-order correlation within the 36 configurations of three-child families. For this subset of configurations, a rank-order correlation between males and females of .95 was obtained.

DISCUSSION

The analyses of variance and covariance for the 1962 samples confirm the relationship between birth order and achievement often noted in the literature. These analyses suggested also that the observed relationship was not attributable to family differences in father's education, mother's education, and family

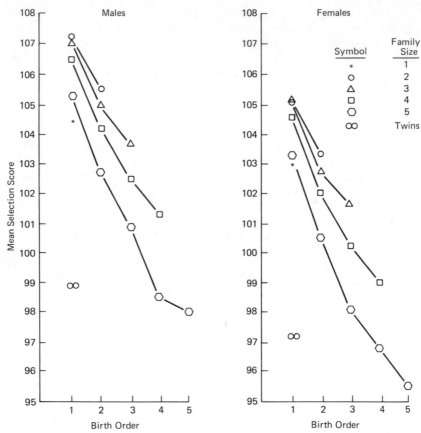

FIGURE 1.   Mean NMSQT Selection Scores, 1965 sample. Symbols for family size: * = 1, ○ = 2, △ = 3, □ = 4,   = 5, ∞ = twins.

income; to family differences in mother's age; or to combinations of these factors. Moreover, the relationship between family size and achievement appeared to be related to some characteristic of family size itself rather than to socioeconomic-status factors associated with family size. Such a result is in close agreement with results obtained and arguments advanced by Nisbet (1953).

That the primary source of the score differences is verbal in nature was indicated by the step-down analyses on the. individual NMSQT tests. After all other sources of variation were removed, the birth-order differences for the most purely verbal of the NMSQT tests (Word Usage) remained. Furthermore, when Word Usage was ordered first, all other differences became insignificant.

The detailed classification of family configurations available for the 1965 sample was useful for substantiating the results of the two smaller 1962 samples as well as for investigation of more subtle effects of sibling spacing and sexes. Although several studies have reported significant differences in birth-order

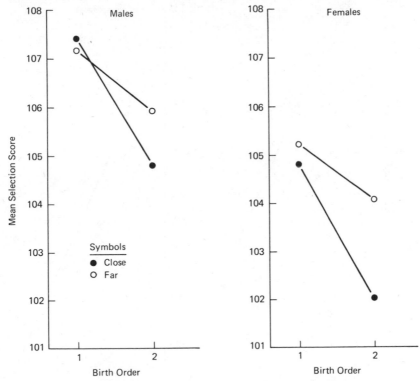

F i g u r e 2.   *Spacing effects in two-child families, 1965 sample.* ● = *close,* ○ = *far.*

effects where the number of like-sexed siblings was varied, the present study indicated no consistent differences at all that were related to sibling sexes. Conversely, the analyses of the 1965 sample data suggested some striking effects associated with sibling spacing. Where a sibling followed closely in age (2 years or less), the scores were depressed. But where the age spacing interval was far (3 years or more), the same score depression did not occur.

Because the birth-order effects on NMSQT scores appear to be attributable to a specific ability of a verbal nature, and because of the apparent importance of spacing effects, one is led to believe that these differences are due to environmental causes. Neither physiological theories nor economic theories would explain differences in verbal achievement but not in nonverbal achievement. And although closeness of siblings might be related to socioeconomic status (poor parents have closer children), the fact that scores are depressed primarily for closely following siblings tends to preclude such a possibility.

Therefore, of the three traditional explanations for birth-order effects (physiological, economic, and social-psychological), the last would seem to offer the most promise—but this is not an expectancy theory. A common denominator tying together low achievement for twins, those of larger families,

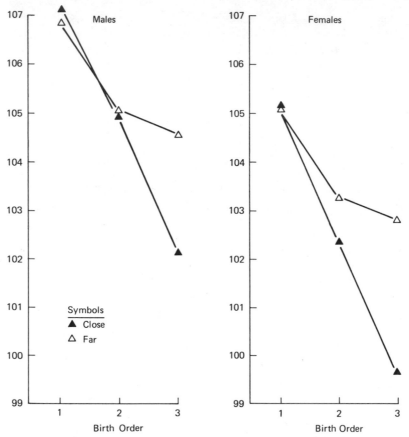

FIGURE 3.   *Spacing effects in three-child families, 1965 sample.* ▲ = *close,* △ = *far.*
Spacing for second born refers only to preceding sibling.

later birth orders, and closely following siblings is what has been called an
"isolation hypothesis" (Faris, 1940). That is, children isolated from other
children during early developmental stages may have an advantage as far as
achievement is concerned. The twin study of Record et al. (1970) serves as
an excellent demonstration of the effect of isolation from other siblings. In this
study, even though normal twins who grew up to the time of testing (age 11)
together had decidedly depressed verbal reasoning scores, surviving twins whose
co-twin died at or near birth had scores about the same as nontwins. What is
not explained by the isolation hypothesis is the case of the only child. As in the
present investigation, Belmont and Marolla (1973) observed that only children
do not appear to fit the same pattern as the other sibship configurations. Mean
scores for only children tend to fall below those of most other firstborns (see
Figure 1). One possible explanation for this anomaly is contained in Kammeyer's
(1967) review of birth-order research. According to Kammeyer, some research
indicates that the firstborn plays a parent-surrogate role relative to later-born

siblings—a role that also may be thought of as a kind of "foreman" role. As long as there are other siblings, therefore, the firstborn serves as interlocutor between parents and later-born. Such a role would appear to be an excellent one for the development of verbal skills.

If one combines the isolation hypothesis with an interlocutor hypothesis, the higher verbal abilities of firstborn in relation to only children would be explained. That is, isolation from other siblings provides for close relationships with parents at their higher verbal level and avoids close relationships with siblings at a low verbal level. But an initial isolation, followed by an interlocutor role, offers the possibility of a further verbal enrichment. What is suggested, then, is a need for a mathematical modeling of these various potential sources of development. It is only with such models that the complex of interacting factors is likely to be understood.

References

ALTUS, W. D. Birth order and scholastic aptitude. *Journal of Consulting Psychology*, 1965, 29, 202–205.

ALTUS, W. D. Birth order and its sequelae. *Science*, 1966, 151, 44–49.

BAYER, A. E., & FOLGER, J. K. The current state of birth-order research. *International Journal of Psychiatry*, 1967, 3, 37–39.

BELMONT, L., & MAROLLA, F. A. Birth order, family size, and intelligence. *Science*, 1973, 182, 1096–1101.

BOCK, R. D. Programming univariate and multivariate analysis of variance. *Technometrics*, 1963, 5, 95–116.

BRADLEY, R. W. Birth order and school-related behavior. *Psychological Bulletin*, 1968, 70, 45–51.

BRELAND, H. M. Birth order and intelligence. (Doctoral dissertation, State University of New York at Buffalo.) Ann Arbor, Mich.: University Microfilms, 1972. No. 72–27. (a)

BRELAND, H. M. Birth order, family configuration, and verbal achievement. *Research Bulletin 72–47*. Princeton, N.J.: Educational Testing Service, 1972. (b)

BRELAND, H. M. Birth order effects: a reply to Schooler. *Psychological Bulletin*, 1973, 80, 210–212.

EYSENCK, H. J., & COOKSON, D. Personality in primary school children: 3-family background. *British Journal of Educational Psychology*, 1969, 40, 117–131.

FARIS, R. E. L. Sociological causes of genius. *American Sociological Review*, 1940, 5, 689–699.

FINN, J. D. Multivariance: univariate and multivariate analysis of variance, covariance, and regression. Ann Arbor, Mich.: National Educational Resources, Inc., 1972.

HSIAO, H. H. The status of the firstborn with special reference to intelligence. *Genetic Psychology Monographs*, 1931, 9, 1–118.

JONES, H. E. Order of birth. In C. Murchison (Ed.), *A handbook of child psychology*. Worcester, Mass.: Clark University Press, 1933.

JONES, H. E. The environment and mental development. In L. Carmichael (Ed.), *Manual of child psychology*. New York: Wiley, 1954.

KAMMEYER, K. Birth order as a research variable. *Social Forces*, 1967, 46, 71–80.

MURPHY, G.; MURPHY, L. G.; & NEWCOMB, T. *Experimental social psychology*. New York: Harper, 1937.

NISBET, J. Family environment and intelligence. *Eugenics Review*, 1953, 45, 31–42.

RECORD, R. G.; McKEOWN, T.; & EDWARDS, J. H. The relation of measured intelligence to birth order and maternal age. *Annals of Human Genetics*, 1969, 33, 61–69.

RECORD, R. G.; McKEOWN, T.; & EDWARDS, J. H. An investigation of the difference in measured intelligence between twins and single births. *Annals of Human Genetics*, 1970, **84**, 11–20.

SAMPSON, E. E. Study of ordinal position. In B. A. Maher (Ed.), *Progress in experimental personality research*. Vol. 2. New York: Academic Press, 1965.

SCHACHTER, S. Birth order, eminence, and higher education. *American Sociological Review*, 1963, **28**, 757–767.

SCHOOLER, C. Birth-order effects: not here, not now! *Psychological Bulletin*, 1972, **78**, 161–175.

SCHOOLER, C. Birth-order effects: a reply to Breland. *Psychological Bulletin*, 1973, **80**, 213–214.

SUTTON-SMITH, B., & ROSENBERG, B. G. *The sibling*. New York: Holt, Rinehart and Winston, 1970.

The Development of Self-Perceptions in Children and Adolescents *

Raymond Montemayor and Marvin Eisen
BROOKLYN COLLEGE AND CALIFORNIA STATE UNIVERSITY AT SAN DIEGO

A small body of research exists in the area of self-concept development. Investigators have concerned themselves with age changes in such things as self-esteem, body image, and the disparity between perceived self and idealized self. However, in few of these studies is self-concept development conceived of as at least partly an outcome of changes in cognitive processes. Yet, developmental changes in self-perceptions and attitudes, and the organization of those perceptions and attitudes may reflect underlying cognitive changes.

The purpose of the present investigation is to explore one implication of such a conception. Specifically, it is hypothesized that with increasing age, self-perceptions, or more accurately self-descriptions, become less concrete and more abstract. It is suggested that young children primarily describe and define themselves in terms of concrete characteristics such as appearance, likes and dislikes, and possessions, while adolescents conceive of themselves more abstractly and describe themselves in psychological and interpersonal terms. This formulation is in agreement with Werner's notion that development leads to increased integration as reflected in the use of abstract constructs.

Few studies in the area of self-concept development bear on this question. However, investigations of the development of impression formation or person perception have consistently found that, with increasing age, other people

Presented at meetings of The Society for Research in Child Development, Denver, 1975. Printed by permission.

* Parts of this research were supported by a grant to the first author from the Faculty Research Award Program of the City University of New York, No. 10702, and by a grant to the second author from the NIH Biomedical Sciences Support Program to Michigan State University.

are viewed in a way that is increasingly more interpersonal, complex, and abstract. To the extent that developmental changes in self-perceptions are similar to changes in person perceptions, one would expect a similar result, i.e., an increasing use of psychological and abstract terms to describe the self.

One hundred and thirty-six males and 126 females served as subjects in this study. The subjects were drawn from five grades—4, 6, 8, 10 and 12— and the average age for the students within each grade was 10, 12, 14, 16, and 18 years, respectively. The subjects were white, middle-class, average and above in intelligence and were from a suburban, academic, midwestern community. Subjects were administered the Twenty Statements Test in class groups. The Twenty Statements Test simply asks the respondent to give 20 answers to the question, "Who am I?" The test takes approximately 15 minutes to complete. A 30-category scoring system, devised by Gordon (1968) was used to classify each answer. Table 1 shows the scoring system and gives a few illustrative examples for each category. For example, category 10, Social Status, was

TABLE 1

Who Am I Scoring Categories with Typical Examples

1. *Sex*: a boy, a sister, a guy.
2. *Age*: 9½, a teenager, a senior.
3. *Name*: Susan, Bobby.
4. *Racial* or *National Heritage*: White, a Negro, Italian.
5. *Religious Categorization*: a Catholic, Jewish, Methodist.
6. *Kinship Role*: a son, a sister, engaged.
7. *Occupational Role*: hoping to become a doctor, paper-boy.
8. *Student Role*: a student, getting bad grades, a "B" student.
9. *Political Affiliation*: a Democrat, an Independent.
10. *Social Status*: middle-class, from a rich family.
11. *Territoriality, Citizenship*: an American, living on Oak Street.
12. *Membership in Interacting Group*: on the football team, in the science club.
13. *Existential, Individuating*: Me, myself, nothing, I.
14. *Membership in an Abstract Category*: a person, a human, a speck in the universe.
15. *Ideological and Belief References*: a liberal, a pacifist.
16. *Judgments, Tastes, Likes*: hate school, like sports.

17. *Intellectual Concerns*: a thinker, likes to read.
18. *Artistic Activities*: a dancer, singer, poet.
19. *Other Activities*: a hiker, a stamp collector, a swimmer.
20. *Possessions, Resources*: have a bike, own a dog.
21. *Physical Self, Body Image*: 5' 10", 125 lbs., fat.
22. *Sense of Moral Worth*: bad, good, honest, a liar.
23. *Sense of Self-Determination*: ambitious, a hardworker.
24. *Sense of Unity*: mixed up, a whole person, in harmony.
25. *Sense of Competence*: good at many things, creative.
26. *Interpersonal Style (how I typically act)*: friendly, fair, shy, cool, nice.
27. *Psychic Style, Personality (how I typically think and feel)*: happy, sad, in love, calm.
28. *Judgments Imputed to Others*: popular, well-liked, loved.
29. *Situational References*: going on a date tonight, bored with this.
30. *Uncodable Responses*: the sea, a flower, dead.

(Adapted from Gordon, 1968).

defined as any reference to the individual's or family's socioeconomic situation, such as middle-class or from a rich family. Category 22, Sense of Moral Worth, was any reference to a moral evaluation of the self. The categories are reasonably exhaustive and rarely was an answer classified as uncodable.

Two undergraduates were trained in the use of the system. Interjudge agreement was tested by having both coders score a sample of 20 tests drawn from the experimental population. Interjudge agreement was 85% (average agreement per test, 17/20 responses). Responses were then summarized for each age group by sex in terms of the number of subjects who answered each category at least once. Age changes for each sex were then determined by chi-square tests performed on each category. Since there were 60 separate chi-square tests performed, the possibility that a test would be significant by chance was high. Therefore, only p values less than .001 were considered significant. Table 2 shows the per cent of subjects at each age using a category at least once.

The results indicated that there were no developmental pattern differences for males and females, i.e., if the use of a category tended to increase or decrease, it tended to increase or decrease for both males and females. However, changes in the use of some categories were significant for only one sex. Females showed a decrease between childhood and adolescence in the use of the categories Name and Territory; while males showed a decrease in the use of the categories Tastes and Likes, and Possessions. Both sexes were more likely to use physical descriptions in childhood than in adolescence.

In addition, for both males and females, there was a significant increase between childhood and adolescence in the use of the following categories: Existential, e.g., I, myself; Abstract Category, a person, a human; Self-Determination, ambitious, a hardworker; Interpersonal Style, friendly, nice; and finally Psychic Style, happy, calm.

The pattern of the data indicates that there is very often more of a change in self-descriptions between ages 10 and 12 than at any other time. Thus, 12-year-olds are to some extent more like 18-year-olds than 10-year-olds. Perhaps reading a few of the protocols will illustrate this finding and will give a better idea of what children at different ages say about themselves. (Original spellings and emphasis have been retained).

These first responses are from a boy, age 9, in the 4th grade. Notice the concrete flavor of his self-descriptions; the almost exclusive use of the categories Sex, Age, Name, Territory, Likes, and Physical Self.

> My name is Bruce C. I have brown eyes. I have brown hair. I have brown eyebrows. I'am nine years old. I *love*! Sports. I have seven people in my family. I have great! eye site. I have lots! of friends. I live on 1923 P. Dr. I'am going on 10 in September. I'am a boy. I have a uncle that is almost 7 feet tall. My school is P. My teacher is Mrs. V. I play Hockey! I'am almost the smartest boy in the class. I *love*! food. I love fresh air. I *love* School.

Next is a girl, age 11½, in the 6th grade. Note that although she uses the category Tastes and Likes quite frequently, there is a heavy emphasis on interpersonal and personality characteristics.

> My name is A. I'm a human being. I'm a girl. I'm a truthful person. I'm not pretty. I do so-so in my studies. I'm a very good cellist. I'm a very good pianist.

TABLE 2

Percent of Subjects at Each Age Using Category at Least Once

AGE	FEMALES					MALES				
	10	12	14	16	18	10	12	14	16	18
Category										
Sex	43	83	46	47	70*	47	63	30	48	74*
Age	33	26	29	21	45	3	44	30	29	37
Name	62	4	4	6	30†	38	15	11	16	32*
Race	0	4	0	12	25**	9	4	4	13	5
Religion	10	0	4	3	15	3	0	4	6	5
Kinship	43	40	25	21	50	31	15	11	29	63**
Occupation	5	9	21	29	50**	3	15	37	26	37**
Student	71	74	29	50	70**	63	44	44	58	74
Politics	0	0	7	6	5	0	0	0	0	5
Social Status	5	0	0	3	5	3	0	0	0	0
Territory	52	17	11	12	5†	44	15	30	13	16*
Inter. Grp.	57	52	46	53	60	56	26	22	23	53**
Existential	0	52	18	26	55†	0	15	19	26	53†
Abstract Category	0	78	39	44	45†	3	81	22	45	59†
Ideological	5	13	32	21	40*	3	15	15	26	37*
Tastes, Likes	71	70	79	50	35*	66	59	81	39	26†
Intellectual	43	26	36	21	20	28	30	44	26	26
Artistic	24	35	29	30	25	22	37	30	26	10
Other Acts.	57	65	75	65	45	69	59	89	84	74
Possessions	52	22	18	18	10*	53	22	30	10	5†
Physical Self	90	65	39	59	15†	84	48	52	39	16†
Moral Worth	5	30	11	21	20	3	15	22	35	32*
Self-Determination	0	4	29	47	45†	9	11	22	42	53†
Unity	0	0	18	18	20	0	0	11	16	21*
Competence	33	26	29	41	40	38	48	59	55	32
Interpersonal	33	96	96	82	90†	50	56	85	90	95†
Psychic Style	29	65	89	74	80†	25	19	41	87	63†
Judgments	24	26	25	21	60*	22	19	22	35	53
Situation	5	9	21	26	10	13	4	19	13	11
Uncodable	10	0	0	6	0	28	30	19	6	16
N	21	23	28	34	20	32	27	27	31	19

* Chi-square significant at .05 level.
** Chi-square significant at .01 level.
† Chi-square significant at .001 level.

I'm a little bit tall for my age. I like several boys. I like several girls. I'm old-fashioned. I play tennis. I am a *very* good swimmer. I try to be helpful. I'm always ready to be friends with anybody. Mostly I'm good, but I lose my temper. I'm not well-liked by some girls and boys. I love sports and music. I don't know if I'm liked by boys or not.

Finally, are the responses from a girl, age 17 who is in the 12th grade. Here, note the strong emphasis on interpersonal descriptions, characteristic mood states, and the large number of ideological and belief references, the beginnings of the establishment of a world view.

> I am a human being. I am a girl. I am an individual. I don't know who I am. I am a Pisces. I am a moody person. I am an indecisive person. I am an ambitious person. I am a very curious person. I am a confused person. I am not an individual. I am a loner. I am an American (God help me). I am a Democrat. I am a liberal person. I am a radical. I am a conservative. I am a pseudo-liberal. I am an atheist. I am not a classifiable person (i.e.—I don't want to be).

Contrast the responses of the previous 11-year-old with both the 9- and 17-year-old and I think you can see that the 11-year-old sounds more like the 17- than the 9-year-old. There may be a transitional period between the ages of 10 and 12 in the area of self-descriptions that corresponds to the transitional period from concrete to formal cognitive operations. To the extent that the 12-year-olds in this sample have begun to acquire the formal operational skills of hypothetical-deductive thinking and propositional logic, their thinking may more closely resemble those older adolescents who are in a similar stage rather than the younger children in a previous stage. Similarily, conceptualizations of the self by the 12-year-old boy may also be more like the older group than the younger group.

As Inhelder and Piaget have pointed out, adolescent thinking is a "second order system" in the sense that the adolescent does not solve problems in terms of concrete givens, but uses those concrete facts to form hypotheses about an underlying reality. Young children seem to characterize themselves in terms of descriptions of their behaviors. One might almost think of them as naïve behaviorists. Adolescents, however, seem to infer from their behavior the existence of an underlying personality trait. For example, it is not uncommon for young children to say that they like to play baseball, football, hockey, soccer, and so on. An adolescent, however will rarely present a list of behaviors such as that. Much more common would be to say: "I am an athlete," or "I like athletics." Thus, there is an integration of behaviors which leads the adolescent to infer a superordinate category.

It might be useful to think of the relationship between increasing cognitive abilities and self-descriptions as an attempt to more accurately and uniquely characterize the essence of the self. One notes an increasing use of descriptions which result in a sharper and more focused picture of the self, and which lead to a clearer differentiation of the self from others. For example, to describe oneself as a boy, 9-years-old, with brown hair and good eyesight is not to say much that will allow for a specific and unique characterization of the self. But, to describe the self as moody, indecisive, confused and a loner results in a picture of this adolescent that is reasonably specific and differentiated from others.

In conclusion, one might say that what appears to be the self for the child is only a set of elements from which the adolescent infers a constellation of philosophical and psychological categories that uniquely characterize himself.

Reference

GORDON, C. Self-conceptions: Configurations of content. In C. Gordon and K. Gergen (Eds.) *The self in social interaction.* Vol. I. New York: Wiley, 1968.

Conservation of Horizontality : Sex Differences in Sixth-Graders and College Students

Lauren J. Harris, Charles Hanley, and Catherine T. Best

MICHIGAN STATE UNIVERSITY

In the classical demonstration of the test for representation of horizontality (Piaget and Inhelder, 1956), the child is shown a bottle half-filled with water, asked to notice the position of the water in the bottle, and then to predict where the water level will be when the bottle is tipped. According to Piaget and Inhelder (1956), the principle that the water level will remain horizontal is mastered by about 12 years of age, the start of the so-called formal operational stage.

Recent studies have shown, however, that many 12-year-olds and even young adults do *not* know the principle (e.g., Liben, 1973; Morris, 1971; Rebelsky, 1964; Thomas et al., 1973), the majority of whom are females— in the case of college-age women, an estimated 50 per cent (Thomas et al., 1973).

This sort of failing of what seems to be a basic principle about nature has sparked much interest generally because it is puzzling in itself, for some psychologists because of its apparent violation of Piagetian theory, and finally because of the sex difference. Why *do* females lag behind? It occurred to us that in all earlier investigations known to us, the subject had to draw or otherwise construct the predicted waterline. With notions about "perception-performance lag" partly in the back of our minds, we wondered what would have happened had the subjects—especially college-age—simply been required to recognize the waterline expected. To find out, we designed a test that required the subject merely to pick that one of several drawings of tilted containers that correctly represented the water level of a standard container shown in upright orientation. We showed a variety of containers, shown in Figure 1—open containers, bottles, and pouring pitchers—one flat-bottomed, one round-bottomed of each type—in questions like those illustrated in Figure

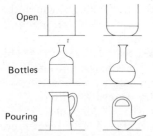

FIGURE 1. *Container types.*

Presented at meetings of The Society for Research in Child Development, Denver, 1975. Printed by permission.

95

If the bowl holding the water, marked *X* at the left, is tipped, which numbered bowl shows where the waterline will be?

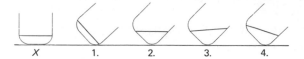

If the sprinkling can holding the water, marked *X* at the left, is tilted, which numbered can shows how the water will look?

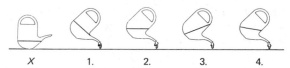

If the can holding water, marked *X* at the left, is tilted, which numbered can shows how the water will look?

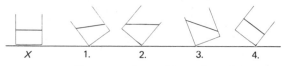

FIGURE 2.   *Types of questions.*

2. For each question, there was one standard in upright orientation with the water horizontal, and four foils showing various degrees and directions of tilt. One foil showed the liquid level at the true horizontal. The other three showed, in various combinations, the water level tilted 10, 20, or 30 degrees, in relation to the true horizontal, or parallel to the base of the container.

Sixteen such questions were printed in booklets. The instructions, appearing above each question read, "If the [container name] holding the water, marked X at the left, is tipped, which numbered [container name] shows how the waterline will look?" [Note: for half the questions, counterbalanced for choice, the instructions ended," . . . how the waterline will be?"] Rebelsky (1964) writes of her college-age subjects who had failed to conserve on a standard drawing task: "Even with a glass of water before them, some *S*s saw the water level was not as they had drawn it, but felt the water level did not look horizontal. A few tried to verify this by looking through the glass at a horizontal plane. *S*s noted that the water was "really" horizontal but reported it "looked" tilted" (pp. 373–374).

We therefore supposed that the wording "which . . . container shows how the waterline will look?" might encourage "phenomenalistic" answers or judgments, even in individuals who knew the principle of invariance, while the wording ". . . how the waterline will be?" would encourage "realistic" answers even for subjects who, like Rebelsky's, might feel that the water level did not actually *look* horizontal. The subject merely had to pick that one of the four foils in which the water level matched the level shown in the standard. It seemed ridiculously simple—to us who had made up the test!—and at least for the adults, we expected practically everybody to pick up the correct foil.

EXPERIMENT 1

Subjects   The subjects in Experiment 1 were 158 undergraduates (48 men and 110 women) and 61 sixth-grade children (33 boys and 28 girls). Both groups were tested in their classrooms.

Results   Contrary to our expectation, many of the university students did not conserve, most of them women. The results are displayed as histograms in Figure 3, which shows the percentages of males and females scoring from 0 to 16 correct for the 16 questions. The adults' scores are on the left. The men averaged 13.4 correct of 16 questions, or 84%; the women, 9.4 correct, or 59%. The difference was significant ($t = 5.16$, $df = 156$, $p < .01$)

The children's scores appear on the right. They did much worse, but once again males were ahead, boys averaging 9.3 correct, or 58%, as well as the university women had done; the girls, 5.9, or 37% ($t = 5.16$, $df = 59$, $p < .01$). Twenty-seven per cent of the boys got from 14–16 correct (15% with perfect scores) compared to only 4% of the girls (all with scores of 14). So a fair number of persons—children and adults alike—did *not* make the horizontal judgment even when they merely had to pick the one horizontal line out of the four foils— and females failed in this respect more than males.

As for the two different wordings of the instructions, item analyses failed to disclose any difference between them. It may be that the subjects simply failed to read them as significantly different instructions (i.e., took them as non-meaningful variants of each other), or that the different wordings were not sufficiently emphasized.

EXPERIMENT 2

One of the men in Experiment 1 who had made predominantly horizontal choices afterwards remarked that he had felt constrained to choose a *non-*

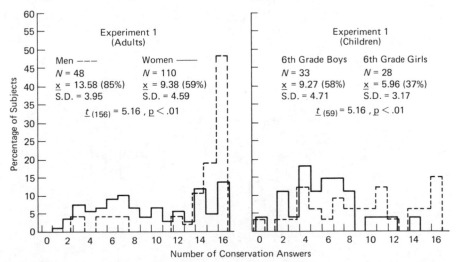

FIGURE 3.   *Percentage of subjects (men, women, boys, girls) giving specified numbers of conservation answers. (Experiment 1.)*

horizontal foil in some cases because the correct foil—the foil showing the water level to be horizontal—did not show the same *volume* of water as the standard. He therefore was unsure whether the test was about water level or water volume. To our chagrin, we discovered that he was right: in making the drawings, we indeed had failed several times to conserve the volume of water in the tilted containers—how fragile are these principles even in the sophisticated!

We doubted that this failing in the test was related to the sex differences found, for if it were, it would mean that females, more than males, had answered on the basis of water volume rather than level—which seemed unlikely. But to be sure, we corrected the mistakes and repeated the test with a new group of undergraduates, 53 men and 105 women. The results were unchanged: the men averaged 13.77 correct (86%), the women 10.3 (64%) ($t = 5.08$, $df = 156$, $p < .01$). As the histograms show, in Figure 4, the distributions of scores were very similar to those for the university sample in Experiment 1.

The question may be raised whether persons with very low or middle scores were simply guessing. Item analyses showed that they were not: errors were *not* distributed haphazardly across the various choices; instead, foils showing the 10 degree tilt—the smallest degree included—were chosen far more often than the others. And the foil showing the water level parallel to the base of the tilted figure was chosen less than 5% of the times it appeared, though more often by females. So the subjects— males and females alike—were making their incorrect choices systematically, usually picking the smallest degree of tilt as though they expected that the water level would be close to but not at the horizontal.

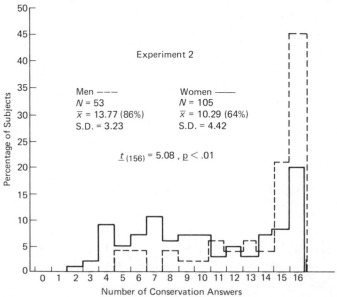

FIGURE 4.   *Percentage of men and women giving specified numbers of conservation answers.*
(*Experiment 2.*)

It is tempting to suppose that the subject's errors were "perceptual"— that they were mistaking the 10 degree tilt for the true horizontal. But the 10 degree tilt was appreciable (adults, men and women alike, have no trouble picking out the foil showing a horizontal line when they are expressly asked to do so, or setting a line at the true horizontal, as other investigators have found; Thomas and Jamison, 1975; Willemsen and Reynolds, 1973), and besides, the foil showing the true horizontal was always available for choice.

So far, then, we merely had satisfied ourselves that the nonconserver's difficulty in previous studies did not stem from the requirement that the predicted waterline be drawn or otherwise constructed, and that females were more affected in this regard than males. Some subjects themselves gave us a clue as to what the real problem might be. These were university students who had failed to conserve and who argued that the instructions ("If the container holding the water . . . is tipped . . .") implied that the water was in motion at that very moment and therefore tilted. As one subject put it, as the container was being tipped, the water would roll to one side. The subject was correct provided the container was tipped quickly and abruptly. But if tipped more smoothly and slowly the water would remain level. Though our instructions did not mention the speed with which the container is tipped, the possibility nevertheless arose that the subjects who failed to conserve horizontality had interpreted the instructions as meaning that the container at that moment was being tipped (quickly and abruptly), and that, for some reason, proportionately more female than males had made this inference. We studied this possibility in a further experiment.

EXPERIMENT 3

Procedure   In Experiment 3, two kinds of instructions were used, in a between-subjects design, with the 16 drawings used in the previous studies. One instruction (Figure 5—top) was designed to imply that the container was still in motion and read, "The pictures . . . show containers of water while they are being tilted. Which picture shows how the waterline will look?" The other instruction (Figure 5—bottom) was designed to imply that the container was still, and read, "The pictures . . . show . . . containers of water, which, several minutes before were tilted at various angles. Which picture shows how the waterline will look?"

Note that we have eliminated the upright standard in this experiment, and that the instructions now imply that the four foils show four *different* containers. With a standard present, as in Experiments 1 and 2, and with instructions saying that all the foils are variants of the standard, it was understandable that at least one subject had been encouraged to compare the foils against the standard in the basis of volume. Even though we were careful, in Experiment 2, to conserve volume in the foils, we worried nonetheless that some subjects would continue to make their judgments in terms of volume in addition to, or instead of, orientation of the waterline. These individuals therefore might make an incorrect choice of orientation because the volumes, in fact equal, nonetheless might appear unequal. This problem is eliminated by eliminating the standard.

". . . While Being Tilted"

The pictures below show containers of water while they are
being tilted at various angles. Which picture shows how the
waterline would look?

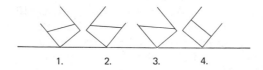

1.   2.   3.   4.

". . . Several Minutes Before"

The pictures below show containers of water which, several
minutes before, were tilted at various angles. Which picture
shows how the waterline would look?

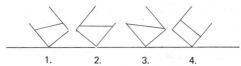

1.   2.   3.   4.

FIGURE 5.   *Examples of questions asked in Experiment 3.*

Subjects   The subjects were a new group of 221 college undergraduates; 45 men and 65 women had test booklets with the "several minutes before" instructions, and 48 men and 63 women had the "while being tilted" instructions.

Results   The results (Figure 6) seemed to have had no effects. In the "while being tilted" and "several minutes before" condition, the men's average scores were 14.1 correct (88%) and 13.4 (84%), respectively, not significantly different from each other or from the combined average for the adult men of Experiments 1 and 2 (all t's < 1.0). The women's average scores were 11.03 correct (69%) and 11.95 (75%), also not significantly different from each other ($t < 1.0$), though slightly better than the combined average of women in Experiments 1 and 2. And in both conditions, the women's scores were behind the men's—by a significant margin in the "while being tilted" condition ($t = 3.88$, $df = 109$, $p < .01$), and marginally so in the "several minutes before" condition ($t = 1.73$, $df = 108$; $.05 < p < .10$, two-tailed). We nevertheless were reluctant to give up on the idea that inferred motion was an underlying factor in the performance of the nonconservers. Perhaps the instructions should have been more explicit. We decided to try again.

EXPERIMENT 4

Procedure   This time we determined to leave no room for doubt as to whether the water was or was not in motion at the moment the subject is asked to represent its level in the container. In one condition, illustrated at the top of Figure 7, the instructions read, "The pictures . . . show containers of water being tilted at various angles. Imagine that this is being done right now, and

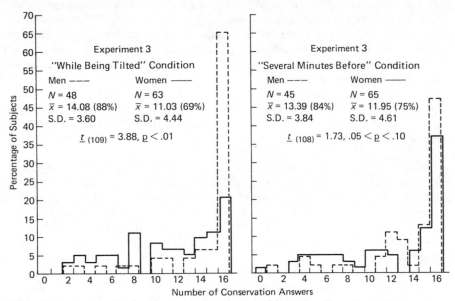

FIGURE 6.   *Percentage of men and women giving specified numbers of conservation answers.*
(*Experiment 3.*)

"Water in Motion"

The pictures below show bottles of water being tilted at various angles. Imagine that this is being done right now, and that the water is still in motion. Which picture shows how the waterline will look?

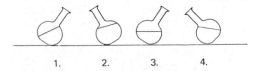

1.   2.   3.   4.

"Water at Rest"

The pictures below show bottles of water which have been tilted at various angles. Imagine that this was done several minutes ago, and that the water has come to rest. Which picture shows how the waterline will look?

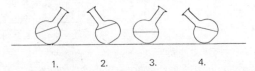

1.   2.   3.   4.

FIGURE 7.   *Examples of questions asked in Experiment 4.*

that the water *is still in motion*. Which picture shows how the waterline will look?" The other instructions (bottom of Figure 7) read, "The pictures . . . show containers of water which have been tilted at various angles. Imagine that this was done several minutes ago, and that the water *has come to rest*." Once again, we eliminated the standard, and this time also shortened the test from 16 to 12 questions.

Subjects   The subjects were a new group of 135 undergraduates. Fourteen men and 55 women had the test booklet with the "water at rest" instructions, and 16 men and 50 women had the "water in motion" instructions.

Results   The results are shown in Figure 8. In the "water in motion" condition—shown at the left—both the men's and women's scores were low, the men averaging 7.37 correct out of 12 (61%), the women, 5.37 (45%). The difference between them was not significant ($t = 1.76$, $df = 64$, $.05 < p < .10$). The subjects given the "water at rest" instructions—shown at the right—did better, the men averaging 9.7 correct out of 12 (81%), the women, 9.58 (80%). For the first time the women's score was clearly equal to the men's (t [difference in men's and women's scores] < 1.0).

This seemed neat: if we assume that the instructions we used in Experiments 1 and 2 ("If the container . . . is tipped . . .") are ambiguous as to the motion of the water, then we now see that where the water is *explicitly* stated to be in motion, men do poorly (about as poorly as women do ordinarily—in

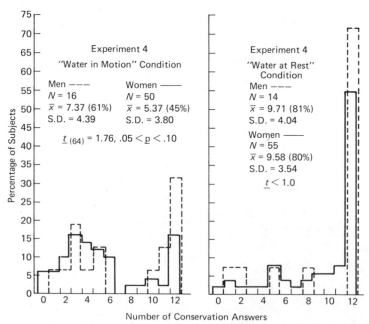

FIGURE 8.   *Percentage of men and women giving specified numbers of conservation answers.* (*Experiment 4.*)

Experiments 1 and 2—with "ambiguous" instructions; and women do poorly too, but no *worse* than they do with ambiguous instructions. And in the "water at rest" condition, men do well, but no better than they do with ambiguous instructions; and women do *better* than they do with ambiguous instructions.

These results suggest a possibly important role for inferred motion on the horizontality task and suggest that the usual male lead stems from men's normally interpreting the task as though the water were still; while women are more likely to think of the water as moving. Unfortunately, it proved to be not quite so neat as this. Again it was a remark by one of the subjects that cued us. This woman was puzzled: "I understand why," she said, "when the water is at rest, it will be level with the tabletop. But as long as the water is in motion, it would have to be tilted." The experimenter allowed how this could be true only if the container was tilted abruptly and quickly, but would stay level if the glass was tilted more slowly and smoothly. In that case, the subject declared, the water would remain level only because the water was *not* in motion.

In fact, of course, she was wrong. When a container of water is tilted, the water moves relative to the container, and the container moves relative to the water, and this is true however quickly or slowly the container is tilted, and however little or much the water "sloshes" around inside. But the subject's error is understandable. It is the container that is actively tilted by some*one*, and so from the subject's point of view—or at least from *some* subjects' point of view—it is the container, and not the water in it, that moves. The psychologically more appropriate way to put the question therefore would have been to emphasize the motion or lack of motion of the *container* rather than the water inside. We therefore did a fifth experiment incorporating this change in instructions.

EXPERIMENT 5

Procedure   In one condition—top of Figure 9—the instructions read, "The pictures . . . show containers of water being tilted at various angles. Imagine that this is being done right now, and that the containers *are still in motion* . . . ." The other instructions—bottom of Figure 9—read, "The pictures . . . show containers of water which have been tilted at various angles. Imagine that this was done several minutes ago, and that the containers are *no longer in motion*. Which picture shows how the water in the container will look?"

Subjects   The subjects were a new group of 220 undergraduates, with 58 men and 52 women assigned to each instruction condition.

Results   The results are shown in Figure 10. The "container in motion" instructions—shown at the left—had nearly the same effect as the "water in motion" instructions in Experiment 4. Both the men's and women's scores again were low, the men averaging only 7.29 correct (61%), again as low as *women* usually do; the women, 6.85 (57%), as poorly as they usually do. Once again men's and women's scores were not different from each other ($t = 1.33$, $df = 101$, $p < .05$).

So for both men and women, and to nearly equal degrees, saying that the *container* is in motion works *against* horizontality conservation. This finding

"Container in Motion"

The pictures below show sprinkling cans of water being tilted at various angles. Imagine that this is being done right now, and that the sprinkling cans <u>are still in motion.</u> Which picture shows how the water in the sprinkling can will look?

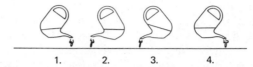

"Container at Rest" (No Longer in Motion)

The pictures below show sprinkling cans of water which have been tilted at various angles. Imagine that this was done several minutes ago, and that the sprinkling cans are <u>no longer in motion.</u> Which picture shows how the water in the sprinkling can will look?

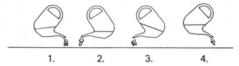

FIGURE 9.   *Examples of questions asked in Experiment 5.*

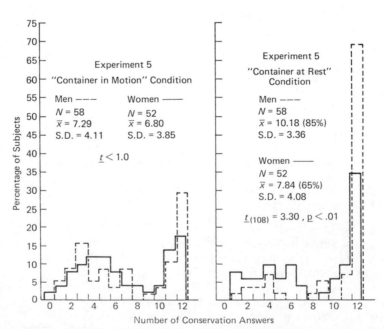

FIGURE 10.   *Percentage of men and women giving specified numbers of conservation answers.*
(*Experiment 5.*)

bolsters our surmise in Experiment 4 that inferred motion is important, and that men typically excel because they conceptualize the water as still, while women see it as moving. Why men and women should be so differently inclined —if indeed they are—we do not know.

This conclusion, however reasonable it may seem, is thrown into doubt when we consider the effects of the "container at rest" instructions—shown at the right. In the "*water at rest*" condition in Experiment 4, both the men and women had done well, the men averaging 81% correct, the women, 80% correct. In the "container at rest" condition in Experiment 5, the men, as expected, again did well, averaging 10.18 correct (85%), with 76% of the subjects getting at least 11 of 12 correct, and only 9% getting as few as 0–3 correct. But the women, as a group, did not do so well. Only 45% got 11 or 12 correct, and 21% got as few as 0–3 correct. As a group, the women averaged only 7.84 (65%), significantly less than the men ($t = 3.30$, $df = 108$, $p < .01$), and also significantly less than the 9.58 (80%) score by the women in the "water at rest" condition of Experiment 4 ($t = 2.35$, $df = 105$, $p < .01$).

Apparently, the "container at rest" instructions are functionally equivalent to the "water at rest" instructions for men but not for women. Describing the *container* requires the subject to *infer* something about the appearance of the water *inside* the container. And women, it seems, are less able, or less likely, than men to make the correct inference. Thus if it is the case that women and girls, more than men and boys, tend to interpret the situation as dynamic—as involving motion—this cannot wholly explain their poorer performance.

Nor can a tendency to infer motion explain certain exceptions to the general findings: combining the "in motion" conditions of Experiments 4 and 5, 29% of the women and 45% of the men gave 10–12 conservation answers. And combining the two "at rest" conditions, 14% of the women and 10% of the men gave as few as 0–3 conservation answers. That is, more than a quarter of the women and nearly half the men *conserved* horizontality even with instructions designed, for the large part successfully, to discourage it; while a small proportion of men and women alike failed in the task even with instructions designed, again for the large part successfully, to make the correct answer obvious.

Perhaps we are thinking about the horizontality task in quite the wrong way. What really seems to puzzle many cognitive developmental psychologists about it is that they conceive of the principle that water seeks its own level, that horizontality is invariant, as strictly a milestone in *logical, analytical* thinking like the principles assessed in tests of abstract reasoning. On these other tasks, adults, for the most part, perform at their expected level of competence, and women are just as good as men, and sometimes better.

But note how Piaget and Inhelder (1956) themselves speak of the water level test, in discussing children's performance:

> Now although it is doubtful whether failure to predict horizontality at this age is by itself proof of inability to conceive of a coordinate system—since it could be due to lack of interest, inattention, and so on—the repeated difficulty in appreciating the material facts themselves carries an entirely different implication. It undoubtedly indicates an inability to evaluate the perceptual data in terms of the orientation of lines and planes, and thereby suggests a failure on the part of

coordination as such. What indeed is a system of coordinates but a series of comparisons between objects in different positions and orientations (p. 390)?

This description sounds not so much like a description of a task involving *logical* principles but of visuo-spatial skills—e.g., perceiving and comparing spatial patterns; turning or rotating an object in 3-space and recognizing a new appearance or position after the prescribed manipulation. In high school seniors, just a bit younger than the college undergraduates we tested, performance on a test of horizontality is correlated significantly with performance on standard tests of spatial visualization (Spatial Subtest or Differential Aptitude Test; Liben, unpublished report), and it is well-established that in this *very particular* skill, males do better than females. The horizontality test, therefore, may well be *primarily* a test of visuo-spatial ability. Like any spatial test, it can be made harder, so that more people fail, or simpler, so that more people do well, though females, on average, still find it more difficult than males do.

The difficulty that many adults and older children have on this task, in particular the greater difficulty experienced by females, therefore might better be examined within the context of current theories about visuo-spatial ability, among them the view that the male's visuo-spatial superiority reflects greater right-hemisphere specialization for visuo-spatial processing (e.g., Knox and Kimura, 1970; McGlone and Kertesz, 1973), and the hypothesis, supported in several studies (e.g., Bock, 1973; Bock and Kolakowski, 1973; Corah, 1965; Hartlage, 1970; Stafford, 1961) that visuo-spatial ability is a sex-linked recessive-gene characteristic (see Harris, 1975, for review).

References

BOCK, R. D. Word and image: sources of the verbal and spatial factors in mental test scores. *Psychometrika*, 1973, **38**, 437–457.

BOCK, R. D. and KOLAKOWSKI, D. Further evidence of sex-linked major-gene influence on human spatial visualizing ability. *American Journal of Human Genetics*, 1973, **25**, 1–14.

CORAH, N. L. Differentiation in children and their parents. *Journal of Personality*, 1965, **33**, 300–308.

HARRIS, L. J. Sex differences in spatial ability: possible environmental, genetic, and neurological factors. To appear in M. Kinsbourne, Ed., *Hemispheric asymmetries of function*. Cambridge: Cambridge University Press (expected publication, 1975).

HARTLAGE, L. C. Sex-linked inheritance of spatial ability. *Perceptual and Motor Skills*, 1970, **31**, 610.

KNOX, C. and KIMURA, D. Cerebral processing of non-verbal sounds in boys and girls. *Neuropsychologia*, 1970, **8**, 227–238.

LIBEN, L. S. Operative understanding of horizontality and its relation to long-term memory. Paper presented at *Biennial Meetings of the Society for Research in Child Development*. Philadelphia, Pa., 1973.

LIBEN, L. S. Individual differences and performance on Piagetian spatial tasks. Unpublished report (mimeo., 28 pages, undated).

McGLONE, J. and KERTESZ, A. Sex differences in cerebral processing of visuo-spatial tasks. *Cortex*, 1973, **9**, 313–320.

MORRIS, B. B. Effects of angle, sex, and cue on adults' perception of the horizontal. *Perceptual and Motor Skills*, 1971, **32**, 827–830.

PIAGET, J. and INHELDER, B. *The child's conception of space.* New York: Humanities Press, 1956 (paperback edition: New York: W. W. Norton & Company, Inc., 1967).

REBELSKY, F. Adults' perception of the horizontal. *Perceptual and Motor Skills*, 1964, **19**, 371–374.

STAFFORD, R. E. Sex differences in spatial visualization as evidence of sex-linked inheritance. *Perceptual and Motor Skills*, 1961, **13**, 428.

THOMAS, H. and JAMISON, W. On the acquisition of understanding that still water is horizontal. *Merrill-Palmer Quarterly of Behavior and Development*, 1975, **21**, 31–44.

THOMAS, H., JAMISON, W., and HUMMEL, D. D. Observation is insufficient for discovering that the surface of still water is invariantly horizontal. *Science*, 1973, **181**, 173–174.

WILLEMSEN, E. and REYNOLDS, B. Sex differences in adults' judgments of the horizontal. *Developmental Psychology*, 1973, **8**, 309.

Chapter 3
Parents, Peers, and the Quest for Identity

BY LAURA S. SMART

STANLEY SUMMER

During adolescence in North America, the youngster's dependence upon her parents lessens while she moves toward the interdependence of equals. The change involves turmoil in parent and child while they learn to play new roles and feel new feelings as the child establishes a mature sense of identity.

Much of the adolescent's social and emotional growth takes place with contemporaries of both sexes. The sense of identity includes a firm concept of where one fits with other people, especially people of one's own generation. The young person's image of himself is built partly on his interpretations of the ways in which others regard him. Is he seen or bold or timid, witty or tongue-tied, handsome or funny looking? Is she considered artistic or "all thumbs," steady or flighty, intelligent or stupid? The reputation will influence his behavior as well as his self-concept. Friendships and love relationships enhance self-concepts and promote constructive behavior and personality growth. Failure to find friendship and love can be threatening.

Friendship and popularity have their sources in the peer group, which is made up of members of both sexes. Relationships with the opposite sex are considered as those that progress toward and include love, sex, and marriage.

Cultural Perspective

The forms of adolescence vary with cultural forms throughout the world and within the United States. For instance, urban, suburban, and rural adolescents differ significantly in this country [20]. Douvan and Adelson found suburban adolescents to be more privileged than the others in range and diversity of leisure activities, dating, group membership, and joint family activity. Rural adolescents were much more restricted in most types of opportunities for development, but city youngsters were also restricted in breadth and were propelled rapidly toward adulthood.

Because we have already discussed other cultural influences, such as social class, in earlier chapters, we go on to features of North American culture that have special meaning for parent–adolescent relationships. Many observers have noted that parents and children have conflicts or disagreements with each other. Sometimes this situation is called a *generation gap*. Some contributors to this situation are:

North American Ideals. Where every individual has a right to life, liberty, and the pursuit of happiness, the attempt to establish a distinct identity is going to be pretty vigorous. Not only does the individual have the right to be himself, but he has a heritage of go-getters—explorers, colonists, pioneers, inventors—young people, full of initiative, not doing what their parents told them, but out on their own, improving on what their parents did. These ideals result in continual social changes, making parents and adolescents unsure of their roles in regard to each other.

The Nuclear Family. Father, mother, and children make up the typical family. The two-generation family is the norm, even though in actual practice many families have additional members living with them, and many also are minus a parent. Children are expected to grow up, move out, and start their own two-generation families. A rupture in parent-child relationships is implicit in this expectation where parents and children intend to be quite independent of each other after the children reach adulthood.

In contrast, in some cultural settings in North America and in other cultures, the joint family or the stem family may be typical. Both types see generations as connected intimately, expecting no break between children and parents. As parents grow old, children take more and more responsibility for them instead of pushing off on their own. Children are not encouraged to develop distinct identities as individuals, but to feel a family identity. An adolescent does not have to work so hard to achieve a sense of identity because it is already partly built for him. Therefore, he stays *with* his family psychologically as well as physically. Even if he goes away for a while to be educated, as some Indian youths do, he still belongs deeply to his whole family and returns to them when he can. This is not to say that Indian adolescents live in complete harmony with their parents but only that they conflict less than do North Americans.

Americans usually believe that you have only one life to live. This however is not the belief of over half of the world's people. A belief in reincarnation usually exists in cultures that have joint family, stem family, or any kind of extended family. An individual's sense of identity is thus part of an identity that extends into the infinite past and future. His religion most likely involves ancestor worship, or at least a duty toward ancestors, with the assurance that his descendants will be obligated to him in the same way. Thus, a person is not alone to find himself. He *belongs* in time and space. He, therefore, feels no necessity to cut himself off from his parents or from the other people who are part of his identity.

A Fast-Changing Society. The rapid pace of science and technology tears an ever-widening gap between generations. From the time when technology produced the automobile, North America has seen continuing changes in behavior patterns and values, especially regarding sex. Society is becoming less work-oriented, more leisure-oriented. Although less socialistic than many countries, the United States and Canada legislate for social welfare, and rugged individualism is favored less than it used to be. Bureaucratic businesses and government have replaced many small, independent operations.

Children are insisting upon honesty, scorning hypocrisy as the sin of sins, while their parents may have made peace with materialism and the concrete fruits of their labors. Adolescents think that parents are hopelessly old-fashioned. Parents know that they are. Parents are often not sure what is right and what standards to insist upon. Here is one of the sources of the loss of moral authority suffered by parents, their uncertainty which comes from the differences between their youthful experience and their children's.

The Mass Media and the Shrinking World. Learning to read once opened a child's eyes to the existence of standards and authorities that differed widely from those of his parents. Now television assaults him in infancy. Children as well as parents are at the mercy of the advertising octopus that exploits childish fears and fantasies, and of the entertainment industry that reduces man to the lowest common denominator. Insofar as parents' values and standards differ from those promoted by the mass media, conflict with adolescents is generated. Easy communication and travel bring youngsters into contact with different worlds of discourse.

Parents' Marital Situation

The way in which parents relate to each other is full of meaning for their children. Not only are they affected as individual persons but as future husbands, wives, fathers, and mothers.

Attitudes toward love were studied in white, middle-class high school seniors [40]. The marriage relationship of the parents was found to be most strongly related to the attitudes held by the young people. When parents were living together, the children were more likely to have realistic attitudes toward love, but more romantic attitudes were held by adolescents whose parents were separated by either divorce or death.

Effects on children of certain kinds of family situations have been investigated. Of these, authority patterns and father absence are of special interest.

AUTHORITY PATTERNS

The traditional pattern of authority in the North American family, as in families in most of the world's cultures, was for the father to be considered the head of the household by all the members. All important decisions and all decisions basic to the countless choices that have to be made from day to day were made by the husband and father. In colloquial terms, the man of the household was the boss. Although it is certainly true that most North American men do not wield the power of men in traditional societies, men in general probably still have more power in the family than do women, because men make the major decisions more often than do women [65]. However, there are many types of power, making family power difficult to assign in absolute terms. As women gain more power in the economic world, their relative power at home is likely to increase, as well.

A study of adolescent perceptions of their parents' conjugal power [3] found that fathers with greater occupational prestige also had more power at home. Working mothers had more power than those who did not work outside of the home. (These findings are consistent with the findings of earlier power studies [64]). Older adolescents saw their parents as less egalitarian than did younger adolescents. Females were more likely to see their mothers as dominant, and males, to see their fathers as dominant. The adolescents also tended to see as the more powerful parent the one with whom they identified more. This study indicates that a person's position in the family influences the way she views power. It may also be, as the authors suggest, that conjugal power differs according to the age and sex of the children.

Black adolescents' perceptions of family power structure were studied by asking over 500 ninth-grade boys and girls how their parents made decisions about work, expenditures, and child rearing [39]. White-collar, blue-collar, and unskilled occupational levels were sampled. Syncratic (shared, democratic) decision making was the most frequent pattern reported. Power structure was found to be more often syncratic than father- or mother-dominated, at all occupational levels. Males reported more father participation than did females, and females reported more mother participation than did males. The black father was seen as more salient and more participating in family life than he has appeared to be in former studies. The study suggests that black men are becoming more important figures in family life.

PARENT ABSENCE

Most one-parent families are those in which the father is absent, and it is the children of these families, especially boys, who have been studied most. Most research has been focused on personality development. However, cognitive development, also, has been found to be depressed in both boys and girls in father-absent homes [8].

The mother's interpretation of the father, whether he is present or absent, is an influence on the personality development of children, especially of boys [8]. For healthy masculine development, it is important that the mother give positive descriptions of the father's masculinity, in terms of characteristics such as competence, strength, and physical prowess. The mother's feelings about masculinity, men, and the father are significant in her relationship with her son.

Fathers are likely to differentiate between boys and girls more than mothers do, thus playing the more salient part in gender typing. Therefore, the single-parent mother who wishes to be more active in gender typing with her children should probably make a conscious effort to do so, or she should see to it that her children interact with appropriate males who will take over this function. Brothers, grandfathers, and uncles may provide a masculine influence for children without a father. Providing such influence, however, need not guarantee that children behave in traditionally "masculine" or "feminine" ways. Just as fathers can encourage their children to experience and display a range of human feelings, so can men who take the father's place. When no male relatives or friends of the mother regularly interact with the father-absent child, a psychologically and interpersonally competent mother may still be able to counteract the effects of father absence in her children's personality development. However, the child's personality development can be facilitated only insofar as the present parent allows the child enough "freedom and responsibility to imitate effective parental behaviors" [8, p. 101].

The development of feminine girls is also highly dependent on the parents' interactions with each other and with their daughters. In his definition of masculine and feminine behavior to his daughter, and in his behavior as a husband with his wife, the father shows his daughter how to be a woman and how to interact with a man. The father's acceptance of the daughter as feminine facilitates her self-acceptance as feminine. Evidence suggests that father-absent girls are likely to show some maladjustment, since they are deprived of the father's important teaching and are likely to have mothers beset with problems that burden single family heads [9]. Hetherington studied adolescent daughters and their divorced, widowed, or married mothers [29]. She found that girls whose fathers had been absent because of divorce or death interacted less "appropriately" with male interviewers than did the daughters whose mothers were married and living with the girl's father. Daughters of widows did not maintain as much eye contact with the male interviewers, and sat rigidly and with closed body posture in relation to the interviewers. Daughters of divorcees sat closest to the interviewer, were friendly and smiling toward him, and maintained open body posture. These girls also reported earlier and more dating and earlier sexual intercourse than the daughters of widows and married women. Daughters of widows started dating at the latest time, and were sexually inhibited. The effects were greater for girls who had lost their fathers at an earlier age. Although the three groups of girls behaved differently in relation to men, all three groups were usually feminine. At the time of the interview, all three groups of mothers had equally positive attitudes toward men. The researcher notes, however, that the divorced mothers had more negative attitudes toward life and were more likely to be anxious and unhappy. Their attitudes toward their ex-husbands were hostile, and they had negative memories of marriage. The daughters of the divorced mothers, too, had a critical attitude toward their fathers.

Little is known about the development of children raised by solo fathers. However, children of full-time employed mothers have been studied in ninth through twelfth graders in Toronto [59]. Children with full-time employed mothers reported more disagreement with their parents than children whose mothers were not employed. However, both groups reported equal feelings of closeness to the mother, with 91 per cent of boys and 83 per cent of girls reporting that they felt very close to the mother. In a study of eighth-grade children, it was found that black inner-city males whose mothers worked full-time had lower self-esteem than those whose mothers did not work full-time. This effect was not found for girls, or for white suburban children [52]. These results suggest the importance of considering variables other than merely whether or not a mother works outside of the home. For example, why is she working, and at what kind of job?

PARENT-CHILD INTERACTION

When members of a group such as a family interact over a period of time, norms or standards for behavior develop. When parents and sons were followed over a ten-year period, both made continuous reference to standards of behavior [41]. For example, a son said of his father, "He's a normal person because there's a lot of people like him around. . . ." A mother said, "I've tried to give (my son) standards to live by." These standards of behavior are important in regulating the interaction of family members, as they prescribe appropriate behavior in particular contexts, and "also set limits on the demands that may legitimately be made." When assessing an action of their sons and deciding how to respond, parents consider the circumstances, the guiding norms, and the attributes of their sons. For example, the parents can respond to their child's interests only if the child *has* interests and reveals them to the parent. The child, in turn, regulates his behavior in accordance with how he anticipates his parents will react. The boy whose parents scoff at his interest in art may choose not to reveal to his parents that he goes to the museum whenever possible.

Communication

Any human relationship is enhanced by mutual understanding, something that is impossible without effective communication. Communication takes place in a social context, and each face-to-face interaction has both verbal and non-verbal components. Facial expression, tone of voice, posture, and silences all modify the literal verbal message, and may negate or support it. Studies of disturbed families have shown that verbal and nonverbal messages in these families often negate each other, leaving the listener confused as to what actually is meant [27].

LISTENING

In addition, really listening to the messages of the other person is essential for effective communication. Not listening may be manifested by speaking before the other is finished, or it may simply be not attending to what the other is saying. In a study comparing parents and normal 12-year-old sons with parents and sons of the same age who had been diagnosed as borderline psychotic, the mothers, fathers, and sons were asked to complete a multiple-choice questionnaire choosing one of three solutions to family problems. Once the questionnaires were completed, the examiner scored them and pulled out four problems for which each member in one family had chosen a different answer. The three family members were told to discuss their answers until they reached complete agreement or decided that they could not agree. Normal families were found to have more agreement resulting from discussion, and parents were more likely to form coalitions, rather than continuing to disagree. Persons in families with disturbed children tended to interrupt each other more and to have overlapping verbal interactions [67]. In other words, they did not listen adequately.

BUILDING ESTEEM

It has been fairly well established that severe family pathology is associated with extremely disrupted communication patterns. *Good* communication apparently facilitates self-esteem in normal families. Among ninth-grade students living with both parents, the adolescents were divided into three groups of self-esteem (SE): High SE, Low SE, and Medium SE. When High SE subjects were compared with Low, the following results emerged: High SEs and their parents all saw their communication as more facilitative than did Low SEs; the parents of adolescents with high SE reported more satisfying marriages and also saw their marital communication as better than did parents of Low SE adolescents [49].

This finding gives support to an idea proposed by Miller and his associates [51] that *esteem building* is essential for effective communication between married individuals. We extend their hypothesis to all intimate relationships, including parents and their adolescent children. Esteem building means taking into consideration what one's message will do for the other person and implies respect for the other and for oneself. Miller notes that subtle, destructive, mixed messages are often the result of communication by a person who is trying to be open but lacks esteem for herself and for the other.

EFFORT REQUIRED

Older studies [21, 66] indicated that adolescents have at least some trouble communicating with their parents about important matters. However, it seems likely that most people have trouble communicating with their intimates at least some of the time on some subjects, and that the hope of parent-adolescent child communication should not be abandoned. One study of 14- to 19-year-olds found that, in general, these adolescents preferred to discuss career and family problems with adults, and preferred to discuss such matters as sex and dating with their peers. However, some young people preferred to discuss most matters with adults; a second group preferred peers for most subjects; a third group showed selective preference for parents and peers [45].

IMPLICATIONS OF RESEARCH

To draw together the results of the research on parent-adolescent communication, we can conclude that good communication in the family is important for normal personality development. When parents communicate well with each other and with their children, children tend to have higher self-esteem. Adolescents vary in their ease of communication with their parents. Adolescents have little control over how well their parents communicate with each other, but parents can work to improve their marriage and their communication patterns.

Realizing that their children may feel they have not enough chances to talk, parents could plan their time so as to make regular and frequent opportunities. Adolescents, too, could point out to their parents that they need more time together in order to understand one another. If mothers realized how important it is to keep confidences in order to continue to receive them, then surely they would be more reluctant to gossip and to share private information with friends. Both parents might try to be more acceptant and less critical of their children as persons while still making clear their own values and standards of behavior.

CONFLICT

Some people think that parent-adolescent conflict is inevitable, whereas others think it avoidable. There are different interpretations of what conflict means and whether it is constructive or destructive. Social change is probably affecting changes in patterning of conflict.

Psychoanalytic Perspective. According to the psychoanalytic viewpoint, the adolescent *must* conflict with his parents in order to strive toward an identity as a distinct and independent being. At the same time, he still wants the love, comfort, and protection that his parents have provided. Thus, to the adolescent, parents are almost always wrong, and children have to pick fights with them. This point of view is often comforting to bewildered parents, since it helps to allay their guilt and feelings of inadequacy. If adolescents have to go through a difficult stage, then parents simply have to wait patiently, confidently, and lovingly until the young people grow out of it into civilized adulthood.

Gestalt Perspective. From a Gestalt perspective, conflict exists *within* a person when her dominant need cannot emerge and organize her behavior toward the meeting of that need [56]. The person who is in conflict within herself stops herself from contacting her needs and striving to meet them. The adolescent faces the emergence of needs that are not necessarily new, but do come on with greater intensity. When what the child needs or wants is not the same as what the parent wants, parent-child conflict in some degree exists. The adolescent in North America begins to break away from standards and values that were learned from her parents and often "swallowed whole." Ideally, the youngster would examine her values closely to see if they fit the way she wants to be, but frequently the adolescent substitutes peer values without really examining them, either.

Conflict within the individual or between individuals has creative potential, because new solutions can be worked out. This view of conflict is in harmony with the North American tradition of breaking away from the old ways that are no longer useful. Each generation is expected to find its own way, and perhaps to "make it" on its own. Disagreements between generations are regarded as not only normal but as essential to the continued vitality of the society.

Conflict as Avoidable. Another point of view is that conflict is neither essential nor inevitable. It has been found that amiable relations between parents and adolescents are the usual situation [2]. A study of high school seniors and parents indicated that large differences in values and goals did not divide the two generations. What conflict was reported was generally not severe [72]. Adolescents mature most easily when parents place reasonable limits on their behavior and when parents are affectionate, interested, and active with their children. College women who recalled their fathers as having been nurturant and involved with them in a positive way had higher self-perceptions than women who recalled that their fathers had rejected them [24]. When students in a small midwestern college were asked if they had been rebellious as adolescents, those who reported having been very or extremely rebellious differed from those who reported moderate or no rebellion. Those students whose parents' marriage was seen as unhappy were more likely to have rebelled. If parents were extremely permissive or extremely restrictive, the young people reported more rebelliousness. And finally, equalitarian parental relationships, as seen by the youth, were associated with *low* levels of rebelliousness [4].

Baumrind found that the parents of exceptionally mature preschool children used firm control, explained their decisions rationally, and encouraged the children to express themselves independently. She states that because the adolescent cannot be forced to comply with her parents' wishes in the way that a young child can be, rational explanation on the parent's part and freedom for the child to express her views is essential if a standoff is to be avoided. The parent does not give the child free rein to do what she pleases, but makes a contract with the child, who is now intellectually capable of holding to such an agreement [6]. Such an agreement is reached through discussion of the problem at hand, and is not dictated by the parent. In this way, the parent gradually moves to a position of less control over the child's life, and the child learns how to be responsible for herself. Parents and child move toward a relationship between equal adults.

Sex Differences in Conflict. Douvan and Adelson's [20] classic study indicated that in the late 1950s adolescent boys had more conflict than did adolescent girls. More recently, parents of 12- to 17-year-olds were asked how much trouble their children had been to bring up [55]. Sixty per cent of parents said that they had had no trouble bringing up their children. However, boys were reported to be more trouble to rear than were girls.

With gender roles in such a state of flux, we cannot say for certain whether parents today would say that boys are more difficult to rear. If girls are no longer expected to be quiet and submissive, but to assert themselves in the same way as their brothers, one could expect that parents and teachers would report even smaller gender differences in the amount of conflict experienced in child rearing.

Areas of Adolescent Conflict. Among tenth-grade students in a rural Pennsylvania high school, it was found that parent-adolescent conflict centered around activities that directly concerned the young people, such as "loafing uptown, staying out late, and failure in school" [13]. These adolescents perceived their parents to be more in agreement with them regarding general items such as divorce, card playing, and smoking. Table 3-1 shows how parent-adolescent disagreement concerning these and other practices has changed since 1947. Conflict regarding some items, such as failure in school and the way young people spend their money, has apparently increased, whereas conflict over staying out late has decreased slightly.

In a study of 14- and 15-year-olds in Sydney, Australia, girls expressed more problems than boys did, and were twice as likely as boys to report family problems. Boys were more concerned with educational problems [15]. An older United States study [1] had similar findings: personal problems (usually relationships with peers) were equally troublesome with parent problems, and for boys, financial concerns also ranked equally with parental and personal concerns. Family problems made up only 10 per cent of the most pressing difficulties reported by boys and 22 per cent of those of girls. Family problems tended to decrease with age, while school problems did not decrease and even increased somewhat for boys. Boys' financial problems also increased. These studies indicate that family conflict is not the most troublesome area for many adolescents. In a comparison of runaway and nonrunaway adolescents [10], it was found that runaways reported more intense conflict, and conflict over more issues, than did nonrunaways. An important issue for the runaways was that parents failed to express love.

Table 3-1. Per Cent of Young People who Disagree with Their Parents' Ideals Concerning Selected Social Practices, 1947, 1960, and 1970.

	Year		
	1947 %	1960 %	1970 %
Youth-Centered Activities			
Failure in school	57.3	58.2	63.1
Loafing uptown	57.0	52.7	56.1
Staying out late	53.3	47.4	51.8
Ways that young people spend their money	42.0	39.9	48.7
Use of makeup	32.3	31.0	35.7
General Activities			
Divorce	55.6	47.2	49.0
Smoking	44.8	45.1	51.1
Social drinking of alcoholic beverages	54.2	51.2	43.9
Irregular church attendance	32.2	31.6	38.9
Card playing	28.6	27.2	22.9

SOURCE: Adapted from I. P. Chand, D. M. Crider, and F. K. Willits. Parent-youth disagreement as perceived by youth: A longitudinal study. *Youth & Society*, 1975, **6**, 365–375.

Parents' Feelings about Adolescents

The parents' feelings and personal development also have some bearing on the production of conflict. Even though children are a burden and annoyance, they also give joy and satisfaction. Most adults who reach the stage of developing a sense of generativity are launched into it and propelled along in it by their children. It is hard to switch from the kind of nurturing role required by offspring into other forms of generativity such as being on the board of education or collecting money for crippled children. Although a few parents have nurtured and created in situations other than their child-raising roles, many have not. Most parents, if not all, feel ambivalent about seeing their children become adults. This is what they have been working toward. For many years they tried to prepare their children for independence. Success, however, means the end of the job of parenthood. Viewing the almost-finished product, at 18 or so, it occurs to many a parent that the job is not perfect. The impact of this realization is twofold. First it seems as though a little more control and direction might improve the son or daughter to the point where future success would be assured. The parent then continues to try to make decisions that the youngster knows he himself must make in order to establish his identity firmly.

Second, the imperfection of the child may reactivate the parent's own adolescent feelings, the fears and pains he knew, his unsolved problems that were almost forgotten until now. Mr. D'Amico relives his sorrow over missing college when Freddie gets a low score on college entrance examinations. Contemplating Brenda's generous proportions, Mrs. Kaufman plumbs the despair she felt over her own bulk when she was 16. The shame and guilt that accompanied youthful sex behavior generate the parental explosion that greets Helen's appearance in a new bathing suit which leaves practically nothing to the imagination. In all these situations, parents seem to their children to be overreacting. To themselves, they are simply trying to protect their children from dangers they know to be much more serious than the children realize.

The real essence of the sense of generativity is wanting the child (or creature or project) to grow in the way that is best for her. Not only does the parent have to let her go on her own at the right point, but the parent also has the problem of knowing what way *is* best, and where to compromise with reality while aiming toward perfection. Sometimes only the threat of disaster will move a parent from a rigid insistence upon making decisions for the adolescent whose growth depends upon making his own. Larry's parents permitted him to drop out of college for a year only when a psychiatrist told them that he was in danger of an emotional breakdown. Janet's parents stopped criticizing her boyfriend when they realized that, if she married him, the breach they were creating would probably be permanent.

It is also possible for parents to be too laissez-faire with adolescents. A hands-off policy can give too little guidance and support to the youngster who needs and wants to stand on her own and yet at the same time needs and wants the security of being held to standards of behavior in which her parents truly believe. Parents who have read about adolescents' need for independence may grant more freedom than their children can profitably use. Some parents are so uncertain about their own beliefs and standards that they cannot be firm in setting limits for adolescents. And some parents don't care enough. They may give up the struggle from fatigue, pressures from other areas of life, or a feeling of hopelessness, as did one divorced mother who moved away, leaving two teenage girls at home with plenty of money, one to go to high school, the other to college. Perhaps the most sophisticated parents of all, appreciating the need for a delicate balance between freedom and control, will agonize over achieving that balance.

Quite aside from the annoyance of adolescent ambivalence, negative parental feelings are engendered from the financial burden that adolescents place upon parents. Probably this feeling is confined to middle-class parents. Although middle-class children often earn money, they are still expensive to keep. Costing more than adults to feed and clothe, adolescents represent a large cash outlay even before they go to college, that fabulously costly place where expenses grow every year. Upper-middle-class parents find that scholarship aid is unavailable or present in such minute quantities as to make little difference in the great drain that education represents. As adolescent children go about their business of athletics, cheerleading, dating, being active in fraternities, telephoning, joyriding, going to beach parties, and shopping, hardworking parents sometimes resent these noncontributing consumers.

In lower socioeconomic levels, the picture is different. Children are expected to earn money as soon as they can and perhaps contribute to family support. Among black families of the lowest socioeconomic stratum, the mother is often the central, powerful figure. She cares for her own children and takes responsibility for her grandchildren who are born to her own adolescent girls [60]. Rainwater sketches a typical family, in which men and boys are constantly demeaned and each member exposes the emptiness of the other members' claims to competence. Human nature is conceived of as bad, destructive, and immoral. The mother, therefore, expects her adolescent to be a bad person unless she is very, very lucky.

SIMILARITY IN VALUES

Two generations holding the same values indicates harmony and positive interaction between them. Although a study of conflicts may give the impression that adolescents usually reject their parents' values, there is much evidence to show that parents and teenagers are more alike than unlike in their values. Researchers asked high school seniors and their parents, "What would you say is the main purpose or task in a person's life?" A considerable number of similarities were found in the responses of both generations. The results are summarized in Table 3-2. For men and boys, answers such as "To prepare oneself educationally, to obtain gainful employment" (a father's answer) or "I guess get educated, get a job" (a son's answer) were frequent answers. Young people were more likely to mention happiness and enjoyment. When asked what they wanted out of life, three quarters of the men and half of the girls said that they most wanted love and understanding. When asked their immediate goal, 88 per cent of the boys and 74 per cent of the girls indicated an instrumental-achievement goal such as getting a job, going to college, or both. Middle-aged men mentioned an instrumental-material concern, and middle-aged women were more likely to list an interpersonal-expressive goal

Table 3-2. "Main Purpose in Life"; High School Seniors and Parents of High School Seniors, by Sex.

	Girls (N = 27)	Women (N = 27)	Boys (N = 25)	Men (N = 27)
Main purpose items				
Happiness	40.7%	22.2%	32.0%	11.1%
Self-realization	37.0	7.4	24.0	11.1
Humanitarian-moral	29.6	25.9	16.0	18.5
Instrumental–				
achievement	29.6	14.8	44.0	40.7
Familial-expressive	25.9	44.4	20.0	33.3
Coping-adjustment	14.8	37.0	12.0	51.9
Religious	3.7	11.1	—	11.1

SOURCE: M. Thurnher, D. Spence, and M. F. Lowenthal. Value confluence in intergenerational relations. *Journal of Marriage and the Family*, 1974, **36**, 308–319.

[72]. A psychiatric study of high school boys showed them sharing their parents' outlooks on life and holding the same middle-class values [54]. College students' values have been found quite similar to their parents' values, no matter whether the students were activists or not [73]. Values included dedication to causes, conventional moralism, intellectualism, and humanitarianism. Resemblances between parents and children were greater for values than for other domains of personality, such as need for recognition or being self-critical.

FEELINGS OF LOVE AND CLOSENESS

Attachment is of vital importance throughout life, although objects of attachment change [11, pp. 207–208]. Adults, as well as infants, seek proximity and contact with people they love at times when they feel threatened or weakened. Adolescents normally continue to be attached to their parents, but not so strongly as they were as children. Girls are often more strongly attached than boys. (This characteristic is seen in many animals, not only among primates but in the herd animals. Female sheep and goats are likely to stay close to their mothers throughout life.)

Several studies indicate that many, or most, adolescents feel close to their parents, and especially to their mother. Among lower-middle-class and middle-class seniors from a large western city and their parents, two fifths of the boys and three fifths of the girls said they were closest to their mothers. Boys saw their fathers as hard workers, but as not hard to get along with. Girls also saw their fathers as hard workers, but as more distant than the boys did. Mothers were described by the girls as "understanding, easy to know, considerate, warm, and there when we need her." Boys saw their mothers as overanxious, worrying, or too emotional [72].

Similar information was obtained in California from high school seniors, newlyweds, and preretired men and women [47]. Persons at all stages of life and both sexes reported that their mother was the parent to whom they felt closer. High school girls and newlyweds were less positive about their mothers; least positive were newlywed women, high school males, and preretired females. Mothers

STANLEY SUMMER

were viewed somewhat more ambivalently than were fathers, as some respondents said that they felt close to them but also saw them negatively. A four-year psychiatric study of suburban high school boys showed that the typical boy liked and admired his parents [54]. At 14, he felt closer to his mother but by 18 was more intimate with his father. The same view of mothers held in Denmark when Danish and United States samples were questioned [37]. Adolescents questioned felt moderately to extremely close to their mothers. Approximately two thirds wanted to be like their mothers in many or most ways. Thirty-five per cent of the adolescents questioned enjoyed doing "many" things with their mothers. (See Table 3-3 for a more complete breakdown.)

Parents Versus Other Influences

The many pulls upon adolescents include those exerted by their parents. Some conflicts are frankly between parents and children. Other problems are created by the opposition of parental and other influences, most important the influences of peers. Teachers and other adults in the community may also put adolescents into the position of having to choose between them and their parents. Other adults can be very influential on the adolescent while reinforcing values held by the parents or opening new vistas that the parents then endorse.

The adolescent realizes that the various meaningful persons in her life vary in

Table 3-3 Adolescents' Perceptions of Patterns of Interaction with Mother and Father, United States and Denmark.

Family Pattern	United States		Denmark	
	Mother	Father	Mother	Father
Affective Relations				
Closeness to Parent				
Extremely close	33%	21%	22%	19%
Quite close	30	29	35	36
Moderately close	26	27	30	31
Not close	11	23	13	14
(Total number)	(967)	(935)	(944)	(936)
Per Cent of Adolescents Who				
Enjoy Doing "Many" things				
with Parent	35	34	35	43
(Total number)	(971)	(937)	(941)	(935)
Modeling:				
Wanting to Be Like Parent in				
Most ways	42	36	30	36
Many ways	21	21	40	38
Few ways	37	43	30	26
(Total number)	(968)	(937)	(941)	(935)

SOURCE: D. Kandel and G. R. Lesser. Parent-adolescent relationships and adolescent independence in the United States and Denmark. *Journal of Marriage and the Family*, 1969, **31,** 348–358.

the expectations that they hold for her [26]. She can see different sets of norms held by her parents, teachers, and peers. There is some evidence that this knowledge helps her to make her own decisions. That is, she can use the demands of her parents when she wishes to make some resistance to demands of peers or teachers, and vice versa.

PARENTS AND OTHER ADULTS

After parents, teachers have the greatest opportunities for influencing the lives of children. High school students have indicated that they consider it most important for teachers to be interested, understanding, and helpful to them [77]. Almost everyone knows at least one case where a teacher had a significant lifelong influence on an adolescent. Ellen's third-grade teacher channeled her sensitivity to nature into careful observation. Her tenth-grade biology teacher refined and deepened her knowledge and enjoyment with the result that she has become a botanist. Almost everyone knows at least one case of a child modeling himself after a teacher in direct contrast to the models available at home. Stan, a big, socially awkward boy, identified strongly with the high school football coach and rejected his librarian father. Stan is majoring in physical education. For many youngsters, a teacher or youth leader provides a welcome and healthy chance to explore a new identity and then to adopt it if it fits. With the variety of personalities, relationships, and situations possible in North American life, parents cannot possibly open up to an adolescent sufficient choices of identity for him to be sure of finding what he needs. Part of the letting-go process that many parents find difficult is the acceptance of these other adult influences as essential relationships for their children.

A successful program is the result of planned efforts to provide adult models for about 2,500 black ghetto boys [46]. In the course of a year, each boy is given opportunities to meet, watch, and talk with 27 or more successful black men in blue-collar and white-collar occupations. IN stands for *Interested Negroes,* of whom more than 1,000 are available to junior high school boys. IN finds out what kinds of work the boy would like to observe and sends him to a man doing that type of work. Often the successful man has come from a community similar to the one in which the boy lives. Thus, the boy has a chance to identify with a man who looks like a hero whom he might dare to emulate.

PARENTS AND PEERS

Peers are of tremendous importance in the lives of adolescents, but what of their influence as compared with that of parents? In some ways, adolescents become closer to their peers as they grow up; in other ways they remain fairly close to their parents. They want to spend more and more time with their friends and less at home. They often feel that friends understand them better and that they are more like their friends than they are like their parents. However, parents are still recognized as sources of guidance and authority.

In order to find out how adolescents might react when parents want them to do one thing and their friends another, hypothetical situations were presented to 1,542 seventh, ninth, and twelfth graders in Oregon [44]. One of the four situations involved going to a party. First, the student was told to imagine that she had been invited to a party that her friends wanted her to attend, but her parents did not. Would she go, or not? Then, she was asked to imagine that she had been invited to a party that her parents wanted her to go to. Her friends, however, had not been invited and were urging her not to go. Would she go? A second situation involved joining a club, against her parents' wishes. In a third situation, she was to imagine that she knew who had broken a door at school. Her friends thought she should tell the principal, and her parents did not. Would she tell? And then, in situation 3-a, her parents thought she should tell and her friends did not. In the final situation, she was to make a choice regarding going into the college curriculum or general curriculum, under two kinds of cross-pressure from parents and peers.

The majority of students chose in terms of the situation, but some were consistent in choosing what parents would want, while others consistently complied with their friends' wishes. Respondents who said they would join the club against their parents' wishes tended to opt for what their friends wanted in other situations. Those respondents who said they would not join against their parents' wishes were more responsive to their parents in other situations. Some students remained compliant to the wishes of one reference group (either parents or peers) when the situation was reversed, but *most* students remained situation-compliant. In other words, most said that they would not be swayed by pressure from either side. The respondents were also asked who best understood their problems, their best friends, parents, or both. Thirty-five and a half per cent of students answered that their parents best understood; 39.3 per cent said that both did, and 25.2 per cent said that their best friends understood them best. These findings are consistent with the findings of studies that we reported earlier concerning feelings of love and closeness.

The Peer Group

Sociologists debate the question of how distinctly adolescence and youth are defined and separated from the rest of North American culture and whether it is accurate to call it a *subculture*. The sharpness with which adolescence is cut off from childhood and adulthood doubtless varies from one situation to another.

For most adolescents, peers (age-mates) play an even more important part in life than they did during childhood. A few adolescents remain outside the social swim from preference, pursuing studies, hobbies, or athletics, perhaps with one or two friends. Some youngsters, rejected by the peer group, exist in isolation or with other isolates in smaller groups of two or three. Among peers, there are two main kinds of groups: *crowds* and *cliques*. Friends, of course, are individuals.

ROBERT J. IZZO

THE CROWD

Both boys and girls belong to "the crowd," but there are occasions when groups of one sex get together. The like-sex crowd is not always identical with the group of boys or girls that participates in the boy–girl crowd. Especially at the younger ages, late maturers and certain nonconforming, independent individuals are unacceptable or uninterested in boy–girl affairs, but they may be cherished members of a like-sex group. Within the crowd are cliques, small groups of close friends, and pairs of best friends.

The crowd is usually based on the school, although neighborhood has some influence. School is the place where most social interaction takes place, in the classroom and library, at basketball and football games, clubs, interest groups, parties, in the corridor and yard (or campus, as it is sometimes called).

One of the basic functions of the crowd is to provide a group identity that separates adolescent from parent, a "we" feeling apart from the family. The adolescent thus strengthens his own sense of identity by being a member of a group that defines his difference from his parents. Joe gets his hair cut (or not cut) like the other boys do, but different from Dad's. The girls wear pretty much the same shade of lipstick and nail polish, as well as standardized coiffures, but if adults adopt those fashions, the fashions are soon dead and are replaced.

The crowd is also for fun and comfortable feelings, for doing things together like bowling and strolling, for hanging around the soda fountain, for just talking and talking and talking. And giggling and shouting. The output in decibels is very large in comparison with the intellectual content of conversation, but with good reason. Everybody is trying out a variety of roles, uncertain and tentative as to what kind of person he can be. There is security and warmth in the company of people who face the same problems, feel the same way, behave the same way, and wear the same symbols of belonging. It feels good to giggle and shout, to be silly and to stand together against those who do not understand.

THE CLIQUE

Smaller and more intimate than the crowd, although often called "the crowd" by its members, a clique is a highly selected group of friends. Usually alike in social background, interests, and experience, the clique members are emotionally attached to each other. Members' feeling for one another is the basic factor holding them together. Some cliques become formalized into clubs, even fraternities and sororities, but most adolescent cliques remain informal and small. Just as the adolescent generation differentiates itself from adults by many symbols, and one crowd from another, so a clique is likely to have ways of proclaiming its difference from others and solidarity within itself. "Everybody" wears blue on Tuesdays. A fraternity pin. The turn of a phrase. A food fad.

Compared with boys, girls show a wider range of emotional needs in peer relationships [33]. Cliques are more important to girls. Belonging to a clique or peer group is more related to status values for girls than it is for boys [14, 33]. Since high status is relative, excluding others from a high-status clique can make the members feel important.

STANLEY SUMMER

Year long observations of ninth graders revealed most boys and girls as belonging to cliques of three to eight members, with an average size of five [16]. As in earlier studies [20], the girls had closer friendships than did the boys. Girls were much more likely than boys to interact socially only with other members of their cliques. Nine girls and three boys were not accepted into cliques and did not form new cliques at the beginning of the year. Eight of the girls were new students. Unlike the new girls who tended to remain loners, the new male students formed a new clique. Only 20 per cent of the students studied were black. Three black females formed a clique; four more remained loners. No social interaction was observed between the black females and white females or males. By contrast, black males dated both black and white females.

Erikson [22, pp. 92–93] tells how clique members can be petty, cruel, and intolerant in order to defend themselves against a sense of *identity diffusion*. By excluding others who are "different" in skin color, religion, class, abilities, or even such trivialities as dress and appearance, the youngster gains some sense of identity from the group to which he belongs. Erikson stresses the importance of understanding this mechanism without condoning the behavior. Adolescents have to be helped to grow beyond the point where they feel the necessity for defending themselves by these cruel methods. (These are the methods of totalitarian systems.) Erikson implies that it can be done by adults living so as to demonstrate "a democratic identity that can be strong and yet tolerant, judicious and still determined."

FRIENDS

The term *best friend* usually indicates a member of the same sex. The best-friend relationship is an important one for the sense of identity, as anyone who shares a telephone with an adolescent will testify. The long conversations are between like-sex friends, especially best friends, and longer for girls than for boys. A best friend is the best audience on whom to project all the roles and identities that you want to test as possibilities, since this audience is just as concerned with testing and trying. A pair may try a role together. "We'd both look better minus ten pounds. Let's go on the same diet! We just won't let each other eat more than 1,100 calories a day." They may play at building a common identity, each gaining security from feeling stronger as a pair than as an individual. "Edna is part of me and I'm part of her. We think the same things. Each of us knows what the other one is thinking. We wear the same kind of clothes and we trade clothes." Communication is easy with someone who faces the same succession of disequilibria—fluctuations in physical balance, emotional upsets, new mental powers, problems with parents, and all the rest. Sometimes the communication is only partial, in that each is a sounding board for the other, not unlike the egocentric conversations of preschool children.

In an upper-middle class community in a midwestern city, high school respondents were asked about their friendships [68]. These adolescents discriminated between "good," "best," and "casual" friends. One girl distinguished among types of friends in this way:

- Q. What are some of the things you expect of a friend?
- A. When you leave (a group), when you walk out, they don't all of a sudden start stabbing knives in your back. It all depends upon the degree of friendship you want (in response to the question).
- Q. What are the various degrees of friendship?
- A. With some girls you just have a casual friendship, and she's got her friends and I've got mine, but we'll sit down and talk. Then like the girls in my club, we are pretty good friends. We know who we are going out with. With the casual friend you don't sit and talk about your boyfriend to them. I have one best friend.
- Q. Are there certain things you share with a best friend that you don't share with a fellow club member (that is, a "pretty good friend")?
- A. You talk about your boyfriends if you had an argument, but you wouldn't tell them personal things (that is, to a "pretty good friend"). I could tell my best friend anything, and she wouldn't think badly of you. You don't have to worry that, will she tell anyone else? While the members of my club, I expect them not to stab knives in my back when I leave, *but my best friend, if someone else does, I expect her to stand up for me. My club members, I wouldn't expect them to stand up for me.*

Friendships tend to become more stable with increasing age, from 11 to 18. Choice stability probably reflects increasing personality maturity. In turn, stability in choice of friends makes possible more opportunities for the development of the sense of intimacy, since intimacy grows within permanent relationships. Erikson writes of the sense of intimacy as "the condition of a true twoness in that one must

first become oneself" [22, p. 95]. Just as all the senses have early beginnings before their periods of critical growth, so we would expect the sense of intimacy to show some expression in childhood and adolescence. In its fullest meaning, intimacy between two people exists on all planes of contact, including sexual, but here, in its beginning stage, it is largely a meeting of minds. Bob tells Tom what he thinks and feels, trying to express it in ways that Tom will understand. Tom listens carefully to Bob and asks pertinent questions, trying to put himself in Bob's place. Each tries to understand and to make himself understandable. Each cares what the other thinks and feels. The stronger a person's sense of identity, the more he can care about the other person's thoughts and feelings. Released from the constant necessity of searching for his identity, he is free to enter into an intimate relationship. Since identity develops slowly throughout the period of adolescence, it is reasonable that it should gradually make way for intimacy.

The years 1946 and 1947 were the dates of studies showing that the best-friend relationship became more stable through the teen years. If the studies were to be repeated today, we wonder (1) would best friend still continue through the teens to mean a member of the same sex? and (2) would friendships with the same sex show increasing stability? Adolescents have less time and energy for like-sex best friends because they are turning increasingly to the opposite sex for companionship. Comparing adolescents of the 1940s and 1960s there was an increase in the choice of cross-sex companions for nine activities, such as studying and going to the movies [43]. Earlier dating and earlier going steady have shortened the period when adolescents can form deep friendships within their own sex. Very early, they come to compete with one another for dating partners, thus lessening the trust they can put in each other. At the age when dating begins, the junior high school age, boys are, on the average, two years behind girls in physiological maturity. Boys and girls of the same age are less suited to be together at this time than at any other time of life. Thus neither can grow at his own pace, in the way that a boy could in male society and a girl in female. The recent increase in identity

129

diffusion, the failure to develop a healthy sense of identity, is attributable to a complex of factors. This could be one of them, the deprivation of a period dominated by strong, deep friendships with members of the same sex.

Sex Differences in Friendship. Douvan and Adelson's [20] nationwide survey of 14- to 16-year-olds revealed important differences in the ways in which boys and girls needed friends and related to them. In order to solve his crucial problem of asserting his independence and resisting adult control, the boy needs a gang or at least a group of friends who band together to present a solid front. The girl's problem is more to understand her own sexual nature and to control and gratify her impulses in the context of interpersonal relationships; for this she needs a few close friends. Girls want friends to be loyal, trustworthy, and reliable sources of emotional support; boys want friends to be amiable, cooperative, and able to control aggressive impulses. Like preadolescent girls, boys between 14 and 16 are not concerned with warmth, sensitivity, and close relationships. The support that boys want from friends is against concrete trouble, especially conflicts with authority, whereas girls want help with their own emotional crises. Since the study did not go beyond age 16 with boys, it is possible that older boys change in the direction of developing warmer and closer relationships with friends.

Popularity. A popular person is one who is chosen or liked by many peers. A youngster may achieve popularity at some expense to his integrity since he may have to make many concessions in order to please a variety of people. He does not necessarily have a deeply satisfying "best friend" with whom he develops intimacy and strengthens his identity. Popularity is a strong value, however.

Although done in the late 1950s, Coleman's study [14] probably still has relevance for adolescents today. From the feminine point of view being a leader in activities and being in a leading crowd and cheerleading were consistently important. A girl's grades and family background influenced her popularity more in relation to girls than to boys. Nice clothes, on the other hand, were more important to her popularity with boys than with girls. Since popularity with boys was important in the status system of girls, the importance of personal attractiveness was increased. Boys saw being an athlete, being in a leading crowd, and being an activities leader as important criteria. Scholarship, though relatively unimportant, appeared to boys as even less important in their popularity with girls, whereas having a nice car was more important.

The basis for sociometric choices was studied by factor analysis of the responses of 10- to 14-year-old boys in a camp [42]. Results showed the two main factors underlying popularity to be perceived athletic ability and perceived conformity to adult standards. The second factor is difficult to square with other investigators' findings as to the importance of friends for support against adults. Perhaps it meant that for these very young adolescent boys, conformity on the part of friends would not get them into trouble with adults.

To the extent that success is measured by popularity and membership in the leading crowd, there is widespread threat to the sense of adequacy of many youngsters. There are not enough places at the top. Nor is there free access to the top for anyone who is willing to work hard for it. The system does have its democratic aspects, however. Social position of families counts for considerably less than athletic achievement. Motor skill is distributed much more evenly throughout the socioeconomic hierarchy than is scholarship. If scholarship and class position were more important than athletics, then the youngsters from more privileged families would have a greater advantage than they do.

THE OPPOSITE SEX: PATTERNS OF ASSOCIATION

Communication between the sexes was explored through a projective picture test used with boys and girls between 10 and 17 [12]. The pictures showed a boy and girl standing side by side, sitting side by side, the girl running after the boy, and the boy running after the girl. The subject was asked, "What is happening now? Why? What will happen next? How will the girl feel then? How will the boy feel then?" Most of the respondents saw the pair as having a romantic potential, although the younger subjects emphasized this aspect less than the older ones did. About a quarter of the subjects saw the boy and girl as friends, whereas only a few (none to 3 per cent) saw them as hostile and exploitative. As the subjects increased in age, they saw communication between the boy and girl as having less to do with matters external to the pair and more with building, maintaining, or repairing romantic relationships.

Dating. Dating, a custom developed by middle-class North American youth, is more of a social relationship than a courtship one. An informant in the study quoted earlier [68] in the section on "Friends" described dating as a game:

> It's one of the most fun games around, too. Because you never know what's going to happen. . . . It's up to you. There are no rules really. There might be a couple of rules that you take for granted . . . (like) not to do anything really nasty. Like go out with his best friend—break a date with him and go out with his best friend or something like that. Nothing really drastic, but aside from that there aren't too many rules, and you've just always got to make sure that you're on top, that you're winning because otherwise if you're not winning you're losing and there's no tie. So you always make sure you're winning.

Informants viewed going steady suspiciously, because in a going-steady relationship, one person would have control and the other would "lose." The boys especially were extremely afraid of being controlled by their girlfriends: such control would result in loss of status among the male peer group. Girls gained popularity by "making out" with a large number of boys but by restraining their dates from sexual intercourse. Some girls who did not date were as attractive physically as those who did date (physical attractiveness was an important attribute for female popularity), but did not want to get caught up in the exploitative system. Instead, these girls would have crushes on entertainers and movie stars.

As early as the late 1950s, most girls had begun dating at the age of 14 and boys at 15 [20]. Some parents still refuse to allow their children to date until a particular age, such as 16, but other parents encourage their fifth graders to take a date to a party or dance. Among black and white adolescents in a southern community before and after integration of the schools (1964 and 1974, respectively), it was found that 6 per cent of whites and 2 per cent of blacks had begun to date by age 11 in 1964. In 1974, the figures were 4 per cent for whites and 8 per cent for blacks. By age 14 in 1964, 77 per cent of the whites and 30 per cent of the blacks had begun to date. In 1974, the percentage of whites who had begun to date by age 14 decreased to 64 per cent, and the percentage of blacks who had begun to date by age 14 had increased to 57 per cent. Almost all subjects had begun dating by the time they were 17 [19].

In the 1970s, changes for which we have only anecdotal evidence began to happen in dating patterns in some communities. Influenced by women's liberation, some females, particularly at the college level but in some instances at the high school level as well, began to ask males for dates and no longer to be as concerned about accepting a date a day or two before it was to occur. In many high schools, the old patterns of female coyness and manipulation in order to get a boy's attention still continue, with little change from previous generations. The change toward female assertiveness represents a broadening of the spectrum of behavior that takes place, rather than an abrupt change.

Personality Development and Dating. Just what is the effect of early dating on personality development? Although much attention has been given to this question in the media, by members of the clergy and by parents, the exact effects are not known. The Roman Catholic Church disapproves of early dating. Another point of view is that dating is educational, giving adolescents experience in human relationships, promoting social skills, and enhancing their ability to choose a mate wisely.

Erikson's theory does not preclude the possibility of developing the sense of identity through association with the opposite sex. In fact, he describes such a boy–girl relationship: ". . . such attachment is often devoted to an attempt at arriving at a definition of one's identity by talking things over endlessly, by confessing what one feels like and what the other seems like, and by discussing plans, wishes and expectations" [22, p. 95]. The danger implied in a boy–girl relationship of this sort is not that it is inadequate for promoting identity, but that it may come to involve a sexual relationship before the pair are ready for intimacy. That is, before the sense of identity is sufficiently established.

ROMANTIC LOVE

One of the effects of love is an emphasis on the loved one's favorable qualities and a playing down of his faults. Romantic love makes this emphasis to an extreme degree. Romantic love is embedded in a complex of beliefs and ideals in Western culture: for every individual there is an ideal mate; love hits suddenly, even at first sight; when ideal mates marry, they live happily ever after; nothing matters but love; fidelity is a natural part of love; moonlight, roses, music, and perfume symbolize and promote love. When a person is in love in our culture, she is expected to be swept away by tumultuous emotion. Movies, magazines, television, and advertising all teach how one is supposed to feel. Walster observes that people are "encouraged to interpret certain mixed feelings as love, because our culture insists that certain reactions are acceptable only if one is madly in love" [76]. For example, sexual intercourse is more acceptable for a woman outside of marriage if she is in love with her partner.

Adolescents are fertile ground for the seeds of romance, although it is likely that some recent cultural developments are causing a decrease in romantic love. In spite of its potential danger, that of leading to a marriage without a realistic basis, romantic love offers opportunities for personality growth, along with a deeply beautiful experience that is worthwhile in itself. Tom sees Alice, the girl of his dreams, as a perfect woman and a perfect person, embodying the qualities that he, in his imperfection, would like to achieve. And Alice loves him! To be loved by such a marvelous creature proves that he is more worthy than he had thought possible. What's more, since they are a pair (unique and perhaps pre-destined), he derives some good qualities from her. The qualities that Tom sees in Alice and then makes his own are his own ideals. His identity becomes firmer as he projects his ideals and then incorporates them, with Alice playing an essential reciprocal role. With Alice, of course, the same process can take place, resulting in a stronger sense of identity for her too.

Tom's and Alice's relationship may develop into one where the sense of intimacy is promoted. Tom may share thoughts and feelings with Alice as he does with Bob, in a search for real understanding of the other person. If Tom and Alice communicate realistically, they will discard some of their romantic patterns, but *after* romantic love has served its identity-building function. If their love affair does grow into a permanent one, they may retain some romantic patterns that can continue to serve each one's sense of identity. After all, none of the crises of personality growth is ever completely solved, and identity, like the other senses, continues to need strengthening throughout life.

SEX BEHAVIOR

Until quite recently, many family life researchers maintained that there was no difference between the sex behavior of present-day adolescents and that of the previous generation of adolescents. Since 1970 there has been increasing evidence that more adolescent females are beginning to have sexual intercourse at a younger age than was true from the 1930s until the late 1960s [7, 32, 38, 70, 75]. Sorensen [70] found that 45 per cent of his female respondents age 13 to 19 and 59 per cent of his male respondents of this age group were nonvirgins. His sample probably excluded some conservative respondents because written parental consent was required for participation in the study. A more accurate estimate of the percentage of nonvirgins in the early 1970s is provided by a national (U.S.) probability sample of females age 15 to 19, of which 30.1 per cent had experienced premarital sexual intercourse [79]. This figure includes women who were married at the time of the study. For those who were unmarried, 27 per cent were nonvirgins. These figures are similar to what Hornick [32] found in a 1974 study in Ontario. Of 16-to-19-year-olds, 28.8 per cent of females and 27.1 per cent of males had experienced premarital intercourse. In a United States college sample also studied in 1974, females were as likely to be nonvirgins as males [5]. Females were found to begin having intercourse at approximately the same age as males, or even younger [48]. What we report here, however, is not the same as saying that "everybody's doing it." Substantial minorities, and among some groups, majorities, of adolescents, both male and female, still do *not* engage in premarital intercourse during their teens and early twenties.

Influence of the Peer Group. The adolescent's peer group, or the individual's perceptions of what her friends are doing may have an influence on an adolescent's sexual behavior. However, most of the sexually inexperienced teenagers in a national survey reported that they themselves had chosen to remain virgins. College students who perceived their friends as being sexually permissive and having "lots of sex" were found to be more likely to be sexually permissive themselves and to engage in intercourse [71]. Those who believed their friends to be inexperienced were also inexperienced themselves. For this result, however, an alternative explanation should be considered. It may be that sexually active individuals perceive their friends to be sexually active, (and inactive individuals perceive their friends to be sexually inactive) in order to give themselves support for their own levels of sexual activity.

The influence of peers was investigated in New Zealand among sexually active teenagers attending a venereal disease clinic [17]. Peers were found to be an influence on the behavior of those with moderate levels of sexual activity but not for those who were the most or least active. The respondents were asked if at the time of their first coitus their friends had also experienced coitus. Of those who had not had coitus or had had coitus with one partner, 50 per cent said that their friends had been sexually experienced at the time they themselves first had intercourse. For those who had sexual experience with two or three partners, 80 per cent reported that their friends had had intercourse, and for those with four or more partners, 60 per cent reported that their friends were nonvirgins at the time of the respondents' first coitus. The most sexually experienced individuals were more likely to report that the media influenced their sexual socialization.

Unfortunately, this study also does not really tell us the extent of peer influence upon sexual activity, whether or not the individuals' friends actually *were* sexually active at the time the individual first had intercourse, and whether or not the individual *at that time* knew of her friends' level of sexual activity and was thereby influenced. It seems logical that a person who believes that her close friends are engaging in an activity will be more likely also to engage in it than one who believes that her friends abstain. Conclusive evidence in the sexual realm, however, has yet to be found.

Noncoital Sexual Behavior. An important flaw in much premarital sex research has been the ignoring of sexual behavior that does not involve sexual intercourse. Sorensen did ask his respondents to indicate whether they had experienced breast fondling and manual contact with the genitals of their partner. Seventeen per cent of his respondents were what he calls "sexual beginners," those persons who have had these experiences but not sexual intercourse. Male petting of the female breast is the most frequent form of sexual activity among these virgins [70, p. 171]. Most sexual beginners either move on to another partner, or to sexual intercourse with their original partner, rather than staying for long periods of time at the "beginning" stage [70, p. 174].

Masturbation. Few people today believe that masturbation causes all maladies from acne to insanity, but a wide range of opinion and feeling about masturbation still exists. Some persons still maintain that masturbation is harmful psychologically, or morally wrong. Others believe that it plays a necessary but temporary role in the sexual development of the adolescent, allowing her or him to integrate childhood sexual experiences with past and future. For others, masturbation provides a sexual outlet to those who are denied heterosexual outlets, either because of separation from a sexual partner or the decision to postpone sexual relations until such a partner can be found, or perhaps until marriage with a present partner. The effect of masturbation upon the individual doubtless is determined by the persons' beliefs and feelings concerning masturbation. The person who believes that masturbation is wrong, or that it is something that she just can't stop doing, would probably find masturbation to induce guilt, shame, or anxiety.

Sorensen [70] asked his teenage respondents when they had last masturbated, how much they enjoyed masturbating, and if and how often they experienced guilt as a result of masturbating. Sixty-nine per cent of nonvirgin boys, and 41 per cent of virgin boys, said that they had masturbated at least once; 53 per cent of nonvirgin girls, and 28 per cent of virgin girls, said that they had masturbated. Of those who masturbated, only 19 per cent of the boys and 12 per cent of the girls reported a great deal of enjoyment from it; approximately three quarters reported "somewhat" or "a little" enjoyment. Of those currently masturbating, 17 per cent of boys and 22 per cent of girls never experienced guilt; 19 per cent of boys and 13 per cent of girls reported that they experienced guilt often. The individuals who were most likely to report guilt as a result of masturbation were those that Sorensen called "sexual adventurers"—those who had sexual relations with a variety of partners in the absence of a stable relationship.

SEXUAL CODES

In the 1960s, Reiss studied the premarital sexual codes of high school and college students [61]. He found that among teenage girls, the most popular standard was petting-with-affection. In other words, teenage girls were most likely to believe that it is all right for a girl to pet with a boy if the two are in love or very fond of each other. Among boys, the dominant sexual code was the double standard; that is, that sexual intercourse is all right for males, but not for females. As indicated previously, since the 1960s there has been an apparent increase in premarital coitus among teenagers, and more acceptance of permissiveness-with-affection among college students [62] and high school students [70]. Seventy-five per cent of Sorensen's virginal 13- to 19-year-olds reported that they had not had sex yet because they were not ready for it [70, p. 149]. Unfortunately, he did not ask them whether they regarded premarital sex as right or wrong. Not being ready for sex could be indicative of an abstinence-before-marriage standard, or it could mean that those interviewed did not feel ready yet, but would not object to having sex before marriage. Although the abstinence standard has lost ground in recent years, many unmarried persons still prefer to save sex for marriage. The range of standards remains the same, from strict abstinence (only kissing is permitted before marriage) to permissiveness-without-affection.

COHABITATION

During the early 1970s, cohabitation or living together without marriage became increasingly common on college campuses [34, 57]. The noncollege population is more difficult to study, but cohabitation most probably is gaining ground among these young people, too. I (LSS) recently talked with students in a high school family-living class, some of whom said that they would prefer to cohabit at least as a prelude to marriage, if not as a substitute for it. They did say, however, that their parents would be furious. Although information from 30 students, nonrandomly selected from one high school in a predominantly working-class city in New England, cannot be used to generalize to the entire population, I don't believe that high school seniors 15 years ago would have considered cohabitation as an option.

Generally speaking, persons who cohabit report that the experience has been beneficial for them. However, it is not clear whether those who cohabit long enough to be counted as cohabitors by researchers (generally, at least three months) are those who would be most likely to benefit [78]. It is not known what effect cohabitation has on relationships. It may be that cohabitation provides a "reality testing" that cannot be obtained in a dating relationship. Partners see each other in many moods throughout the day and night, as do married couples. They share the financial burden, (although doubtless many college students are still supported by their parents). On the other hand, some individuals may be pushed toward greater commitment to their partners simply by virtue of the intensity of the relationship and not because the quality of the relationship has been tested.

Early Marriage

As early as 1900, the marriage rate for the United States females aged 15 to 19 was considerably lower than the rate for other industrialized nations [69]. The percent of ever-married females aged 15 to 19 rose dramatically in the 1950s and remained high until the mid 1960s, when it dropped again. Figure 3-1 shows the trend from 1890 to 1970. The smaller proportion of teenage marriages is reflected in a rise in the average age at marriage. Another indication of this trend is that in 1960, 41 per cent of women aged 18 to 24 were unmarried, compared with 48 per cent in 1972 [74].

From the standpoint of personality development, one would expect adolescent marriages to be less satisfactory than those between adults. With one partner or both in the crisis of developing a sense of identity, the relationship cannot be one of mutuality and intimacy, which is the essence of the ideal North American marriage. Both partners expect happiness from marriage, and yet their own immaturity prevents the establishment of the relationship that yields lasting happiness. The theory is borne out by statistics. Figure 3-2 shows the per cent distribution of divorces by age of husband and wife at marriage for 1969. Almost half of the divorces involved women who were married under the age of 20. A nationwide survey in 1967 made by the Office of Economic Opportunity found that 27 per cent of women who had married in their teens, compared with 14 per cent of those who had married after they reached their twenties, were divorced within 20 or more years of marriage. Since women in the past have tended to marry slightly older men, the comparable figures for men are 28 per cent who married before the age of 22, versus 13 per cent of those who married after 22 [30]. Furthermore,

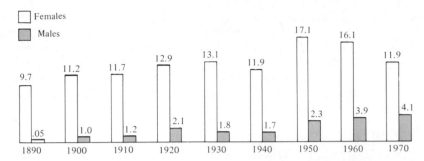

Figure 3-1. Per cent of teenage population ever married, by sex and age, United States, 1890–1970.

SOURCE: A. M. Hetzel and M. Capetta. *Teenagers: marriages, divorces, parenthood, and mortality.* Vital Health Statistics Series 21, No. 23. DHEW Publication No. (HRA) 74–1901. Washington, D.C.: U.S. Government Printing Office, 1973.

women whose first marriage ended in divorce have been married about two years younger, on the average, than married women whose marriages did not end in divorce [25].

Many factors contribute to early marriage. The insecurity of modern life leads to a desire for loyalty, warmth, and affection that an adolescent hopes to find in marriage. Personal happiness is understood as inherent in family life. A bandwagon effect may operate, as friends marry young. Marriage is overevaluated because of the romantic, glamorous image promoted by the mass media. Economic

Figure 3-2. Per cent distribution of divorces by age of husband and wife at marriage: divorce-registration area, 1969.

SOURCE: A. A. Plateria. *Divorces: analysis of changes, United States, 1969.* DHEW Publication No. (HSM) 73–1900. Washington, D.C.: U.S. Government Printing Office, 1973.

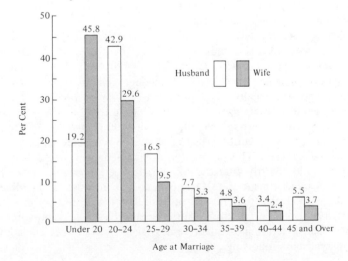

restraints are reduced by prosperity, employment of wives, contribution of parents, and occupational fringe benefits. Increased heterosexual behavior at younger years, earlier dating and going steady, plus increased stimulation of sex drives by mass media, leads to increased premarital sexual intercourse, pregnancy, and forced marriages. Some early marriages are precipitated by the desire to escape from unhappy situations in home, school, or community or to solve other emotional problems.

PROBLEMS RESULTING FROM EARLY MARRIAGE

In addition to the disasters of marriage dissolution and the hazards to personality development already mentioned, young marrieds face curtailment of education and reduction of level of aspiration. (This problem is a serious one from the standpoint of society, as well as for the individuals involved, since it results in individuals less able to do society's productive and creative work.) Not only do married high school students face restrictions and some hostility from teachers and principals but economic pressures also may force them out of school.

Females who marry during their teens are likely to have conceived a child before marriage. In a national probability sample of women aged 15 to 19, it was found that 76 per cent of all infants born to these women were conceived prior to marriage. About 45 per cent of all live births occurred out of wedlock, and 31 per cent were premaritally conceived but born to married couples. When looking only at legitimate births to women aged 15 to 19, the researchers found that 56.4 per cent were conceived prior to marriage [79]. The arrival soon after marriage of a child puts an added strain on the marital relationship. A number of studies have indicated that marital satisfaction declines with the advent of children [63]. In a longitudinal study of 37 couples who married while still in high school, the satisfaction of husbands and wives regarding child rearing and of husbands regarding sex relations dropped significantly between the third and thirtieth month of marriage. Wives in this study reported a great deal of unhappiness about their social relations after they married, complaining that they had been "dropped" by most of their friends. The husbands continued to spend time socially with their male friends, who did not make the wives feel welcome [18].

Couples who marry too soon, either while still teenagers or during their twenties but without adequate dating experience, may later suffer from what two marriage counselors call the "Lost adolescence syndrome" [36]. Persons suffering from this syndrome define themselves as having "romantically" loved only one person—their spouse. Usually, they were married early, but in some cases the couple remained in a monogamous, intimate long-term relationship until they could marry, sometimes throughout all of high school and college. In the early years of marriage, persons with the lost adolescence syndrome usually have happy marriages with little stress. This peaceful period sometimes lasts until the first child is a year or two old. Shortly after the childbearing period begins, however, one or sometimes both spouses begin to feel trapped, and to view the single adolescent life as the ideal existence that they missed out on. The dissatisfaction grows, and the unhappy partner seeks a way out. Not infrequently the result is a divorce, followed by loneliness and a rapid subsequent remarriage, with another cycle of the lost adolescence syndrome following.

The most obvious problem in teenage marriages concerns children. The higher instability of these marriages implies that they will involve more children in divorce than will other marriages. The average adolescent is two stages behind the stage of maturity required by parenthood. Since most teenagers are deeply involved in the identity crisis and barely started on the problems of intimacy, the sense of generativity is far beyond them. One has to grow far beyond mutual give and take, understanding, and communicating in order to nurture a completely dependent being, to fit one's own existence in with hers, to enjoy giving without receiving immediate understanding and appreciation.

Unwed Parenthood

The drop in teenage marriages has been accompanied by an increase in unwed parenthood, and an increase in unwed mothers who keep their infants [69]. The social penalty for having a baby out of wedlock has decreased in recent years, and welfare makes it possible for a woman and her child to survive. The increasing prevalence of single parenthood-by-adoption may also serve to remove the stigma from single parenthood-by-pregnancy.

A national probability sample of women aged 15 to 19 was conducted in 1971 to determine the extensiveness of premarital sexual experience, pregnancy, and changes in marital status [79]. We have reported some of the other findings elsewhere in this chapter. Of those women who were premaritally pregnant at the time of the study (15.1 per cent of the sample), 19.4 per cent planned to marry before the baby was due, and 80.6 per cent had no plans to marry. Of those illegitimate children born to women in the sample, 85.6 per cent were living with their mothers; 4.7 per cent were living with relatives or friends, and only 7.8 per cent had been adopted.

The physical strain on mother and child that exists when a teenager becomes pregnant is discussed in Chapter 1. In addition, the unwed teenage mother faces the same psychological problems that the married teenage mother does, only without the help of a husband. If she continues to live with her own mother, she may get considerable support from her mother and from other family members. Nonetheless, the teenage mother is not as prepared as a more mature woman to nurture her child.

Gender Identity

The development of the sense of identity includes the development of identity as a man or a woman. As noted in previous chapters, sex typing occurs from birth onward. By the time a child reaches adolescence, he or she has done a great deal of growing toward becoming what is culturally defined as "masculine" or "feminine."

The adolescent asks, "Just what does it mean to be an adult of my sex and what sort of acceptable adult am I capable of becoming?" Since the cultural prescription is not clear-cut and in fact permits many different interpretations, each young person has to select from the variety of possibilities, without the certainty of knowing that his choice is right. Although freedom of choice is a cherished democratic right, it does carry the disadvantage of uncertainty and anxiety. Students reflect the strain of this burden in their current practice of dropping out for a semester or a year or two in order to "find themselves." Dropping out began with college students but is also done by high school students who "run away" if they have to in order to attain a moratorium from demands.

MASCULINE IDENTITY

Since masculinity is defined in terms of activity and achievement, boys are encouraged to develop assertiveness and independence [20]. A boy has to come to terms with authority while maintaining his autonomy, neither submitting nor fighting too much. He has to come to terms with assertiveness, becoming neither timid nor cruel but controlled and purposeful. He has to come to terms with his sexuality, which he experiences directly as sexual desires. In order to control and gratify his sex impulses, he must loosen his family ties and make new ones. But before he can develop a sexual identity in relation to the opposite sex, he needs a foundation in the identity that requires achievement and assertiveness. Some sort of vocational success, perhaps a plan or commitment, will serve.

The adolescent boy knows and has known from early childhood that he must achieve and produce. Even though the high school peer group in general rewards athletes more than it does scholars, the adult male's vocational role is that of breadwinner, both before and after marriage. This fundamental is clear, even though expectations of husbands are not so definite. Also, there is continuity between the two roles. Research shows that husband–wife relationships are strongly influenced by the husband's vocational role. The very importance of work as part of a man's role makes vocational decisions serious and problems anxiety-producing. Farrell [23] notes that boys are pushed into becoming either "student strivers" or "physical strivers." The physical striver is the boy who proves himself in sports, the All-American hero. The "student striver" (who later becomes a "job striver") strives to achieve through manipulating the system, by "psyching out" teachers and writing for them, instead of writing and analyzing the way he himself wants to. Student strivers learn to pick apart the arguments of others, rather than to give positive and negative criticism. Farrell argues that the tremendous emphasis upon male achievement causes men to lose sight of their "more human" qualities of tenderness, emotion, humility, and sensuality. He does not mean that men should give up striving completely, but that achievement striving is only one of life's desirable goals.

A recent study suggests that higher creativity in adolescent males is associated with lower masculinity, as rated by teacher and peers [53]. More masculine boys received lower Originality and Fluency scores than did boys who were rated "low" on masculinity. Girls who were rated highly feminine, however, scored higher on these two scales. In another study, [58] adolescent females who were highly feminine had better academic records than those who were not highly feminine. Among boys, however, low masculinity scores were associated with higher academic achievement.

There is evidence that the ideal masculine role is changing from the picture of a man as a go-getter, a competitive individual who initiates, invents, saves for the future, and pushes ahead. Modern bureaucratic society seems to influence men to be cooperative, relaxed group members, enjoying the present and letting the company or the union take care of the future. Mead [50] decries the shift from longtime goals to immediate gratification, which means early marriage and early forcing into a pattern of domestication, focusing on earning a living instead of on ambitions for the future, curtailing the period of freedom in which a youth can dream.

FEMININE IDENTITY

In the early 1960s, Douvan and Adelson [20] studied the gender identity of adolescent boys and girls. Autonomy, assertion, and occupational goals had no significance for feminine identity. Interpersonal competence was important for girls, and it was within a framework of interpersonal relations that they came to understand their sexuality. Girls who measured high on a femininity test measured high on ego strength. Whereas the boy gained masculine identity by focusing on a future job, the girl gained feminine identity by projecting herself into the future as wife and mother, carrying on nurturing interpersonal activities. The girls who were most feminine were responding to the cultural stereotype of woman as nurturant, centered on relationships involving love, reproduction, homemaking, and dependent upon a man to define her status in society.

Recent research has focused much more upon the gender identity of the college woman than the high school girl. Horner [31], for example, asked college students to write stories about Anne, who headed her class in medical school, or about a male counterpart. Sixty-five per cent of women wrote stories that indicated a "fear-of success"; Anne was disliked by her classmates, or in the second semester she did not work as hard and allowed a man to be first.

Fifty-four per cent of ninth-grade girls in home economics classes wrote fear-of-success stories [28]. They were then told to find mistakes in photographs that illustrated food preparation and service. Half of the girls were told to set a goal for themselves of how many mistakes they would find. The control group was not told to set goals. It was found that the girls who were encouraged to set goals found more mistakes than those who did not set goals. Of the control group, girls who wrote fear-of-success stories found fewer mistakes (that is, achieved less) than those who did not write fear-of-success stories. The author suggests that if girls are encouraged to set goals for themselves, they may be less likely to be afraid of success.

Fear-of-success is but one small part of feminine identity. Other researchers have investigated how junior high students see themselves in relation to the opposite sex [35]. Girls saw themselves as more nervous than boys, more easily embarrassed, more likely to feel worthless, and more sensitive than other people. However, they also believed more often than boys that men should not make the major decisions in marriage, that men are not more aggressive than women, and that men are not better leaders than women. Boys believed that men are more able to reason logically than women, that it is a fact of life that a woman can work only when her family duties allow her to, that men should be given preference in hiring since if a woman is hired it means a man will not be, and that women are more suited to the care of young children than are men. In summary, this study indicated that although girls viewed themselves as more emotional and less competent than boys, they also saw women's roles in a more equalitarian manner than did the boys.

Unfortunately, the research does not tell us whether girls still believe that their main place is in the home, or whether girls still wait for a man to define their identity. As with many other cultural aspects, we believe that the range of beliefs and behaviors is increasing. Many adolescent girls probably still look forward to spending their childbearing years at home, without considering that even if they have their last child at age 30 they will have 20 or more years without a child in the home. Other girls declare that they will not get married, or that they will remain childfree, or that they will have both families and career.

It is unfortunate that many girls still do not believe that they have a range of options open to them. Boys, too, could benefit from not having to fit into a preconceived mold of what is manly. Just as women can learn and grow from close association with their infants and children, men's horizons are increased when they *share* child rearing rather than "helping out." It is a burden for a man to have to provide an identity for his wife, when she is certainly capable of being her own person with her own interests.

Summary

American parents and adolescents are likely to have considerable trouble with each other as the child, in accordance with cultural demands, establishes his independence and sense of identity. Some of their conflicts are intensified by the emotional concentration of the nuclear family, rapid social changes, and the impact of mass media and easy travel. Some authorities consider conflict inevitable, but others, noting the existence of many harmonious parent–adolescent relationships, doubt the necessity of conflict. Boys challenge parental authority more than girls do. Adolescents generally like, love, and admire their parents, even though they are concerned about problems regarding their parents.

An adolescent is influenced by her parents' marital situation. If the father has been absent from the home, the adolescent is likely to be disadvantaged cognitively and emotionally. The effect of mother-absence has not been adequately explored. Positive communication patterns between parents and among parents and children contribute to normal personality development of children.

Most adolescents have some trouble in communicating with their parents. When husband and wife communicate well with each other, parent-child communication tends to be satisfactory, as well.

Parent-adolescent conflict is seen as normal from a psychoanalytic viewpoint, as important for continued growth from a Gestalt perspective, and as minimal and nonessential from a third viewpoint. Low levels of rebelliousness in adolescents is associated with their seeing their parents' marriage as happy and equalitarian, and with nonauthoritarian treatment of children by parents. When conflict occurs, it usually centers around activities that concern the adolescent in his daily life, rather than broader goals or values.

Parents usually have complex feelings about their teenage children, often with considerable ambivalence. Not only do they worry about the child's adequacy in coping with his life but they also relive some of their own adolescent feelings and problems. Parents often find it difficult to achieve a satisfactory balance between controlling their almost-grown children and allowing them sufficient freedom. Adolescents generally report feeling close to their parents, especially to their mothers.

Although adolescents are usually influenced more by their parents than by any other adults, youngsters often use several adults for models. Teachers, youth leaders, and such people may build relationships that are important in adolescents' development. Although teenagers move from family orientation toward peer orientation, the family retains strongest influence in certain areas, but peers become stronger in places where adolescents see them as knowing more than their parents.

The adolescent peer group is fairly distinct as a cultural group. Peer interaction provides opportunities essential to the growth of the sense of identity. The crowd offers the adolescent a group identity that helps him to separate himself from his family, drawing a distinct line between generations. Because he feels comfortable when identified with the crowd, he can try out a variety of roles. The clique is a small, select group of close friends, usually alike in interests and background, giving one another security and status, often behaving cruelly to outsiders.

Friendship contributes to the sense of identity, especially close relationships such as "best friends" enjoy. When the sense of identity has reached a certain level of strength, friends can achieve true intimacy. It is easier and safer to develop the first intimate friendship with members of the same sex. Boys need a group of friends for support in resisting adult authority. Girls need close individual friends for emotional support in understanding themselves.

Greatly valued by many adolescents, popularity may exact a price of those who achieve it. Popularity, along with other attributes, gives high status. Many adolescents feel inadequate and inferior because they are assigned low or moderate statuses in systems that offer little room at the top.

Early dating has been the norm for at least 20 years, but recently the age at first marriage has risen slightly. High school students often view dating as a game, and may be manipulative in their cross-sex relationships. In some high schools, girls are beginning to ask boys for dates, but in many schools this is still rare or unheard of.

Romantic love is an aspect of American culture that sometimes confuses adolescents and yet also strengthens and beautifies their relationships with the opposite sex. Romantic love can promote the development of the sense of identity.

Adolescents are more likely to have had premarital intercourse than was true in the early 1960s and before. Some researchers report that males are more likely to be nonvirgins, but others have found males and females equally likely to have had intercourse. The influence of peers on sexual activity is not adequately understood. Permissiveness-with-affection is a sexual code that is gaining popularity, but many adolescents continue to hold the abstinence standard.

Early marriage is less of a problem than it was in the 1950s, but more adolescent girls who become premaritally pregnant are bearing and keeping their infants. Cohabitation also decreases the number of young marriages. For those who begin their families while still in adolescence, either through childbearing, marriage, or both, many problems still exist.

The development of a masculine identity requires a boy to come to terms with his assertiveness, independence, and sexuality. Vocational interest is basic. Boys are pushed to strive, and are not encouraged to develop their tenderness, emotion, and sensuality. Traditionally, girls' identity remained more fluid than did boys' and was often defined in relation to their husbands once they married. Adolescent girls are now more egalitarian than boys in their view of gender roles, but feel less sure of themselves than they think boys do.

References

1. Adams, J. F. Adolescent personal problems as a function of age and sex. *Journal of Genetic Psychology,* 1964, **104,** 207–214.
2. Adelson, J. What generation gap? *New York Times Magazine,* January 18, 1970.
3. Bahr, S. J., C. E. Bowerman, and V. Gecas. Adolescent perceptions of conjugal power. *Social Forces,* 1974, **52,** 357–367.
4. Balswick, J. O., and C. Macrides. Parental stimulus for adolescent rebellion. *Adolescence,* 1975, **10,** 252–259.
5. Bauman, K., and R. R. Wilson. Sexual behavior of unmarried university students in 1968 and 1972. *Journal of Sex Research,* 1974, **10,** 327–333.
6. Baumrind, D. Authoritarian vs. authoritative parental control. *Adolescence,* 1968, **3,** 255–272.
7. Bell, R. R., and J. B. Chaskes. Premarital sexual experience among coeds, 1958 and 1968. *Journal of Marriage and the Family,* 1970, **32,** 390–392.
8. Biller, H. B. *Paternal deprivation.* Lexington, Mass.: D. C. Heath 1974.
9. Biller, H. B., and S. D. Weiss. The father-daughter relationship and the personality development of the female. *Journal of Genetic Psychology,* 1970, **116,** 79–93.
10. Blood, L., and R. D'Angelo. A progress report on value issues in conflict between runaways and their parents. *Journal of Marriage and the Family,* 1974, **36,** 486–491.
11. Bowlby, J. *Attachment and loss. Vol. 1: Attachment.* London: Hogarth, 1969.
12. Broderick, C. B., and J. Weaver. The perceptual context of boy-girl communication. *Journal of Marriage and the Family,* 1968, **30,** 618–627.
13. Chand, I. P., D. M. Crider, and F. K. Willits. Parent-youth disagreement as perceived by youth: A longitudinal study. *Youth and Society,* 1975, **6,** 365–375.
14. Coleman, J. S. *The adolescent society.* Glencoe, Ill.: The Free Press, 1961.
15. Collins, J., and J. Harper. Problems of adolescents in Sydney, Australia. *Journal of Genetic Psychology,* 1974, **125,** 187–194.
16. Damico, S. B. The effects of clique membership upon academic achievement. *Adolescence,* 1975, **10,** 93–99.
17. Davis, P. Contextual sex saliency and sexual activity: The relative effects of family and peer group in the sexual socialization process. *Journal of Marriage and the Family,* 1974, **36,** 196–202.
18. deLissovoy, V. High school marriages: A longitudinal study. *Journal of Marriage and the Family,* 1973, **35,** 244–255.
19. Dickinson, G. E. Dating behavior of black and white adolescents before and after desegregation. *Journal of Marriage and the Family,* 1975, **37,** 602–608.

20. Douvan, E., and J. Adelson. *The adolescent experience.* New York: John Wiley & Sons, Inc., 1966.
21. Dubbe, M. C. What teen-agers can't tell parents and why. *Family Coordinator,* 1956, **4**:3, 3–7.
22. Erikson, E. H. *Identity and the life cycle.* New York: International Universities Press, 1959.
23. Farrell, W. *The liberated man.* New York: Bantam Books, Inc., 1975.
24. Fish, K., and H. B. Biller. Perceived childhood paternal relationship and college females' personal adjustment. *Adolescence,* 1973, **8**, 414–420.
25. Glick, P. C. A demographer looks at American families. *Journal of Marriage and the Family,* 1975, **37**, 15–38.
26. Goodman, N. Adolescent norms and behavior: Organization and conformity. *Merrill-Palmer Quarterly,* 1969, **15**, 199–211.
27. Haley, J. An interactional description of schizophrenia. In D. D. Jackson (ed.). *Commnnication, family and marriage.* Palo Alto, Ca.: Science and Behavior Books, 1968.
28. Harvey, A. Goals setting as compensation for fear of success. *Adolescence,* 1975, **10**, 137–142.
29. Hetherington, E. M. Father absence and personality development in adolescent daughters. *Developmental Psychology,* 1972, **7**, 313–326.
30. Hetzel, A., and M. Capetta. *Teenagers: Marriages, divorces, parenthood, and mortality.* Vital and Health Statistics, Series 21. No. 23. DHEW Publication Number (HRA) 74–1901, Washington, D.C.: U.S. Government Printing Office, 1973.
31. Horner, M. S. A bright woman is caught in a double bind. *Psychology Today,* 1969, **3**:6, 36 ff.
32. Hornick, J. Premarital sexual attitudes and behavior: A reference group contingent-factor theory. Unpublished Ph. D. Dissertation, University of Waterloo, 1975.
33. Horrocks, J. E., and S. A. Weinberg. Psychological needs and their development during adolescence. *Journal of Psychology,* 1970, **74**, 51–69.
34. Huang, L. J. Research with unmarried cohabiting couples: Including non-exclusive sexual relations. Paper presented at meetings of the National Council on Family Relations, St. Louis, 1974.
35. Joesting, J. and R. Joesting. Sex differences in equalitarianism and anxiety in ninth-grade students. *Adolescence,* 1975, **10**, 59–61.
36. Jurich, A. P. and J. A. Jurich. The lost adolescence syndrome. *Family Coordinator,* 1975, **24**, 357–361.
37. Kandel, D., and G. R. Lesser. Parent-adolescent relationships and adolescent independence in the United States and Denmark. *Journal of Marriage and the Family,* 1969, **31**, 348–358.
38. Kantner, J. Teenage sexual and reproductive behavior. Paper presented at meetings of the American Psychological Association, New Orleans, 1974.
39. King, K. Adolescent perception of power structure in the Negro family. *Journal of Marriage and the Family,* 1969, **31**, 751–764.
40. Knox, D. H. Conceptions of love at three developmental levels. *Family Coordinator,* 1970, **19**, 151–157.
41. Kotlar, T. Characteristics and correlates of parent-son interactions. *Genetic Psychology Monographs,* 1975, **91**, 121–168.
42. Krieger, L. H., and W. D. Wells. The criteria for friendship. *Journal of Social Psychology,* 1969, **78**, 109–112.

43. Kuhlen, R. G., and N. B. Houlihan. Adolescent heterosexual interest in 1942 and 1963. *Child Development,* 1965, **36,** 1049–1052.
44. Larson, L. E. The influence of parents and peers during adolescence: The situation hypothesis revisited. *Journal of Marriage and the Family,* 1972, **34,** 67–74.
45. Lauer, R. The generation gap as sociometric choice. *Youth and Society,* 1973, **5,** 227–241.
46. Lewis, E. A new set of heroes. *American Education,* 1970, **6:**1, 23.
47. Lurie, E. Sex and stage differences in perceptions of marital and family relationships. *Journal of Marriage and the Family,* 1974, **36,** 260–269.
48. Macklin, E. Colloquium presented at the University of Connecticut, May, 1975.
49. Matteson, R. Adolescent self-esteem, family communication and marital satisfaction. *Journal of Psychology,* 1974, **86,** 35–47.
50. Mead, M. The young adult. In E. Ginzberg (ed.). *Values and ideals of American youth.* New York: Columbia University Press, 1961, pp. 37–51.
51. Miller, S., R. Corrales, and D.-B. Wackman. Recent progress in understanding and facilitating marital communication. *Family Coordinator,* 1975, **24,** 143–152.
52. Miller, T. Effects of maternal age, education, and employment status on the self-esteem of the child. *Journal of Social Psychology,* 1975, **95,** 141–142.
53. Oberlander, M. I., J. Smilansky, E. E. Lessing, and K. Vroegh. Sex-role development and creative functioning in preadolescent and adolescent students. Paper presented at meetings of the Society for Research in Child Development, Denver, 1975.
54. Offer, D., D. Marcus, and J. L. Offer. A longitudinal study of normal adolescent boys. *American Journal of Psychiatry,* 1970, **126,** 917–924.
55. Oliver, L. *Parents' ratings of behavioral patterns of youths 12–17 years: United States.* Data from the National Health Survey. Series 11. No. 137. Washington, D.C.: U.S. Government Printing Office, 1974.
56. Perls, F. S., R. Heferline, and P. Goodman. *Gestalt therapy.* New York: Data, 1951.
57. Peterman, D. J., C. A. Ridley, and S. Anderson. A comparison of cohabiting and noncohabiting college students. *Journal of Marriage and the Family,* 1974, **36,** 344–354.
58. Ponzo, Z., and W. Strowig. Relations among sex-role identity and selected intellectual and non-intellectual factors for high school freshmen and seniors. *Journal of Educational Research,* 1973, **67,** 137–141.
59. Propper, A. M. The relationship of maternal employment to adolescent roles, activities, and parental relationship. *Journal of Marriage and The Family,* 1972, **34,** 417–426.
60. Rainwater, L. Crucible of identity: The Negro lower-class family. In A. E. Winder and D. L. Angus (eds.). *Adolescence: Contemporary studies.* New York: American Book Company, 1968, pp. 166–181.
61. Reiss, I. L. *The social context of premarital permissiveness.* New York: Holt, Rinehart and Winston, Inc., 1967.
62. Robinson, I. E., K. King, and J. O. Balswick. The premarital sexual revolution among college females. *Family Coordinator,* 1972, **21,** 189–194.
63. Rollins, B., and K. L. Cannon. Marital satisfaction over the family life cycle: A reevaluation. *Journal of Marriage and the Family,* 1974, **36,** 271–282.
64. Safilios-Rothschild, C. The study of family power structure: A review 1960–1969. *Journal of Marriage and the Family,* 1970, **32,** 539–552.
65. Safilios-Rothschild, C. The dimensions of power distribution in the family. In J.

Christ and H. Grunebaum, (eds.). *Marriage problems and their treatment*. Boston: Little, Brown and Company, 1972.

66. Schmuck, R. Concerns of contemporary adolescents. *Bulletin of the National Association of Secondary-School Principals*, 1965, **49**, 19–28.

67. Schuham, A. I. Activity, talking time and spontaneous agreement in disturbed and normal family interaction. *Journal of Abnormal Psychology*, 1972, **79**, 68–75.

68. Schwartz, G., and D. Merten. The language of adolescence: an anthropological approach to the youth culture. *American Journal of Sociology*, 1967, **57**, 453–468.

69. Sklar, J., and B. Berkov. Teenage family formation in postwar America. *Family Planning Perspectives*, 1974, **6**, 80–90.

70. Sorensen, R. C. *Adolescent sexuality in contemporary America*. New York: World Publishing Co., 1973.

71. Teevan, J., Jr. Reference groups and premarital sexual behavior. *Journal of Marriage and the Family*, 1972, **34**, 283–292.

72. Thurnher, M., D. Spence, and M. F. Lowenthal. Value confluence and behavioral conflict in intergenerational relations. *Journal of Marriage and the Family*, 1974, **36**, 308–319.

73. Troll, L. E., B. L. Neugarten, and R. J. Draines. Similarities in values and other personality characteristics in college students and their parents. *Merrill-Palmer Quarterly*, 1969, **15**, 323–336.

74. U.S. Department of Commerce. *We: The Youth of America*. Washington, D.C.: U.S. Government Printing Office, 1973.

75. Vener, A. M., C. S. Stewart, and D. Hager. Adolescent sexual behavior in middle America revisited: Generational and American-British comparisons. *Journal of Marriage and the Family*, 1974, **36**, 728–735.

76. Walster, E. Passionate love. In B. Murstein (ed.). *Theories of attraction and love*. New York: Springer, 1971. 85–99.

77. Won, G., and D. Yamamura. Expectations of youth in relating to the world of adults. *Family Coordinator*, 1970, **19**, 219–224.

78 Workshop on Non-Marital Cohabitation. Groves Conference on Marriage and The Family, Myrtle Beach, S.C., 1973 (mimeo).

79. Zelnick, M., and J. F. Kantner. The resolution of first pregnancies. *Family Planning Perspectives*, 1974, **6**, 74–80.

Readings in
Parents, Peers, and the Quest for Identity

The sense of identity is an integrating concept in the study of adolescent personality development. Identity is approached from many different perspectives. Physiological development produces changes that a person must integrate into the self-concept. Cognitive transformations equip the individual to think in more complex ways about the self and its relation to the world, the past, present, and future. Emotional experiences add another dimension. Two of the articles in this chapter place the adolescent in a broad context. The third deals with limited aspects of teenage and parent behavior.

The excerpt from Erik H. Erikson's book is very concentrated in meaning, although short in length, summarizing his ideas on the development of the sense of identity in adolescence. We hope that this small piece from Erikson will stimulate students to read his books. Erikson is a model for human developmentalists in relating the individual to his bodily and intellectual growth, to his personal history, and to his society and its place in history.

In analyzing support systems, or where adolescent boys go for help, Benjamin H. Gottlieb also gives much information about the social structure of a high school. He describes variety and meaning in peer relationships, illustrating them vividly with direct quotations. Gottlieb, like Erikson, takes a broad viewpoint of the ways in which adolescents interact with many different representatives of the social environment.

Jack O. Balswick and Clitos Macrides consider adolescent rebellion, as interpreted by adolescents themselves, in relation to the parents' marriage and disciplinary practices with children. Erikson's article offers a framework in which to view the relevance of both rebellion and parental behavior to the whole of the development of adolescent personality. Balswick and Macrides focus on a small area of the whole scene, as must be done in order to understand these particular relationships. However, the reader should not exaggerate the importance of what parents do, even though it is shown to relate to one aspect of adolescent behavior.

Excerpt from "'Identity Crisis' in Autobiographic Perspective"

Erik H. Erikson

To say, then, that the identity crisis is psycho *and* social means that:

1. It is a subjective sense as well as an observable quality of personal sameness and continuity, paired with some belief in the sameness and continuity of some shared world image. As a quality of unself-conscious living, this can be gloriously obvious in a young person who has found himself as he has found his communality. In him, we see emerge a unique unification of what is irreversibly given—that is, body type and temperament, giftedness and vulnerability, infantile models and acquired ideals—with the open choices provided in available roles, occupational possibilities, values offered, mentors met, friendships made, and first sexual encounters.

2. It is a state of being and becoming that can have a highly conscious (and indeed, self-conscious) quality and yet remain, in its motivational aspects, quite unconscious and beset with the dynamics of conflict. This, in turn, can lead to contradictory mental states, such as a sense of aggravated vulnerability and yet also an expectation of grand individual promise.

3. It is characteristic of a *developmental period*, before which it cannot come to a head, because the somatic, cognitive, and social preconditions are only then given; and beyond which it must not be unduly delayed, because the next and all future developments depend on it. This stage of life is, of course, *adolescence and youth*. The advent and solution of the identity crisis thus partially depends on *psychological* factors, which secure the somatic basis for a coherent sense of vital selfhood. On the other hand, *psychosocial* factors can prolong the crisis (painfully, but not necessarily unduly) where a person's idiosyncratic gifts demand a prolonged search for a corresponding ideological and occupational setting, or where historical change forces a postponement of adult commitment.

4. It is dependent on the *past* for the resource of strong identifications made in childhood, while it relies on new models encountered in youth, and depends for its conclusion on workable roles offered in young adulthood. In fact, each subsequent stage of adulthood must contribute to its preservation and renewal.

The "socio" part of identity, then, must be accounted for in that communality within which an individual finds himself. No ego is an island to itself. Throughout life the establishment and maintenance of that strength which can reconcile discontinuities and ambiguities depends on the support of parental as well as communal models. For youth depends on the ideological coherence of the world it is meant to take over, and therefore is sensitively aware of whether the system is strong enough in its traditional form to "confirm" and to be confirmed by the identity process, or so rigid or brittle as to suggest renovation, reformation, or revolution. Psychosocial identity, then, also has a *psycho-historical* side, and suggests the study of how life histories are inextricably interwoven with history. The study of psychosocial identity, therefore, depends on three complementarities—or are they three aspects of one complementarity? —namely, the personal coherence of the individual and role integration in his group; his guiding images and the ideologies of his time; his life history—and the historical moment.

All this sounds probable enough and, especially when shorn of its unconscious dimension, appears to be widely, and sometimes faddishly, acceptable in our day. The unconscious complexities often ignored can be grouped thus:

1. Identity formation normatively has its dark and negative side, which throughout life can remain an unruly part of the total identity. Every person and every group harbors a *negative identity* as the sum of all those identifications and identity fragments which the individual had to submerge in himself as undesirable or irreconcilable or which his group has taught him to perceive as the mark of fatal "difference" in sex role or race, in class or religion. In the event of aggravated crises, an individual (or, indeed, a group) may despair of the ability to contain these negative elements in a positive identity. A specific rage can be aroused wherever identity development thus loses the promise of an assured wholeness: an as yet uncommitted delinquent, if denied any chance of communal integration, may become a "confirmed" criminal. In periods of collective crisis, such potential rage is shared by many and is easily exploited by psychopathic leaders, who become the models of a sudden surrender to total doctrines and dogmas in which the negative identity appears to be the desirable and the dominant one: thus the Nazis fanatically cultivated what the victorious West as well as the more refined Germans had come to decry as "typically German." The rage aroused by threatened identity loss can explode in the arbitrary violence of mobs, or it can—less consciously— serve the efficient destructiveness of the machinery of oppression and war.

2. In some young people, in some classes, at some periods in history, the personal identity crisis will be noiseless and contained within the rituals of passage marking a second birth; while in other people, classes, and periods, the crisis will be clearly marked off as a critical period intensified by collective strife or epidemic tension. Thus, the nature of the identity conflict often depends on the latent panic or, indeed, the intrinsic promise pervading a historical period. Some periods in history become identity vacua caused by the three basic forms of human apprehension: *fears* aroused by new facts, such as discoveries and inventions (including weapons), which radically expand and change the whole world image; *anxieties* aroused by symbolic dangers vaguely perceived as a consequence of the decay of existing ideologies; and, in the wake of disintegrating faith, the *dread* of an existential abyss devoid of spiritual meaning. But then, again, a historical period may (as, for example, the American Revolution did) present a singular chance for a collective renewal which opens up unlimited identities for those who, by a combination of unruliness, giftedness, and competence, represent a new leadership, a new elite, and new types rising to dominance in a new people.

If there *is* something to all this, why would insights concerning such universal matters first come from psychoanalysis, a clinical science? The fact is that in all periods of history, mental disturbances of epidemiological significance or special fascination highlight a specific aspect of man's nature in conflict with "the times" and are met with by innovative insights: as happened to hysteria in Freud's early days. In our time, a state of *identity confusion*, not abnormal in itself, often seems to be accompanied by all the neurotic or near psychotic symptoms to which a young person is prone on the basis of constitution, early fate, and malignant circumstance. In fact, young individuals are subject to a more malignant disturbance than might have manifested itself during other stages of life, precisely because the adolescent process can induce the individual semi-deliberately to give in to some of his most regressed or repressed tendencies in order, as it were, to test rock bottom and to recover some of his as yet undeveloped childhood strengths. This, however, is safe only where a relatively stable society provides collective experiences of a ceremonial character, or where revolutionary leaders (such as Luther) provide new identity guidelines which permit the adolescent individual to take chances with himself. Historical crises, in turn, aggravate personal crises; and, indeed, many young people have in the recent past been judged to suffer from a chronic malignant disturbance, where we now know that an aggravated developmental crisis was dominant. This, then, is the clinical anchorage for the conception of an identity crisis.

The Contribution of Natural Support Systems to Primary Prevention Among Four Social Subgroups of Adolescent Males

Benjamin H. Gottlieb
UNIVERSITY OF GUELPH

In a recent chapter of the *Annual Review of Psychology,* "Social and Community Interventions," Cowen (1) presents an overview of the fields of community mental health and community psychology. While acknowledging that this title is "little more than a polymorphous, perverse locus designator," he nevertheless identifies a preventive orientation in mental health programming as its critical hallmark, based on his readings of the theoretical underpinnings of these community approaches. Following his review of specific avenues toward implementing a preventive model, however, he voices two strong reservations about the field: a lack of programming efforts in *primary* prevention and a deficit of empirical research.

This paper describes one pathway toward establishing an empirical research base in primary prevention with a population of adolescents. It centers upon an examination of natural support systems in the community which aid

From *Adolescence,* 1975, **10,** 207–220. Reprinted by permission of Libra Publishers, Inc.

the coping efforts of adolescents. The natural support system is composed of two categories of informal helping agents: community gatekeepers or caretakers such as family physicians, employers, clergymen, teachers, counselors and school administrators. These persons' normal work roles in the community bring them into contact with large segments of the population and they are therefore in strategic frontline positions to aid the coping efforts of people who are experiencing problems in living. The second category of informal helpers are primary group members including kin and kith. Research on the contribution of natural support systems to primary prevention integrate three theoretical propositions underlying the community mental health movement: an orientation toward practice which aims to promote health, not to remediate illness; a programmatic orientation toward serving the needs of groups or populations-at-risk, not individuals and a commitment to utilizing all the mental health resources within any locality, not only the professional clinical services. Interlacing these propositions, this study assesses how the coping efforts of a population of adolescents are strengthened by the helping relationships they form with a range of informal community resources.

Two considerations prompted the specific choice of high school seniors as a critical population for the study of informal helping relationships. First, a number of important decisions and problems are compacted within the last year of high school and are fequently accompanied by emotional and role strains within the family and peer group contexts. This period of heightened stress thus offers an excellent opportunity for documenting the helping transactions which occur. Second, the use of adolescent subjects presents an opportunity to determine whether contrasting social subgroups within a given population prefer and value different qualities in the helping agents whom they engage for the management of problems.

Elsewhere (4), the author has presented a detailed account of the procedure used to reliably identify peer social subgroups within the Senior class of high school adolescents. Essentially, this procedure called for 20 peer raters who independently classified a random half of their classmates into social subgroups, and provided descriptions of the bases of their classification. That report also presented an analysis of the quantitative data gathered about the major current concerns of each of the four identified social subgroups and their contrasting preferences for informal help sources.[1] This paper begins with a summary of these latter findings and sketches a profile of the social characteristics of each subgroup of youth. The major focus of this paper, however, is on qualitative data which illuminates the bases of group preferences for different informal help sources. Specifically, the qualitative data are the recurrent themes expressed by the members of each social subculture in describing the qualities of helping relationships which they prize most highly. These emergent themes provide a sensitive record, from the adolescents' interior perspectives, of the helping experiences which have an impact on their lives.

PROFILES OF THE FOUR SUBGROUPS

The first three group sketches below are derived from the common perceptions of the fourteen reliable peer raters. These were the raters who inde-

[1] Copies of this report, including analysis details of the procedure used to identify social subgroups and their members, are available on request from the author, Dr. Gottlieb.

pendently generated these group classifications and were in agreement about their memberships. The membership of the fourth group was also generated by the peer rating procedure, but since this group's classification rested on its members' anonymity to the raters, the group's descriptive profile is based solely on self-report data drawn from its members' family background and social activities questionnaires. Thus the final sample of 20 adolescents interviewed in this study was composed of the five youths in each subgroup who received the highest interrater agreement scores. No single label can faithfully describe each group. For ease of reference, however, assignments have been made on the basis of the raters' consensus about the outstanding typing characteristic of the group as a whole.

Elites   Members of this group are highly visible, competitive, and successful in both academic and extra-curricular school programs, especially in varsity athletics, the major prerequisite for entry into this high status social subgroup. Raters perceived the group as cliquish, populated by talented, but conceited individuals. In the words of one rater: "They stick together; they've got their own clique; in the hall you know them right away; the in-crowd. They're all very good at something. Everybody knows it; they know it too." Members of this group are described as moderate users of both alcohol and marijuana.

Isolates   Members of this social subgroup are involved exclusively in the school's academic program. Raters describe members as lacking self-confidence and as deficient in those social skills demanded by extra-curricular group participation. The major typing characteristic of the group is its members' isolation from the overall peer social structure of the class. A typical rater comment was: "They have no true friends; they keep to themselves; they just don't know how to relate." Isolates are "straights" who abstain both from drug and liquor use.

Deviants   These youths are involved neither in the academic nor in the extra-curricular programs of the high school. The hallmark of the group is its members' tendencies to engage in certain excesses of behavior which are perceived as inappropriate within the school setting and directly linked to members' high use of soft drugs. This low status social subgroup included only a small number of students who neither constitute a cohesive group nor maintain ties to the overall peer social structure. One rater noted: "They have their own group, but it's not that big; they don't have too much to do with other people; they tend to go to more extremes than others; they come to school high."

Outsiders   A more limited sketch of the anonymous social subgroup is drawn from members' self-reports of family background, involvement in social and extra-school activities and future plans following high school. First, three of the five group members do not participate in any school or community-based social clubs or teams. In comparison to the three other social subgroups, the group contains the largest number of youths who plan to work full time during the coming year while they attend the local junior college. Four of the five group members are employed and have been working 35-hour weeks for the past ten months. Two of the members have already left home and the majority report that their best friends are located at their places of employment. Taken together, these findings help to account for the apparent anonymity of these youths within the high school and the complementary salience of extra school settings in their lives. The commonalities between this group and the others include similar middle class status on socio-economic indicators (Father's and Mother's Educations, Father's Occupation), similar family sizes and similar lengths of school and community tenure.

MAJOR PROBLEMS AND PREFERRED HELP SOURCES

Intensive private interviews were conducted with the 20 youths, five from each of the four social subgroups. Each youth was requested to review a list of twelve everyday problems, whose relevance to the youths' lives was suggested by pretest interviews with adolescent informants and underscored by the literature on the tasks of adolescent development including the instrumental (goal achievement), expressive (relationship), and integrative (values and identity) domains. After reviewing the list, the youth was asked to rate his relative current concern about each problem. The interview then focused on the three problems rated of greatest relative concern, inquiring in particular about the help sources the youth had involved in his attempts to cope with these problems. A summary follows of the differences among the major life concerns of the four subgroups and their contrasting preferences for informal helping agents.

Elites   Three problems are of greater concern to Elites than to any other group: their current school performance, their plans following graduation and their fears about disappointing their parents. The first concern is congruent with aters' characterizations of group members as high achievement competitors, and the second complements the self-reported intentions of four of the five group members to attend college outside the local area on a full-time basis. Clearly, the two concerns mesh since Senior grades have an important bearing on college admission. Members' third major concern about disappointing parents is also tied to the former concerns since these youths' parents are highly invested in their son's successes. These parents not only passively communicate their high expectations, but represent the single most active helping agents engaged by Elites.

School-based adult personnel rank second, and account for 37% of all mentions of help sources used by the Elites for current problems. This figure is twice as large as any other group's percentage use of school-based sources and is inflated by the Elite's access to and engagement of a team coach who appears to serve in an exclusive and comprehensive helping role to members. Teachers and counselors are also engaged by members, but represent second and third preference, respectively, as helping agents in the school. These findings appear consistent with raters' description of Elites as highly visible and successful in the athletic and academic programs of the high school.

The third outstanding finding is that peers account for only 7% of all mentions of help sources used by Elites, while peers represent at least 30% of the mentions for each of the other subgroups in the study. This is particularly striking in view of members' reputed participation in a cohesive peer group and their shared team memberships. This finding is best accounted for in the following section which reveals that peers do not possess qualities which Elites value in a helping relationship.

Isolates   Problems within the expressive task domain are of great concern to Isolates and reflect members' social isolation. Specifically, they are more worried than are members of other groups about their relations with peers, family members and girls, and deviate most sharply from other group scores in their high concern about "What classmates think of me." A single problem in the instrumental task domain is of greatest concern of all, however: "Managing my time better." In members' detailed accounts of this problem, they express an inability to initiate or complete daily responsibilities, such as school assignments, finding employment and submitting applications to college. For instance, one youth summarized his feelings about the problems of tasks left undone:

> I should be getting out but I don't have the drive. Not motivated I guess. I want to move too, you know. It kinda motivates me a little bit to see them [peers] going . . . I want to go too. It might motivate me for a while. I do care but I just haven't got on it.

These examples, combined with our knowledge of members' social isolation, yield a group portrait of unmotivated, passive individuals.

Isolates' passivity, however, does not extend to their help seeking behavior. Theirs is the most inclusive pattern of choices, revealing an almost even distribution of relationships with all helping agents, including parents, kin, peers, counselors, teachers, employers, and clergymen. Only peers are favored slightly more than others. Thus Isolates' passivity is complemented by a coping style which communicates their dependency on any other persons in the natural environment who can either stimulate them to action or simply provide interpersonal contact and feedback. One of the Isolates' remarks about his inability to complete school assignments illustrates this point:

> Every time I've tried, I get going good for a couple of weeks and then, Bang!, I'm right back where I started from. It goes on and off. When somebody like you talks to me . . . a counselor, my parents or somebody . . . then it sort of motivates me.

It is likely that this bond of passivity and dependence contributes to their peers' rejection of them, and so perpetuates members' social isolation.

Deviants   The portrait composed from the raters' comments about the Deviant subgroup highlighted members' reputed heavy drug use and their tendency to engage in unconventional, even bizarre behavior in school. Within the group, these perceptions are mirrored in two integrative problems which members experience most intensely, relative to the other groups: they feel a need to achieve a greater measure of understanding of themselves and their "hang-ups," and they express concern about their drug involvements. The two problems are interdependent since members feel that their use of drugs may be retarding or compromising their own personal development. One youth expressed this relationship as follows:

> The main reason I started drugs was because at the time, people were telling me that drugs create peace, love, harmony and great insight. You can find your problems. Well, it took me a long time to find out that it wasn't, so I'm just starting back where I was.

Their desire to gain a deeper insight into themselves is, in part, an expression of their felt need to alter those aspects of their behavior which feed peers' stereotype of them as "dopers."

Primary group members, including parents, siblings, and peers, constitute 70% of the mentions of helping sources engaged by Deviants for their problems. No single other category is prominent among the remaining help sources mentioned. In the category of school-based personnel, a single work-study program teacher is mentioned three times and is described by members as unconventional because he reaches out to help both within and outside school.

Outsiders   Relative to the other groups, Outsiders express greatest concern about two problems which reflect their marginal status in their families and their preoccupation with problems of economic self-maintenance in the community: "Getting a job to have enough money" and "Worry about family members." Since two of the members have already left home, one is paying rent at home and all are more highly employed than members of the other groups, decreased contact with home naturally prompts a greater concern about family welfare. Their intense involvement with matters which pertain to supporting themselves in the community also helps to explain their relative anonymity to peers at school and their low relative concern about school performance.

Of all groups, the Outsiders reveal the strongest preference for peer helping sources, who account for 57% of all mentions. The peers who are cited, however, are encountered outside the school setting. The unique relational qualities which characterize these helping transactions are discussed in the following section. Parents rank second in preference as helping resources, receiving 30% of all mentions. Mere contact with parents constitutes help since it reassures members of family well-being.

VALUED QUALITIES OF THE HELPING RELATIONSHIPS

Follow-up interviews were conducted with two members of each of the social subgroups for the purpose of gaining greater insight into the qualities differentiating more from less preferred helping agents. The two youths were selected on the basis of the fit between the pattern of preferences for helping agents which they reported in the first interview and the pattern of preferences which emerged for their group as a whole. It was felt that individuals who approximated their group preference pattern most closely would be in the best position to serve as spokesmen in communicating the bases of these preferences. Thus, each youth was given a "feedback card," which displayed, in categories of high, moderate, and low, the total subgroups' profile of preferences for helping agents. Only those themes appearing in both youths' descriptions of the valued qualities of the most preferred helping agents are presented below.

Elites   Elites prefer helping relationships with expert sources of help who recognize and reinforce their high social status. Particularly, they value helpers whose past experience can be drawn upon in those areas of instrumental tasks which are of greatest concern: their current school performance and future career plans. They do not mention process variables in their accounts— the opportunity to share their feelings and reflect upon their own psychological selves—but instead stress the importance of outcome decisions and problem resolutions which expert sources of advice can provide. Members also prefer helping agents who acknowledge, or even call attention to their "significant" status in the school, which separates them from the mass of students. The coach is one prototype of the ideal help source. He combines authoritative advice in specific task areas with the exclusivity of attention the Elites desire. In the words of one youth:

> My coach has done everything for me—got a job for me, given me advice during football and stuff like that; helped me extra. You can always count on him to give you some pretty good advice. He'll give you both sides but he'll tell you what he thinks is best for you. He knows me, too. I mean that's a different thing. He's seen me in action, I guess.

Parents as help sources, however, are most highly valued and most frequently engaged since they combine expert knowledge with the greatest investment of all persons in their sons' special academic and athletic status.

Teachers and counselors, sources of help potentially available to all students, do not meet members' needs for special attention which reinforces their status. One youth dismissed teachers and counselors because ". . . they've got too many kids to worry about, and the don't really get to know me."

Peer sources of help are strongly rejected, since contemporaries experience precisely the same problems, can therefore not impart expertise and perhaps could harm the youth by offering misleading advice. One youth summed up his opinion of friends as helpers:

> Sometimes they let other things influence them, stuff like that. I'd just rather go to somebody who knows a little bit more about the situation . . . gone through that time and can look back and give you the best advice.

And, according to the second youth:

> Maybe I don't trust them as much. I don't know if I'd want to listen to them as much. Someone your own age—they're not experienced as much.

The matter of trust among peers is especially salient for the Elites since a facade of "machismo" may be required among athletes, inhibiting the disclosure of personal emotional problems which both signify weakness and endanger in-group status.

Isolates   The Isolates do not identify any specific valued qualities among the helpers they prefer, nor do they engage others for outcomes. What they deem most important in a helping relationship are feelings of ease in the partner's company and a sense of security that the partner values their company. Those rare social transactions which contain an element of mutuality are highly prized since Isolates do not participate in cooperative group activities at school. The theme of reciprocity is expressed in one youth's account of an important helping relationship with a peer: "Frank and I exchange ideas and feelings about a lot of problems. I feel more at ease with him than I do with my parents."

Isolates welcome occasions to convene with a peer: such meetings offer a pleasurable break from isolation, as well as an opportunity for realistic social comparison. Peers provide more solid feedback about how members are perceived, while members themselves compare their feelings and responses to events with those of their peers. In the words of one Isolate:

> Mostly from talking to them [peers] I get to understand my problems. Sometimes I don't exactly understand what's going on and by talking to my friends I sort of like analyze myself. It's kinda a funny way of doing it, but it works a lot.

Isolates report that interpersonal problems with girls and parents—problems which members rate of high concern—are the main subjects of these dyadic exchanges.

A second theme drawn from the Isolates' reports of helping relationships is that of "appropriateness." They firmly believe that the problem should be suited to the helper's formal role specialization. Thus, all community-based and school-based adult gatekeepers are deemed inappropriate for addressing personal emotional problems, although they are used for their specialized functions. For example, in reference to his employer, one youth remarked:

> I would be inclined to take some problems to him, but not all. I think that I would trust him to some extent—it would be more like the Principal—I would tend to take more of a work problem to him instead of a personal problem.

In response to a question about approaching counselors and teachers for help with personal problems, the second youth interviewed responded:

> With them it goes back to what I said about the boss and family doctor. They're for school-related problems only. It's their role, and I think that's their place.

Deviants   The Deviants value helping relationships which permit the expression of mutual authenticity. Regardless of the helper's formal role, members engage for help persons who allow the stereotype of the "Doper" to recede, and who take a genuine interest in and appreciate the member's personal identity. The following remarks of one member not only reveal the link between his drug use and his desire to renegotiate his public and private identity, but also suggest that only intimates, not "people in general," are acceptable helping agents:

> I have a hard time being myself around *people in general*, 'cause like, I play a part, and as time progresses, you get tired of the part you're playing, and you try to change, and people act as if they expect you to be your old self . . . the drug-crazed hippy, which I played pretty good.

Congruent with their high concern about obtaining a deeper understanding of themselves is the fact that Deviants prize helping relationships with persons who accept their expression of more idiosyncratic and private feelings. Primary group helpers—close peers and parents—are thus the preferred helping sources. As one youth explained:

> Well, the people who know me really well are really close . . . the others are people you try to put up a front for . . . like a teacher . . . to get a better grade; your kin . . . to make your parents look good; your family doctor . . . just be healthy; a boss . . . you're always kind, precise, and polite around him. These people make me be more an outgoing person, like friendly. But it's kinda like a front.

Neither requirements of helper's formal expertise, experience, status or age are prerequisite to the helping relationships preferred by Deviants. Nor do the formal roles of school- and community-based adult gatekeepers prevent their engagement as personal helpers if they are open and sincere. As an example, one member described the qualities which he feels make the school biology teacher an approachable helping resource:

> I think that I would probably talk to him about anything, [even though] everybody thinks that he's a nut. He's an honest guy . . . he's open about stuff . . . if he feels one way or the other about things he just tells you—he doesn't try to hide anything or put on a show or cover up about anything.

Outsiders   The following description of several friends in the community captures the qualities which the Outsiders value most highly in their preference for helping relationships with peers:

> When I'm around them, I don't feel apprehensive, just relaxed. They make me feel comfortable. We're pretty good friends and none of us would want to do anything to hurt the other person. We've all had hassles with our parents and stuff like that—some a little worse than others.

Outsider's preference for helpers who share their life style and values is partially based upon the fear that others, both peers and adults, who live more conventional lives will use the helping relationship as an opportunity to make negative judgments or to prescribe solutions to problems which demand that Outsiders conform to age-graded norms. Thus, in supplying reasons why teachers and counselors were least preferred sources of help, one Outsider maintained:

> Oh, it just doesn't seem that there would be that much they could do for me . . . the most they could do is tell you to cut it out and that kind of stuff. So, if that's what they're going to say, why bother?

Peers who are on their own and working in the community, however, hold values which are generated from life experiences compatible with members', and are therefore naturally most relevant as helpers. One member described the basis of his willingness to confide in his roommate as follows:

> He's lived and had everything that you shouldn't have had . . . you know, and he's come out of it pretty decent. Any time we want to share a problem I feel open towards him . . . more open than towards other people.

Far from attaching any stigma to the Outsider, friends who have prematurely opted out of traditional home life also provide a substitute for family support and personal warmth. Nevertheless, Outsiders remain ambivalent about preserving their emotional ties to parents since, on the one hand, they express the highest relative concern of all groups about family welfare, yet on the other hand, they must safeguard their own independence from the family.

DISCUSSION

Before offering any firm recommendations for future program design in primary prevention with adolescents, this study or a variant should be replicated on a larger scale and with a strictly representative population of adolescents. Similarly, a group-based case study such as this cannot yield conclusive statements regarding the theoretical properties of informal support systems engaged by adolescents. The purpose of this study has been to generate, not test, hypotheses.

One outstanding pattern in the results which begs for future probing is the fit of each social subgroup's major life problems and preferred qualities of help sources with the group's observed social characteristics. Each group occupies a unique ecological niche within the overall peer social structure of the class. Members' original assignment to these niches and their subsequent tenure is, in part, a function of the labelling process — practiced by school-based peers and adults. Certain values, attitudes, needs, and pressures are unique to each group niche and members experience common emotional and interpersonal stresses. Similarly, each group expresses distinctive preferences for resources in the environment. Some categories of persons are less attractive as helpers because of their cultural distance from members and the accompanying censure they reflect, while others are attractive because of the coincidence of values and the esteem and cultural acceptance they offer. Thus, the cultural environment of each social subgroup mediates both the particular stresses which members experience and their access to and preferences for different helping agents. This hypothesis appears to support the social ecology model of research and theory which examines the reciprocal and dynamic interplay of person and setting variables on the behaviors of persons occupying a given ecological niche. Thus, this hypothesis represents a specific example of the general proposition which asserts the importance of the ecological niche in the organization of behavior:

> ... the understanding of behavior requires systematic study of the characteristics of the environmental pattern defining the ecologic niche of each species and the adaptations required by that environment as well as of response processes (5, p. 48).

Several issues arise in considering the implications of this study for programmatic efforts in primary prevention. First, the study reveals the existence of a natural support system which aids the coping efforts of adolescents in the community. To the degree that these informal helpers are available during the early stages of problem recognition and crystallization, and are accepted as naturally relevant during the problem-solving process, they function as a first line of defense against potential loss of social and emotional equilibrium. As such, their early intervention makes a contribution toward secondary prevention. More important for primary prevention, however, is the fact that repeated occasions of collaborative management of stress generate independent problem-solving skills and the social competence necessary for successful coping with future developmental and situational stressors. There is no implication here that the individual will become autonomous, functioning apart from his personal support community. Rather, we suggest with Erikson (2, 3) that the successful resolution of developmental crises throughout life instills enhanced ego functioning and increased openness to alternative sources of support available in the environment.

Practically, the findings of this study suggest that mental health professionals must re-examine their assumption that community gatekeepers are in need of further education through consultation in mental health helping skills. In fact, helping professionals may risk injury to the process of natural support by replacing intuition and compassion with technique and objectivity. Instead, this study suggests that a close collaboration between professional and lay helper is desirable on account of the benefits which the professional would receive. These benefits would accrue both from more extensive diagnostic consultation with laymen who have been involved in the early pre-referral stages of problem-solving with adolescents, and from directly involving the subculturally appropriate informal helpers in the process of strengthening a fragile or incomplete support system in the adolescent's natural environment.

References

1. COWEN, E. "Social and Community Interventions," *Annual Review of Psychology*, 1973, 24, 423–472.
2. ERIKSON, E. H. *Childhood and Society*. New York: Norton, 1950.
3. ERIKSON, E. H. "Identity and the Life Cycle," *Psychol Issues*, 1959, 1, No. 1.
4. GOTTLIEB, B. H. "Natural Support Systems: An Analysis of Preferred Helping Relationships Among Four Social Subgroups of Adolescent Males," Unpublished Manuscript, 1974.
5. SELLS, S. B. "Ecology and the Science of Psychology," in R. H. Moos and P. M. Insel (Eds.), *Issues in Social Ecology*. Palo Alto, California: National Press Books, 1974, pp. 45–64.

Parental Stimulus for Adolescent Rebellion *

Jack O. Balswick and Clitos Macrides
UNIVERSITY OF GEORGIA AND LANITION GYMNASIUM (CYPRUS)

Abstract
Utilizing the responses of 417 college students to questionnaires, self-defined adolescent rebellion is correlated with perceived parental marital happiness, restrictive-permissiveness of child rearing practices, and division of authority.

From *Adolescence*, 1975, **10**, 253–266. Reprinted by permission of Libra Publishers, Inc.

* We wish to acknowledge our thankfulness to Daniel Hobbs for his most helpful critical reading of the paper.

Adolescent rebellion is found to be the product of a home thought to be patriarchal and unhappy, patriarchal and very restrictive, and patriarchal and very permissive. Whether parents are restrictive or permissive is not as important as the extent of their restrictiveness or permissiveness. A very restrictive home leads to frustration and then to aggression, while a very permissive home leads to frustration, in not knowing what the parental expectations are, which then leads to aggression, in search of norms. Frustration-aggression theory is used to explain how parental stimulus can produce frustration in an adolescent child which can result in the child's aggression.

INTRODUCTION

Research on adolescent rebellion has focused attention on cultural conditions at large. Most of the literature has followed the trend initiated by such pioneer social scientists as Margaret Mead and, later, Kingsley Davis. Mead (1928) was perhaps the first to demonstrate that adolescence *per se* is not necessarily a time of stress and strain, but cultural conditions may make it so. Davis (1940) identified certain "universals" in the parent-child relation (e.g., the age differential between parents and child) which tended to produce conflict. He suggested that cultural variables (e.g., the rate of social change) will determine whether or not the universals produce conflict.

The present paper deviates from the above explanations and suggests that certain structural components *from within* the family may be contributing factors to adolescent rebellion. Although youth in American society may be exposed to the cultural variables discussed above, the nature of the actual parent-child relationship may vary greatly, producing little or no conflict or rebellion.

Although this is an exploratory study, and it is designed more as an attempt toward hypothesis-forming than hypothesis-testing, it is motivated by research which has been conducted within the frustration-aggression hypothesis. A recent summary of the research conducted on the frustration-aggression hypothesis can be seen in Zigler and Child's chapter on "Socialization" in *The Handbook of Social Psychology* (1969). Radke (1946), based on a number of early studies, concluded that parental behavior is a key variable in explaining frustration of the child which results in aggression. Sears (1953) found that frustration itself depends upon such factors as the child's perception of other's behavior, and Berkowitz (1964, 1965) found that the type of frustration-produced-aggression that will occur depends to a large extent upon the kind of stimuli present. Using these studies as a starting point, the parents (or the child's perception of parental behavior) become the stimuli in producing his frustration-aggression level. One of the dynamics of family interaction especially present when the child is a teenager, is parentally induced frustration which leads to the adolescent's aggression. The possibility of heightened frustration-aggression interaction during the parental-adolescent period suggests the fruitfulness of examining the relationship between adolescent rebellion and certain perceived parental conditions. The specific questions with which this study was concerned included the correlation between the extent of a youth self-defined rebellion and 1) perceived parental marital happiness; 2) the restrictiveness or permissiveness of perceived child rearing practices; and 3) perceived division of authority between parents. Another concern was with the possible inter-relationship between each of these variables and the differences which may exist between males and females in regard to each of the above.

METHODOLOGY

This study is based upon the responses to mailed questionnaires of an entire student body of 720 undergraduate students attending a small mid-western liberal arts college. The actual data are drawn from the 417 (59%) returned questionnaires. The characteristics of the sample include an average age of 20 years, 43% male, 57% female, and 95% white and 5% black. The liberal arts college is a church related school which might be considered theo-logically conservative although not predominantly fundamentalistic.

Four scales, consisting of forced category responses to four questions, were used to measure the four major variables. Adolescent rebellion was measured by the following scale: Some teenagers seem to go through a period of stress and strain or rebellion toward parents and other authorities. During this period would you say that you were: Extremely rebellious; Very rebellious; Slightly rebellious; Not rebellious at all. Perceived parental marital happiness was measured by the following scale: Taking all things together; how would you describe your parent's marriage? Very unhappy; Not too happy; Just about average; A little happier than average; Extremely happy.

Perceived parental restrictive/permissive child rearing practices was meas-ured by the following scale: In regard to bringing you up, would you de-scribe your parents' child rearing as: Very restrictive; Slightly restrictive; Just about average; Slightly permissive; Very permissive. Perceived division of authority between parents was measured by the following scale: Taking all things together, how would you describe the division of authority between your mother and your father: Would you say your: Mother had much more authority than your father; Mother had slightly more authority than your father; Mother and father had equal authority; Father had slightly more authority than your mother; Father had much more authority than your mother.

In the initial analysis of the data all of the separate categories within each variable were maintained in cross-tabulating the variables. In collapsing the categories care was taken not to obscure any nonlinear relationships. In con-sidering the relationship between each of the three independent variables and rebellion, the remaining two variables were held constant.

FINDINGS

In the sample as a whole, 14% of the males and 21% of the females replied that they did not go through a period of rebellion, 65% of the males and 56% of the females replied that they had experienced slight rebellion and 21% of the males and 23% of the females replied that they were very rebellious or extremely rebellious.

PARENTAL HAPPINESS AND REBELLION   Table 1 shows that youths who see their parents' marriage as unhappy rather than happy, are more likely to rebel. This relationship holds when sex, rearing practices, and parental

TABLE 1
Parental Happiness and Rebellion*

PARENTAL HAPPINESS**	TOTAL SAMPLE		SEX				REARING PRACTICES						AUTHORITY†			
			Male		Female		Very Restrictive or Very Permissive		Slightly Restrictive or Slightly Permissive		Average		Non-Patriarchal		Patriarchal	
	%	N	%	N	%	N	%	N	%	N	%	N	%	N	%	N
Unhappy	29	(137)	29	(55)	30	(81)	49	(33)	23	(69)	22	(35)	27	(70)	31	(67)
Happy	19	(280)	18	(125)	19	(155)	23	(47)	21	(155)	10	(78)	22	(93)	17	(187)
	χ^2 = 6.06 P < .01		G = .32		G = .27		G = .51		G = .05		G = .44		G = .15		G = .38	

* In this and all following tables, the number in each cell represents the percentages who are rebellious and the number in parenthesis represents the N upon which the percentage is based. "Rebellious" includes the categories "extremely rebellious" and "very rebellious" of the Rebellion Scale. χ^2 is the symbol for Chi Square and G is the symbol for Gamma. As a rule of thumb, two Gammas which differ by at least .20 will be discussed as significantly different. For a discussion of the use of Gamma as the choice for a measurement of Association see Costner (1965).

** In this and all following tables "Happy" includes the categories "a little happier than average," and "extremely happy," while "unhappy" includes "just about average," "not too happy," and "very unhappy."

† In this and all following table Non-Patriarchal includes the categories "mother much more than father" and "mother slightly more than father" and "mother and father had equal authority," while Patriarchal includes "father much more than mother," and "father slightly more than mother."

authority are held constant. However, there is the tendency for rebellion to be associated with the combined conditions of unhappy parental marriage and very restrictive or very permissive rearing practices, and for low rebellion to be associated with the combined conditions of a happy marriage and average restrictive/permissiveness in rearing practices. There is also the tendency for parental happiness and rebellion to be more strongly related where the home is patriarchal.

PARENTAL CHILD REARING PRACTICES AND REBELLION   The child rearing scale measures child rearing on a continuum from very restrictive to very permissive. Table 2 shows that when the five points on this continuum are related to rebellion, the resulting relationship is bimodal rather than linear. Although rebellion is higher where parents are perceived as being very permissive or slightly permissive rather than very restrictive or slightly resrictive, rebellion is higher the more the child rearing practice is in either the permissive or restrictive direction. The data were reorganized into a new ordinal scheme with the three categories of very permissive or restrictive, slightly permissive or restrictive, and about average in restrictive/permissiveness. The logic behind and justification for using the data in this way will be elaborated on in the discussion section.

Table 3 shows that there is a positive relationship between the extremes in child rearing practices and rebellion. Thirty-four percent of those who defined their parents' child rearing as very restrictive or permissive are rebellious, 22% of those who define their parents as slightly restrictive or permissive are rebellious, while only 14% of those who define their parent child rearing as average are rebellious. The relationship continues to hold when sex, parental happiness and parental authority are used as control variables. Females (42%) are more likely to rebel under very restrictive or permissive child rearing practices than are males (23%). Parental authority seems to have a specifying effect upon the positive relationship between extremes in child rearing practices and rebellion; the relationship declines among those who perceive their home as non-patriarchal and is intensified among those who perceive their home as patriarchal.

PARENTAL AUTHORITY AND REBELLION   The relationship between parental authority and rebellion is not linear (See Figure 1). The highest

TABLE 2

Parental Child Rearing Practices for All Five Child Rearing Categories

	PERCENTAGE REBELLION IN TOTAL SAMPLE	
	%	N
Very Restrictive	29	(60)
Slightly Restrictive	19	(142)
About Average	14	(113)
Slightly Permissive	24	(82)
Very Permissive	45	(20)

TABLE 3

Parental Child Rearing Practices and Rebellion

	Total Sample		Sex				Parental Happiness				Parental Authority			
			Male		Female		Unhappy		Happy		Non-Patriarchal		Patriarchal	
	%	N	%	N	%	N	%	N	%	N	%	N	%	N
Very Restrictive or Permissive	34	(80)	23	(31)	42	(48)	49	(33)	23	(47)	30	(30)	36	(50)
Slightly Restrictive or Permissive	22	(224)	24	(103)	20	(121)	23	(69)	21	(155)	25	(88)	20	(136)
Average	14	(113)	13	(46)	15	(67)	22	(35)	10	(78)	18	(45)	12	(68)
	$\chi^2 = 10.47$ $P < .005$		G = .20		G = .40		G = .35		G = .29		G = .20		G = .40	

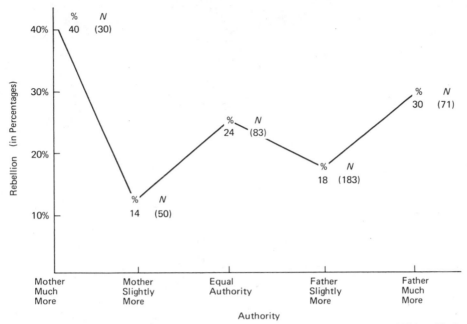

FIGURE 1.   *Parental authority and rebellion: All five authority categories. (This table is presented in graph form so as to illustrate the tri-modal curve in this relationship.)*

amount of rebellion occurs in homes where either the mother or the father is perceived as having much more authority than the other, with a considerably higher percentage where it is the mother who has greater authority. The lowest amount of rebellion occurs in homes where either the mother or the father is seen as having only slightly more authority than the other. An equalitarian marriage relationship tends to be related to a moderate amount of rebellion.

The lack of linear relationship between parental authority and rebellion makes it almost impossible to collapse the authority categories in further analyzing the relationship. Therefore, a choice was made to collapse the categories into traditional patterns of parental authority (patriarchal) and non-traditional patterns (non-patriarchal).

Table 4 demonstrates that parental authority, based upon the patriarchal-non-patriarchal distinction, is not related to rebellion. However, an examination of how the control variables affect this relationship is of interest. In regard to child rearing practices, the relationship between parental authority and rebellion is highest among those who see their parents as moderate in rearing practices, declines among those with slightly restrictive or permissive parents, and becomes a negative relationship among those who feel they have very restrictive or permissive parents. Parental happiness has a similar effect upon the relationship between parental authority and rebellion: Among unhappy parents it is a negative relationship and among happy parents it is a positive relationship. The greatest amount of youth rebellion occurs where the marriage

TABLE 4

Parental Authority and Rebellion: Non-Patriarchal/Patriarchal

| | TOTAL SAMPLE | | SEX | | | | REARING PRACTICES | | | | PARENTAL HAPPINESS | | | | | |
| | | | Males | | Females | | Very Restrictive or Permissive | | Slightly Restrictive or Permissive | | Average | | Unhappy | | Happy | |
	%	N	%	N	%	N	%	N	%	N	%	N	%	N	%	N
Non-Patriarchal	24	(163)	25	(59)	23	(103)	30	(30)	25	(88)	18	(45)	27	(70)	22	(93)
Patriarchal	21	(254)	19	(121)	23	(133)	36	(50)	20	(136)	12	(68)	31	(67)	17	(187)
	$\chi^2 = .53$ NS		$G = .19$		$G = .02$		$G = -.14$		$G = .15$		$G = .24$		$G = -.10$		$G = .14$	

relationship is patriarchal and unhappy, while the least amount of rebellion occurs where the marriage relationship is patriarchal and happy.

DISCUSSION

PARENTAL HAPPINESS   The evidence presented in this paper suggests that parental variables may help to explain youth rebellion. The finding that rebellion is higher in unhappy homes than in happy homes is not surprising, as unhappy homes have been found to be related to juvenile delinquency (Glueck and Glueck, 1950; Monahan, 1957) and mental illness (Nye, 1957). Parental unhappiness may produce frustrations in the youth, resulting in aggression expressed in the form of rebelling. Where parents are perceived as being unhappy in their marital relationship the child is likely to discount them as a desirable source of authority and may even see this as an opportunity to "conquer the divided." A child may find it much easier to justify a defiant attitude toward parents who have not shown themselves to be models of contentment, than he would if his parents were getting along well. Unhappiness undoubtedly involves a certain amount of verbal and/or physical aggression on the part of the parents, thus providing aggression models to the child who comes to be aggressive also. Applicable here would be Bandura and Walters' (1963) modeling theory of aggression, where aggressiveness on the part of the child is seen as an imitation of the aggressiveness on the part of his parents. In the unhappy home the child may find aggression models in the parents and come to aggress also if he observes parental aggression. Also, children of unhappy parents may participate in strong rebellion as a way of expressing their distinctiveness from their unhappy parents.

CHILD REARING PRACTICES   The traditional argument between the restrictive and the permissive school of child rearing may be an over-simplified one. The question is not whether parents are restrictive or permissive, but rather concerns the extent of their restrictiveness or permissiveness. Extremes in either of the two directions tend to be associated with high rebellion. The dynamics of the parent-child relationship can be described as the process of the child moving through time from a state of rather complete dependence upon his parents, to a state of relative independence from his parents. The change from a dependent to an independent relationship may be smoother when parents are moderate in their disciplinary practices. The overly restrictive parent holds the reins too tight upon his children, and does not allow for a gradual development of independence. This tight hold on children creates a situation where independence can come about only by the child initiating a drastic break with his parents. High parental restrictiveness leads to frustration in the child. The frustrated child then becomes aggressive toward his parents and sometimes toward society in general; this aggressiveness is then interpreted as rebellion.

The extremely permissive home may produce a state of confusion for the child, within which the parents are so permissive that the child does not perceive any clearly defined rules for behavior. The extremely permissive parent not only allows the child to make his own decisions, but he may also fail to set the limits for the child's behavior. Dr. Spock has emphasized that he had been greatly misinterpreted by modern parents. Whereas he has argued for greater permissiveness in the sense that a child should be free to begin making his own decisions, he feels that he has been falsely interpreted as proposing that parents not set any limits upon their children. When parents don't clearly state what the rules and limits are, the child has only the option to behave in increasingly extreme ways in an attempt to discover the parental limitations. The brand of permissiveness which may be exemplified by permissive American parents may include a great deal of ambiguity about just how the child is expected to behave. This ambiguity produces behavior which is defined as rebellion, but which in fact may be considered behavior in search of norms.

An alternative interpretation of the relationship between high permissiveness and high rebellion may be that the child of permissive parents interprets this permissiveness as a lack of interest in him. Parents are seen as permissive because they just don't care what the child does. Having reached such a conclusion, the child then rebels as a way of receiving attention from his neglecting parents.

PARENTAL AUTHORITY   The relationship between the division of parental authority and adolescent rebellion is both interesting and confusing. A trimodal relationship develops where rebellion is high at the extremes (where either the father or mother has much authority), low where either parent has moderate authority, and high in an equalitarian home (See Figure 1). Tentatively, it may be suggested that extreme inequality in parental authority may result in a state of confusion for the child as to the nature of the disciplinarian role of the subordinate parent. When authority is perceived as being primarily in the hands of one parent, the child may have problems interacting with both parents as authority figures. Rebellion may then be the best solution to this confused situation. Much authority on the part of one parent may also mean much domination over the child. Such domination, regardless of the tyrant, is still frustrating to the child and may result in aggressiveness. Thus the frustration-aggression hypothesis may also be applied here. A different type of confusion may be experienced in the equalitarian home, where the problem for the child is one of not being able to identify with whom the ultimate authority resides. The situation where least rebellion will occur will then be in the home where one of the parents clearly has a little more authority over the other, but the authority is not so complete as to usurp the authoritative role of the other or to put the other down. Parental authority may be best where one of the parents has enough more authority than the other as to be a "tie breaker" in the decision making process, but who can break the tie in a non-authoritarian way.

Both the extreme highs and extreme lows in adolescent rebellion seem to be produced in a patriarchal home. The two combinations of a patriarchal and unhappy home and patriarchal and very restrictive or permissive home both produce a high rate of rebellion. The lowest amount of rebellion is produced when the home is patriarchal and happy and patriarchal and average in permissiveness. When the home is matriarchal and very restrictive or permissive, rebellion is less than it is when it is patriarchal. When a child aggresses toward his father, it may be tolerated, but when he aggresses toward his mother it will not be tolerated. Children are taught not to aggress toward females in general, and especially not toward *mother* in particular. The child may be in a bind when his mother is in control of the home, for although she may act very restrictively or permissively and thus produce frustration in the child, the child must be gentle toward her.

CONCLUSION

The frustration-aggression hypothesis may be relevant in both very restrictive and very permissive situations. A very restrictive home leads to frustration and then to aggression and to further frustration, etc. A very permissive home leads to frustration, in not knowing what the parental expectations are, which then leads to aggression—in search of norms. But where there are no checks on the aggression, there is then an increased amount of aggression expressed.

This study has been concerned with perceived parental conditions which may contribute to adolescent rebellion. Further research is needed which is based upon more exacting measurements of the major variables. With this suggestion it may be helpful to offer the following tentative hypotheses in conclusion:

1. The lower the parental marital happiness, the greater will be the adolescent rebellion.

2. The greater the parental restrictiveness or permissiveness, the greater will be the adolescent rebellion.

3. The less the parental marital happiness and the greater the father's authority, the greater will be the adolescent rebellion.

4. The greater the parental restrictiveness or permissiveness and the greater the father's authority, the greater will be the adolescent rebellion.

5. The greater the parental marital happiness and the greater the father's authority, the less will be the adolescent rebellion.

6. The less the parental restrictiveness or permissiveness and the greater the father's authority, the less will be the adolescent rebellion.

It could be argued that the hypotheses do not have a clear cut theoretical tie to the frustration-aggression hypothesis. Some researchers may, in fact, wish to use the above hypotheses as part of an alternative theoretical framework in explaining adolescent rebellion. It is hoped that this paper will serve as a challenge to researchers to further explore the possible effects of familial variables upon the phenomena of adolescent rebellion.

References

BANDURA, A. and R. H. WALTERS. *Social Learning and Personality Development.* New York: Holt, Rinehart, and Winston, 1963.

BERKOWITZ, L. "Aggressive Cures in Aggressive Behavior and Hostility Catharsis," *Psychological Review,* 71, 104–122, 1964.

"The Concept of Aggressive Drive: Some Additional Considerations," *Advances in Experimental Social Psychology,* edited by L. Berkowitz. Vol. 2. New York: Academic Press, 301–329, 1965.

COSTNER, H. L. "Criteria for Measures of Association," *American Sociological Review*, 30, 341–353, 1965.

DAVIS, K. "The Sociology of Parent-Youth Conflict," *American Sociological Review*, 2, 523–535, 1940.

GLUECK, S. and E. GLUECK. *Unraveling Juvenile Delinquency*. Cambridge, Mass.: Harvard University Press, 1950.

MEAD, M. *Coming of Age in Samoa*. New York: William Morrow and Co., 1928.

MONAHAN, T. "The Trend in Broken Homes Among Delinquent Children," *Marriage and Family Living*, 362–365, 1957.

NYE, F. I. "Child Adjustment in Broken and in Unhappy Homes," *Marriage and Family Living*, 356–361, 1957.

RADKE, M. "Relation of Parental Authority to Children's Behavior and Attitudes," *University of Minnesota Institute of Child Welfare Monograph*, No. 22, 1946.

SEARS, R. and J. WHITING, V. NOWLIS, and P. SEARS. "Some Childrearing Antecedents of Aggression and Dependency in Young Children," *Genetic Psychology Monograph*, 47, 135–236, 1953.

ZIGLER, E. and I. CHILD. "Socialization," *The Handbook of Social Psychology*, Vol. 3. 450–589, 1969.

Chapter 4
Growth in Self-Direction

BY LAURA S. SMART

The development of the sense of ego identity involves a search for something to which one can be true. *Fidelity* is a virtue that adolescents have to achieve in order to move forward in psychosocial development. ". . . fidelity is that virtue and quality of adolescent ego strength which belongs to man's evolutionary heritage but which—like all basic virtues—can arise only in the interplay of a life stage with the individuals and the social forces of a true community." [21, p. 235]. Bowlby [6, p. 207] describes these phenomena in terms of attachment. During adolescence, as the bonds to parents grow weaker, the individual's attachment behavior is directed not only to other people but to institutions other than the family, such as schools, colleges, and political and religious organizations. Thus, the attachment behavior and resulting fidelity to institutions and groups are expressions of the growing sense of ego identity and contributors to it.

Not only does the young person seek cultural values worthy of her commitment but she also needs a conviction of autonomy, the feeling that she is in charge. Convictions of adequacy and achievement are also basic, for one must have personal resources in order to offer herself in commitment. Adolescence can be viewed

173

through a series of developing goals and values and as attempts to reach the goals and to be true to the values.

Responsibility and Achievement

Boys and girls at every age level from 12 through 20 indicated a strong desire to be self-directing, to establish and work for worthwhile goals, and to be productive [38]. The subjects answered a questionnaire consisting of portrayals of social roles. For example, "Nothing stops Caroline from doing the best she can." After each item, the subject answers two questions: Am I like her (him)? Do I want to be like her? Answers at all ages showed significant interest in work-success, indicated by choice of goals in which initiative and action were involved. The young people showed eagerness to put forth their best efforts and to reach high goals. They were not looking for material rewards but the satisfaction of attaining their own goals and meeting their own standards for achievement. Self concept and self-evaluation are closely associated with these goals. Since the goals were held by the youngest subjects studied, it seems that the desire for a more effective, adequate self is already established by the age of 12 or 13. Erikson's theory is thus confirmed in that the development of a sense of industry and resulting feelings of adequacy are crucial during the elementary school years. The development of responsibility and achievement motivation can be seen as further development of the sense of industry and as essential to the sense of ego identity.

RESPONSIBILITY

A responsible person is one who consistently does his work, contributes his share, and carries his load without being watched or coerced by someone else. In their answers to questions about goals, adolescents showed that they wanted to conform to standards set by home and other institutions at the same time that they wanted to be independent and adequate [38]. A goal called *adequacy—self-assertion,* important to girls over 16 and boys over 17, is illustrated by these items: the people at home treat Steve like a grown man; Janet is seldom shy with a boy. The investigators suggest that a major change in adolescence is the acquisition of social skills that serve goals already established: the internalized values for mastery of the environment.* Thus, the child begins adolescence knowing that he wants to be adequate and to achieve, but he has to learn to do so with and through other people. In indicating that he wants to conform to established standards, he shows that he wants to achieve within the cultural framework. Fair success in so doing

---

* The alert reader may notice some contradiction between this section and the discussion of masculine and feminine identity on pages 140–142. Douvan and Adelson found that masculine identity required assertiveness, achievement, and internalization of standards, whereas feminine identity required interpersonal competence. Perhaps the difference between the two studies lies in the study on values being concerned with all aspects of the development of the self and identity, whereas Douvan and Adelson focused on masculinity and femininity. Perhaps self-assertion is relevant to developing a whole sense of identity but not important to the feminine aspects of it. Perhaps masculine identity does not require achieving within a framework of interpersonal competence, but being a whole person requires some development of feminine characteristics in a man and masculine ones in a woman.

would normally be called *responsibility* by parents and other adults. Responsibility in tenth graders was shown to be positively associated with having companionship with their parents, and negatively associated with parental rejection and neglect [10]. This does not say what caused children to be responsible, or that rejecting, neglectful parents caused irresponsibility. More likely, a certain quality of inter-action between parent and child builds companionship, mutual involvement, and responsibility. High school boys who were low in social responsibility were found to be more interested in participating in youth culture and to have lower per-formance in school, than boys who scored high on social responsibility. The low socially responsible boys were also more likely than the "highs" to be in the general curriculum rather than the college [2]. College-preparatory high school seniors saw themselves as being concerned primarily with intellectual activities and as needing to achieve more than did seniors in the vocational curriculum. Vocational students were thing-oriented rather than people-oriented, and saw success in terms of concrete activities. They were also more socially conforming than college-prep seniors [17].

The meaning of her work to the adolescent probably has a great deal to do with the responsibility she feels and shows. A serious, significant, and demanding job is likely to evoke more responsible effort and more satisfaction than is a simple routine task. Compare lifeguarding with tidying the garage, or making a wedding cake with doing a week's ironing! Paid work outside the home tends to give the youngster a greater feeling of responsibility than does working for her family, since in the former situation, she is judged entirely on her own performance, whereas her

EDWARD C. DEVEREUX

family has to keep her anyway. Responsibility is shown also in school, with friends, in the community, in work and play.

INDEPENDENCE

Independence or self-reliance is a characteristic that can be seen early in life, probably in infancy. From preschool years through adolescence, it is a fairly stable characteristic, more so for girls than boys [44]. The investigators who studied independence defined its opposite, dependency, in terms of passive behavior in the face of obstacles or stress; seeking support, nurturance, and help when under stress; seeking affection and emotional support from female adults; seeking help with specific problems. Dependency in adults was rated on seeking dependent gratifications in choice of an occupation; dependent behavior toward a love object (sweetheart, husband, wife); dependent behavior with parents; dependent behavior with nonparents; withdrawing in face of failure; conflict over dependent behavior. Relating childhood behavior to adult behavior, results showed that girls who were generally dependent as children tended to be dependent adults, but boys often changed during childhood. Probably these findings reflect the pressure that is placed upon boys to become more and more independent as they grow up.

ACHIEVEMENT

Children develop standards of performance for themselves from their parents' expectations of them, depending on the ways in which the parents encourage children, set tasks for them, and make demands upon them. Children doubtless take parents as models for achievement behavior and aspirations, just as they do in other areas.

Success or failure at school contributes also to aspirations. By the time the child reaches adolescence, he has many experiences that affect his desire for excellence, his definition of it, and his expectations as to what he will be able to accomplish. Achievement expectations and life span expectations were compared in two groups of adolescents, one white and upper-middle-class, the other largely black and lower–class [85]. Both groups saw themselves as having lived about a third of their lives, thus underestimating their biological futures. The lower-class boys and girls saw their present achievements representing 43 per cent of their total life's achievements, whereas the other group saw present achievements as 31 per cent of the whole. Ideal achievement scores (what they would like to achieve) were quite similar for the two groups.

Attitudes Related to School Success. Although successful students are more likely to come from middle-class homes than from disadvantaged, some advantaged students do poorly in school and some from poor backgrounds do well. When certain attitudes were explored in over 1,000 grade 10 students, some conditions for success in school were discovered [31]. Successful students from both types of background shared three conditions and in these they differed from the unsuccessful students from both types of background. Successful students believed that it is possible for man to gain control of his environment. This finding is consistent with the importance of children's belief in an internal locus of control, as discussed on page 67. The significance of this attitude for school success is very understandable. A student who believes that a person can control his environment would logically try to gain mastery of his own.

The second significant attitude was the position that it is worthwhile to associate with formal and informal school groups. A student holding this belief would, of course, share interests and activities related to the school. A third important dimension was believing that one's peer group valued education. The student agreed with items such as "Most of your friends will probably go on to college."

An attitude that did not distinguish between successful and unsuccessful students was that education is important. Students generally admitted that education is important. The extent to which they were able to make use of school was apparently much more related to the other three dimensions of attitudes and beliefs. One of the most interesting results of the study was that home background was significant only because of the differences in peer group attitudes. Advantaged students were more convinced than disadvantaged students that their peers valued education highly. The study did not explore all aspects of home background and does not prove that no other differences exist. It only shows that among the dimensions studied, only one difference was significant.

Stability of Achievement Behavior. At the Fels Foundation, 71 subjects were followed from birth to early adulthood [55]. Ratings of achievement behavior at age 10 to 14 showed significant relationships to ratings of adult achievement behavior, particularly in the intellectual sphere. In this area, ratings at 10–14 accounted for at least a quarter of the variation in ratings in adulthood. The true figure may be greater than 25 per cent, since other kinds of observations, interviews, and ratings might reveal more. Even if childhood experience determined as much as half of the adult achievement behavior, there is still room for the adolescent years to be extremely important in the development of achievement motivation.

Parental Influence. When parent–adolescent relationships are studied for insight into achievement behavior, one has to consider that some of the measured results will be caused by past parent–child relationships rather than by only the present situation. With this limitation in mind, let us see what is offered by some research on parents and adolescents. Achievement orientation in adolescents was found to be associated with getting along with parents, never having used illicit drugs, obeying rules willingly, and seeking social acceptability [3]. Adolescents whose parents demanded high achievement were also more likely to deliver it [11].

Achievement motivation is closely related to independence. Especially for economically advantaged girls, too much parental warmth is associated with less achievement. Dominance in relation to peers is associated with purposive behavior in girls [4]. The settings in which parents communicate their expectations make a difference in children's reactions to those expectations. Children tend to develop high levels of aspiration when their parents make appropriate demands at appropriate times, rewarding success liberally, and holding standards of excellence for them while also giving them freedom to work out their own problems in their own ways [80]. Both of these conditions seem to be necessary for high achievement motivation: a demand for achievement, and plenty of opportunities for independent work and decision making. Parental faith is implicit. The youngster and everyone else must realize that if a parent expects his offspring to do well, while giving her autonomy within wide limits, then the parent believes strongly in the child. Such a relationship has meaning for an adolescent's sense of identity, as well as for her desire to excel. She is faced with the problem of believing in herself, her abilities and potential, with the questions of whether she will be able to play the roles in life that she wants to play and of what *are* the roles she would like to play. The demonstrated faith of parents shows her that significant people are sure she can accomplish what she must.

BACKGROUND FACTORS

What kinds of setting produce the types of parent–child relationships that lead to high-achievement motivation? Research shows that culture, class, family size, position in the family, and family structure all have some bearing on the question.

Race Differences. Southern white and black adolescents (ages 14 to 17), of low socioeconomic status, were compared on two dimensions that are related to school success [86]. *Delay of gratification* was tested by offering real choices, such as one candy bar now or a box of candy bars three weeks from today. The white students were more likely to wait three weeks for a larger reward. *Internal versus external control* was assessed by a questionnaire that measured the extent to which the adolescent believed in luck, chance, fate, or powers beyond his control rather than in his own abilities and activities. For example, one question was, "When somebody gets mad at you, do you feel that there is nothing you can do about it?" White students were much more likely than black students to locate the source or control inside themselves. The authors point out that a recent study of preschool children of low socioeconomic status showed no difference between blacks and whites in locus of control. Therefore, they say, significant differences in experience occur during the elementary school years, convincing the black students that they have little control over what happens to them and that it is better to take a small reward now than to trust others to deliver a larger reward promised for later.

Class Differences. Comparisons show the middle class to be most concerned with achievement and most intent upon training its children thus. The successful middle-class parent serves as a model of academic and occupational achievement, thereby actively perpetuating middle-class behavior in his child.

The joint effects of social class and family size were studied for boys only [65]. Although the middle class averaged the highest achievement scores, scores within a given class varied greatly with the sizes of the families. The lowest aspiration levels were seen in large lower-class families, the next lowest in large upper-class families. Medium-sized upper-class families produced about the same aspiration levels as middle-class families.

Position in the Family. Ordinal position makes a difference in achievement orientation. The popular notion is that eldest children are most ambitious. When

During her summer as a camp counselor, this young woman was able to find out whether she wanted to be a teacher.

class and family size are also taken into account, the eldest child does not always show up as the one most interested in achievement, although he often does. When scores of reading ability and achievement motivation were compared for firstborn and later-born high school students, it was found that firstborn children of fathers with at least a high school education scored higher than their later-born siblings, but that this relationship did not hold for children whose fathers had not graduated from high school. Third-born children, however, tended to score lower than their earlier-born siblings regardless of their father's education [24]. When scores of a highly achieving group, National Merit Scholarship examination participants, were compared firstborns of smaller families scored higher, even when parents' educations and family income were controlled [8]. A third study indicated that the highest achievement scores of all belonged to children born into intermediate positions in large families of the upper and middle classes. Eldest children scored high in medium-sized families in the upper and middle class. The youngest child in a small upper- or middle-class family was likely to be just as achievement-oriented as the eldest. Least ambitious of all was the eldest in a large lower-class family. Second place for lack of achievement motivation went to the youngest in a large upper or middle-class family [65].

VOCATIONAL DEVELOPMENT

A major concern of adolescents is the choosing of a vocation and getting established in it. A firm sense of identity requires successful working and producing a role acceptable to the young person and to the adults and peers important to him [69]. In contrast to the situation in simple societies, where there is little choice of occupation, modern youth is faced with a bewildering array of possibilities. Even though his parents may be ready with advice or even urging, the young person feels the necessity for self-direction in choosing his occupation. To be adequate and successful in an acceptable work role is usually a requirement of adulthood. In actually doing adult work, a young person learns to distinguish between what he thinks and hopes he might become, and what he hopes and thinks he could do in order to make a better world [40].

The background for vocational choice lies in the development of the sense of industry, in the stage previous to adolescence, for here is where work skills and attitudes take on great importance. The child identifies with his parents as workers and with older children and with other workers. He begins to learn to organize his time and to put work ahead of play appropriately. He experiments with different vocational roles, observing, learning about them, sometimes choosing one. Thus he shapes his concept of himself as a potential worker [5].

A summer job in construction offers opportunities to explore different kinds of work and to develop valuable skills.

ROBERT J. IZZO

Vocational guidance means helping with both the choosing and the preparation. In a broad sense, all of education is preparation for work roles. The youngster's interaction with his school depends upon many influences, including the important ones of his desire for achievement and his intellectual resources. Educational achievement and vocational preparation depend also on the opportunities offered.

Teenagers profit from opportunities to try out occupational roles in volunteer work or summer jobs. As the photograph on page 179 suggests, working as a camp counselor, for example, gives a young person a chance to know whether she would like to be a professional in child development.

The Schools. The purpose of formal education is to prepare young people for future participation in society. How well this purpose is achieved by the schools has long been a subject of intense debate. Schools are a middle-class institution, and children from lower socioeconomic levels do not come to school as well equipped to function within it as do middle-class children. It has been argued that a major purpose of the schools is custodial, to keep children from the labor market. Middle-class parents have more money with which to support their children through their years of schooling than do lower-class parents, who may need the additional income that their children could earn if they worked [15].

Failing to finish high school, of course, lowers a person's future earning ability. Black youngsters and youngsters from lower socioeconomic levels have been suspended and expelled at higher rates than have white, middle-class children. Very often, the black child is also a child from a poor family. A national study of schoolchildren in all grades reported that more than a million children were suspended from school one or more times during the school year 1972–73 [13]. For black secondary school children, the suspension rate was one out of eight. According to the report, almost two thirds of the suspensions were for "non-dangerous, nonviolent" offenses such as smoking, tardiness, truancy, or cutting in on the lunch line. One black girl was suspended for five days because she did not wear a gym suit, something that she probably could not afford to buy.

Although most suspensions of schoolchildren are for nonviolent acts, vandalism in schools is on the rise. In the United States, school vandalism is estimated to cost about $500 million per year, according to a Senate subcommittee study. Between 1970 and 1973, assaults on teachers rose 77 per cent to 70,000 "serious" assaults, and assaults on students rose 85 per cent [15]. Some observers of the high school scene believe that much of the problem lies in the newly won rights of students, rights that are not accompanied by responsibilities. Students have recently won the right to wear what they want to school. In some cases, courts have reduced the amount of time for suspension set by school authorities "because it was said to be unduly harsh" [32]. School officials have been prevented by the courts from capriciously searching students' lockers. To protect the rights of students, teachers, and administrators alike, it has been suggested that high schools should function as democracies [15, 32]. If students truly had a voice in their daily decisions, they would be less likely to resort to sabotage.

Some schools are experimenting with innovative programs that allow students greater flexibility in choosing courses. Across the country, about 1,000 schools,

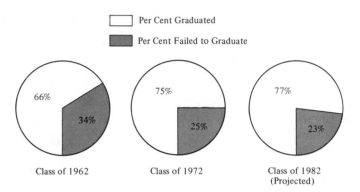

Per Cent Graduated

Per Cent Failed to Graduate

66%

34%

75%

25%

77%

23%

Class of 1962   Class of 1972   Class of 1982
                                              (Projected)

Figure 4-1. Percentages of high school graduates and dropouts for 1962 and 1972, and percentage of dropouts projected for 1982, United States.

SOURCE: C. R. Herron and D. Johnston. There is less dropping out. *New York Times,* August 24, 1975.

about half of which are located in the suburbs have alternative programs. In most alternative schools, teachers discuss rather than lecture. In some alternative programs students pursue their studies outside of the school. They may study the stars at a university observatory, work with computers at a local business, learn baking at the corner bakery, or discuss the Renaissance with a historian in his home—all for academic credit. (Like regular high schools, alternative schools must comply with state academic standards, and the students must work in required subjects such as English and American history [43].)

More students are graduating from high school now than ever before. Figure 4-1 illustrates the percentages of high school graduates and dropouts for 1962 and 1972, as well as the projected figures for 1982. Nonetheless, academic achievement among high school students has been dropping over the past 20 years. A study released by the College Entrance Examination Board shows that from 1957 to 1975, the average of verbal scores dropped from 473 to 434, or 39 points, and mathematical scores dropped from 496 to 472, or 24 points. Between 1974 and 1975, scores dropped an average of 10 points. No reasons for the drop in scores was given, but a number of speculations have been made, including an increase in the number of hours spent watching television, poorer teaching, and a change in the mix of students taking the tests [22].

Opportunities for Education. In the United States and Canada, everyone who wishes to do so can take a college preparatory course in secondary school. Completion of such a course does not grant one automatic entrance to college. The institutions of higher learning apply their own systems of selection. For many years, it has been possible for anyone who could pay, to get into a college, although not necessarily the one of his first choice. The State of California has practiced open access for some time, admitting all high school graduates who desired to a two-year college, all those in the upper third of their high school graduating class to a state college, and those in the upper 12 per cent of their class to a state university [35]. Starting in September 1970, City College of New York (CCNY) not only began to practice open education for all city residents but also provided the education free of cost. The result was an immediate increase of enrollments by about 75 per cent. Half of the new students needed remedial reading and math. However, CCNY's 1970 class of freshmen remained enrolled at rates comparable to freshmen in other colleges throughout the nation. Enrollment of blacks and Puerto Ricans doubled between 1969 and 1975. Students with low high school grade point averages who participated in a special program that provided remedial courses and stipends and free books for poor students did as well academically as students with higher high school averages who did not participate in the program [30]. What CCNY's experiment suggests is that disadvantaged students can succeed in college when they are allowed to attain the skills that middle-class children more easily acquire as they grow up.

Educational opportunities are more available for the middle class than for the poor, and for whites rather than for minority students. Of 18- and 19-year-olds, under 4 per cent of whites and 7 per cent of blacks have an education of eight years or less; 9 per cent of whites and 21 per cent of blacks have one or two years of high school; 73 per cent of whites and 63 per cent of blacks have three or four years of high school; and 13 per cent of whites have one to four years of college, versus 7 per cent of blacks [16]. Children from a family with an income of less than $3,000 per year are one-third less likely to go to college than children from families that earn $15,000 or more per year [30]. Since 1970, some gains have been made, since in that year children from $3,000-per-year families were only a fifth as likely to go to college as children from $15,000-per-year families [35].

The American plan also includes terminal education for those electing it in high school, with preparation for some vocations possible. The junior high school is an American invention designed to accommodate to the variety of physical, intellectual, and emotional growth encountered in people between about 11 and 15. Ideally, the junior high provides a time and a place where the young adolescent can explore vocational identities and find at least the broad outlines of the one that fits, if not the exact form. Guided by teachers and counselors, he tests himself as to interests, talents, and achievements. With self-knowledge in these areas, he is helped to choose the high school course that will lead him to an appropriate work role. Whether the junior high school is fulfilling its obligations or not, some sort of system like this is required by the basic values in American democracy.

The probability of going to college is greater for low-achieving boys than for low-achieving girls, but is the same for high achievers of both sexes [81]. When fathers were associated with academia, their offspring had similar college attendance rates. Birth order is also associated with college opportunities [28].

In recent years, tests that are used as criteria for admission to college have come under attack, for such tests are claimed to be culturally biased. Disadvantaged students as a group perform less well on tests such as SCAT (School and College Ability Test). However, it has been demonstrated that such tests are generally useful predictors of grade-point average in college [12]. What is needed are programs designed to teach disadvantaged students the necessary skills and study habits so that they may compete successfully with their middle-class contemporaries. Such a program is the Job Corps, which in the ten years since its founding has given basic education and job training to disadvantaged youth age 16 to 21. Forty-five per cent of Job Corps trainees were illiterate or poor readers when they entered the program. Trainees get the opportunity to develop behavior patterns that will improve their chances of getting and keeping jobs, and they may earn high school equivalency certificates. While in the program, they get complete medical, dental, and mental health care. Over two thirds of those who complete the program have been placed in jobs [9]. In order to give more disadvantaged and marginal young people an equal access to education, programs such as the Job Corps should be greatly expanded.

Education Required by Various Occupations. Educational level is related to occupational level. As one ascends the occupational scale, more and more years of academic achievement are required, with the professions necessitating education that extends into adulthood. A college education has become almost essential for success in the professions and management occupations. The average professional or technical worker has had more than four years of college. In some jobs, the worker can learn while doing, through an apprenticeship, an in-service training program, or a probationary period after an appropriate amount of formal education. Such jobs include many skilled crafts, salesclerk, policeman, and college professor. For other jobs, especially those where licensing is required, an institutional training period and examination are required before the worker is allowed to operate. Examples of these occupations are hairdresser, optometrist, schoolteacher, and physician. The increasing technological complexity of the modern world creates an increased demand for workers who are competent in using various scientific techniques. Many technicians are trained by the companies who need them, others by educational institutions. In addition to finding out which work roles he wants and which he could achieve, the adolescent has to find and obtain the education necessary for the job. Many young people also face the problem of being educated for jobs that do not exist.

Intellectual Factors. Intelligence as measured by IQ tests is positively related to occupational level, but correlations between intelligence and success on the job are quite low. For high school boys who were not going to college, good predictors of occupation were grade point average and post high school education [34]. The occupations can be arranged in a hierarchy according to average intelligence of those following them, but with each occupation, there is a wide range of intelligence scores, with considerable overlapping between levels [77]. For example, a teacher with a score of 110 scored higher than 10 teachers out of 100, but a lumberjack with a score of 60 scored higher than 10 lumberjacks out of 100. The top 10 per cent of lumberjacks, however, scored higher than the bottom 10 per cent of teachers.

Highly creative adolescents were found to have very different career choices than highly intelligent (high IQ) adolescents [23]. The creatives mentioned significantly more occupations and more unconventional ones. They were also more likely to mention expressive occupations such as writing and dancing. High IQ adolescents chose occupations such as engineering, architecture, science, medicine, law, and teaching. They judged success by conventional standards and planned for careers to conform to what others expected of them. The creatives diverged from stereotyped meanings, rejected the models provided by teachers, and sought careers that did not conform to the expectations of others.

Special Abilities. In addition to intelligence tests, occupational aptitude tests are used for occupational selection. A factor analysis of 59 different tests given to 2,156 subjects yielded these factors as pertinent in the various occupations [64]: verbal meaning, number, manipulation of spatial relations, general intelligence, perception of geometric forms, perception of words and numbers, aiming, accuracy or precision of movement, speed, finger dexterity, manual dexterity, and logic. Vocational guidance includes measuring such abilities and matching the individual to the requirements of the occupation. A given ability can be desirable, undesirable, or neutral for a certain job. Social ability, for example, although not listed in the factors given, is very valuable to an insurance salesman, of indifferent use to a fireman, and possibly distracting to a theoretical physicist.

High school athletes have been found to have higher vocational goals than nonatheletes, and boys on the starting team were more likely to plan to attend college than substitute players [71]. Encouragement by their coaches was seen as an important influence on their aspirations by boys who planned to attend college.

Personality Factors. Good adjustment at 10 and 11 years predicts education and vocational achievement at 17 and 18 [14]. Personality factors contribute to choice of occupation as well as to achievement in the work role selected. Insofar as interests are considered an expression of personality, then a great deal of research has been done in this area. Interest inventories are questionnaires that reveal a pattern of interests. The pattern is then matched to the interest pattern of people engaged in a certain occupation. In the Strong Vocational Interest Test, for example, occupations are grouped by similarity of interest pattern, and the individual's test results are examined to see which group or groups they fit. Thus, a person may find that his pattern fits that of Group IX, consisting of sales manager, real estate salesman, and life insurance salesman. Or he may go into Group II, mathematician, engineer, chemist, physicist. When the results of interest tests are factor-analyzed, these broad types of interest show up as distinct: scientific, linguistic, social, and business [64, p. 86]. Interests in children are quite unstable. Interest patterns increase in permanence as adolescents progress through high school and college. A longitudinal study concludes that the interests characteristic of scientists become crystallized in boys between ages 10 and 14, but that the temperamental pattern basic to the interests becomes established much earlier. Girls who are interested in careers, as contrasted with those who are not, show certain characteristics. The career girls scored higher on scales measuring responsibility, self-control, and achievement. Their career interests began to take shape at or before the age of 14 [79].

Cultural and Family Influences. Vocational plans will be affected by cultural values and by the type of jobs available in the country or region in which the adolescent lives. Economic factors are closely bound up with cultural influences. Children from economically deprived areas have fewer opportunities to learn values and behaviors that will facilitate their success. As much as parents want their children to succeed, they may be unable to help them much if survival is of primary importance. Children from lower socioeconomic groups have lower occupational aspirations [29, 59] and lower academic success [56].

The higher the socioeconomic level of the family, the better are the children's chances of going to college, graduating from college, achieving high-level occupations, and achieving eminence. The reasons for these conditions are complex. They include differences in all sorts of opportunities as well as the personality structure produced by middle- and upper-class families and the values held by these families. Studies of eminence and achievement at high levels usually show a larger-than-chance proportion of firstborns and only children. The same is true in studies of gifted children and children with high IQs [64, 75].

Generally speaking, when parents have high occupational aspirations for their children, the children are more likely to go on to posthigh school education. Parents who had low aspirations for their children were less likely to perceive their children's plans accurately, and appeared to be alienated from their childhood [18]. However, it is important for parents to perceive realistically their children's capabilities when encouraging them to set goals for themselves. When parents of children of low intelligence set high goals, the children become withdrawn and discouraged [4].

Boys who strongly identify with their fathers were found to have higher levels of occupational aspiration, more self-confidence, and greater satisfaction with high school than boys with low father-identification [42]. When the same subjects were studied a year later, 64 per cent of the High Identification males had gone on to some form of higher education, versus 26 per cent of the Lows [41]. Of those boys enrolled in educational programs, 81 per cent of the Highs and 67 per cent of the Lows were in four-year programs. Employed Highs were more likely to work two jobs than employed Lows. When asked about what they would be doing in five years, 42 per cent of the Highs and 13 per cent of the Lows said they would be in professional or managerial positions. Both Highs and Lows were more optimistic about their futures than they had been a year previously, but the optimism of the Lows had increased more. Perhaps this is because the Lows, who had expressed less satisfaction with school than did the Highs, felt better about themselves once they were out of school.

Sex and Cultural Differences in Vocational Goals. Most of the available research on vocations concerns boys and men, a reflection of the general traditional attitude that men's work is more important than women's work. Vocational goals as indications of self-concept were studied in boys and girls from 16 to 19 years of age, in the United States, East and West Germany, Chile, Poland, and Turkey [68]. Samples were equalized for educational level and socioeconomic background. Subjects reported their vocational goals for after graduation. Goals were classified as major professional (such as medicine and architecture), minor professional (such as nursing and photography), clerical-commercial, and undecided. Girls, in comparison with boys, were much more likely to choose minor rather than major professional goals. This sex difference was even more striking in the United States than in other countries. American students set lower goals for themselves than did any of the others measured, and American girls set the lowest goals of all. This finding suggests that American women were still responding to the traditional expectation that girls make a career of domesticity, using jobs outside the home as short-time stopgaps. Although American girls are supposed to have equal opportunities with boys, they did not pick up the option. The authors point out that in many cases, women's so-called emancipation means only adding an outside job to a full-time domestic load, amounting to a new type of double standard.

The cross-cultural findings may be misleading. Although Americans were seen to have lower occupational aspirations than students in the other countries, this may be the result of a difference in samples. Since large numbers of Americans go to college, this group is not very similar to the small elite groups who have access to higher education in other countries. Even though the investigators equated fathers' occupational backgrounds, it is possible that social-class differences were great enough to influence the results.

Sex differences in occupational goals are also influenced by parents. Students and parents in Wisconsin were studied for six years, beginning when the children were in seventh and eighth grade and ending when they were in the twelfth grade [58]. In the seventh and eighth grades, the more intelligent and achieving girls with fewer problems wanted to pursue occupations through which they could become independent. In the ninth and tenth grades, the children became more concerned with work fulfillment, and parents began to stress to their daughters the importance of preparing to become housewives. Boys began to place more emphasis upon using their unique abilities in their work and showed less concern with security.

In grades 10 and 11, boys were more concerned than girls about earning a good income. Girls were more interested in helping others, having time for a family, and working with people. In the eleventh grade, girls correctly perceived that their parents also thought that their earning an income was less important than their using their abilities to work with people. Boys accurately saw their parents as stressing the importance of earning a good income and using their talents. Senior girls were more likely than boys to say that the job they wanted did not require a college education. Workers in dead-end jobs tend to deal with their vocational frustration by giving up hope of advancement and concentrating on developing strong relationships with peers [44a]. Many more women than men have jobs in which little or no advancement is possible. It is likely that many of the parents in the Wisconsin study, perceiving the reality of the marketplace, prepared their daughters to accept the kinds of jobs that they were likely to get. They prepared girls to build happy social relationships instead of encouraging them to be ambitious, assertive, and prepared for advancement.

Student and parent values in the lower years of secondary school were correlated with the values held by seniors. Figure 4-2 illustrates these correlations. For example, seventh- and eighth-grade students who had more family problems were generally the same students who as seniors valued job security.

Vocational Maturity. Based on the idea that growth occurs through solving certain problems at each age, a project called the Career Pattern Study is concerned with finding out what is appropriate vocational behavior at various ages. Selecting

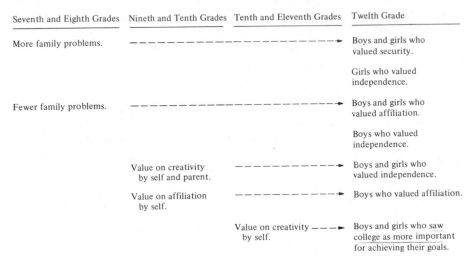

Seventh and Eighth Grades	Nineth and Tenth Grades	Tenth and Eleventh Grades	Twelth Grade
More family problems.	— —▶		Boys and girls who valued security.
			Girls who valued independence.
Fewer family problems.	— —▶		Boys and girls who valued affiliation.
			Boys who valued independence.
	Value on creativity by self and parent.	— — — — — — — — — —▶	Boys and girls who valued independence.
	Value on affiliation by self.	— — — — — — — — —▶	Boys who valued affiliation.
		Value on creativity — — — —▶ by self.	Boys and girls who saw college as more important for achieving their goals.

Figure 4-2.   Correlations across time of values held by high school students and their parents.

SOURCE: P. A. Perrone. A longitudinal study of occupational values in adolescents. *Vocational Guidance Quarterly*, 1973, 116–123.

and preparing for an occupation is one of the essential tasks of adolescents. In order to understand better how this task is achieved, and thus to know better how to help adolescents with it, the investigators started with the handling of the task in early adolescence, using boys entering the ninth grade [74]. They were concerned with the competence of these adolescents to make important decisions about their vocational futures. From analyses of tests and interviews and a factor analysis, the following vocational maturity in the ninth grade was defined. The essence of vocational maturity was *planfulness* shown by looking ahead in preparation for vocational choice. Vocational planfulness was the general factor in the four kinds of behavior that indicated vocational maturity, planning orientation, and taking the long view ahead, the short view ahead, and the intermediate view. Wisdom of choice was not characteristic of boys this age. Almost half the subjects had vocational preferences that were inappropriate for their intelligence levels. Almost half chose vocations that did not agree with their interest patterns as shown on a standard vocational interest test.

Those boys who did express wise preferences, however, were more likely to be among the more successful young men at age 25, as shown by a follow-up study [73]. Other ninth-grade predictors of success at age 25 were concerned with education and vocational choices, acceptance of responsibility for choice and planning, planning itself, consistency of field preferred, parental occupational and educational levels, cultural stimulation, out-of-school activities, and high school grades.

This research shows, then, that at the beginning of adolescence, vocational maturity is an expression of the whole personality rather than a narrow part of it. Preparation for taking adult roles has a broad base. The study also yields evidence that it is unwise to let boys this age make vocational choices that will limit their experience and education, since they tend not to choose appropriately.

Moral Development

Increasing self-direction is possible through the development of moral judgment and moral action. The sense of identity includes a concept of oneself as a moral person, behaving responsibly and acceptably in his own eyes and in the eyes of his fellow men. The adolescent, then, is concerned with what is right and with doing right. Moral knowledge and moral actions are not the same, although both are essentials of morality.

MORAL KNOWLEDGE

As the child interacts with a social and moral environment, he constructs and reconstructs the thought processes with which he thinks about moral issues, comes to decisions, and carries out actions. "These changing structures represent successive transformations of ways of thinking and feeling about the social world, about right and wrong, and about the self in relation to these" [78]. "Moral development involves a continual process of matching a moral view to one's experience of life in a social world" [46]. Because he experiences conflict, the child changes his moral structures in an effort to make them fit with reality as he knows it. Achievement of formal thought and broader experience make possible a more comprehensive kind of thinking about morality. The adolescent can think more objectively than the child, who is more influenced by his own needs and desires. Greater flexibility of thought makes it possible to go beyond the immediate situation to consider many factors that might have a bearing on the question. Therefore, he can judge an act right or wrong or in-between in terms of the intentions and the setting in which it happened, whereas a child is more likely to judge an act in terms of results and to declare it good or bad rather than shaded. An adolescent can accept, understand, and invent flexible rules because he is flexible in thought. His ability to control thought empowers him to hold different aspects of a conflict situation in mind while considering all, and thus to avoid the conflicting statements often produced by younger children.

Adolescent potential for independence in moral thinking (as in all thinking) contrasts with the dependency of the child, who thinks that rules are unchangeable, given by adults or by God, or by some obscure and rigid agent. An adolescent can easily take the role of another. He can understand duty and obligation as based on reciprocal rights and expectations that people have of one another, whereas the childish concept of duty is obedience to a rule or to an adult. Children are likely to believe in an eye-for-an-eye, tooth-for-a-tooth type of justice, in which people must pay for their misdeeds by enduring inevitable punishment given by some authority. Adolescents can grasp a concept of justice based on making amends for misdeeds, repairing and restoring what has been spoiled or taken away by the wrongdoing. They can conceive of individual responsibility, equality before the law, and impartiality in justice [45].

This is not to say that all adolescents think in the most mature ways possible at their age, or that children do not occasionally think on the levels designated as adolescent. Everyone has heard of a little child making an extraordinarily sage moral comment and everyone knows that adolescents (and adults) sometimes think childishly. Furthermore, what is "mature" moral judgment in one cultural milieu may not be so in another. Cross-cultural research has not substantiated that individuals in all cultures go through invariant stages of moral development [50, 70], as is claimed by Kohlberg and others [62]. What is clear is that a young child's moral reasoning is usually less complex than that of an adult or an adolescent.

MORAL BEHAVIOR

Although there is some relationship between moral reasoning and action, people often fail to do what they say is right [50, 53]. Moral behavior depends not only upon cognitive functioning such as role taking, the ability to consider more than one person's viewpoint at a time, but also upon affect or feeling [37, 53]. Hogan [37] suggests that moral behavior is governed by five relatively independent dimensions that emerge gradually as the individual's cognitive processes develop. As the person moves from infancy to adulthood, he encounters an expanding social world that presents him with new situations to be mastered. The infant is concerned with building a sense of trust, and must be nurtured and protected. When he becomes mobile, it is essential for survival that he be able to obey the commands of his caretaker. At this stage, the first of Hogan's five dimensions emerges: the individual becomes aware of rules. Knowledge of rules allows the beginnings of self-control to develop. When a child starts school, he begins to interact with peers in relationships that involve reciprocity; adequate social functioning requires that he take into consideration the viewpoints of others. (Parents and siblings, of course, can facilitate role taking before a child reaches school age.) The second dimension of moral development, role-taking ability (or empathy), enables the child to comply with group expectations and to interact more flexibly with others. The person with role-taking skills is able to consider the implications of his actions for others.

A very young child believes that rules cannot be broken, but older school-age children realize that rules are made by people and can be changed. The third dimension of moral development is the awareness of the changeability of rules. The individual attaches importance to some or most of the rules that exist in her cultural environment, and determines which will be obeyed and under what circumstances. As an adolescent and young adult, the individual in Western culture must establish her own life-style and sense of identity. She is often caught between the expectations of her family, internalized during childhood, and the external demands of the peer and larger culture. The fourth dimension of moral development involves a freedom to deviate from the standards set down by others, peer pressure, and the desire for prestige. And finally, the individual is somewhere along a continuum of preferring to follow patterns of moral behavior established by the culture in which she lives, and preferring to make moral decisions on the basis of intuition and personal ethical codes. Other writers [53] suggest that the choosing of one moral act over another depends upon the individual's motivation and desire for one outcome or another, for example, immediate reward or a more temporally distant one. For instance, an adolescent may be tempted to cheat on an exam for the immediate reward of a higher grade, but decides against it because she believes that cheating is wrong or that in the long run it would work against her.

FAMILY INFLUENCES

As cognitive and social interactions permit continuous reorganizing of moral judgments and moral actions, certain kinds of experiences stand out as particularly significant. Family relationships are, of course, one of the important areas of experience. How do families influence moral development?

Peck and Havighurst were concerned with the family relationships of the boys whose character development was followed and analyzed [57]. Each subject was assigned a character type (which was really a description of his moral judgment and conduct), on the basis of ratings, interviews, and tests. Peck and Havighurst found that some of their subjects remained at immature levels, some showed mixed behavior, typical of two levels, and some reacted fairly consistently at the highest level. Family correlates are given for each of the character types (levels of moral judgment and behavior):

Type 1: The *amoral* person acts largely on impulse, motivated by immediate rewards and punishments. . . . Egocentric, he sees other people as means to ends. He is unsuccessful and ineffectual because of his inability to set realistic goals, to adapt his behavior, and to control his impulses. This type did not occur in pure form in any of the 34 subjects, but was mixed with other kinds of moral behavior.

Amoral adolescents' families were chaotically inconsistent, rejecting the children, giving them neither gratification nor any rules or principles to guide them. With no chance of gaining pleasure through pleasing his parents, the child used impulse gratification. Sometimes he was punished for it, sometimes not. Therefore, he never learned behavior that was acceptable and useful for carrying on in the outside world.

Type 2: The *expedient* person considers other people's welfare and reactions only in order to gain her own ends. She is more successful than the amoral type in understanding other people and hence more successful in gratifying herself through others. She fits in when she has to do so in order to gain her ends, but takes the easiest way in avoiding as many demands as possible. She respects the reward–punishment power of adults and behaves correctly in their presence, as does a three-year-old. She is often tense from suppressing impulses and seeking the human warmth that she cannot find.

Expedient adolescents' families were mostly lenient, giving in ꞌriminate freedom and unthinking, inconsistent approval. One different pattern consistency, high severity, and autocratic control by mistrustful parer. sistency without affection and affection without consistency were equ. effective. The child who had had superficial success at home approach᷍ world sensitive to approval, but placing his own desires above everything Since his parents had neither demanded from him nor controlled him, he did internalize rules, nor did he learn to adapt to other people's points of view.

Level II: The *conforming* person follows rules rather than principles. He plays the role assigned to him by his society and says and does what others want and expect of him. A variation at this stage of development is the *irrational-*

conscientious person, who follows rules compulsively. He does not realize that rules are man-made to serve human purposes, and he follows them without regard for feelings and motivation.

Conforming adolescents' families were largely consistent, autocratic, and severe punishers. Mutual trust existed in some, mutual distrust and disapproval in others. Consistent authoritarianism seemed to be the key factor in producing conforming adolescents. It provided the children with stable behavior patterns that they used unquestioningly and fairly successfully as long as they could remain in a similar community. These adolescents tended to feel positively toward their parents and to like their family life. Irrational-conscientious adolescents' families were severe to extremely severe in their discipline.

Level III: The *rational-altruistic* person is spontaneous, friendly, perceptive, and concerned with the well-being of other people. His impulses are usually in accord with his own principles and with what society approves. He feels little hostility and guilt. This type of person matches Erikson's concept of an individual with firm identity, well-developed intimacy, and a strong sense of generativity. About a quarter of the subjects in the study showed a considerable component of rational-altrustic character.

Rational-altruistic adolescents' families were consistent, strongly trustful, loving, democratic, and lenient. They encouraged their children to make an increasing number of decisions as the children's judgment matured, but reserved the right to decide what they considered necessary for the children. Mature parental love and rational discipline seemed to be interrelated and overlapping. Both appeared to be essential, joint determinants of good character.

Peck and Havighurst found significant relationships between personality and family relationships in four areas: mutual trust and approval, consistency of family life, democratic control, and severity of punishment. They concluded that the child learned to feel and act morally as just the kind of person his mother and father had been in their relationships with him.

Values and the Social Order

The virtue of *fidelity,* a product of the developing sense of ego identity, requires a community to which the young person can be true. The adolescent has to examine his social order, to make sense out of it, to accept or reject, commit himself or withdraw. Cognitive development makes a large contribution to this process, just as it does to the closely allied process of moral development. Information and experiences are processed to produce a transformed view of the family, politics, law, religion, and other institutional aspects of his community. His concept of community is restructured as he moves from a concrete, face-to-face notion to one of a social order. If a child lives in a complex culture, he may alter his concept of community as neighborhood to community as the world. (Not necessarily, though. We knew an 18-year-old ricksha driver in Banaras, a most complex culture, who had never heard of Delhi or Calcutta.)

When cultural values and purposes are clearly stated and strongly held, it is

A young women's band parades on National Day in Peking. When cultural values are clearly stated, as they are in China, adolescents can be expected to experience less uncertainty and ambivalence.

easier for adolescents to commit themselves to their society, thus achieving fidelity. Recent visitors to China report a unanimity of purpose in that society.

POLITICS AND LAW

A child has a concrete concept of his community, country, and government. He cannot imagine an abstract collectivity. An example from a study [36] of 17,000 elementary schoolchildren is the answer of 7-year-old Tommy to the question "What is the government?"

> The government is like the president but he isn't actually a president. The builders, the street makers and all these people work for the government. The sidewalks and streets are the government's property and he lets people walk in them.
>
> He has a moneymaking machine and he makes a lot of money, but he doesn't use it. I think he uses money for decoration—some money is put on necklaces with little things.
>
> . . . Probably he works in the capital, like the President. He does! He lives in Washington. He doesn't live in the White House. He has his own home.
>
> He's the judge of the wildlife service. I sent him a letter about banding birds and he told the wildlife service to send me that pamphlet. . . .

The young child views the president as personal, nurturant, benevolent, and very powerful [36]. He sees his country and language as superior. National symbols, especially the flag and Statue of Liberty, are points of attachment. By the eighth grade, the concept of nation has some abstraction and ideological content. When asked why they were proud to be American, "freedom" and "the right to vote" became frequent answers by eighth graders. Also at this age, our country was seen as part of a larger, organized system of countries. A child's political knowledge is understandably influenced by current events, and his answers to questions reflect the imminence of an election, the shooting of a president or candidate, and the turmoil over a war [61].

Even in early adolescence, between 13 and 15, the child understands government in terms of its concrete agents, such as the police, the mayor, and the president [1]. In later adolescence, he grasps the structure and processes of the community. He comes to realize that the agents of the government are servants of the social order, and that politics involves interactions of citizens and community.

Concepts of law undergo significant transformations during the adolescent years. Adelson and his associates [1] interviewed 120 subjects between 10 and 18 years of age, beginning with the premise that 1,000 people had moved to a Pacific island to build a community. Questions dealt with a wide range of political and legal topics. Answers showed the years from 13 to 15 to be the time when the following important changes occurred:

1. *From a concrete to abstract level of discourse.* When asked, "What is the purpose of laws?" a typical 13-year-old response was, "To keep people from doing things they're not supposed to do, like killing people and like . . . if you're in the city, like speeding in the car and things like that."

   A 15-year-old said, "To keep us safe and free," while an 18-year-old answered, ". . . to set up a standard of behavior for people, for society living together so that they can live peacefully and in harmony with each other."

2. *From a restrictive to a beneficial view of the law.* The examples given also show the change from emphasis on constraint to appreciation of the positive, constructive aspects of law. The younger adolescent thinks in terms of restrictions because he himself is controlled by benign authority at home and at school, and also because he thinks of individual conduct rather than of total community. The older adolescent can conceive of community needs and processes, past, present, and future. Although he realizes that law inhibits for the common good, he sees that law fulfills many social functions.

3. *From an absolute to a functional view of the law.* The younger subjects tended to think that existing laws should be upheld, no matter how involved enforcement was. Adolescents over 15 were more likely to revise an unworkable law, reflecting their increased flexibility of thought.

4. *From concern with outer effects to concern with inner effects.* Younger subjects saw the law in terms of restraining external conduct. When asked what would happen if there were no laws, they suggested pillage, chaos, and the rule of the strong and evil. Older subjects mentioned this sort of result but stressed inner corruption, such as personal confusion and dwindling of moral capacity.

The older adolescents saw the law as a human product, made to serve the social and spiritual good. With formal thought at their disposal, they were able to criticize a proposal from many angles, recognizing many of man's foibles and anticipating future results from one or another course of action. They understood that the law must accommodate competing interests and must balance short-term against long-term effects. Thus does an adolescent come to know his community in the complexity of its political and legal institutions, and on this basis he can and will pledge his fidelity.

Race and Class Differences in Political Views. Views of the political and legal system are affected by the life experiences of the individual. Black adolescents who felt the effects of racial discrimination expressed "less support for the President and the police and reject(ed) a paternalistic, benevolent view of the government" [27]. Knowledge of high school civics apparently increased the political cynicism and lowered the feelings of political power of black adolescents in a rural, poor community in the South [63]. Black adolescents were found to feel less powerful politically, and more alienated from the political system, than white students from the same inner-city high school [51]. Black adolescents, however, are not alone in their feelings of powerlessness. When rural, blue-collar, and white-collar youth were compared, the white-collar youth were found to be "more independent, more alienated from traditional values, more accepting of sexually permissive behavior, and (to feel) less able to affect the world around them" [7].

RELIGION

In developing his sense of identity, the adolescent has important interactions with the religious institution of his culture. He asks, "Who am I?" and "To what and whom can I be true?" His religion answers, "A child of God" and "To God and Jesus" or "To Buddha's teachings" or "To the god of your choice—Shiva, Vishnu, Durga, Sarasvati—as you decide." His church confirms his identity as a child of God through a confirmation ceremony. If the church waits for confirmation until the child has achieved some facility with formal thought, then his asking of questions and pondering on conflicts and issues will make the church pertinent to his developing sense of identity [72, p. 294]. Initiation ceremonies typically take place at puberty, in order to establish an individual as an adult in his own eyes and in the eyes of God and the social order.

Just as increased cognitive and social growth underlie the moral development of adolescence, so they also contribute to religious and philosophical development. The adolescent, in his urge for self-direction, tries to find out for himself the meaning of life. To find his identity involves placing himself in new relationships. What eventually results from a successful search is called by Erikson the sense of integrity [20, pp. 268, 269].

Typical Concepts. Adolescents are intellectually capable of viewing religion abstractly and seeing their own denominations as systems-among-systems. Religious beliefs and practices were explored in the context of personality development in 30 young adolescents who were the subjects of a longitudinal study at the Menninger Foundation [72]. The adolescents had clearer beliefs about Jesus than about God. God was personal and somewhat physical to a third of the subjects and abstract to another third. Moralistic teaching shows in their beliefs about heaven, hell, right, and wrong. Seeing God primarily as lawgiver and judge seems to be related to the young adolescent's being under the control of parents and teachers. This finding is consistent with those of the studies on adolescents' conceptions of law, described previously.

Four religious orientations were distinguished in the Menninger group of adolescents. The largest number were traditional, accepting the forms of the church with little question, integrating it weakly into their lives. The second group was conventional, echoing parents, pastors, and priests, maintaining a childhood orientation. The third group conformed to peers, believing much that was neither traditional nor conventional. The fourth group held beliefs that resulted from their own struggles in coping with the environment. This group led the investigator to the conclusion that vulnerability or openness to stress is an important predisposition to religious experience. As the adolescent tries actively to cope with conflict in solving identity problems, he is likely to recall symbols, myths, and rituals, and to appeal to loyalties larger than his immediate group and to open himself to novelty, mystery, and creative life forces.

In recent years, adolescent participation in religion has been increasing. A 1975 Gallup poll indicated that 55 per cent of American young people had "quite a lot" or "a great deal" of confidence in organized religion, and that 35 per cent usually attended weekend religious services [84]. New forms of Christianity such as the Children of God, old forms of Judaism such as Hassidism, and Eastern religions such as Hinduism and Buddhism are attracting followers. Transcendental Meditation also appears to be gaining popularity, although its followers claim that it is not a religion. It does represent another variation of the new spiritualism that began in the 1960s and continued to grow through the mid-1970s.

DELINQUENTS

Technically, a juvenile delinquent is one whose behavior is brought to the attention of law enforcement agencies because it endangers the juvenile, other individuals, or the community [67]. Thus, identical pieces of behavior may or may not be legally delinquent. Juvenile delinquency may be thought of as a deviancy from the dominant middle-class behavior norms, or it may be seen as an outgrowth of the "undercurrent" of middle-class norms that endorse (or at least do little to discourage) illegal acts such as perjury by high government officials. At the lowest socioeconomic levels, delinquent gang behavior is a product of a culture that values "getting into trouble" and being tough and smart [52]. The excitement of potential danger lends spice to an otherwise dull existence. Belief in luck and fate is strong and planning for the future may be unknown [49]. Desires for belonging and status are answered to some degree by the peer group, although it has been argued that intimate personal relationships are absent from most delinquent gangs, and that gang members generally hold each other in low esteem [19]. Delinquents' perceptions of factors promoting happy, successful living revealed emphasis on dominance, aggression, and exhibition [76]. Nondelinquents put more stress on the value of nurturant, deferent, affiliative behavior.

The traditional sociological perspective on gangs is that they are held together by strong bonds of personal loyalty. However, research evidence suggests that members of delinquent gangs are united against external forces, and that when

BRYAN JONES

the threats are removed, group cohesion splinters. School authorities, police, parents, and other gangs provide rallying points for gang members [19].

Socioeconomic Factors. Although many people think that juvenile delinquency is much more widespread among lower socioeconomic groups than among middle and upper, recent studies indicate that this is not the case. High school students were asked to check delinquent behaviors in which they had engaged at least once. Upper- and middle-class males had committed an average of 7.6 types of delinquent acts, compared with 7.4 for lower-class males. For girls, the corresponding figures were 3.5 and 3.8. The kinds of acts included ranged from truancy to assault and stealing [48].

Delinquent acts of lower-class youngsters are more likely to be recorded by police than are the same acts when committed by middle-class youngsters [19]. Males are more likely to become delinquents than are females. Middle-class girls now engage in a number of delinquent acts that were once regarded as typically masculine [82]. It has been estimated that about 75 per cent of delinquent acts are committed by groups. Rather than being carefully planned, group acts of delinquency are often spontaneous, rarely involving all gang members acting together. Individual members generally attribute to other gang members a greater commitment to delinquency than they themselves feel [19].

Family Influences. Although family problems are associated with delinquency, they are not a sufficient explanation by themselves. Of 246 delinquent boys in court for the first time, two thirds came from "ordinary" families that were intact and without serious, persistent problems. However, the delinquent boys were more likely than a group of working-class nondelinquent boys of the same age to have come from homes that were broken or had problems. In a follow-up study two years later, 25 per cent of the boys from "ordinary families" had become repeat offenders, and 33 per cent of the boys from problem families had reappeared in court [60]. Delinquent girls often report bad relationships with their parents, who are often economically deprived. Many have an image of an adult as a person who is brutal (especially men), ineffectual, vacillating (especially women), "phony," or an anonymous authority [47]. Delinquents who come from middle- and upper-income families may be lacking in care and protection. Needs for dependency, submission, and being cared for were emphasized in the early recollections of delinquent boys and girls [83].

Sometimes delinquency in middle-class children is an attempt, perhaps an unconscious one, by these children to make their parents pay attention to them or to express their dissatisfaction or desperation with school. Runaways usually leave home because of a conflict with parents that may be severe or minor. Some runaways leave home for several days, but others roam around the country for long periods of time. Running away from home has become a national concern. In 1974 the Runaway Youth Act became law, establishing shelters and counseling for runaways, as well as a national toll-free number that handles about a thousand calls per month. The average age of runaways is 16 years old. Thirty-six per cent are male, and 64 per cent are female. The incidence of male runaways is probably underreported [54]. Runaways who had returned home were asked why they had run away. All mentioned problems with parents, school, or both. Relationships with fathers were more difficult for both boys and girls. Seventy-four per cent of the boys and 86 per cent of the girls reported that their lives were "much better" after returning home, and approximately two thirds said that leaving home had been a positive experience [39].

In New York City, prostitution among teenage runaways as young as 14 has become a problem. The girls come from all kinds of families, often broken or unstable ones. Some parents of runaways have told police officers flatly that they do not want their children back [54].

Juvenile shoplifting, a growing problem, has also been studied in relation to parents [78a]. Almost 2,000 teenagers responded to questions concerning their attitudes, behavior, and family relationships. Opposition to shoplifting was found more often in students who had some freedom to spend money but who spent relatively little (less than $3 weekly, rather than $11 to $16), whose parents were the main source of financial advice, who took part in family financial planning and family chores, who were younger and female. The authors believe that the study has the following implications: because family values are transmitted to children, it is worthwhile to support parental efforts in teaching sound values, and to teach parenting practices; parents encourage honesty in children by being honest themselves and by giving children positive discipline and emotional support; parents should teach children financial management and encourage discussions on money and ethical problems. Family studies show personal and marital inadequacy in parents associated with inadequacy in children. For example, delinquent boys are more likely to have emotionally disturbed fathers than are normal boys. An investigation of this question showed 44 per cent of delinquent boys, as contrasted with 18 per cent of a normal group, to have disturbed fathers [26]. A scale of parental behavior revealed significant differences between the parents of a group of normal boys and girls and a group of 81 institutionalized delinquent 12- to 18-year-old boys [66]. The parents of delinquents were more likely to grant extreme autonomy and to provide lax discipline. Delinquent boys' fathers were less positive and less loving, while mothers were more positive and more loving than those of normal youngsters.

If the family is so important an influence, how can one family produce both a delinquent and a civically responsible adolescent? The answer is twofold. Siblings do not have identical experiences with their family, nor with any situation. Siblings are different individuals, different in physical constitution as well as in life experience. A classic [33] study on delinquent and nondelinquent pairs of brothers concludes that the delinquent boy had had little satisfaction from his family relationships, while his brother had had a much more fulfilling family life. The former was likely to feel rejected, unloved, deprived, insecure, blocked, jealous, guilty, and confused. He was often intensely unhappy over family shortcomings, such as lack of harmony and parental mistakes and misconduct.

Physical Factors. Physical constitution has been found to have a bearing on delinquency in boys [11, 25, 26]. Delinquents were more likely to be solid, muscular, closely knit, rather than linear and fragile. The interplay between physical, social, and psychological factors is shown in the series of studies from which this information comes. For example, linear and fragile boys tended to be more sensitive and responsive to the environment than did chubby types, who were more stolid and matter-of-fact. When a linear boy had an emotionally disturbed father, he was more likely to be delinquent than was a chubby boy with an emotionally disturbed father.

Limited moral development, as expressed in delinquency, is the result of a complex of interactions between the individual and the environment. This topic constitutes a whole area of specialized study.

Summary

Fidelity is a virtue developed by the adolescent as he seeks and finds ways of committing himself as a participant in his community. Adolescents want to be self-directing, productive, responsible, and yet cooperative with expectations at home and at school. Achievement within the cultural framework is seen as responsibility by parents and teachers. The assumption of responsibility in adolescence seems to be related to warmth, friendliness, and companionship of the home in which the adolescents grew up. Highly responsible boys did better in school than boys who were judged low in responsibility. Girls tend to maintain about the same level of dependency on others as they grow up, but boys often change, probably because the culture calls for more independence from adolescent and adult males.

Achievement is related to standards and attitudes developed by the adolescent in the various contexts of his life. Success or failure at school influences what the child expects of himself, although what he would like to achieve may be far beyond what he thinks he can actually do. Success in school is related to the child's perceptions of the peer group's evaluation of education. Motivation to achieve is related to the extent to which parents have expected achievement from their children and given them chances to achieve on their own. Cultural background and class position of the family are related to adolescents' measured need for achievement. Democratic, equalitarian families tend to produce children with a high need for achievement. Factors that help to build a strong sense of identity also bring about the building of independence, responsibility, and drive for achievement because of the relationship of the latter characteristics to a sense of identity. Race differences that are significant for achievement motivation include willingness to delay present gratification for future rewards and the belief in internal rather than external control of events.

In North American culture adolescents are expected not only to prepare for a vocation, as is true in all cultures, but to decide from a vast array of vocations for which one to prepare. Although the schools have as their purpose the preparation of young people for future life in society, the quality of education varies widely. Suspensions and vandalism are problems. More students are completing high school, but their achievement scores are dropping. Opportunity for a good education varies widely.

Because some vocations demand education beyond high school, vocational choice and preparation are related to educational achievement and aspirations. Although individuals in any occupation differ widely in intellectual capacity, it is possible to arrange occupations from low to high as to average level of intelligence of people engaged in them.

Intellectual level, therefore, is one of the factors involved in occupational choice. Cognitive style, particularly creativity, is another such factor. Specific abilities are required in differing degrees in various occupations. Not only are specific interests important in occupational success but patterns of interests also have been found to be so related. These patterns of interests are unstable in childhood, but are very stable from late adolescence onward through adulthood.

Family background is related to vocational success, not only because of differences in wealth and prestige but also because of differences in personality of the children. Children are more likely to continue their education beyond high school when their parents have high occupational aspirations for them. Boys who identify highly with their fathers have higher educational and occupational goals than boys who do not identify with their fathers. Often taught thus by their parents, girls tend to have lower occupational aspirations than boys and to be more interested in helping people than in earning a good income.

Many adolescents state vocational choices that are inappropriate for them as to their intelligence level or interest patterns. The earlier a wise choice is made, the more likely the adolescent is to become successful in his vocation in young adulthood. The wisdom of choice can be increased by greater knowledge of vocational possibilities and greater insight into one's own abilities. Adolescents can be helped to achieve both of these by sympathetic guidance from adults.

Moral development proceeds as the child becomes more flexible cognitively and socially, becoming more complex as the child grows up. People do not always do what they say is right. The very young child first becomes aware of rules. Next, she begins to be able to take the role of others. Later, she learns that rules can be changed, and then that she must balance her own needs with family and societal demands. The mature individual is somewhere on a continuum of preferring personal or situation ethics and following the moral dictates of the culture in which she lives. Parents are highly influential in the moral development of their children.

In developing the virtue of fidelity, the adolescent chooses values and makes them his own. The more complex his community, the more opportunities he may have for complex interactions, leading to abstractions in values. As he structures and restructures his concepts of law and politics, he makes value judgments and commitments. He examines and chooses in the field of religion, influenced by the religion of his family and by his education, intelligence, and sex.

Delinquency is not confined to lower-class adolescents, but the delinquent acts of lower-class youngsters are more likely to be recorded. Delinquent acts are more often spontaneous than planned. The bonds that hold delinquent gangs together are probably external rather than internal. The problem of young runaways is increasing. Delinquency is often a cry by the child for help and attention. Parents can influence their children to develop ethical patterns of thought and behavior.

References

1. Adelson, J., B. Green, and R. O'Neil. Growth of the idea of law in adolescence. *Developmental Psychology,* 1969, **1,** 327–332.
2. Askov, W. H., J. C. LaVoie, and R. E. Grinder. Social responsibility and interests in school and youth culture. *Adolescence,* 1975, **10,** 175–186.
3. Baumrind, D. Authoritarian versus authoritative parental control. *Adolescence,* 1968, **3,** 255–272.
4. Baumrind, D. Early socialization and adolescent competence. In S. E. Dragastin and G. Elder, Jr. (eds.). *Adolescence in the life cycle.* Washington, D.C.: Hemisphere, 1975, pp. 117–143.
5. Borow, H. The adolescent in a world of work. In J. F. Adams (ed.). *Understanding adolescence.* Boston: Allyn & Bacon, Inc., 1968, pp. 337–360.
6. Bowlby, J. *Attachment and loss.* vol. I: *Attachment.* London: Hogarth, 1969.
7. Boyd, R. E., J. P. Mockaitis, N. A. Hedges. Socio-political liberalism in three adolescent samples. *Adolescence,* 1973, **8,** 455–462.
8. Breland, H. M. Birth order, family configuration and verbal achievement. *Child Development,* 1974, **45,** 1011–1019.
9. Brennan, P. J. Report on manpower requirements, resources, utilization and training by the U.S. Department of Labor. *Manpower report of the President.* Washington, D.C.: U.S. Government Printing Office, 1975.
10. Bronfenbrenner, U. Some familial antecedents of responsibility and leadership in adolescents. In L. Petrullo and B. M. Bass (eds.). *Leadership and interpersonal behavior.* New York: Holt, 1961, pp. 239–271.
11. Clarke, H. H., and A. L. Olson. Characteristics of 15-year-old boys who demon-

strate various accomplishments or difficulties. *Child Development,* 1965, **36,** 559–567.

12. Cleary, T. A., L. G. Humphreys, S. A. Kendrick, and A. Wesman. Educational uses of tests with disadvantaged students. *American Psychologist,* 1975, **30,** 15–41.

13. Coming to the defense of children. *Carnegie Quarterly,* 1975, **13:**3, 1–4.

14. Crites, J. O., and I. J. Semlar. Adjustment, educational achievement and vocational maturity as dimensions of development in adolescence. *Journal of Consulting Psychology,* 1967, **15,** 489–496.

15. DeCecco, J. P., and A. K. Richards. Civil war in the high schools. *Psychology Today,* 1975, November, 51–56.

16. DeLury, G. E. *1974 World Almanac,* New York, Doubleday & Company, Inc., 1974.

17. Dittenhafer, C. A. Students' perceptions of personality needs and environmental press as a function of program separation. *Journal of Vocational Behavior,* 1974, **4,** 155–172.

18. Dolem, A. A. Aspirations of blacks and whites for their children. *Vocational Guidance Quarterly,* 1973, **22,** 24–31.

19. Empey, L. T. Delinquency theory and recent research. In R. E. Grinder, (ed.). *Studies in adolescence.* New York: Macmillan Publishing Co., Inc., 1975.

20. Erikson, E. H. *Childhood and society.* New York: W. W. Norton, & Company, Inc., 1963.

21. Erikson, E. H. *Identity: Youth and crisis.* New York: W. W. Norton, & Company, 1968.

22. Fiske, E. B. College entry test scores drop sharply. *New York Times,* September 7, 1975.

23. Getzels, J. W., and P. W. Jackson. *Creativity and intelligence.* New York: John Wiley, & Sons, Inc., 1962.

24. Glass, D. C., J. Neulinger, and O. G. Brim. Birth order, verbal intelligence, and educational aspiration. *Child Development,* 1974, **45,** 807–811.

25. Glueck, S., and E. Glueck. *Physique and delinquency.* New York: Harper & Row, Publishers, Inc., 1956.

26. Glueck, S., and E. Glueck. *Family environment and delinquency.* Boston: Houghton Mifflin Company, 1962.

27. Greenberg, cited in S. Long. Sociopolitical antecedents of political alienation among black and white adolescents: Social deprivation and/or political reality? Paper presented at the Annual Meeting of the American Sociological Association, San Francisco, 1975.

28. Greene, R. L. and J. R. Clark. Birth order and college attendance in a cross-cultural setting. *Journal of Social Psychology,* 1968, **75,** 289–290.

29. Haller, A. O., L. B. Otto, R. F. Meier, and G. W. Ohlendorf. Level of occupational aspiration: An empirical analysis. *American Sociological Review,* 1974, **39,** 113–121.

30. Harrington, M. Keep open admissions open. *New York Times Magazine,* November 2, 1975.

31. Harrison, F. I. Relationship between home background, school success, and adolescent attitudes. *Merrill-Palmer Quarterly,* 1968, **14,** 331–334.

32. Hartman, S. G. Students' rights and the school administration. *Thresholds in Secondary Education,* 1975, **1:**1, 28–31.

33. Healy, W., and A. F. Bronner. *New light on delinquency and its treatment.* New Haven: Yale University Press, 1936.

34. Heath, B. R. G., and R. W. Strowing. Predicting occupational status for non-college-bound males. *Personnel Guidance Journal,* 1967, **14,** 331–334.
35. Hechinger, F. Taking the politics out of open access. *New York Times,* March 15, 1970.
36. Hess, R. D., and J. V. Torney. *The development of political attitudes in children.* Chicago: Aldine Publishing Co., 1967.
37. Hogan, R. The structure of moral character and the explanation of moral action. *Journal of Youth and Adolescence,* 1975, **4,** 1–15.
38. Horrocks, J. E., and S. A. Weinberg. Psychological needs and their development during adolescence. *Journal of Psychology,* 1970, **74,** 51–71.
39. Howell, M. C., E. B. Emmons, and D. A. Franx. Reminiscences of runaway adolescents. *American Journal of Orthopsychiatry,* 1973, **43,** 840–853.
40. Inhelder, B., and J. Piaget. *The growth of logical thinking from childhood to adolescence.* New York: Basic Books, Inc., 1958.
41. Jackson, R. M., and N. M. Meara. Father identification, achievement, and occupational behavior of rural youth: One year follow-up. *Journal of Vocational Behavior,* 1974, **4,** 349–356.
42. Jackson, R. M., N. M. Meara, and M. Arora. Father identification, achievement and occupational behavior of rural youth. *Journal of Vocational Behavior,* 1974, **4,** 85–96.
43. Johnston, D. Made-to-order high schools. *New York Times,* August 31, 1975.
44. Kagan, J., and H. A. Moss. The stability of passive and dependent behavior from childhood through adulthood. *Child Development,* 1960, **31,** 577–591.
44a. Kanter, R. M. Why bosses turn bitchy. *Psychology Today,* 1976, **9:**12, 56-ff.
45. Kohlberg, L. Moral development and identification. In H. W. Stevenson (ed.). *Child psychology,* The Sixty-second Yearbook of the National Society for the Study of Education. Chicago: University of Chicago Press, 1963, pp. 277–332.
46. Kohlberg, L., and R. Kramer. Continuities and discontinuities in childhood and adult moral development. *Human Development,* 1969, **12,** 93–120.
47. Konopka, G. *The adolescent girl in conflict.* Englewood Cliffs, N.J.: Prentice-Hall, Inc., 1967.
48. Kratcoski, P. E., and J. E. Kratcoski. Changing patterns in the delinquent activities of boys and girls: A self-reported delinquency analysis. *Adolescence,* 1975, **37,** 83–91.
49. Krisberg, B. Gang youth and hustling: The psychology of survival. *Issues in Criminology,* 1974, **9,** 115–131.
50. Kurtines, W., and E. B. Grief. The development of moral thought: review and evaluation of Kohlberg's approach. *Psychological Bulletin,* 1974, **81,** 453–470.
51. Long, S. Sociopolitical antecedents of political alienation among black and white adolescents: Social deprivation and/or political reality? Paper presented at the Annual Meeting of the American Sociological Association, San Francisco, 1975.
52. Miller, W. B. Lower-class culture as a generating milieu of gang delinquency. In A. E. Winder and D. L. Angus (eds.). *Adolescence: Contemporary studies.* New York: American Book Company, 1968.
53. Mischel, W., and H. N. Mischel. Moral behavior from a cognitive social learning viewpoint. Paper presented at meetings of the Society for Research in Child Development, Denver, 1975.
54. Morgan, T. Little ladies of the night. *New York Times Magazine,* November 23, 1975, 34–50.
55. Moss, H. A., and J. Kagan. Stability of achievement and recognition-seeking be-

haviors from early childhood through adulthood. *Journal of Abnormal & Social Psychology,* 1961, **62,** 504–513.

56. Page, W. F. Self-esteem and internal *vs.* external control among black youth in a summer aviation program. *Journal of Psychology,* 1975, **89,** 307–311.

57. Peck, R. F., and R. J. Havighurst. *The psychology of character development.* New York: John Wiley & Sons, Inc., 1960.

58. Perrone, P. A. A longitudinal study of occupational values in adolescents. *Vocational Guidance Quarterly,* 1973, **23,** 116–123.

59. Picou, J. S., and E. W. Curry. Structural, interpersonal, and behavioral correlates of female adolescents' occupational choices. *Adolescence,* 1973, **8,** 421–432.

60. Power, M. J., P. M. Ash, E. Schoenberg, and E. C. Sirey. Delinquency and the family. *British Journal of Social Work,* 1974, **4,** 13–38.

61. Rebelsky, F., C. Conover, and P. Chafetz. The development of political attitudes in young children. *Journal of Psychology,* 1969, **73,** 141–146.

62. Rest, J. R., E. Turiel, and L. Kohlberg. Level of moral development as a determinant of preference and comprehension of moral judgements made by others. *Journal of Personality,* 1969, **37,** 225–252.

63. Rodgers, H. R., Jr. Toward explanation of the political efficiency and political cynicism of black adolescents: An exploratory study. *American Journal of Political Science,* 1974, **18,** 257–282.

64. Roe, A. *The psychology of occupations.* New York: John Wiley & Sons, Inc., 1956.

65. Rosen, B. C. Family structure and achievement motivation. *American Sociological Review,* 1961, **26,** 574–585.

66. Schaefer, E. S. Children's reports of parental behavior: An inventory. *Child Development,* 1965, **36,** 414–424.

67. Sebald, H. *Adolescence: A sociological analysis.* New York: Appleton-Century-Crofts, 1968.

68. Seward, G. H., and R. C. Williamson. A cross-national study of adolescent professional goals. *Human Development,* 1969, **12,** 248–254.

69. Shacter, B. Identity crisis and occupational processes: An intensive exploratory study of emotionally disturbed male adolescents. *Child Welfare,* 1968, **47,** 26–37.

70. Simpson, E. L. Moral development research: a case study of scientific cultural bias. *Human Development,* 1974, **17,** 81–106.

71. Snyder, E. E. Athletic team involvement, educational plans, and the coach-player relationship. *Adolescence,* 1975, **10,** 191–200.

72. Stewart, C. W. *Adolescent religion.* New York: Abingdon Press, 1967.

73. Super, D. E. Ninth-grade vocational maturity and other predictors of career behavior and occupational criteria at age 25. Paper presented at the meeting of the American Psychological Association, August 30, 1963.

74. Super, D. E., and P. L. Overstreet. *The vocational maturity of ninth-grade boys.* New York: Columbia University Press, 1960.

75. Taft, R. A note on the characteristics of the members of MENSA, a potential subject pool. *Journal of Social Psychology,* 1971, **83,** 107–111.

76. Thompson, G. G., and E. F. Gardner. Adolescents' perceptions of happy-successful living. *Journal of Genetic Psychology,* 1969, **115,** 107–120.

77. Thorndike, R. L., and E. Hagen. *Measurement and evaluation in psychology and education.* New York: John Wiley & Sons, Inc., 1961.

78. Turiel, E. Developmental processes in the child's moral thinking. In P. H. Mussen, J. Langer, and M. Covington (eds.). *Trends and issues in developmental psychology.* New York: Holt, Rinehart and Winston, Inc., 1969, pp. 93–131.

78a. Turner, J. and H. Potter. Teenage shoplifting. *Journal of Home Economics,* 1976, **68:**3, 24–26.

79. Tyler, L. E. The antecedents of two varieties of vocational interests. *Genetic Psychology Monographs,* 1964, **70,** 177–227.

80. Veroff, J. Theoretical background for studying the origins of human motivational dispositions. *Merrill-Palmer Quarterly,* 1965, **11,** 3–18.

81. Werts, C. E. A comparison of male vs. female college attendance probabilities. *Sociology of Education,* 1968, **41,** 103–110.

82. Wise, N. Juvenile delinquency among middle-class girls. In E. Vaz, (ed.). *Middle class juvenile delinquency.* New York, Harper & Row Publishers, Inc., 1967.

83. Wolman, R. N. Early recollections and the perception of others: A study of delinquent adolescents. *Journal of Genetic Psychology,* 1970, **116,** 157–163.

84. Woodward, K., and E. Woodward. Why are teens turning to religion? *Seventeen,* July, 1975, 96, 97+.

85. Zelen, S. L., and G. J. Zelen. Life-span expectations and achievement expectancies of underprivileged and middle-class adolescents. *Journal of Social Psychology,* 1970, **80,** 111–112.

86. Zytkoskee, A., B. R. Strickland, and J. Watson. Delay of gratification and internal versus external control among adolescents of low socioeconomic status: *Developmental Psychology,* 1971, **4,** 93–98.

Readings in
Growth in Self-Direction

This chapter is concerned with the adolescent's control of his own life. Significant topics include moral thought and behavior, beliefs about source of power and influence, planning, and the ability to influence society as well as oneself.

Recent literature on moral development abounds in cognitive interpretations, or how and what children think about moral questions. Another line of inquiry yields information on altruistic behavior, the motivations behind this behavior, and the circumstances under which children share or help. In his article, "Legal Socialization," Robert Hogan pulls together many different threads of thought. He provides an account of moral development that integrates cognitive and motivational sources of morality, and acknowledges the historical sources of his ideas. Furthermore, Hogan draws upon the new ethological views of human beings as having inherited potential for cooperative social behavior that has survival value for the group.

Following a comprehensive study on United States high school students, Amos Handel investigated the relationships of certain attitudes, beliefs, and aspirations to cognitive functioning in Israeli students. Locus of control, self-concept, and educational aspiration were found to be more predictive of achievement and intelligence than were socioeconomic, home, and parental education measures. This study and the United States studies suggest that the particular salience of each measure may vary with the ethnic or socioeconomic group studied.

Legal Socialization

Robert Hogan
THE JOHNS HOPKINS UNIVERSITY

By human goodness is meant not fineness of physique, but a right condition of the psyche. That being so, it is evident that the statesman ought to have some inkling of psychology.

Aristotle, *The Nichomachean Ethics*

Reprinted by permission of the publisher, from *Psychology and the Law* by Battelle Memorial Institute (Lexington, Mass.: Lexington Books, D.C. Heath and Company, 1976).

I. AN OVERVIEW OF LEGAL SOCIALIZATION

As the foregoing quotation suggests, Aristotle thought there was a natural relationship between law and psychology. The two disciplines are most clearly joined in what psychologists call the socialization process. The *Oxford English Dictionary* defines the verb "to socialize" as "to render social, to make fit for living in society." As used by social psychologists, socialization refers to those events that cause people to develop their particular (and usually favorable) orientations to the rules, values, and customs of their society. Legal socialization, then, is concerned with the development of people's attitudes and behaviors with regard to a particular set of social rules, the manifest law.

Since the mid-1950's social psychologists have become increasingly interested in legal socialization. Their writing on this topic can be divided into two broad classes depending on whether it is concerned with content or process. The content literature describes children's attitudes toward the law at various age levels. Adelson, Green, and O'Neil (1969), Gallatin and Adelson (1971), Hess and Torney (1968), and Tapp and Kohlberg (1971) have made important contributions to this topic. It is a rather extensive literature, difficult to summarize briefly, but Adelson et al.'s findings convey the flavor, i.e., over time children are increasingly able to think in terms of legal principles, to see law in a relativistic, pragmatic, utilitarian way as an instrument for achieving social ends.

There are two principle process theories of legal socialization. The first, outlined by Hess and Torney originally in the context of political socialization, assumes four different processes underlying the manner in which children orient themselves to the legal system:

(a) The Accumulation model describes legal socialization as a process wherein children steadily acquire over time units of knowledge about the law; the Accumulation model explains the contribution of the school system to legal socialization.

(b) The Interpersonal Transfer model holds that a child transfers to authority figures (policemen, judges, etc.) attitudes and behavior developed *vis à vis* its parents; this model is used to explain the emotional loading of a child's relationship to authority.

(c) The Identification model describes legal socialization in terms of a child directly imitating adult attitudes toward some aspect of the law rather than transferring their attitudes from an earlier object; this model would explain such phenomena as a child's attitude toward capital punishment.

(d) The Cognitive-Developmental model maintains that a child's conception of the law is modified by its stage of intellectual development; this model is primarily useful for explaining how a child develops complex and abstract legal ideas such as distributive justice and natural rights.

The second process theory of legal socialization, described in detail by Tapp and Levine (1974) and Tapp and Kohlberg (1971), is probably the best known view of this subject. Here legal socialization is equated with the development of legal reasoning (defined in terms of how laws are justified); this reasoning is seen as evolving through three levels. At the preconventional level, legal reasoning is grounded in physical fear of authority and deference to power. At the second or law maintenance level, laws are justified in terms of their ability to regulate society. Level three is called post-conventional; it is a "law-creating, legislative perspective" wherein laws are justified in terms of certain abstract and personally defined conceptions of justice. This second process theory is primarily concerned with the development of conscious, publicly stated attitudes toward the law; as such it is a very "rational" model: ". . . the ultimate appeal of a cognitive-developmental explanation of legal thought is its emphasis on rationality and its refusal to accept the preeminence of irrationality" (Tapp & Levine, 1974, p. 11).

These two process theories of legal socialization were imported from other (related) fields—Hess and Torney are students of political socialization, the Tapp and Kohlberg model comes from moral development—and this is no accident. Only content studies of legal socialization contain subject matter specific to the field. Process theories necessarily belong to the study of socialization broadly defined, and they take *legal* socialization as a special case.

The process models discussed above are important contributions to the study of legal socialization and they have stimulated some very useful research. At the same time, however, they tend to foster a serious misconception—i.e., that a child's consciousness of rules is important in itself, that its actual behavior with regard to these rules is irrelevant or at least not very important. Process research consists almost exclusively of inquiring about children's conscious attitudes toward the law, or of asking them to comment on hypothetical legal dilemmas and situations. But this resarch repeatedly demonstrates that even fairly young children distinguish between what they think they should do or say in a situation, and what they actually would do or say (cf. Zellman and Sears, 1971, p. 119). That children can do this points up the importance of Ichheiser's (1970) distinction between "views in principle" and "views in fact." As Ichheiser notes, views in principle are those we have about social and legal issues in general, and they have no serious implications for our actions; they reveal only how we think we would or should act in certain hypothetical situations. In contrast with our views in principle, our views in fact actually determine our actions. The problem is that most people don't know what their views in fact actually are, and when asked, they typically state their views in principle. The point is that to the degree that legal socialization research studies only children's theoretical legal judgments, it is sampling their views in principle and is studying the social psychological equivalent of phlogiston.

There is a second misconception fostered by this research. The rationalist view that motivates it—the view that people's conscious opinions and judgments are the cause (or at least a major determinant) of their actions —represents what Freud, Jung, and William James called the intellectualist fallacy (cf. McDougall, 1908; p. 323; Rawls, 1971, p. 470). The problem is that once we know a person can state a rule or legal principle, why should we assume that person will follow it? Similarly, this rationalism accounts for the fact that these models contain no reference to the moral passions, no mention of guilt, remorse, and painful moral introspection, no description of man's irrational sense of honor; they seem unconcerned with the kinds of conflicts between private belief and respect for public authority that can cause one to resign from high public office, or push one to the edge of madness and despair. We have instead tepid accounts of how children's theoretical legal attitudes change over time.

II. AN ALTERNATIVE MODEL OF LEGAL SOCIALIZATION

In a very influential analysis, Kelman (1961) identified three sets of reasons for following a socially defined rule, three types if you will of legal socialization. The first set of reasons, labeled *compliance*, results in relatively superficial rule observance. Compliance occurs when one follows a rule with the hope of gaining a favorable reaction from certain others. Here rule observance is a function of the degree to which one is observed by the relevant others. In the second case, which Kelman calls *identification*, one follows a rule in order to preserve a social relationship that is personally rewarding, a relationship that enhances one's feelings of self-esteem. If a person finds a particular relationship satisfying he will tend to act in accordance with the expectations of the others with whom he is involved, and these expectations coincidentally will reflect the norms and rules of the group. Identification is similar to compliance in that the rules aren't seen as intrinsically worthwhile; it differs from compliance in that the person actually believes in the norms and rules that he adopts. Moreover, the person will follow these rules in private as long as the role relationship remains satisfying.

Kelman's third type of rule compliance is called *internalization*. It occurs when a law is seen as congruent with a person's own value system. In such cases the law is assimilated effortlessly to a person's character structure and it is thereafter followed and defended in an unambivalent, almost unconscious manner. Kelman emphasizes that internalization is not necessarily or even primarily a rational process. Laws are internalized essentially without regard for their logical consistency with one's existing values, and they are subsequently observed whether or not one is being watched and regardless of the wishes of one's friends and associates.

Only when laws have been internalized in Kelman's sense can legal socialization be considered complete. The next question is, What social experiences and development processes produce an internalized orientation to the law?

In the remainder of this paper I will describe a model of legal socialization that focuses on the processes underlying internalization of the law. Like the Tapp and Kohlberg theory described earlier, this model was initially derived from the study of moral development. Before moving into the details of the model itself, I should describe the assumptions on which it is based—the model assumes that beyond his survival requirements man needs social interaction, predictability and order, and that his cultural and legal systems reflect these needs.

Three separate lines of research support these assumptions. For example, recent work in anthropology suggests that for the major portion of his time on earth man lived in small hunting groups and seemed largely concerned with killing game and members of competing groups as efficiently as possible. Individual survival depended on the quality of the group rather than the talent of particular members; efficient social organization (defined in terms of laws, language, leadership structure, etc.) rather than brain size promoted man's survival and ultimately his evolutionary success. This line of reasoning suggests, then, that man has a deep organic need for his culture, and that legal systems are not arbitrary accretions of history continually threatened with obsolescence. Rather, part of what it means to be human is to have a system of law.

A second line of research, ably summarized by Bowlby (1969), suggests that children (and people in general) require social interaction with preferred others on a predictable basis. Conversely, they fear unpredictability and isolation. (In man's evolutionary past he was most vulnerable when alone and in a strange environment.) People seem happiest in the company of familiar companions in a predictable environment; infants in particular become severely disturbed—in some cases even die—when these requirements aren't met.

A third line of research, conducted by my colleagues at Johns Hopkins, points to the conclusion that children need social interaction (probably from birth), and they rapidly develop (i.e., by age $3\frac{1}{2}$) a considerable range of conventional, rule-governed means for carrying out this interaction. Moreover, the rules that structure their interaction often become so important that many small children stop playing rather than allow the rules to be broken—e.g., when playing with girls many little boys will quit rather than be "Mommy."

Restating the main point, three lines of research suggest that man needs social interaction on a predictable and orderly basis, and that his cultural and legal systems reflect these needs. In brief, we have the image of man as a rule-formulating and rule-following animal, and these rule-oriented tendencies reflect human biology and promote human survival. With this image in mind we can now turn to a discussion of how internalized attitudes toward the law develop.

Starting from an initial unsocialized state, internalized compliance with legal and social rules seems to pass through three forms or levels; the attainment of each level is precipitated by changes in a child's life circumstances. The first is characterized by *attunement to rules*; the second is marked by *sensitivity to social expectations and concern for the well-being of others*; the third is defined by *ideological maturity*. As a graduate student I came to these three levels from a consideration of what counts as an adequate explanation of social conduct. I have subsequently discovered that at least three distinguished writers have proposed the same stages, although arriving at them from very different perspectives. Emile Durkheim (1961) described a person's integration into his social groups as passing through three stages. The first is defined by a sense of loyalty and duty to the rules of the group; the second is achieved by adopting impersonal, group-defined goals for one's actions; the third is reached by a conscious and rational understanding of the group's purposes. William McDougall (1908) described moral development in terms of three stages. In the first, one's conduct is regulated by fear of punishment; in the second, conduct is governed by social praise and blame; and in the third, one's conduct and sense of self-worth depend on the maintenance of certain abstract moral principles.

Rawls (1971) elaborates his discussion of a theory of justice by describing moral development in terms of three stages that he calls the ethics of authority, the ethics of association, and the ethics of principle. The parallels between Rawls' views and those presented below are obvious and extensive.

A. ATTUNEMENT TO RULES

Among the many problems confronting a very young child, two stand out—procuring care and attention from adult caretakers, and making sense out of the social world that surrounds it. For the social scientist a key problem is to explain why the initially amoral infant would allow itself to be guided by adult rules. This is a puzzle because, as Rawls (1971) notes, "The child's having a morality of authority [being attuned to rules] consists in his being disposed without the prospect of reward and punishment to follow certain precepts that not only may appear to him largely arbitrary but which in no way appeal to his original inclinations" (p. 466). This distinguishing feature of the first level of internalization has nothing to do with the rules *per se*, i.e., the child doesn't internalize a set of rules much as it would eat a box of cookies. Rather, the critical transformation concerns the accommodation that a child makes to adult authority. If a child sees its parents as benevolent and trustworthy sources of support and guidance, it will be disposed to accept their rules and commands regardless of their content. If the parents are not so viewed, a child will tend to regard authority with suspicion and even resentment—it will be resistant to rules regardless of their content.

The specific chemistry of the parent–child interaction that engenders attunement to rules is not well understood. Nonetheless, two points about this early transformation are apparent. First, Waddington (1967) points out that the survival of culture necessarily requires the role of authority accepter; children would be unable to learn language (or the safe foods to eat, or danger signs) unless they were willing to accept the arbitrary pairing of certain random sounds with various meanings. And there is in principle no difference between language learning and the acquisition of any other rule system or aspect of culture. Second, there is evidence to suggest that within the first twelve months of life, maternal warmth and sensitivity to an infant's needs are sufficient to produce compliance to maternal commands; given the "proper" parent–child atmosphere, infants seem innately disposed toward compliance (cf. Stayton, Hogan & Ainsworth, 1971). As an infant begins to creep around, however, its caretakers must increasingly restrict its behavior. Generally speaking, a child will be most attuned to rules if it is treated in a warm but restrictive fashion, if it receives love and nurturance combined with prompt and consistent disapproval for disobedience. Warm but permissive parents, on the other hand, produce self-confident children who are not attuned to rules. Cold restrictive parents tend to have children who are hostile toward authority but who publicly conform to rules. Cold permissive parents tend to produce delinquent children.

To restate the point, the first level of legal socialization (in developing internalized compliance with the law) involves attunement to rules; this entails recognizing that social situations are governed by rules, learning what they are, and adjusting to them in an effortless, unambivalent way. Moreover, by adopting parental rules (e.g., language, etc.), a child is able simultaneously to secure parental care and to begin making sense of its environment. As Rawls (1971) notes, a child will become attuned to the rules under the following conditions: "First, the parents must love the child and be worthy objects of his admiration. In this way they arouse in him a sense of his own value and the desire to become the sort of person that they are. Secondly, they must enunciate clear and intelligible (and of course justifiable) rules adapted to the child's level of comprehension. In addition they should set out the reasons for these injunctions in so far as these can be understood, and they must also follow these precepts insofar as they apply to them as well. The parents should exemplify the morality which they enjoin, and make explicit its underlying principles as time goes on (pp. 465–466)." The point, however, is that a child doesn't internalize rules *per se*, rather it becomes attuned to the existence and operation of rules so that when it enters any given situation it expects rules to apply; its job is to determine what they are.

Understanding this permits us to make sense of some otherwise rather curious findings in the legal socialization literature. For example, Torney (1971) notes that relative to lower-class and to upper-middle-class children, lower-middle class children have favorable attitudes toward the police. She explains these findings in terms of different social-class-related experiences with policemen. Her explanation requires that lower-middle-class children have generally positive experiences with the police while the experiences of lower-class and upper-middle-class children must be generally negative. But how many normal seven-year-olds have had significant contact with the police? A more parsimonious answer is that social class differences in child rearing lead to differences in attunement to rules and orientation to adult authority generally.

Finally, I might note that if a child is attuned to rules, if it loves and trusts its parents, it will tend to feel guilty when it breaks these rules. The guilt associated with this stage is a composite of fear of parental punishment and fear of parental rejection—rejection in particular is a blow to a child's self-esteem and symbolizes parental abandonment. Rawls (1971) disagrees; he observes that ". . . love and trust will give rise to feelings of guilt once the parental injunctions are disobeyed. Admittedly in the case of the child it is sometimes difficult to distinguish feelings of guilt from the fear of punishment, and especially from the dread of the loss of parental love and affection . . . I have supposed, however, that even in the child's case we can separate (authority) guilt feelings from fear and anxiety" (p. 465).

B. SENSITIVITY TO SOCIAL EXPECTATIONS

The second level of legal socialization entails developing internalized compliance with the norms, values, and principles of one's society. How does this come about? Throughout the history of mankind very young children have been faced with the problem of making an accommodation to adult authority. Typically, however, by the time a child is five it has been replaced at the center of family attention by a younger sibling. Changes within the family in conjunction with a child's naturally expanding sociability cause it to spend increasing time away from its parents, usually with its peers. Making one's way in the peer group is a major problem at this point in life, and to the degree that a child remains scrupulously loyal to parental rules and adult authority, its way will be hindered. At this point, a child must accommodate itself to a greatly altered (i.e., more general and abstract) set of rules or risk becoming a social isolate. To the degree that the children of a culture are sensibly supervised, the norms of the peer group will approximate the norms of adult society.

As Mead (1934) and Piaget (1964) pointed out so well, the major vehicle for the socialization of children at this age is games and the experience of cooperation. Through games children are exposed to a range of adult values, including most importantly the norms of reciprocity and the concept of fairness. In the first period of legal socialization children become attuned to *rules*. In the second period, however, they develop internalized compliance with adult *norms* and *values*—through peer group experience. And, as Rawls (1971) points out, the notions of reciprocity and fairness in childhood turn into the concept of justice in adulthood.

Although the preadolescent child is able to articulate many adult values and principles (cf. Adelson et al., 1969), the question remains as to how they become internalized. In very general terms, this is a function of the development of empathy (Hogan, 1973), which can be broken down into two psychological processes. The first is sensitivity to social expectations. I remember a boy in my seventh grade class who was vastly unpopular; he routinely alienated his classmates and was sublimely indifferent to their attempts to socialize him. He was one of the most obtuse and insensitive people I have ever met—and remained so into adulthood. I watched him one day in the company of his parents at a supermarket. The parents obviously worshipped the ground the boy walked on; apparently their solicitude and unqualified affection made it unnecessary for him to develop the introspection and attentiveness to social cues that leads to sensitivity to social expectations. This sensitivity in turn provide cues for regulating one's behavior.

The second process that seems to engender internalized compliance with norms and values is concern for the welfare of those people with whom one interacts—in a child's case, the extended family and the peer group. How do people come to care about the welfare of their social groups? Freud (1960) suggested that when people work together toward a common goal, ties of affection "naturally" spring up. Rawls (1971) is more specific. Sensitivity to social expectations develops as children experience reciprocity in the family, school, neighborhood, and peer group. "Thus if those engaged in a system of social cooperation regularly act with evident intention to uphold its just (or fair) rules, bonds of friendship and mutual trust tend to develop among them, thereby holding them even more securely to the scheme" (Rawls, 1971, p. 470). Thus, ". . . the evident intention to honor one's obligations and duties is seen as a form of good will, and this recognition arouses feelings of friendship and trust in return" (p. 471). These bonds of friendship and trust lead to a concern for the welfare of others and to an internalized orientation to the norms and values appropriate to this second level of legal socialization.

Once a set of norms and values has been internalized, a person will tend to feel guilty if it is violated. These feelings of guilt are perhaps rooted in fear of social disapproval; they are manifested in a willingness to make reparations, to admit blame, and to be less indignant when others violate the same norms. If this capacity for guilt is missing, then there are no genuine ties of friendship and mutual trust among the members of the group, and one's compliance with these norms and values is not internalized.

To summarize this discussion, the second level of legal socialization consists in developing an internalized orientation to the norms, values, and principles implicit in the laws of one's society. This process starts when a child leaves the exclusive care of its parents and begins to accommodate itself to the demands of its peer group, neighborhood, and school. Being required to cooperate with others, experiencing reciprocity in peer play, perceiving that certain ideals are upheld by attractive members of the group, all these factors sensitize a child to social expectations and engender a concern for the welfare of the group. This leads to what Rawls (1971) calls the ethics of association; here the ideals and norms of one's social group are seen as one's own, and one feels guilty when these norms are violated.

C. IDEOLOGICAL MATURITY

According to Jung (1934) the critical problem facing an adolescent is choosing a mate and a career. According to Erikson (1950), however, neither choice is possible unless a person has a sense of personal identity, some knowledge of who he is and what he stands for. Another way of putting this, it seems to me, is to say that a major problem for an adolescent is to make sense of the competing and often contradictory lessons learned in the family, neighborhood, and peer group. From the viewpoint of legal socialization, the problem is to explain a person's internalized compliance with the rules and principles of law when such compliance runs counter to the wishes and expectations of his parents and peer group. From the viewpoint of social theorists the problem is that a person who is attuned to rules, sensitive to social expectations, and concerned about the welfare of his social groups will be necessarily committed to the status quo. Consequently, a proper model of legal socialization must make provisions for constructive nonconformity, for prosocial deviation from established patterns of conduct.

At the first level of legal socialization one must learn to live with authority; at the second level, one must learn to live with other people; but at the third level, one must learn to live with oneself. Rawls (1971) calls this final level of internalized compliance with the law the ethics of principle. As he remarks, although a person at the second level ". . . understands the principles of justice, his motive for complying with them . . . springs largely from his ties of friendship and fellow feeling for others, and his concern for the approbation of wider society . . .. Once a morality of principle is accepted, however, moral attitudes are no longer connected solely with the well-being and approval of particular individuals and groups, but are shaped by a conception of right chosen irrespective of these contingencies" (p. 475).

We are concerned here with what in another context I called autonomy or autonomous observance of legal and social rules. The problem of autonomy has vexed social psychology for years. Part of the difficulty is methodological— e.g., it is hard to distinguish autonomous behavior from simple, immature anti-conformity (cf. Hollander and Willis, 1967). Perhaps the biggest problem, however, is conceptual and definitional. The tradition of ethical individualism exemplified by Friedrich Nietzsche, for example, defines autonomous moral behavior as conformity to internal rather than external laws; truly moral (and autonomous) conduct is guided by one's personally derived standards of right and wrong. Although this individualistic view is widely popular (e.g., Kohlberg, 1963), it is untenable for practical and psychological reasons. On the one hand, society would be impossible if citizens refused to comply with any laws but their own. On the other hand, the unpredictable and anomic society that would follow from the Nietzschean ethic violates man's need for a predictable and orderly social environment. Nietzschean autonomy, like the existentialist's notion of authentic existence, presupposes a stable social order; if everyone adopted Kohlberg's stage six post-conventional morality, there would soon be no society in terms of which they could be post-conventional.

It seems to me then that autonomous conduct has to be defined not with regard to the rules, values, and principles of a society, but with regard to other people—peers and authority. The autonomous or principled person upholds the moral and legal ideals of his society without regard for their contemporary popularity.

How does autonomous or principled rule compliance come about? The best empirical work on the subject has been conducted by Baumrind (1971). She has identified a set of child-rearing practices that characterize "authoritative" parents. Such parents provide clear guidelines for their children's behavior, explain their rules, allow for rational discussion of specific prescriptions, but adhere to the principle that there will be some rules in any event. Perhaps the truly critical feature of such parents is that they are themselves autonomous—they provide models of autonomous adult behavior, and this may be more important than any discrete pattern of child-rearing practices.

William James and William McDougall proposed definitions of autonomy similar to that presented above; i.e., that one is autonomous with regard to other people rather than social rules and principles. They explained the development of autonomous rule observance in terms of what is today known as reference group theory. That is, over time some people come to be concerned about the approval and censure of a group of judges more distinguished or elevated than their own family and friends. These judges may be historical personages, even in the case of Socrates, for example, semi-fictional characters. They no longer have a temporal existence and they embody the best traditions of one's culture or society. By being concerned with their approval rather than that of one's peers, one achieves a measure of autonomy while remaining generally in tune with the rules and precepts of one's society. McDougall was particularly clear about this; as he remarked: "The man who stands up against the prevailing public opinion . . . has found some higher court of appeal, the verdict of which he esteems more highly . . . and whose approval he desires more strongly, than that of the mass of mankind . . .. In short, he has learned to judge his conduct as it would appear to a purely ideal spectator . . .. In this way . . . a man may become, as it is said, a 'law unto himself'" (1923, pp 441–442).

There is an alternative view, however, that emphasizes the role of ideology in promoting autonomous rule compliance. As mentioned above, one of the major problems facing an adolescent is to integrate the conflicting requirements of parents, peers, school, and neighborhood. This integration is made possible through ideological maturity. Ideological maturity is a function of having organized one's experiences and aspirations in terms of a coherent philosophy, political perspective, religion, or set of family ideals. To achieve ideological maturity the adolescent needs two supporting features in the environment— adult models of autonomy, and a history, a tradition, a political philosophy, or a culturally based ideology on which he can draw. Problems will develop, of course, when the relevant adult models and cultural traditions are absent.

Erikson (1950) also emphasizes the role of ideology in adolescent identity formation, and Gallatin and Adelson (1971) provide evidence that 18 year olds are in fact inclined to formulate ideologies. As they remark: "To lend coherence to his anticipated adult life, some order to his decisions, the adolescent needs to develop what Erikson (1959) has loosely termed an 'ideology of religion' or what Inhelder and Piaget (1958) call 'a feeling for ideals'" (p. 105).

In addition to providing a structure for organizing his life, an ideology also gives an adolescent a sacred rationalization for the rules adopted from his parents, and the norms and principles learned in the peer group. The sacred or numinous quality of ideologies in part accounts for the extraordinary tenacity and independence of the views of persons at this level of legal socialization. When the rules and principles of one's culture have been organized under an ideology, they become a part of one's identity, and their violation produces the most profound psychological distress.

III. CONCLUSION

The complete argument can now be stated very quickly. For the rules, values, and principles of one's society to be fully internalized in Kelman's (1961) sense, legal socialization must pass through three levels. In the first, one internalizes *rules* by accommodating oneself to loving but controlling parents. At the second level, one internalizes *principles* by accommodating oneself to a peer community in which certain standards (e.g., fairness, cooperation) are maintained by virtue of judicious adult supervision. At the third level, one organizes these rules and principles under an ideology usually by accommodating oneself to one's cultural and ethnic history; this gives the rules and principles acquired earlier a sacred quality that makes their violation almost unimaginable.

References

ADELSON, J., GREEN, B., & O'NEIL, R. Growth of the idea of law in adolescence. *Developmental Psychology*, 1969, 4, 327–332.

BAUMRIND, D. Current patterns of parental authority. *Developmental Psychology Monograph*, Part 2, January, 1971, pp. 1–103.

BOWLBY, J. *Attachment and loss* (Vol. I): *Attachment*. New York: Basic Books, 1969.

DURKHEIM, E. *Moral education*. New York: Free Press, 1961.

ERIKSON, E. *Childhood and society*. New York: Norton, 1950.

ERIKSON, E. Identity and the life cycle. *Psychological Issues*, 1959, 1(1, Whole Monograph 1).

FREUD, S. *Group psychology and the analysis of the ego*. New York: Bantam, 1960.

GALLATIN, J., & ADELSON, J. Legal guarantees of individual freedom: A cross-national study of the development of political thought. *Journal of Social Issues*, 1971, **27**, 93–108.

HESS, R. D., & TORNEY, J. V. *The development of political attitudes in children*. New York: Anchor Books, 1968.

HOGAN, R. Moral conduct and moral character. *Psychological Bulletin*, 1973, **79**, 217–232.

HOLLANDER, E. P., & WILLIS, R. H. Some current issues in the psychology of conformity and nonconformity. *Psychological Bulletin*, 1967, **68**, 62–76.

ICHHEISER, G. *Appearances and reality*. San Francisco: Jossey-Bass, 1970.

INHELDER, B., & PIAGET, J. *The growth of logical thinking from childhood to adolescence*. New York: Basic Books, 1958.

JUNG, C. G. *Modern man in search of a soul*. New York: Harcourt Brace, 1934.

KELMAN, H. C. Processes of opinion change. *Public Opinion Quarterly*, 1961, **25**, 57–78.

KOHLBERG, L. The development of children's orientation towards a moral order. *Vita Humana*, 1963, **6**, 11–33.

McDOUGALL, W. *Social psychology*. London: Methuen, 1908.

McDOUGALL, W. *Outline of psychology*. New York: Scribners, 1923.

MEAD, G. H. *Mind, self, and society*. Chicago: University of Chicago Press, 1934.

PIAGET, J. *The moral judgment of the child*. New York: Free Press, 1964.

RAWLS, J. *A theory of justice*. Cambridge, Mass.: Harvard University Press, 1971.

STAYTON, D., HOGAN, R., & AINSWORTH, M. D. S. Infant obedience and maternal behavior: The origins of socialization reconsidered. *Child Development*, 1971, **32**, 1057–1069.

TAPP, J. L., & KOHLBERG, L. Developing senses of law and legal justice. *Journal of Social Issues*, 1971, **27**, 65–92.

TAPP, J. L., & LEVINE, F. J. Legal socialization: Strategies for an ethical legality. *Stanford Law Review*, 1974, **27**, 1–72.

TORNEY, J. V. Socialization of attitudes toward the legal system. *Journal of Social Issues*, 1971, **27**, 137–154.

WADDINGTON, C. H. *The ethical animal*. Chicago: University of Chicago Press, 1967.

ZELLMAN, G. L., & SEARS, D. O. Childhood origins of tolerance for dissent. *Journal of Social Issues*, 1971, **27**, 109–136.

Attitudinal Orientations and Cognitive Functioning Among Adolescents [*]

Amos Handel

UNIVERSITY OF HAIFA

The purpose of this study was to examine the pattern of relations of attitudinal orientations to cognitive functioning in a sample of Israeli seventh-grade students ($N = 950$). Following Coleman et al.'s 1966 study, attitudinal orienta-

From *Developmental Psychology*, 1975, **11**, 667–675. Copyright © 1975 by The American Psychological Association. Reprinted by permission.

* This research was supported by a grant from the University Research Council, University of Haifa. The author is indebted to D. Yagil, S. Shur, T. Spanglet, and S. Bar for their assistance in various phases of the investigation and to M. Lakin for his most helpful and constructive criticism of the manuscript.

tions were represented by measures of locus of control, self-concept, and educational aspirations. Multiple regression analyses showed that 18.1% to 31.6% of the total variance in four measures of cognitive functioning was associated with attitudinal orientations, while only 10.6% to 18.9% of the total variance in these measures was associated with socioeconomic background variables. In the economically least advantaged group, locus of control was the most potent attitude variable; in the complementary two groups of higher socioeconomic status, more of the variance in cognitive functioning was associated with self-concept and aspirations than with locus of control.

In their survey of equality of educational opportunity, Coleman and his co-workers (Coleman, Hobson, McPartland, Mood, Weinfeld, & York, 1966) included brief measures of three attitudinal orientations: (a) academic self-concept, (b) interest in school and educational aspirations, and (c) sense of control of the environment. These student orientations, along with sets of measures of family background and of characteristics of their schools, were examined in relation to the dependent variable of verbal achievement. One of the striking findings in the Coleman report is the indication that of all independent variables measured in the survey, attitudinal orientations showed a strong relation to verbal achievement and contributed more of its variance than did a set of eight family background and socioeconomic variables.

While Coleman et al. (1966) based this conclusion on attitudes expressed by the students themselves. Other investigators arrived at similar conclusions based on measures of parents' achievement-related attitudes and of their stimulation of the child. Such measures, obtained through extensive home interviews, contributed more to variance in cognitive performance of the child than did various indices of the socioeconomic status of the family (Marjoribanks, 1972a, 1972b; Plowden, 1967; Werner, 1969; Wolf, 1966).

The growing interest in various expressions of attitudinal orientations seems to reflect a recent trend in studies of the determinants of cognitive development. This trend focuses on process variables. That is, the actual experiences of children which contribute to their cognitive growth, rather than on status variables (social class, race), which are presumed to represent only surface characteristics of the environment (Wolf, 1964, 1966). This trend has been stimulated by the anticipation that investigation of attitudinal orientations and process variables could have one of the following advantages: (a) increase the predictability of cognitive functioning above the level of predictions afforded by standard indices of socioeconomic status (SES); (b) elucidate the factors underlying the observed correlations between SES and the level of cognitive functioning (Deutsch & Katz, 1968; Jensen, 1968); or (c) indicate a class of variables that would be amenable to intervention and manipulation (Wolf, 1966; Whiteman & Deutsch, 1968). However, in spite of the consistency of social class differences in cognitive functioning across various countries (Thorndike, 1962), no attempt has yet been made to examine the cross-cultural consistency of Coleman et al.'s (1966) frequently cited finding about the prepotency of students' attitudinal orientations in relation to achievement.

Coleman et al. (1966) also found substantial differences in the relative amount of variance associated with the three attitudinal orientations within the racial and ethnic groups included in his survey. Thus, for blacks, sense of control of environment was clearly the most important attitude, associated with from two to several times as much of the variance as either of the other two attitudinal orientations. For whites (and native-born Orientals), the order of importance was different: Self-concept was more highly related to the level of verbal ability than was sense of control of environment.

The implications of these findings for the education of disadvantaged children have been widely discussed (Coleman et al., 1966; Hess, 1970; Katz, 1967, 1969; Pettigrew, 1968; Tulkin, 1972). Notwithstanding this extensive discussion, no attempt has ever been made to determine whether these findings are unique to the social structure of the United States or would be duplicated in other sociocultural settings.

The purpose of the present study was to examine the pattern of relations of attitudinal orientations to cognitive functioning in a sample of adolescents in Israel. There were two specific goals for this study: (a) to determine whether the class of attitudinal orientations is associated with more of the variance in various measures of cognitive functioning than is the class of socioeconomic background variables, as indicated by Coleman et al. (1966); and (b) to determine whether the particular patterns of relations of attitudinal orientations reported by Coleman et al. (1966) for whites and blacks obtain among the more and less advantaged students in Israel.

METHOD

Most of the measures used by Coleman et al. (1966) were adopted with only slight modifications, In addition, the following modifications were made in the design of the present study in order to extend the scope of its relevance and increase its potential significance:

1. The criterion of cognitive functioning was extended to include measures of scholastic achievement and measures of nonverbal intelligence in addition to verbal ability, which was the primary criterion of achievement in the analyses presented by Coleman et al. (1966). The choice of both verbal and nonverbal criterion measures was made in view of differences found in the degree of relation of verbal and nonverbal abilities with socioeconomic status (Cropley, 1964; Karp, Silberman, & Winters, 1969; MacArthur & Elley, 1963; Marjoribanks, 1972a, 1972b) and with parents' achievement-related attitudes (Marjoribanks, 1972a, 1972b).

2. A second questionnaire, in addition to that used by Coleman et al. (1966), was used to measure control of environment in view of the importance accorded to this orientation in their report.

3. Socioeconomic background variables were restricted to measures of "objective" background conditions (crowdedness of home, items in the home which indicate its economic standing) and did not include such "subjective" factors as parental educational aspirations for the child.[1] This differs from the Coleman et al. (1966) study in which these subjective factors were contained within the class of socioeconomic background variables.

[1] This more limited definition of the home background seemed to be called for in order to contrast the relative contributions of socioeconomic background and of attitudinal orientations to the variance in cognitive functioning. Moreover, the broad definition originally used by Coleman et al. (1966) appears to have eventually obscured differences in the relationships of objective and subjective background variables to achievement (Smith, 1972).

4. The differentiation between more and less advantaged students was based on a measure of socioeconomic background (crowdedness ratio of the home) rather than on a criterion of ethnicity[2] as in the Coleman et al. (1966) study. This was done on the assumption that the use of a direct measure of socioeconomic background is preferable to the use of ethnic classifications, which generally represent a confounded index of socioeconomic background (Edwards, 1974; Hess, 1970).

5. The degree of association of attitudinal orientations with the variance in cognitive measures was determined with socioeconomic background variables held constant. Likewise, attitudinal orientations were partialed out in estimating the degree of association of socioeconomic background variables with the variance in cognitive measures. Unlike this symmetric approach to the two classes of independent variables, Coleman et al. (1966) only controlled for family background variables and did not assess their degree of association with attitudes partialed out.

MEASURES OF COGNITIVE FUNCTIONING   Four tests were used to assess the relevant areas of cognitive functioning: a comprehensive test of scholastic achievement, a verbal intelligence test, and two nonverbal intelligence tests. These tests were (a) Achievement Test A, covering the areas of arithmetic, Hebrew language, and social studies; this multiple-choice test was prepared by the Ministry of Education in Israel (Ortar, 1967) and was originally used in 1958 for selection and guidance of graduates of all elementary schools throughout the country; (b) Otis, a modified Hebrew version (Handel, 1973a) of the Otis Beta Quick-Scoring Mental Ability Test; (c) Standard Progressive Matrices, Raven's (1960) nonverbal intelligence test; (d) The D48 Test (Centre de Psychologie Appliquée, 1959), a nonverbal analogies test that shares about 45% of its variance with Progressive Matrices among adolescents (Handel, 1973a).

The information about socioeconomic background and attitudinal orientations was gathered by a student questionnaire. Most of its items were adopted, with slight modifications, from the 6th- and 9th-grade questionnaire used in the survey of Coleman et al. (1966).

MEASURES OF SOCIOECONOMIC BACKGROUND   The assessment of socioeconomic background was based on information provided by the student about items in his home, crowdedness conditions in his home, and education of his parents.

All six "items in home" listed in Coleman et al.'s (1966) questionnaire were included and coded 1 and 2 for presence or absence, respectively, of each in the home (TV, telephone, record player, refrigerator, automobile, vacuum cleaner).

Crowdedness ratio of the home (number of persons divided by number of rooms) provided another index of economic level, as used in studies of SES

[2] Ethnicity in the Jewish population in Israel is defined by the country of origin of the parents. Two major groups are distinguished: (a) the Oriental Jews whose origin is Asia (usually, the Arab countries of the Middle East) and North Africa; (b) the Western group whose origin is Europe and North and South America. Oriental Jews are predominant in the Israeli lower class; the Western group is usually of a higher socioeconomic status.

effects in the United States (Bloom, Whiteman, & Deutsch, 1965; Deutsch, 1967; Tulkin, 1968; Tulkin & Newbrough, 1968), in Canada (Marjoribanks, 1972a), in England (Swift, 1967), and in Israel (Handel, 1973c; Yaffe & Smilansky, 1958).

The information obtained about education of parents was eventually discarded because 25% of the students responded "don't know" with respect to father's education and 32% with respect to mother's education. These two items received similarly high rates of "don't know" responses (36% and 31%) among sixth-graders in the Coleman et al. (1966) survey (Jencks, 1972).

MEASURES OF ATTITUDINAL ORIENTATIONS   Self-reports of students provided measures of self-concept, educational aspirations, and locus of control (control of environment).

Self-Concept   Academic self-concept was assessed by three items from the Coleman et al. (1966) questionnaire: (a) How good a student are you? (3-point scale, from 1 = low self-esteem to 3 = high self-esteem); (b) I sometimes feel I just can't learn (1 = agree—low self-concept, 2 = disagree— high self-concept); (c) I would do better in school if teachers didn't go so fast (1 = agree—low self-concept, 2 = disagree—high self-concept).

Educational Aspirations   Included were two items from the Coleman et al. (1966) questionnaire, both scored on a 5-point scale: (a) Mark the highest grade you want to finish in school (from 1 = low aspirations—finishing elementary school to 5 = high aspirations—finishing college); (b) how good a student do you want to be in school? (from 1 = high aspirations to 5 = low aspirations).

Locus of Control   This orientation (subsequently referred to as "control") was assessed by three items adopted from the Coleman et al. (1966) questionnaire: (a) People like me don't have much of a chance to be successful in life. (b) Every time I try to go ahead, something or somebody stops me. (c) Good luck is more important than hard work for success. Each of the three items was dichotomously scored (1 = agree—external control, 2 = disagree—internal control). In addition, a specifically constructed scale of internal control was used. This scale was developed from a pool of items selected from the Intellectual Responsibility Questionnaire (Crandall, Katkowsky, & Crandall, 1965) and from the Internal–External Control Scale (Rotter, 1966). Experimental versions of this scale were applied to different groups of adolescents in Israel. The final version of the scale (Handel, 1973b) was composed of 20 forced-choice items. Each item of this scale referred to a positive achievement experience in the student's daily life or to various success and failure experiences of people in general. Each item was followed by two alternatives representing an internal and external control interpretation of these events. The score was the total number of internal choices endorsed by the student. The Kuder–Richardson (KR 20) estimate of internal consistency of this scale in a sample of 161 seventh-grade pupils yielded a value of .63, which is comparable to estimates of internal consistency reported by Rotter (1966) for his original scale.

The tests and questionnaires were administered to groups of 12–15 students at a time during a 2-month period at the beginning of the autumn term in 1969. The testing was conducted by two male and two female graduate students.

SUBJECTS   The sample, which intended to draw from all socioeconomic groups, consisted of seventh-grade students in four newly established junior high schools in Haifa. It included all seventh-grade students enrolled in these schools in 1969, with $N = 950$, 440 boys and 510 girls. The range of ages was from 11 years 9 months to 13 years 3 months, with about the same mean for the boys (12 years 4 months) and the girls (12 years 3 months) and a standard deviation of 5 months for both groups.

The socioeconomic composition of this sample corresponded closely with the 1969 census data for the total Jewish population in Israel (Central Bureau of Statistics, 1970, Table F/16, p. 181). This comparison was based on the crowdedness index as a gross and comprehensive indicator of socioeconomic status. The medians of this index in our sample and in the census data were 1.58 and 1.60, respectively. The percentage of those living in relatively crowded conditions (dwellings with a crowdedness ratio of 2.0 or more) were also highly similar: 25.7% in our sample and 27.7% in the total Jewish population.

The ethnic composition of this sample also corresponded closely with the 1969/1970 census data for the junior high schools in Israel (Central Bureau of Statistics, 1972), with the following proportions of students of a distinctly Oriental origin: 15.2% in our sample and 13.2% in the total population of students in junior high schools. The corresponding complement (84.8% and 86.8%) comprised children of a distinctly Western origin and second-generation Israeli children of either Western or Oriental origin.

ANALYSES OF DATA   The relations of individual background and attitude variables with each measure of cognitive functioning were analyzed by means of zero-order correlations between these variables. These data provided a base line from which to view the results of multiple regression analyses inasmuch as the latter procedure was the primary method used to analyze the pattern of relations obtained in the total sample and in its subgroups.

Multiple regression analyses were used to assess the degree to which the two major classes of independent variables—attitudinal orientations (nine variables) and socioeconomic background variables (seven variables)—were associated with each dependent (cognitive) measure. It was recognized that significant relations between the class of attitudinal orientations and cognitive measures might be spurious due to the common variance shared by both of these with the background variables. Therefore, the degree of association of attitude variables with the dependent measures was determined both before and after partialing out of background variables. Similarly, the degree of association of background variables with the dependent measures was computed with and without partialing out of attitude variables.

Multiple regression analyses were also applied to three sets of variables within the class of attitudinal orientations: measures of aspirations (two variables), self-concept (three variables), and control (four variables).

TABLE 1

Zero-Order Correlations Between Independent Variables and Cognitive Measures

INDEPENDENT VARIABLE	ACHIEVE-MENT TEST A	OTIS	PRO-GRESSIVE MATRICES	THE D48 TEST
Items in home				
TV	−03	−02	−05	−03
Telephone	−27†	−32†	−24†	−26†
Record player	−15†	−16†	−10**	−09**
Refrigerator	−07*	−11†	−09**	−07*
Automobile	−21†	−26†	−20†	−22†
Vacuum cleaner	−18†	20†	−16†	−20†
Crowdedness ratio	−32†	−36†	−27†	−28†
Aspirations				
Highest grade	37†	36†	28†	31†
Achievements	−24†	−25†	−17†	−15†
Self-concept				
Achievements	35†	27†	17†	18†
Can't learn	20†	19†	18†	15†
Teachers' pace too fast	31†	37†	31†	27†
Control				
Don't have chance	27†	29†	25†	22†
Don't go ahead	19†	19†	21†	17†
Luck more important	27†	30†	21†	21†
Internal control	32†	31†	24†	21†

Note. Direction of scores is as follows: for items in home, crowdedness ratio, and the second item (achievements) of aspirations, a high score = absence of item in home, high crowdedness, and low aspirations; for the first item (highest grade) of aspirations and for variables of self-concept and control, a high score = high aspirations, high self-concept, and internal control. All decimal points have been omitted.
* $p < .05$.
** $p < .01$.
† $p < .001$.

The relation of each of the three sets of attitude variables with measures of cognitive functioning was further examined in three distinct SES groups. For this purpose, the distribution of scores of the crowdedness ratio was divided at two points that roughly coincided with the values of Q_1 and Q_3 in the distribution of these scores for the total Jewish population in Israel (Central Bureau of Statistics, 1970). The resultant three subgroups were as follows:

low crowdedness: ratio of 1.1 and below, $N = 224$
average crowdedness: ratio of 1.2 to 2.2, $N = 583$
high crowdedness: ratio of 2.3 and above, $N = 143$.

Separate regression analyses were also performed to identify possible differences in the pattern of relationship in each sex group.

RESULTS

ATTITUDINAL ORIENTATIONS AND SOCIOECONOMIC BACKGROUND VARIABLES   All attitude measures and background variables, with the exception of one (possession of TV), are significantly related to each of the four measures of cognitive functioning (Table 1).

The multiple regression analyses computed for successive sets of the independent background and attitude variables (Table 2) clearly indicate that attitudinal orientations as a group (Set J) are associated with more of the variance than is the class of socioeconomic background variables (Set C). This major finding applies to each of the four measures of cognitive functioning. Furthermore, predictions from even two attitudinal orientations (Sets G, H, I) are superior to predictions based on the total class of socioeconomic background variables.

The data in Table 3 further demonstrate the relatively strong relation between the dependent cognitive variables and the class of attitudinal orientations. With the total class of background variables partialed out, attitudinal

TABLE 2

Multiple Regression Analyses (R^2) of Cognitive Measures by Sets of Independent Variables

INDEPENDENT VARIABLE	TOTAL NO. OF MEASURES IN EACH SET	OTIS	ACHIEVEMENT TEST A	PROGRESSIVE MATRICES	THE D48 TEST
A = crowdedness*	1	.13	.10	.07	.08
B = items in home	6	.15	.10	.08	.10
C = A + B = background	7	.19	.14	.11	.12
D = aspirations	2	.16	.16	.09	.10
E = self-concept	3	.18	.19	.12	.10
F = control	4	.18	.16	.10	.12
G = D + E	5	.25	.26	.16	.15
H = E + F	7	.26	.26	.17	.14
I = D + F	6	.27	.26	.17	.16
J = D + E + F = attitudes	9	.32	.31	.20	.16
K = C + J	16	.40	.36	.24	.23

Note. All R^2 values are significant ($p < .001$).
* For crowdedness ratio, R^2 values are based on zero-order correlations.

TABLE 3

Proportions of Variance of Cognitive Measures Accounted for by
Classes of Independent Variables

INDEPENDENT VARIABLE*	% VARIANCE (R^2) ACCOUNTED FOR		
	TOTAL SAMPLE	BOYS ($n = 440$)	GIRLS ($n = 510$)
Otis			
K	39.5	37.2	42.6
J	31.6	29.3	34.5
C	18.9	17.3	20.7
L	7.9	7.9	8.1
M	20.6	19.9	21.9
Achievement Test A			
K	36.5	34.5	39.2
J	31.3	29.5	33.7
C	14.2	17.3	15.8
L	5.2	5.0	5.5
M	22.3	17.2	23.4
Progressive Matrices			
K	23.7	20.1	27.3
J	19.8	15.9	23.8
C	10.6	9.6	11.5
L	3.9	4.2	3.5
M	13.1	10.5	15.8
The D48 Test			
K	23.5	22.3	26.0
J	18.1	16.6	20.8
C	12.2	11.4	13.4
L	5.4	5.7	5.2
M	11.3	10.9	12.6

Note. The total numbers of measures included in each class of independent variables are: 16 in K, 9 in J, and 7 in C.
* K = background + attitudes; J = attitudes; C = background; L =
K − J = background, attitudes partialed out; M = K − C = attitudes, background partialed out.

orientations are associated with from two to four times as much of the variance in cognitive measures as is the class of background variables with attitudes partialed out. This is true for the total sample as well as for both sex groups.

ATTITUDINAL ORIENTATIONS WITH MORE AND LESS ADVANTAGED SUBGROUPS   The estimates of variance associated with the three sets of attitudinal orientations are much the same both in the total sample (Table 2, Sets D, E, and F) and in the two sex groups. Further comparisons of these estimates within the subgroups of low, average, and high crowdedness, however, indicate highly consistent differences[3] between the proportions of variance associated within each subgroup (Table 4).

For the high-crowdedness group, control seems to be the most important attitude and shows the strongest relation to performance on different measures of cognitive functioning. In this group, the variable of control is associated with considerably more of the variance than are either of the other two attitude variables, and the association of measures of control (Set O) is even larger than the association of the combined set of variables of self-concept and aspirations (Set N).

In the average- and low-crowdedness group, the variables of self-concept and aspirations are of more importance, and their joint association with the variance in cognitive measures is about two to four times as large as the association of the measures of control.

The apparent similarity of the pattern of relations between attitude and cognitive measures in the two groups of higher socioeconomic status was further examined by a cross-validation analysis. For this purpose, regression weights from the low-crowdedness subgroup were applied to scores of students in the average-crowdedness subgroup, and vice versa. The resultant R^2 values[4] are very similar in magnitude to the original R^2 values in both subgroups, especially for Otis and Achievement Test A, thus indicating the comparability of the pattern of relations between attitude and cognitive measures in the two subgroups of higher socioeconomic status.

DISCUSSION

The results of this study suggest that attitudinal orientations represent meaningful constructs and potent correlates of the cognitive functioning of adolescents in Israel. Specifically, our data support the consistency of two major findings of Coleman et al. (1966): (a) Attitudinal orientations are more highly associated with the variation in cognitive functioning than are socioeconomic background variables. (b) For the disadvantaged group, locus of control shows the strongest relation to cognitive functioning, while for the more advantaged subjects, self-concept and educational aspirations seem to be of more importance.

The specific estimates of variance associated with attitudinal orientations and socioeconomic background variables also show close agreement with estimates reported in the United States (Coleman et al., 1966; Kohn & Rosman,

[3] These differences are not attributable to differences in the sizes of variances of these measures, since these variances do not differ widely (see Footnote 4).
[4] The table containing the results of this cross-validation analysis (Table A) and the table of the means and variances of all measures in the total sample and in the three subgroups of crowdedness conditions (Table B) may be obtained from the author, Dr. Handel.

TABLE 4

Proportions of Variance in Cognitive Measures Accounted for by Sets of Attitude Variables in Subgroups of High, Average, and Low Crowdedness

INDEPENDENT VARIABLE	CROWDEDNESS SUBGROUP*	% VARIANCE (R^2) ACCOUNTED FOR			
		Otis	Achievement Test A	Progressive Matrices	Test D48
J = aspirations + self-concept + control	High	35.0	31.9	22.3	15.8
	Average	29.1	30.2	18.0	16.7
	Low	25.7	20.7	13.7	14.2
D = aspirations	High	8.5	9.8	2.8	5.3
	Average	16.9	17.6	10.2	10.9
	Low	11.9	8.6	4.0	4.9
E = self-concept	High	14.9	14.0	12.2	4.6
	Average	14.8	17.4	9.4	8.3
	Low	15.4	15.3	9.5	8.2
F = control	High	28.6	23.6	16.5	12.5
	Average	13.6	12.4	8.9	7.0
	Low	11.6	8.4	5.9	6.8
G = D + E = aspirations + self-concept	High	22.6	22.5	14.1	9.2
	Average	23.9	26.0	15.2	15.0
	Low	19.4	17.5	10.6	10.0
N = J − F = aspirations + self-concept; control partialed out	High	6.4	8.3	5.8	3.3
	Average	15.5	17.8	9.1	9.7
	Low	14.1	12.3	7.8	7.4
O = J − G = control; aspirations + self-concept partialed out	High	12.4	9.4	8.2	6.6
	Average	5.2	4.2	2.8	1.7
	Low	6.3	3.2	3.1	4.2

* *ns* for high, average, and low-crowdedness subgroups are 143, 583, and 224, respectively.

1973) and in Canada (Marjoribanks, 1972a). Thus, the estimates of total variance for the criterion of verbal ability (Otis) in this study, and the corresponding estimates in the study of Coleman et al. (1966) for ninth-grade[5] whites, are as follows: 39.5% and 38.8% for the attitude and socioeconomic variables, 31.8% and 31.1% for the attitude measures, and 18.9% and 23.3% for the socioeconomic variables, respectively. Comparable estimates of variance associated with multiple indices of socioeconomic background were found by Kohn and Rosman (1973) for the Stanford Binet (19.1%) and for the Caldwell Preschool Inventory (22.0%), and by Marjoribanks (1972a) for the verbal subtests of SRA Primary Mental Abilities (28.1%).

Furthermore, the fact that Otis and Achievement Test A seem to be more predictable than the nonverbal tests of Progressive Matrices and D48 by both attitude and socioeconomic measures further replicates the findings from multiple regression analyses of Marjoribanks (1972a) for the SRA Primary Mental Abilities.

In contrast to the consistencies and similarities in the findings discussed so far, two findings deviate from this general trend. These findings pertain to further characteristics of the economically disadvantaged group in our sample (high-crowdedness group) and to the characteristics of the complementary two groups of higher socioeconomic status.

First, the disadvantaged group scored one standard deviation or less below the mean of the most advantaged group on the measures of cognitive functioning and about one half of a standard deviation below its mean on various measures of attitudinal orientations (see Footnote 4). In contrast, Coleman et al. (1966) found that southern blacks scored about one standard deviation or more below the mean of northern whites on different measures of cognitive functioning, and fell even farther behind in their level of internal control, while their academic self-concept and educational aspirations were as high as those of the northern whites.

Unlike the low-achieving black student who showed lack of realism in his educational aspirations (Coleman et al., 1966) and may have used expressions of high ambition and interest in education as a verbal substitute for behaviors he is unable to enact (Katz, 1968), the typical low-achieving student from the economically disadvantaged group in our sample seemed to be more diffident in the expressions of his academic self-concept and educational aspirations. Furthermore, his feelings about low control of the environment were consonant with the level of his other attitudinal orientations, unlike the discrepancy found between the level of focus of control and that of the other two attitudinal orientations among southern blacks (Coleman et al., 1966).

Second, the data of the present study indicate the similarity of the two groups of average and high socioeconomic status. This is suggested by the fact that students living in homes of average and low crowdedness differ only slightly in their scores on the dependent cognitive measures, while they score about the same on the independent attitude measures and produce highly

---

[5] For this comparison, the ninth-grade data were selected from the Coleman et al. (1966) survey, since Grade 9 was the lowest grade at which students were tested by uncurtailed scales of attitude measures in this survey.

similar patterns of relations between the two classes of variables (see Footnote 4).

Thus, the division of SES between average- and high-crowdedness conditions yields two relatively homogeneous groups. This might reflect a particular characteristic of the measure chosen to represent the continuum of SES in the present study, or a particular feature of the social structure of the Jewish population in Israel, or both.[6]

Alternatively, the division in terms of crowdedness might be viewed in the context of other observations which suggest that social class variation does not represent a psychologically equidistant continuum (Kohn, 1963; Lorion, 1973; Pavenstedt, 1965). Specifically, dichotomization at a point near the lower end of the continuum of social class variation is especially relevant to he psychological functioning of individuals from low-SES groups. Such individuals may lack sufficient resources and relevant experiences to develop a favorable view of self in school-related activities and of the environment. Consequently, they have feelings of inadequate control of the environment, low self-esteem, and depressed aspirations in contrast to the more favorable outlook of individuals located anywhere above the critical point of social class variation.

Further exploration of the determinants of attitudinal orientations at different ages, under different cultural conditions, may indicate the generality of this interpretation and further contribute to the clarification of some critical questions in the research on disadvantaged groups: (a) the extent to which the characteristic patterns of attitudinal orientations of children from poverty groups are directly influenced by various objective "realities of life" and the extent to which the impact of these "reality" factors is mediated by parental styles and socialization practices (Allen, 1970; Gurin & Gurin, 1970; Hess, 1970; Tulkin, 1972); (b) the extent to which the attitudinal orientations of disadvantaged groups are amenable to educational intervention and modifiable in a time perspective of years or decades (cf. Rappaport, 1974; Sarason, 1973); and (c) the extent to which changes in the attitudinal orientations of these groups will be reflected in corresponding changes in the level of their cognitive performance (cf. Hunt & Hardt, 1969).

Reference Note

1. OKADA, T., COHEN, W. M., & MAYSKE, G. W. *Growth in achievement for different racial, regional, and socioeconomic groupings of students.* Washington, D.C.: U.S. Office of Education mimeograph, May 16, 1969.

---

[6] Such a particularistic interpretation may be at least partially defended in view of the specific form of the regressions of the various cognitive measures on the crowdedness ratio in the total sample. While no significant deviations from linearity were found for these regressions, the increments in the level of cognitive performance at the lower end of the SES continuum (between high and average crowdedness) consistently exceeded the increments at the upper end (between average and low crowdedness) for the various criteria of cognitive functioning (see Footnote 4). This is at variance with the findings of monotonicity in the relationships between cognitive performance and indicators of SES in the original data of the Coleman et al. (1966) survey (Okada, Cohen, & Mayeske. Note 1), as well as with other findings that suggest either monotonicity (Curry, 1962; Deutsch & Brown, 1964) or infrequent departures from this type of relationship (Kohn & Rosman, 1973).

References

ALLEN, V. E. Theoretical issues in poverty research. *Journal of Social Issues*, 1970, **26**, 149–167.

BLOOM, R., WHITEMAN, M., & DEUTSCH, M. Race and social class as separate factors related to social environment. *American Journal of Sociology*, 1965, **70**, 471–476.

Central Bureau of Statistics. *Statistical Abstract of Israel*, 1970, **21**.

Central Bureau of Statistics. *Demographic characteristics of pupils in kindergartens and schools 1963/4–1969/70*. Jerusalem, Israel: Author, 1972.

Centre de Psychologie Appliquée. *Manuel: Test D48*. Paris: Editions du Centre de Psychologie Appliquée, 1959.

COLEMAN, J. S., HOBSON, C. J., McPARTLAND, JR., MOOD, A. M., WEINFELD, F. D., & YORK, R. L. *Equality of educational opportunity*. Washington, D.C.: U.S. Government Printing Office, 1966.

CRANDALL, V. C., KATKOWSKY, W., & CRANDALL, V. J. Children's beliefs in their own control of reinforcement in intellectual-academic achievement situations. *Child Development*, 1965, **36**, 91–109.

CROPLEY, A. J. Differentiation of abilities, socioeconomic status, and the WISC. *Journal of Consulting Psychology*, 1964, **28**, 512–517.

CURRY, R. L. The effect of socio-economic status on the scholastic achievement of sixth-grade children. *British Journal of Educational Psychology*, 1962, **32**, 46–49.

DEUTSCH, M. Minority groups and class status as related to social and personality factors in scholastic achievement. In M. Deutsch et al. (Eds.), *The disadvantaged child*. New York: Basic Books, 1967.

DEUTSCH, M., & BROWN, B. Social influences in Negro–white intelligence differences. *Journal of Social Issues*, 1964, **20**, 24–35.

DEUTSCH, M., & KATZ, I. Introduction. In M. Deutsch, I. Katz, & A. R. Jensen (Eds.), *Social class, race, and psychological development*. New York: Holt, 1968.

EDWARDS, D. W. Blacks versus whites: When is race a relevant variable? *Journal of Personality and Social Psychology*, 1974, **29**, 39–49.

GURIN, G., & GURIN, P. Expectancy theory in the study of poverty. *Journal of Social Issues*, 1970, **26**, 83–104.

HANDEL, A. The applicability of the WISC for pre-school children. *Megamot*, 1973, **19**, 255–267. (a)

HANDEL, A. Cognitive styles among adolescents in Israel. *International Journal of Psychology*, 1973, **8**, 255–267. (b)

HANDEL, A. The D48 as a measure of general ability among adolescents in Israel. *Journal of Cross-Cultural Psychology*, 1973, **4**, 302–213. (c)

HESS, R. D. Social class and ethnic influences upon socialization. In P. H. Mussen (Ed.), *Carmichael's manual of child psychology* (3rd ed.). New York: Wiley, 1970.

HUNT, D. E., & HARDT, R. H. The effect of upward bound programs on the attitudes, motivation and academic achievement of Negro students. *Journal of Social Issues*, 1969, **25**, 177–229.

JENCKS, C. S. The quality of data collected by the equality of educational opportunity survey. In F. Mosteller & D. P. Moynihan (Eds.), *On equality of educational opportunity*. New York: Random House, 1972.

JENSEN, A. R. Basic processes in intellectual development: Introduction. In M. Deutsch, I. Katz, & A. R. Jensen (Eds.), *Social class, race, and psychological development*. New York: Holt, 1968.

KARP, S. A., SILBERMAN, L., & WINTERS, S. Psychological differentiation and socioeconomic status. *Perceptual and Motor Skills*, 1969, **28**, 55–60.

KATZ, I. Some motivational determinants of racial differences in intellectual achievement. *International Journal of Psychology*, 1967, **2**, 1–12.

KATZ, I. Academic motivation and equal educational opportunity. *Harvard Educational Review*, 1968, **38**, 57–64.

KATZ, I. A critique of personality approaches to Negro performance, with research suggestions. *Journal of Social Issues*, 1969, **25**, 13–27.

KOHN, L. M. Social class and parent–child relationships: An interpretation. *American Journal of Sociology*, 1963, **68**, 471–480.

KOHN, M., & ROSMAN, B. L. Cognitive functioning in five-year-old boys as related to social-emotional and background-demographic variables. *Developmental Psychology*, 1973, **8**, 277–294.

LORION, R. P. Socioeconomic status and traditional treatment approaches reconsidered. *Psychological Bulletin*, 1973, **79**, 263–270.

MACARTHUR, R. J., & ELLEY, W. B. The reduction of socioeconomic bias in intelligence testing. *British Journal of Educational Psychology*, 1963, **33**, 107–119.

MARJORIBANKS, K. E. Environment, social class, and mental abilities. *Journal of Educational Psychology*, 1972, **63**, 103–109. (a)

MARJORIBANKS, K. E. Ethnicity and learning patterns: A replication and explanation. *Sociology*, 1972, **6**, 417–431. (b)

ORTAR, G. Educational achievements of primary school graduates in Israel as related to their socio-cultural background. *Comparative Education*, 1967, **4**, 23–34.

PAVENSTEDT, E. A. A comparison of the child rearing environment of upper-lower and very low lower-class families, *American Journal of Orthopsychiatry*, 1965, **35**, 89–98.

PETTIGREW, T. F. Race and equal educational opportunity. *Harvard Educational Review*, 1968, **38**, 66–76.

PLOWDEN, B. *Children and their primary schools* (Report to the Central Advisory Council for Education, England). London: Her Majesty's Stationery Office, 1967.

RAPPAPORT, H. Jewishness, blackishness, and the impending retreat of psychology. *American Psychologist*, 1974, **29**, 570–571.

RAVEN, J. C. *Guide to the Standard Progressive Matrices: Sets A, B, C, D, and F*. London: Lewis, 1960.

ROTTER, J. C. Generalized expectancies for internal versus external control of reinforcement. *Psychological Monographs*, 1966, **80** (1, Whole No. 609).

SARASON, S. B. Jewishness, blackishness, and the nature–nurture controversy. *American Psychologist*, 1973, **28**, 962–971.

SMITH, M. S. Equality of educational opportunity: The basic findings reconsidered. In F. Mosteller & D. P. Moynihan (Eds.), *On equality of educational opportunity*. New York: Random House, 1972.

SWIFT, D. F. Family environment and 11+ success: Some basic predictors. *British Journal of Educational Psychology*, 1967, **37**, 10–21.

THORNDIKE, R. L. International comparison in the achievement of 13-year-olds. In, *Educational achievements of thirteen-year-olds in twelve countries*. Hamburg: UNESCO Institute for Education, 1962.

TULKIN, S. R. Race, class, family, and school achievement. *Journal of Personality and Social Psychology*, 1968, **9**, 31–37.

TULKIN, S. R. An analysis of the concept of cultural deprivation. *Developmental Psychology*, 1972, **6**, 326–339.

TULKIN, S. R., & NEWBROUGH, J. R. Social class, race, and sex differences on the Raven (1956) Standard Progressive Matrices. *Journal of Consulting and Clinical Psychology*, 1968, **32**, 400–406.

WERNER, E. E. Sex differences in correlations between children's IQs and measures of parental ability, and environmental ratings. *Developmental Psychology*, 1969, **1**, 280–285.

WHITEMAN, M., & DEUTSCH, M. Social disadvantage as related to intellective and language development. In M. Deutsch, I. Katz, & A. R. Jensen (Eds.), *Social class, race, and psychological development*. New York: Holt, 1968.

WOLF, R. *The identification and measurement of environmental process variables related to intelligence*. Unpublished doctoral dissertation, University of Chicago, 1964.

WOLF, R. The measurement of environment. In A. Anastasi (Ed.), *Testing problems in perspective*. Washington, D.C.: American Council on Education, 1966.

YAFFE, E., & SMILANSKY, M. The extent and causes of early school leaving. *Megamot*, 1958, 9, 275–285.

Chapter 5
An Overview of Human Life and Growth

All of existence is continuous and related. A search for beginnings and causes of life reveals psychological, physiological, biological, biochemical, and physical structures built upon and of each other.

Every organism and its environment have dynamic, reciprocal relationships. Affecting each other and being affected by each other, neither can be understood without the other, nor can either be what it *is* without the other. The cool air under the tree does not exist without the tree, nor would the tree exist without air. An interesting interaction between plants and landscape can be seen in coastal areas where conservation projects are carried out. A beach that was washed away by a hurricane now stretches smoothly into the Atlantic Ocean, backed by sand dunes built by plants. The plants were dead Christmas trees stuck into the sand and then reinforced by living plants which, finding nutrients and moisture enough in the sand, sent down a network of tough roots, which held the sand in the dunes.

More remarkable even than the building of beaches is the interaction of the human baby with his environment, his family. A human baby grows into a human

233

child as he lives in a human family, calling forth maternal and paternal responses from two adults whose behavior could not be parental if he were not there.

Varieties of Interaction Between the Individual and His World

The story of child development begins with the interactions of a small package of DNA and ends with an adult human being living in a complex social network. Everyone has some beliefs and hypotheses as to how these many changes take place. Nobody has explained it all in a comprehensive theory, but many theorists have described and explained parts of it. A theory depends first of all on the point of view from which the observer looks at the human scene and consequently on the phenomena that he observes. Theories of growth and development usually have a biological flavor. Learning experiments may suggest the influence of physics. Research in social relationships often involves sociology and perhaps anthropology. This chapter deals with six types of interactions that represent different ways of looking at human phenomena. They are equilibration, growth and development, learning, maturation, evolutionary adaptation, and heredity.

Equilibration

The organism constantly regulates its life processes so as to maintain physical and mental states within certain limits.

HOMEOSTASIS

Homeostasis is a balance that the organism maintains within itself during the processes of living and as environmental influences affect its internal conditions. Since the balance is continually upset and re-created, through a complex of interactions, it can be called a *dynamic equilibrium*. Through activities that are mostly unconscious, the individual keeps his blood sugar at a definite level, his water content within a given range, his oxygen content just so. Breathing and heartbeat speed up or slow down from their average rates to restore disturbed balances. The mechanisms of homeostasis regulate sleeping and waking states, activity and rest. Pressures and depleted tissues may register consciously as felt needs, leading to such purposeful interactions with the environment as eating, drinking, and eliminating.

Looming large in the life of a newborn infant, the problems of homeostasis dwindle throughout infancy and childhood. By about 3 months of age, basic physiological processes are well controlled. At any time throughout the life span, however, when the balance is seriously threatened, when biological demands become crucial or urgent, the individual drops his higher-order activities, such as giving a lecture or playing tennis, in order to restore the balance within his body.

PSYCHOLOGICAL EQUILIBRIUM

The search for balance occurs in the mental realm as well as in the physical. Equilibration is the process of achieving a state of balance. Sooner or later, the state of equilibrium is upset and a new one must be created. Equilibration includes selecting stimuli from the world, seeking this or that kind, more or less, paying attention to some of them and using some in more complex mental operations. When you consider all the sounds, sights, tastes, and other perceptions available, it follows that a person could not possibly attend to all of them at once. The mother or principal caretaker protects the infant and young child from excessive stimulation, helping the child gradually to take over the functions of selecting and ignoring stimuli [65].

Equilibration is one of Piaget's principles of mental development [50, pp. 5–8]. Action can be provoked when equilibrium is upset by finding a new object, being asked a question, identifying a problem; in fact, by any new experience. Equilibrium is re-established by reaching a goal, answering a question, solving a problem, imitating, establishing an effective tie or any other resolution of the difference between the new factor or situation and the mental organization already existing. Equilibration results in the successive stages of intelligence that Piaget describes.

Equilibration, in Piaget's theory, includes two complementary processes through which the person proceeds to more complex levels of organization— *assimilation,* which is the taking in from the environment what the organism can deal with and *accommodation,* the changing of the organism to fit external circumstances. Just as the body can assimilate foods and not other substances, so the mind can take in certain aspects and events in the external world and not others. Existing structures or *schemas* incorporate experiences that fit them or that almost fit them.

A schema is a pattern of action and/or thought. A baby develops some schemas before he is born and has them for starting life as a newborn. With simple schemas, he interacts with his environment, working toward equilibration. He achieves equilibrium over and over again, by using the schemas available to him at the moment. For example, a baby has a furry toy kitten that he knows as *kitty.* When given a small furry puppy he calls it *kitty,* strokes it and pats it, assimilating the puppy to an existing schema. A new little horse on wheels requires accommodation, since it is too different to be assimilated into the schema for dealing with *kitty.* It looks different; it feels different; it is not good for stroking and patting, but something can be done with the wheels that cannot be done with *kitty.* A new pattern of action is required. The child accommodates by changing and organizing existing schemas to form a schema for dealing with *horsey.* Thus the child grows in his understanding of the world and his ability to deal with his experiences in meaningful ways. Assimilation conserves the structural systems that he has while accommodation effects changes through which he copes more adequately with his environment and behaves in increasingly complex ways.

When homeostasis presents no problems, such as hunger, thirst, or fatigue, a person looks for something to do, something interesting, a new experience. If equilibrium were completely satisfying in itself, then surely he would sit or lie quietly doing nothing. In looking for action, the child seems to be trying to upset his state of equilibrium, as though equilibration were fun! And so it is. Activity is intrinsic in living tissue, brain cells included. The nervous system demands input, just as the digestive system does. Curiosity, exploration, competence, and achievement motivation are all outgrowths of the human propensity for enjoying the process of equilibration. The first stage of the process, perception of a problem, an incongruity or discrepancy, involves tension and a feeling of incompleteness. Something is missing or something is wrong.

The baby pushes himself forward to grasp a toy that is out of reach. The 4-year-old makes a mailbox that is necessary for his game of postman. The first grader sounds out a new word. Each child reduces a feeling of tension as he creates a new equilibrium. The equilibration (achievement of new balance) makes him into a slightly different person from what he has been, a person who can move forward a bit, a person who has made his own mailbox and can therefore make other things, a person who can read another word. Thus, equilibration is a way of describing behavior development. New and more complex behavior occurs as it is demanded by the person's relationship with his surroundings.

When a person's schemas are adequate to deal with the situation in which he finds himself, he reacts automatically. For example, the response of a hungry breast-fed baby of 3 months would be quite automatic when offered his mother's breast. A 10-year-old would automatically answer the question "What is two times two?" When the schemas are not quite adequate to the situation, the child uses what he has, changing them slightly into actions which do solve the problem. For instance, the baby would change his behavior sufficiently to cope with a bottle and the 10-year-old with "$2x = 4$. What does x equal?" The change that takes place at the same time within the child is the development of a new behavior pattern or schema. A pleasant feeling of curiosity and satisfaction accompanies successful adjustments to demands for new behavior.

A person feels uneasy when he encounters a situation in which his resources are very inadequate. In order to provoke uneasiness, the problem must be somewhat similar to those that a person can solve, but not similar enough for him to succeed with. Such a problem for the baby mentioned might be a cup of milk. For the 10-year-old it might be an equation such as $5x - 49/x = 20x/5$. If the situation is so far removed from a person's past experience that his schemas for dealing with it are extremely inadequate, then he will have no reaction to it. He will not notice it. He will not select from the environment the stimuli that would pose the problem. The baby will not try to drink out of a carton full of cans of milk. The child won't attempt to solve:

$$5x + 6y = 145$$
$$12x - 3y = 21$$

Familiar objects in unfamiliar guise produce unpleasantness, uneasiness, or even fear. (Chimpanzees are afraid of the keeper in strange clothes, an anesthetized chimp, or a plaster cast of a chimp's head. Human babies are afraid of strangers.) In order to be frightened or to get the unpleasant feeling, the subject must first have residues of past experience with which to contrast the present experience. Thus does incongruity arise, with its accompanying unpleasant feeling tone. If the individual can cope with the situation successfully, he achieves equilibration and its accompanying pleasant feeling tone. Stimuli preferred and chosen are those that are slightly more complex than the state of equilibrium that the individual has already reached. Thus he moves on to a new state of equilibrium [51].

Growth and Development

The child's body becomes larger and more complex while his behavior increases in scope and complexity. If any distinction is made between the two terms, growth refers to size, and development to complexity. However, the two terms are often used interchangeably, and this is what we have done. The terms *growth* and *development* were borrowed from the physical field, but they are commonly understood in connection with mental and personality characteristics. One can say, "He has grown mentally," or "He has developed mentally." The statement means "He is now functioning on a more complex intellectual level." Or one can speak of growth of personality and development of attitudes. Listening in on second-grade and fifth-grade classrooms in the same school building will reveal differences in subject matter interests and in mode of thinking.

Growth or development can be shown to have taken place either by comparing younger and older individuals at the same moment of time or by comparing the same individuals at two different points of time. When the measures of some characteristic of a number of individuals are averaged by age groups, the averages of the successive age groups show what growth has taken place. If each individual is measured only once, that is, if there are different people at each age, the study is *cross-sectional.* If the same individuals are measured at each successive age, the study is *longitudinal.* If some individuals do not remain available for continued study and new ones are added, the study is called *mixed longitudinal.* In a cross-sectional study, growth status at each age is investigated, and inferences regarding growth are drawn from *differences* between any groups. *Change* in status from age to age can be inferred only if the individuals at the two ages can be assumed to be comparable in all relevant ways. In a longitudinal study both growth status at each age and change in status from age to age can be investigated more precisely, because the same individuals are involved and actual growth patterns are established for individuals.

PRINCIPLES OF GROWTH

There are a number of generalizations about growth that are more apparent with respect to physical growth but that, as far as research can show, are also true for psychological growth. We elaborate on nine such statements about growth at this point, some of them with subheadings.

Variation of Rates. Rates of growth vary from one individual to another, and they vary within one individual. An organism grows at varying rates, from one time to another. The organs and systems grow at varying rates and at different times. There is a sex difference in rates and terminals. Various group differences can be shown. It is no wonder that comparisons of growth require facts obtained by highly controlled methods.

An organism and its parts grow at rates that are different at different times. The body as a whole, as measured by height and weight, shows a pattern of velocity that is fast in infancy, moderate in the preschool period, slow during the school years, and fast in the beginning of adolescence. Figure 5-1 illustrates growth

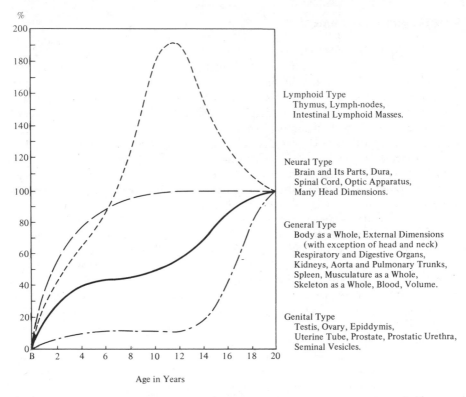

Figure 5-1. Growth curves of the body as a whole and of three types of tissue. Values at each age are computed as percentages of values for total growth.

Source: Reproduced by permission from J. A. Harris, C. M. Jackson, D. G. Paterson, and R. E. Scammon. *The measurement of man.* Minneapolis: University of Minnesota Press, 1930.

of four types of tissue, expressed at each age as percentages of the values for total growth. The general type of growth, which represents not only height and weight but muscles, skeleton, and most of the internal organs, is illustrated by a sigmoid curve, an elongated S. The brain and related tissues grow in a different pattern of velocity, very fast during the first 2 years, moderately until about 6, and very little after that. The growth curve for genital tissue is almost the reverse of that of neural tissue. The genital system grows very little during infancy and childhood and very fast in adolescence. The fourth curve in Figure 5-1 represents the lymph system which grows rapidly throughout infancy and childhood, reaches a peak just before puberty, and then decreases in size throughout adolescence.

Rates of growth vary from one individual to another. Some children are fast growers, some moderate, and some slow in regard to the number of years taken to reach maturity. Periods of fast and slow growth vary as to when they occur and for how long. One child begins the pubescent growth spurt earlier or later than another, grows faster or slower during the spurt, and finishes sooner or later.

There are sex differences in rates. Early in fetal life, girls show evidence of maturing faster than boys, especially in skeletal development. At birth, girls are four weeks ahead of boys skeletally. Boys' skeletal development is about 80 per cent of that of girls' from birth to maturity [59, p. 43]. Girls are ahead of boys in dentition, as measured by eruption of permanent teeth. Although sex differences in height and weight before the preadolescent growth spurt are very slight, favoring boys, sexual maturity and its antecedent growth spurt occur in girls about two years before they do in boys. Therefore, there is a period of about two years when girls are taller and heavier than boys. At all ages, girls are more mature physiologically than boys.

Individual Differences in Terminals. It is obvious, yet it is essential in understanding growth, to recognize that for different people maturity comes at different points. You have only to walk down the street to observe that some people grow until they are over six feet tall, others stop at five feet, and most people stop in between. Measurable mental growth stops at different times for different individuals too. The average girl reaches height and weight terminals before the average boy. Little is known about mental growth terminals.

Dynamic Interrelations in Growth. It would be surprising if different measures of growth were not related to each other. A tremendous number of studies have probed into the question of interrelationships of growth-controlling and regulating mechanisms.

Correlations between measures of growth can be between measures in the same field (physical–physical, mental–mental, and so on), or in different fields (physical–mental, mental–emotional). Skeletal development, assessed by X rays of the wrist, is at present the best indicator of physiological maturity, although if body proportions could be quantified and scaled in some manageable way, this might prove even more useful. Fat thickness in childhood is also a measure of general physiological maturity [24]. Sexual maturity and eventual height can be predicted with good accuracy from measurements of skeletal maturity. A general factor of bodily maturity operating throughout the growth period influences the child's growth as a whole, including his skeleton, size, physiological reactions, and possibly intelligence. Influencing factors of more limited scope operate independently of the general factor and of each other. One of these limited factors controls baby teeth, another permanent teeth, another the ossification centers in the skeleton, and probably several others regulate brain growth. This is why various measures of physical growth have low positive correlations with each other. If there were only one controlling factor, then the different measures would presumably all correlate highly or even perfectly with one another [59].

Studies of the relation between physical and mental growth show a small but consistent positive correlation, bearing out the hypothesis of a general factor that influences all growth processes. This relationship has been documented by a variety of studies [1, 9, 11, 33, 56, 57]. A study of children at the extremes of distributions of mental traits showed gifted boys to be significantly ahead of retarded boys in measures of physical growth [33]. A small positive correlation between mental ability and size is also found in adults [60]. As an example of the relationships between growth and personality, there is evidence that early maturers feel more adequate and more comfortable about themselves than do late maturers [32, 45].

Optimal Tendency. An organism behaves as though it were seeking to reach its maximum potential for development in both structure and function. Even though growth is interrupted, such as in periods of inadequate food supply, the child (or organism) makes up for the lean period as soon as more and better food is available, returning to his characteristic pattern of growth. Only if the deprivation is severe, or if it occurs throughout a critical period, will he show permanent effects from it. During the deprivation period, the organism adapts by slowing growth and cutting down on the use of energy.

All sorts of adaptive arrangements are worked out when there are interferences with the normal course of development, as though the child is determined to reach his best potential by another route when one is blocked. The child with poor eyesight seeks extra information from his other senses. Babies with a tendency toward rickets drink cod liver oil freely if permitted to, selecting their own diets from a wide variety of simple foods [14]. For white children in the northern United States, the characteristics of the home were found to be most important in determining how well the child did at school, but for southern black children the characteristics of the school were more important than those of the home. "It is as if the child drew sustenance from wherever it was available. When the home had more intellectual stimulation to offer, it became more determining; but when the school could provide more stimulation than the home, then the school became the more influential factor." [10, p. 106].

Gesell has stated the principle of optimal tendency as follows. "Every breach in the normal complex of growth is filled through regenerative, substantive, or compensatory growth of some kind. . . . Insurance reserves are drawn upon whenever the organism is threatened. . . . Herein lies the urgency, the almost irrepressible quality of growth" [26, p. 165]. This principle has been recognized as working in physical realms as well as organic, where there seems to be a self-stabilizing or target-seeking property of certain systems [62].

Differentiation and Integration. From large global patterns of behavior, smaller, more specific patterns emerge. Later the small, specific patterns can be combined into new, complicated, larger patterns. For example, a photographic study of human beginnings shows an 11½ weeks' fetus reacting to being stroked on the right cheek [26, p. 25]. The fetus contracted the muscles of its neck, trunk, and shoulder, causing its whole body to bend away from the stimulus and the arms and hands to move backward. When a newborn infant is stroked on the cheek he turns toward the stimulus, pursing his lips and opening his mouth when his lips touch something. Thus, he shows a new, specialized response pattern that involves a small part of his body instead of the whole. As he grows older, the rooting response changes and becomes integrated with other behavior patterns. Instead of turning toward food when he is touched near the mouth, he turns toward the breast or bottle when he sees it. His hands come into play in guiding food toward his mouth. Later he uses a knife and fork. He is integrating behavior patterns of eyes and hands with the rooting pattern, forming a smoothly functioning whole.

Bower analyzes the process of reaching and grasping in terms of differentiation and integration. The newborn baby will reach for a seen object, opening the hand before contact and closing it on contact, but too quickly for hand closure to have been released by the contact. The reaching and grasping is a unitary act. Reaching rarely occurs after 4 weeks, but reappears at around 20 weeks, in a different form. The infant can now reach without grasping and can also combine them. Reaching and grasping are differentiated. Either reaching or grasping can be corrected during the act instead of having to be corrected by starting again. Reaching and grasping are integrated. They are separate but combinable [7, pp. 150–166].

Examples can also be taken from purely intellectual fields, such as mathematics. There is a stage of maturity at the end of infancy when a child knows *one, two* and *a-lot-of*. At 5, he has differentiated *three* and *four* out of *a-lot-of*. By 6, numbers up to ten have true meaning. Using these differentiated concepts, the child next combines them in addition and subtraction to form new and more complicated concepts. Conceptual differentiation and integration are at work as the student moves up through algebra and geometry into higher mathematics. There remains an undifferentiated sphere where each person stops in his progress in mathematics.

Developmental Direction. Certain sequences of development take place in certain directions, in reference to the body. The motor sequence takes two such directions, *cephalocaudal* (head to tail) and *proximodistal* (midline to outer extremities). Like all animals, the child grows a relatively large, complex head region early in life, whereas the tail region or posterior is small and simple. As he becomes older, the region next to the head grows more, and finally, the end region grows. Coordination follows the same direction, the muscles of the eyes coming under control first, then the neck muscles, then arms, chest, and back, and finally the legs. The motor sequence illustrates the proximodistal direction by the fact that the earliest controlled arm movements, as in reaching, are large movements, controlled mostly by shoulder muscles. Later the elbow is brought into play in reaching, then the wrist, and then the fingers.

Normative Sequence. The sequence of motor development has long been noticed and understood as one of the ways of nature. "A child must creepe ere he walke."

As the structures of the body mature in their various sequences, they function in characteristic ways, provided that the environment permits appropriate interaction. The resulting behavior patterns appear in an orderly sequence. Sequences have been described for locomotion, use of hands, language, problem solving, social behavior, and other kinds of behavior [12, 27, 28]. During the decade of the 1930s, the bulk of research in child development was normative, delineating sequences of development and designating average ages for the patterns observed. The classic studies, exemplified by Gesell's work, viewed normative sequences as an unfolding. Although the role of the environment was implicit in these early writings, the focus was on regulation from innate forces. Today interaction between organism and environment is emphasized as basic to development. The change in viewpoint has come about to some extent because of the broadening of areas of child study to include a variety of cultures, at home and abroad. Although child development continues to take place in orderly sequences, exceptions can be found [16]. Hence normative sequences cannot be considered as universal, but must be understood as occurring in particular kinds of environments.

Epigenesis. Growth takes place upon the foundation that is already there. New parts arise out of and upon the old. Although the organism becomes something new as it grows, it still has continuity with the past and hence shows certain consistencies over time. Through interactions with the environment, the organism continues to restructure itself throughout life, being at each moment the product of the interaction that took place in the previous moment between organism and environment. A toddler's body results from interactions of a baby's body with food, water, and air. The motor pattern of walking is derived and elaborated from creeping and standing. Writing is built from scribbling.

Critical Periods. There are certain limited times during the growth period of any organism when it will interact with a particular environment in a specific way. The result of interactions during critical periods can be especially beneficial or harmful. The prenatal period includes specific critical periods for physical growth. The first three months are critical for the development of eyes, ears, and brain, as shown by defects in children whose mothers had rubella during the first three months of pregnancy. Apparently those organs are most vulnerable to the virus of rubella when they are in their periods of rapid growth.

Experiments on vision with human and animal infants reveal critical ages for the development of visual responses, times when the infant will either show the response without experience or will learn it readily [21]. If the visual stimulus is not given at the critical age (as when baby monkeys are reared in darkness), the animal later learns the response with difficulty, or not at all.

Psychological development also shows critical periods in the sense that certain behavior patterns are acquired most readily at certain times of life. Critical periods in personality development include the period of primary socialization, when the infant makes his first social attachments [55] and develops basic trust [18]. A warm relationship with a mother figure is thought to be essential among the experiences that contribute to a sense of trust [8]. This type of critical period is probably not so final and irreversible as is a critical period for the development of an organ in the embryo. If the term *critical period* is applied to the learning of skills such as swimming and reading, then it should be understood that it signifies the most *opportune* time for learning and not the only one [43].

STAGE THEORIES OF DEVELOPMENT

The last three principles of growth are incorporated in theories of child development that present growth occurring in stages. Each stage is created through *epigenesis,* behavior patterns being organized and reorganized or transformed in an orderly sequence. Thus, past, present, and future development are related and can be understood as an ongoing process. Small pieces of behavior can be interpreted in terms of the stage when they occur instead of being invested with one meaning. For example, crying at 1 month of age was seen to be an active attempt to overcome interference with sucking, whereas crying at 1 year of age was found to be a passive mode of response to environmental frustration [36]. Stage theories encourage research that establishes ways of predicting future development [31].

This book is organized in stages of development, leaning heavily on two stage theories: Erikson's theory of personality growth, and Piaget's theory of the growth of intelligence. The ages corresponding with the various stages are only approximations or rough landmarks. Although it is useful to be able to anchor stage concepts to some sort of chronology, it is important to realize that stages are only age-related and not age-determined. The growth principle, *variation of rates,* applies here.

Erikson's Stages. Erikson's theory might be called epigenetic in a double sense. Not only does it portray epigenetic stages but it was built upon Freud's theory and yet is a new organization and a unique creation. Freud proposed psychosexual stages of development, each of which used a certain zone of the body for gratification of the *id* (the unconscious source of motives, strivings, desires, and energy). The *ego,* which mediates between the demands of the id, the outside world, and the superego, "represents what may be called reason and common sense, in contrast to the id, which contains the passions" [23, p. 15]. The *superego* or ego ideal corresponds roughly to *conscience.* Freud's psychosexual stages are *oral,* when the mouth is the main zone of satisfaction, about the first year; *anal,* when pleasure comes from anal and urethral sensations, the second and third years; *phallic,* the third and fourth years, a time of pleasure from genital stimulation; *oedipal,* also genital but now, at 4 and 5 years, the child regards the parent of the opposite sex as a love object and the same-sex parent as a rival; *latency,* from 6 to around 11, when sexual cravings are repressed (made unconscious) and the child identifies with the parent and peers of his own sex; *puberal* when mature genital sexuality begins.

Erikson uses Freud's concepts in his theory of psychosocial development, adding to the complexity of each stage and also adding three stages above the puberal, thus dealing with adulthood as a time for growth. Progress through the stages takes place in an orderly sequence. In making his stages psychosocial as well as psychosexual, Erikson recognizes the interaction between individual and culture as contributing to personal growth. Although Freud's theory has a great deal to say about pathology, Erikson's offers a guide to both illness and health of personality. For each stage, there are problems to be solved within the cultural context. Thus, each stage is a critical period for the development of certain attitudes, convictions, and abilities. After the satisfactory solution of each crisis, the person emerges with an increased sense of unity, good judgment, and capacity to "do well" [19, p. 92]. The conflicts are never completely resolved nor are the problems disposed of forever. Each stage is described with a positive and negative outcome of the crisis involved. The stages are [18, pp. 247–274]:

1. *Basic trust versus basic mistrust.* Similar to Freud's oral stage, the development of a sense of trust dominates the first year. Success means coming to

trust the world, other people, and oneself. Since the mouth is the main zone of pleasure, trust grows on being fed when hungry, pleasant sensations when nursing, and the growing conviction that his own actions have something to do with pleasant events. Consistent, loving care is trust-promoting. Mistrust develops when trust-promoting experiences are inadequate, when the baby has to wait too long for comfort, when he is handled harshly or capriciously. Since life is never perfect, shreds of mistrust are woven into the fabric of personality. Problems of mistrust recur and have to be solved later, but when trust is dominant, healthy personality growth takes place.

2. *Autonomy versus shame and doubt.* The second stage, corresponding to Freud's anal period, predominates during the second and third year. Holding on and letting go with the sphincter muscles symbolizes the whole problem of autonomy. The child wants to do for himself with all of his powers: his new motor skills of walking, climbing, manipulating; his mental powers of choosing and deciding. If his parents give him plenty of suitable choices, times to decide when his judgment is adequate for successful outcomes, then he grows in autonomy. He gets the feeling that he can control his body, himself, and his environment. The negative feelings of doubt and shame arise when his choices are disastrous, when other people shame him or force him in areas where he could be in charge.

3. *Initiative versus guilt.* The Oedipal part of the genital stage of Freudian theory, at 4 and 5 years, is to Erikson the stage of development of a sense of initiative. Now the child explores the physical world with his senses and the social and physical worlds with his questions, reasoning, imaginative, and creative powers. Love relationships with parents are very important. Conscience develops. Guilt is the opposite pole of initiative.

4. *Industry versus inferiority.* Solutions of problems of initiative and guilt bring about entrance to the stage of developing a sense of industry, the latency period of Freud. The child is now ready to be a worker and producer. He wants to do jobs well instead of merely starting them and exploring them. He practices and learns the rules. Feelings of inferiority and inadequacy result when he feels he cannot measure up to the standards held for him by his family or society.

5. *Identity versus role diffusion.* The Freudian puberal stage, beginning at the start of adolescence, involves resurgence of sexual feelings. Erikson adds to this concept his deep insights into the adolescent's struggles to integrate all the roles he has played and hopes to play, his childish body concept with his present physical development, his concepts of his own society, and the value of what he thinks he can contribute to it. Problems remaining from earlier stages are reworked.

6. *Intimacy versus isolation.* A sense of identity is the condition for the ability to establish true intimacy, "the capacity to commit himself to concrete affiliations and partnerships and to develop the ethical strength to abide by such commitments" [18, p. 263]. Intimacy involves understanding and allowing oneself to be understood. It may be, but need not be, sexual. Without intimacy, a person feels isolated and alone.

7. *Generativity versus self-absorption.* Involvement in the well-being and development of the next generation is the essence of generativity. While it includes being a good parent, it is more. Concern with creativity is also part of it. Adults need to be needed by the young, and unless the adults can be concerned and contributing, they suffer from stagnation.

8. *Ego integrity versus despair.* The sense of integrity comes from satisfaction with one's own life cycle and its place in space and time. The individual feels that his actions, relationships, and values are all meaningful and acceptable. Despair arises from remorseful remembrance of mistakes and wrong decisions plus the conviction that it is too late to try again.

Figure 5-2 shows the normal timing of Erikson's stages of psychosocial development. The critical period for each stage is represented by a swelling of the rope that stretches throughout life. The ropes indicate that no crisis is ever solved completely and finally, but that strands of it are carried along, to be dealt with at different levels. As one rope swells at its critical period, the other ropes are affected and interact. As Chapter 4 showed, solutions to identity problems involve problems in all the other stages. The metaphor of the rope can also be extended by thinking of the personalities of a family's members as being intertwined ropes. When the parents' Generativity strands are becoming dominant, the infant's Trust strand is dominant. The two ropes fit smoothly together, indicating a complementary relationship between the personalities of infant and parents.

Piaget's Stages. Figure 5-2 shows Piaget's stages in the development of intelligence. Piaget is concerned with the nature of knowledge and how it is acquired. His studies of infants and children have revealed organizations of structures by which the child comes to know the world. The structural units are *schemas,* patterns of action and/or thought. As the child matures, he uses his existing schemas to interact, transforming them through the process of equilibration. Each stage of development is an advance from the last one, built upon it by reorganizing it and adapting more closely to reality. Reorganization and adaptation go on continuously, but from one time to another the results differ from each other. Piaget has broken this series of organizations of structures into units called *periods* and stages. There are three periods, each of which extends the previous one, reconstructs it, and surpasses it [51, pp. 152–159]. Periods are divided into stages that have a constant sequence, no matter whether the child achieves them at a slow or fast pace. Progress through the periods and stages is affected by organic growth, exercise and experience, social interaction or equilibration. The periods are

1. *Sensorimotor.* Lasting from birth until about 2, sensorimotor intelligence exists without language and symbols. Practical and aimed at getting results, it works through action-schemas [51, p. 4]. Beginning with the reflex patterns present at birth, the baby builds more and more complex schemas through a succession of six stages. Figure 5-2 lists the names of the stages. During this period the baby constructs a schema of the permanence of objects. He comes to know that things and people continue to exist even when he cannot see them and he realizes that they move when he is not looking. He learns con-

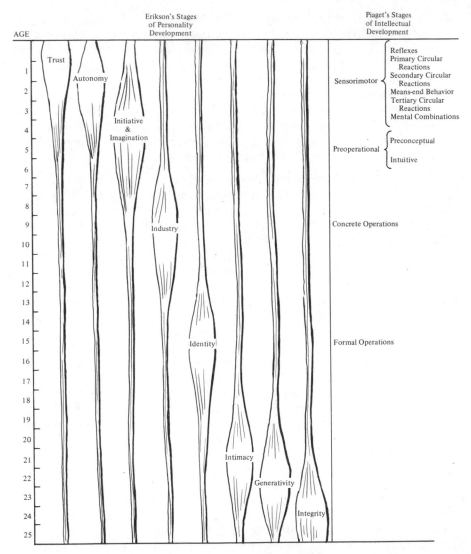

Figure 5-2. Schematic representation of Erikson's stages of psychosocial development, with names of Piaget's stages of the development of intelligence.

trol of his body in space. He begins to use language to imitate and to make internal representations of reality.

2. *Preoperational.* Sometimes this period, from about 2 to 7, is considered a subperiod of the whole time from 2 to 11. It is distinctly different, however, from the sensorimotor period and the period that comes around 7, the period of concrete operations. Two stages, preconceptual and intuitive thought, are

included. The preoperational period is marked by the *semiotic* function and imitation. The semiotic function, often called *symbolizing,* is the use of an indicator or sign as distinct from the object or event to which it refers [51, pp. 52–91]. For example, the bell that announces dinner is perceived as distinct from the food but as indicating food. Achievements show much use of his new representational abilities, in deferred imitation (imitation starting after the model has disappeared), symbolic play, drawing, mental images, and verbal representation. The child thinks that names are essential parts of the objects to which they refer. When he gives a reason, it is in terms of how he wants things to be. He sees no need to come to the same conclusions as anyone else because he does not realize the existence of viewpoints other than his own. Throughout this stage the child becomes more flexible in his thinking, more able to use past experience, and to consider more than one aspect of an event at a time.

3. *Concrete operations.* The period from about 7 to 11 years of age is essentially the time when the child can think about real, concrete things in systematic ways, although he has great difficulty in thinking about abstractions. He orders, counts, classifies, and thinks in terms of cause and effect. He develops a new concept of permanence, called *conservation,* through which he realizes that amount, weight, volume, and number stay the same when outward appearances of objects or groups are changed. Although he finds it difficult to change his hypotheses, he learns to take other people's points of view and comes to feel that his reasoning and his solutions to problems should check with other people's. His thinking has become socialized.

4. *Formal operations.* The period of formal operations or logical thought begins at about 11 and continues to develop until about 15, when the individual has the mental operations for adult thinking. Instead of having to think about concrete objects, he can think and reason in purely abstract terms. He can think systematically, combining all factors in a situation so as to exhaust all possibilities. He makes hypotheses and tests them. This type of thinking is basic to logic and to the scientific method. The limitation of this stage is a confusion of what could and should be with what is practically possible. The adolescent resists the imperfections in the world when he can construct ideal arrangements in his mind.

Memory

Both remembering and learning refer to changes in the organism that result from interactions with the environment. In remembering, as in all interactions, the child brings his own resources to bear on the particular environment in which he lives. Some cultures stress memorizing more than others do. Children may be encouraged and assisted in remembering what is considered important to remember. Until recently, it was important for a Maori to be able to recite the names of his ancestors, right back to the one who came to New Zealand in a particular one of the canoes that brought the first Maoris. Because textbooks are scarce in India, college students memorize extensively. In North America, organizing and understanding are often preferred to memorizing.

Memory means the storing of experience within the person, in all likelihood in his brain, in such ways that he can hold it and retrieve it. *Learning* occurs when behavior changes as a result of experience. Therefore, many learning experiments involve memory and many memory experiments involve learning. For many years, psychologists have been exploring the conditions under which children learn everything from swimming to moral behavior. More recently, scientists from different disciplines have been trying to discover the processes by which human beings take in information from their senses, process it, store it, and take it out for use when they need it.

THE STRUCTURES AND PROCESSES OF MEMORY

The *hippocampus,* a deep part of the brain, is a place where memories are made, or, more exactly, the hippocampus is essential for the process of long-term storing of new experience in retrievable form [44]. Biochemical changes occur in the brain as the processes of memory are carried on. One of the mysteries of the process is the form in which the brain stores experience and the method by which it converts perceptual input into items that can be stored and found for later use. Pribram suggests that memory works on the principle of the *hologram* (a construct from physics), a mechanism that codes 10 billion bits of information in the space of about a cubic centimeter [52].

The various sense organs react to stimuli. The processes of attention select certain features. *Perception* involves analyzing stimuli, first in terms of physical or sensory features and later matching them with stored memories and extracting meaning. If processing continues to a deeper level, the material is enriched by associating it with additional stored material. Thus, more meaning is added. A theory of memory holds that the more deeply a stimulus is processed, the longer and more fully it is remembered [13]. Some researchers think that there are different storage structures for long-term and short-term memory, but others think that the same processes are at work and that the level of processing determines how long and how well an experience will be remembered.

The term *control processes* refers to the ways in which an individual uses his perceptual processes, puts material into his memory store (or stores), and finds (retrieves) the stored material when he wants it. The methods of analyzing and coding material and extracting meaning from it will depend, of course, on the type of mental operations used. As Piaget has shown, mental operations are stage-related, depending upon the maturity and experience of the child. Some control processes can be modified by the individual as he adapts to new conditions and learns new techniques [53]. "Learning to learn" includes adopting new patterns of control that improve remembering.

Developmental research deals with age-related changes in the various aspects of memory. Topics include long-term and short-term memory and their connections with each other and with input, response, and control systems. Experimenters vary input, such as visual or verbal, color or form. They require different responses, such as recall or recognition, after different time lags. They consider the effects of intelligence and nutrition, and even of sibling position [13, 53].

Learning

Learning occurs when behavior changes as a result of experience. Behavior includes inner processes as well as actions. Different approaches to the study of learning give different emphases. Some of the terms of behaviorism focus on something being done to the learner. Thus, the learner may be seen as passive. *Behavior shaping,* for example, sounds very much like a "psychosculptor" hewing out a neat set of behavior patterns from a rough bundle of mass activity. (Such is not really the case, as is seen later.) Presently, however, the self is seen as an active shaper of personal destiny, as evaluator, decision-maker, and active learner. The view of self as active is illustrated in the following section on academic learning and in the discussion of social learning. The self can also be seen as active in reinforcement and conditioning.

ACADEMIC LEARNING

A new way of measuring and understanding school learning is offered by Bloom's use of *time* as a yardstick [6]. A child takes a measurable length of time to reach criteria of achievement in reading, mathematics, science, literature, a foreign language, and so on. Bloom reviews studies of the length of time required by children in different countries to reach the same criteria. The average student in the highest-scoring of the developed nations achieved 12 years of learning in 12 years. For children in low-scoring developed nations, the achievement was 8 years in 12 years. The average child in an underdeveloped country achieved 6 years in 12 years. United States research has shown that if the highest 20 per cent of students reach the criterion level one year, 50 per cent will reach it the next year and 80 per cent in 2 years. When mastery teaching is used and students spend extra time during the first year in learning, 80 per cent can reach the same criterion as the upper 20 per cent in one year. (Mastery teaching includes identifying gaps in learning and then using corrective procedures designed especially for the child's particular needs.)

When mastery learning procedures are first offered to students who are not learning fast, the slowest 5 per cent of learners take about five times as long to reach criterion as do the fastest 5 per cent of learners. After achieving several learning units through mastery procedures, the slowest learners reach criterion in three times or less what was required by the fastest. Thus, it pays off to help the slow learners in the early stages. Most likely they will increase in self-esteem and self-confidence as they achieve more and as they learn more effective ways of learning.

Further studies reviewed by Bloom show that the fastest learners spend more time *on task,* or actually learning. From both observation and interviews, the fast learners were found to spend large amounts of time in school actively engaged with the subject matter. Slower learners were likely to spend the first 20 minutes talking, arranging their materials, and fixing their hair and clothing. Then they worked for about 20 minutes. The next 15 or 20 minutes were spent getting ready to leave. *Time on task* explains many of the differences between fast learners and slow learners. In ghetto schools, apathy and hostility depress the amount of time spent on task. Here and in poor countries, hunger and malnutrition contribute to apathy.

Although human beings vary in their initial learning ability, all need to learn basic academic subjects in order to get along in the modern world. Nearly all can learn them if enough time is allowed, but nearly all can learn them much faster and with greater satisfaction if teaching procedures enlist all of their learning potential.

Social Learning

One of the most remarkable features of human beings is that they learn so much and so easily from one another. People learn from the experience of those who lived in the past as well as from face-to-face encounters, learning from others' errors and successes instead of having to try out all kinds of actions. Very often, a person can acquire a new piece of behavior by simply watching another person perform it or by listening to the other person telling how to do it. However, a learner does not imitate everything she sees or hears. She chooses to do what is rewarding, or what she thinks will have positive reinforcement value.

SOCIALIZATION

Children learn by observing their parents and listening to them. Parents teach children through a variety of techniques, as they *socialize* the children. *Socialization* is the teaching done by members of a group or institution in order that the individual will learn to think, feel, and behave as a member of that group. Socialization occurs in people of all ages, but much of it takes place during childhood, as the developing person acquires appropriate values, attitudes, and behavior patterns. Parents are the primary socializers. Siblings and other family members also teach. Teachers and peers are important socializing agents as are, to a lesser extent, other members of the community.

Socialization refers to both the present and the future. The child learns to behave appropriately as the child he now is, but he also learns attitudes, values, and skills that he will use in the future. From interacting with his father, he learns the father role as well as the son role. Similarly, he observes his various socializers as worker, manager, host, citizen, and teacher, and in all the many roles that they play in his society. The child learns some specific information and skills, as well as values and attitudes. Thus, he is gradually socialized into his family, community, and nation through a process that maintains the values and behavior patterns of that group.

MODELING

Infants begin to imitate toward the end of the sensorimotor period. Piaget observes that imitation is always active, never automatic or nonintentional [49]. Imitation is accommodation, a way of modifying present schemas. Imitation is the child's first mode of representing an action. Throughout life, imitation continues to serve as an important mode of learning.

Bandura, who has conducted basic experiments on observational learning, concludes that "virtually all learning phenomena resulting from direct experience can occur on a vicarious basis by observing other people's behavior and its consequences for them" [4]. An action can be learned from one observation. It can be stored for a long time, to be used if and when an appropriate time comes.

Influences on Modeling. Although children will imitate spontaneously, various factors and circumstances have been shown to affect whether they do imitate. Age and developmental level are related to whether children will imitate the ways in which toys are manipulated [22]. The child's past experience with peers affects his tendency to imitate peers [29]. Children who had often been reinforced by peers were more likely to imitate a rewarding peer; children who had seldom been reinforced by peers were more likely to imitate a nonrewarding peer. What happens to the model also has an effect on the child. In one of Bandura's famous experiments, children saw a film of an aggressive model either being punished, rewarded, or having no consequences [3]. Then they were left in a room with the aggressed-against clown and the instruments of aggression, as well as other toys. Those who saw the model being punished did less imitating of his aggressive behavior than did those who saw the model being rewarded or having no consequences. When the children were offered reinforcers for imitating the aggression, the difference between the groups disappeared. Boys imitated more aggressive acts than girls after seeing the model punished, but when rewards were given, the sex difference disappeared. Thus, it seems that children inhibit aggressive imitation when they see the model punished, but they learn the behavior just as readily. Girls are more inhibited than boys by punishment for aggression, but they learn the behavior just as well. Bandura says that one of the most interesting questions in regard to modeling is whether one can keep people from learning what they have seen [4]. Presumably the answer is *no*.

These experiments, and many additional ones, give insight into modeling, but they cannot predict what a given individual will imitate. The situation is analogous to language. One can test a child's level of language development, but one cannot tell just what the child will say. Modeling involves abstracting from what is observed, storing it in memory in some symbolic form, making generalizations and rules about behavior, mentally putting together and trying out different kinds of behavior, and choosing which forms to act out at what times. Thus, other people's behavior is used creatively by the individual in an extraordinarily efficient way of developing new ways of acting that are suited to the particular occasion. Bandura has summarized the component processes of observational learning [4].

Component Processes. First, *attention* regulates the perception of modeled actions. Second, what is observed is transformed into representations that are preserved in *memory*. Coding and symbolic rehearsal make these transformations. Memory keeps the symbolically represented actions available as guides to performance. Third, new response patterns are integrated from *motor* acts. Fourth, *incentive* or *motivational* processes govern the choice of action patterns to be used.

Thus, it is the *person* who actively observes, remembers, judges, decides, and creates a response. The person's own values are the context in which the processes of modeling occur.

CONDITIONING

Conditioning, or learning by association, is the establishing of a connection between a stimulus and a response. In *classical conditioning,* the kind made famous by Pavlov, a neutral stimulus is presented with another stimulus that elicits an innate response. After several such presentations, the neutral stimulus is given without the other stimulus and the response occurs. Pavlov sounded a buzzer when he gave food to his dog. Eventually the dog salivated at the sound of the buzzer.

Operant, or *instrumental,* conditioning is done by rewarding the desired response whenever it occurs. Operant conditioning techniques have been developed for use in a wide variety of situations, with animal and human subjects. By rewarding small pieces of behavior, complex patterns can be built up, thus "shaping" or modifying the behavior of the subject. This technique has proven to be very useful in treating behavior disorders in infants, children, retardates, and the mentally ill.

Conditioning has been used to explore the abilities of infants and to show that newborn babies do learn [37]. Papoušek taught newborn babies to turn their heads to the sound of a buzzer by using a combination of classical and operant conditioning methods [47]. A bell was sounded and if the infant turned to the left, he was given milk. If he did not turn, head turning was elicited by touching the corner of his mouth with a nipple. Then he was given milk. Newborns were slow to condition, taking an average of 18 days, whereas at 3 months, only 4 days were required and by 5 months, 3 days were required. Two-month-old infants learned to operate a mobile by means of pressing their heads on their pillows [63].

REINFORCEMENT

Reinforcements are consequences of events, or so they are seen by the subject. A *positive* reinforcement makes the reoccurrence of the event more likely, a *negative* reinforcement, less likely. Positive reinforcement functions not only through being pleasant or rewarding but because it gives information, such as, "That was right," "You succeeded." Likewise, negative reinforcement is not only unpleasant; it informs the person, "You did wrong." Reinforcement is, therefore, not just a mechanical procedure by which one person manipulates another, but a means by which people can regulate their own behavior [4].

Reinforcement comes from both external and internal sources. People reward themselves when they think they have done well and punish themselves when they fail or do wrong. Or they may try to cheer themselves up after failure, by a reward. The reinforcement may be just a comment to oneself, such as "That was a great job!" Or a person may buy a present for herself or indulge in a fancy dessert. Children's self-rewarding behavior has been studied under various conditions. Although preschool children tend to reward themselves liberally [35], school-age children make complex judgments about giving themselves appropriate reinforcements. School-age children rewarded themselves differently for different types of altruistic behavior [40]. They also apparently considered the length of task and quality of performance in dispensing self-rewards [39]. Thus do children evaluate and direct their own behavior. When children receive inappropriate reinforcement at school, their learning behavior is likely to be depressed [30].

Modern behavior modification programs take account of the individual's capacity for self-regulation rather than simply administering external reinforcements [4]. The person who wants to change his behavior is helped to plan inducements for the desired behavior, to evaluate his own performance, and to dispense the reinforcers.

Successful socialization of children also makes use of children's growing powers of self-regulation. Even if behavior could be controlled by extrinsic rewards and punishments, the result would be a child who could not control herself. And, of course, external rewards and punishments will not give predictable results because the child herself is also active in the process. Experiments with adults have shown that external rewards and punishments sometimes decrease self-motivation [46]. The reason may be that the person sees himself as less self-controlled and with less freedom of choice when someone else is dispensing reinforcements.

Punishment especially is a risky technique of influence. Although punishment is often effective in suppressing behavior, it does not teach new, positive behavior. Parke has summarized the effects of punishment on children as shown by research [48]. Punishment suppressed behavior more effectively when it occurred close in time to the deviation. High-intensity punishment was more effective than low, but when it occurred promptly, high- and low-intensity punishment were equally effective. When the adult withdrew affection or was inconsistent with affection, children were likely to suppress undesired behavior in order to win back the affection. When reasoning and explanation accompanied punishment, light punishment was as effective as severe. Reviewing the deviance had the same effect. Inconsistency delayed the effect. Indiscriminate and harsh punishment may make the child avoid the punisher or may lead to passivity and withdrawal.

Maturation

As the child's bodily structures grow, they change in size and complexity, becoming more and more the way they will be in the mature state. Bodily functions likewise change as the structures do. The whole process is called *maturation*. Although maturation is controlled by hereditary factors, the environment must be adequate to support it. The growth principle of normative sequence is reflected in maturation, since structures and functions mature in an orderly, irreversible sequence. Since maturation is little affected by experience, its effects are the same throughout a species. An impoverished environment slows the process of maturation more than it changes quality or sequence.

Certain behavior patterns are the result of maturation more than of learning because they are relatively independent of experience. Many developmental processes involve both maturation and learning. Examples of processes that are largely maturational are the motor sequence and the emergence of language. In all but the most abnormal environments, infants go through regular sequences of raising the head, raising the chest, sitting, creeping, standing with support, and so on.

Another explanation of maturation is that certain experiences are encountered by everyone and are, therefore, not recognized as experience. Behavior patterns attributed to maturation are really the results of interactions with the universal environment. For instance, everyone makes postural adjustments to gravity, but nobody notices gravity. Another example is that everyone learns to chew food because everyone receives food. The emergence of language is a response to an almost universal experience, the hearing of spoken language.

Some theories of development, such as Gesell's, emphasize the role of maturation in determining behavior. Gesell's descriptions of behavior stages led some parents to think that they could do little to influence their children's behavior and that they must enjoy his good stages and wait patiently while he grew out of unattractive, annoying, or disturbing stages. In contrast, although Piaget recognizes that the body matures, he stresses the necessity for the child to interact, explore, and discover for himself in order to build his mental structures. Mental growth cannot be forced or hurried, however, since its counterpart is physical maturation. "Mental growth is inseparable from physical growth: the maturation of the nervous and endocrine systems, in particular, continues until the age of 16" [51, p. vii].

Evolutionary Adaptation

Evolutionary changes can be considered in terms of behavior patterns or behavior systems.

ETHOLOGY

The behavior patterns that develop through maturation can be traced back in the history of the species or the phylum. These fixed action patterns evolved as the animal adapted to a certain environment. *Ethology,* the study of the relation between animal behavior and environment, has influenced the study of human development, offering insight into certain kinds of behavior that cannot be explained as learning or fully understood as maturation. Lorenz pointed out the implications of ethology for understanding certain forms of human behavior [38]. Bowlby has integrated psychoanalytic theory with ethology [8]. Ainsworth [2] has done extensive research on attachment behavior, a main focus of the ethological approach to human development.

The adaptive behavior pattern becomes fixed in form, appearing as an innate skill in every member of a species, even though he has not had opportunities to learn [17]. A specific stimulus from the environment activates the particular behavior pattern, as though it were a key, unlocking the mechanism. Thus, the behavior is sometimes called an *innate response mechanism,* or IRM. For example, a toad's catching response is released by a small, moving object, a nine-week-old gosling gives an intense fear reaction to his first sight of a hawk, and a stickleback fish will attack a red spot that resembles the red underbelly of another stickleback.

Bowlby points out that the environment to which a species is adapted is the environment in which it evolved into its present form [8, p. 59]. Most likely, when man first emerged as a distinct species, he lived by hunting and gathering in a savannah environment, much like today's most primitive societies and not unlike the ground-dwelling primates [2]. Mother–infant reciprocal behavior was adapted to protecting the infant so as to ensure his survival. The baby's unlearned, spontaneous patterns of crying, clinging, and sucking brought him (and still bring him) into contact with the mother. Other aspects of attachment behavior, maturing a little later, serve to maintain and strengthen the contacts with the mother, who was (and still is) adapted or genetically programmed to respond with specific action patterns. In the urban environment of today, close physical contact of mother and baby is not necessary for protecting the baby from predators, but babies still behave as though it were and mothers still respond to their infants' behavior with innate action patterns. Closeness of mother and baby has other advantages, however, in terms of normal development.

BEHAVIOR SYSTEMS

Ascending the evolutionary scale, the nervous system and brain become more complex. Their first function is to control and integrate the other bodily systems and organs. In the higher animals and most notably in man, the cognitive system has its own needs and demands, in addition to its function as controller and coordinator. Curiosity, information seeking, and exploration are modes of obtaining what the cognitive system must have in order to function optimally. Dember maintains that the brain is not like a computer that acts only on demand, but rather it is "an instrument with needs of its own" [15]. Cognitive actions may even result in states that oppose the demands of other systems. Ideas or ideologies can be so strong that the person harms his own body or even kills himself. Such is the case with martyrs, political prisoners resisting torture, and people who accept dares.

Disharmony between behavioral systems is also discussed by Wolff [64]. He points out that different behavioral systems have evolved at different times and with considerable independence between them. Autonomic reactivity appears first followed by organized reflex action and diffuse nonreflex activity. Next, the voluntary behavior system develops and then language. Although all systems influence each other to some extent, there are times when a person's actions do not coincide with her feelings, or words with actions. Many therapies and techniques are presently trying to bring these systems into closer relationships. Such methods include Gestalt techniques, yoga, meditation, brain-wave conditioning, and control of the autonomic system. Wolff suggests that success in these efforts will have survival value for the species and may bring happiness to the individual.

Heredity

Although most students of child development will study the mechanisms of heredity in a biology course, we include a brief account here. After all, the mechanisms of heredity are what start the child developing and guide the course of development.

BIOLOGICAL INHERITANCE

The human being is composed of two main types of cells. By far the larger number of cells are the *body* cells. These are the cells that compose the skeleton, skin, kidneys, heart, and so on. A minority of cells are the *germ* cells. In the male, germ cells are called *spermatazoa* (the singular is *spermatazoon*), usually shortened to *sperm:* in the female, the germ cells are *ova* (the singular is *ovum*).

Each body cell is composed of several different parts, the most important of which for our present discussion are the *chromosomes,* of which there are 46, arranged in 23 pairs. The sizes and shapes of the chromosomes can be determined by viewing a prepared cell through an electron microscope. Twenty-two of the pairs of chromosomes are composed of two highly similar chromosomes, though each pair differs in certain respects from every other pair. These 22 pairs are similar in males and females. In males, the twenty-third pair is composed of two chromosomes that are unequal in size. The larger one is an *X chromosome;* the smaller is a *Y chromosome.* In females, the twenty-third pair is composed of two X chromosomes. When, in the course of growth, a body cell divides to form two

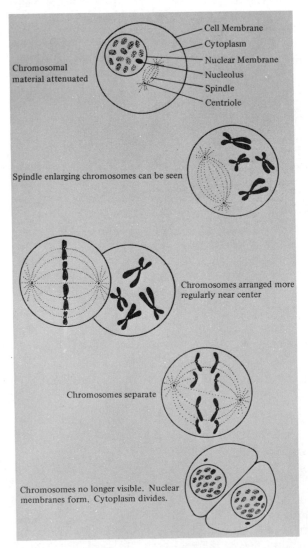

Chromosomal material attenuated

Cell Membrane
Cytoplasm
Nuclear Membrane
Nucleolus
Spindle
Centriole

Spindle enlarging chromosomes can be seen

Chromosomes arranged more regularly near center

Chromosomes separate

Chromosomes no longer visible. Nuclear membranes form. Cytoplasm divides.

Figure 5-3. Stages in the process of mitosis.

SOURCE: Adapted from P. A. Moody. *Genetics of man.* New York: W. W. Norton & Company, Inc., 1967. Figure 3–2, p. 28.

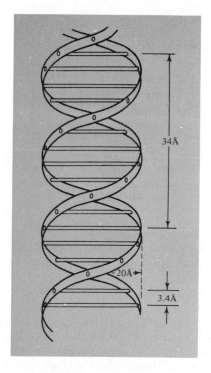

Figure 5-4. DNA takes the form of a double helix.

Source: Adapted from G. W. Burns. *The science of genetics*. New York: Macmillan Publishing Co., Inc. 1969. Figure 14–9, p. 258.

new cells, it goes through the process of *mitosis*. The result of mitosis is that each of the new cells has exactly the same kind and number of chromosomes as the first cell had before it divided. Figure 5-3 shows the process of mitosis.

DNA, a substance in the chromosomes, is the carrier of the genetic code that transmits characteristics from one generation to the next. Figure 5-4 shows a model of the DNA molecule, in the shape of a double helix or spiral ladder. The *genes,* carriers of specific instructions for growth, are arranged in linear order on the spirals. The two spirals can come apart like a zipper. Then each half produces another half.

Dominant and Recessive Genes. A story [58] that might be called *science prediction* rather than *science fiction* went like this: a young couple had been quietly holding hands in a secluded corner of the campus. Then one of them said, "Let's match cards." Each pulled out a printed card containing a few holes. They put one on top of the other. None of the holes matched. They embraced happily. Like most human beings, each carried a few dangerous recessive genes out of the thousand or more that can cause birth defects. Since it takes a recessive gene from each parent to produce a characteristic that does not show in either parent, the young couple could safely plan to have children. Or if not with complete assurance, at least they would know that they were not endangering their future children as far as their own dangerous recessives were concerned. Suppose two of the holes had matched such that each of the couple was carrying a recessive gene for cystic fibrosis. For each conception, chances would be one in four for a child with two recessives and hence having cystic fibrosis, two in four for a child carrying one recessive, like the parents, and not showing the defect, and one in four for a normal child with two normal genes. And suppose they conceived a defective embryo. It could be diagnosed early in pregnancy and aborted, if they so chose.

Although at the moment when this is being written, the story is only prediction, the technology on which it is based is of the present. Many physical characteristics, including a large number of defects, are inherited according to simple Mendelian law, as illustrated in our story. Some other defects, such as color blindness, are sex linked, which means that they are dominant in the male and recessive in the female. A male shows the defect when he carries only one gene for it, but the female does not suffer unless she has two such genes.

Heredity works in more complicated ways, also. Genes work in concert with one another and with the environment. The mechanisms of *crossing over* and *independent assortment* add enormously to the variety of genetic combinations that are possible. Genes "turn on" and off at various times during the life cycle. For example, the control of sexual maturation is considerably influenced by heredity.

Gene Blends. Many characteristics are the results of more than one pair of genes. Skin color in human beings is such a characteristic. It is not determined in all-or-none way, as is seed color in peas. Rather, in spite of popular belief to the contrary, a child's skin color is almost never darker than the skin of the darker parent, nor lighter than the skin of the lighter parent. If the child's skin is darker than either parent's, it is only a shade darker. At least two pairs of genes are considered to be active in determining skin color; there may be three or more.

Standing height is another human characteristic that is the result of many different genes working at least in part in a literally additive way, although blending of the kind that determines skin color may also be operating. A human being's height is the sum of the lengths of many different bones and many pieces of cartilage. Each bone's length is probably determined by one or more genes, and varies somewhat independently of the length of every other bone. Height is, therefore, a *polygenic* trait. (In addition, of course, the variation in heights of a group of individuals is affected by environmental factors such as diet and disease.)

Meiosis. Although each individual receives the chromosomes from germ cells of the parents, the offspring of the same parents do not receive identical chromosomes. The explanation of this difference between brothers and sisters lies in the process of *meiosis,* the formation of germ cells, sperm and ova.

Figure 5-5 shows the development of sperm that contain only two single chromosomes, since to show 23 chromosomes would unnecessarily complicate the diagram. In the diagram the primordial germ cell, the *spermatogonium,* is shown as containing two pairs of chromosomes. In the process of meiosis, the spermatogonium divides into two cells called *secondary spermatocytes,* each of which has one of the members of each pair of chromosomes. Each chromosome is composed of two *chromatids.* Each spermatocyte divides into two *spermatids,* each of which has one of the chromatids from the eight chromatids that are shown to have been in the original spermatogonium. From each spermatid develops a sperm. Therefore,

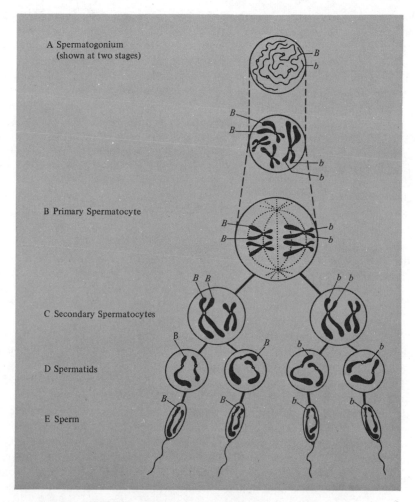

A Spermatogonium
(shown at two stages)

B Primary Spermatocyte

C Secondary Spermatocytes

D Spermatids

E Sperm

Figure 5-5. Meiosis provides the mechanism by which a heterozygous male produces sperm of two kinds: half of them containing the dominant gene, *B*, half of them containing its recessive allele, *b*.

SOURCE: Adapted from P. A. Moody. *Genetics of man.* New York: W. W. Norton & Company, 1967. Figure 3–7, p. 34.

from each male primordial germ cell result four sperm, each containing 23 single chromosomes.

The development of each ovum is similar to the development of each sperm, except that from each female primordial germ cell (called an *obgonium*) there result not four ova, but one. But it, like each sperm, contains 23 chromatids from among the 92 chromatids present in the obgonium. Since the obgonium begins meiosis with two X chromosomes, every ovum contains an X chromosome. The spermatogonium, which begins meiosis with one X and one Y chromosome, results in four sperms, two of which contain an X apiece and two a Y. If an X-bearing sperm fertilizes an ovum, the new individual will have two X chromosomes, and will be female. If a Y-bearing sperm fertilizes an ovum, the new individual will have one Y chromosome and one X chromosome, and will be a male.

In the same way, if one parent has two genes for any trait, each offspring will receive from that parent the same kind of genetic material as any other offspring. But if a parent has unlike genes for a trait, half of the offspring (other things being equal, which they often are not) will receive one kind of gene (for example, the dominant gene) and half will receive the other. The process of meiosis explains part of the genetic difference between brothers and sisters, including the fact that a given father and mother are likely to have both sons and daughters.

BEHAVIOR GENETICS

Not only are body form and coloration inherited from generation to generation but different kinds of functioning are, also. The ability to roll the tongue is one of these functions. One of the authors of this book (MSS) can roll her tongue; RCS cannot. All three of their daughters can. Since this ability is known to be a dominant characteristic, we know that RCS is homozygous recessive. Some of our grandchildren may turn out to be like Grandpa. Our daughters are heterozygous for this characteristic. If their husbands are also heterozygous, we could predict that our grandchildren will be tongue-rollers in the ratio of 3:1.

(Incidentally, the genetic ratios hold only for large populations, not for small samples. Since we expect that the total number of our grandchildren will be no more than six, they might all be tongue-rollers.)

The inheritance of certain defects in mental functioning can be described in terms of chromosomes [42]. Down's syndrome (Mongolism), a type of mental retardation accompanied by distinctive physical anomalies, occurs when an extra chromosome is attached to the chromosome numbered 21, making a total of 47 instead of the normal 46 chromosomes. Klinefelter's syndrome, incomplete sexual development along with lowered intelligence in males, involves two X chromosomes in addition to a Y. Turner's syndrome, in which females have only one X chromosome, includes defective spatial abilities. Males with an XXY condition are more likely than normals to be tall, aggressive, and mentally defective.

The transmission of all-or-none traits, such as tongue-rolling and Down's syndrome, can be explained by basic rules of genetics. When many genes are involved and when the characteristic is highly complex, such as intelligence or emotional stability, *heritability* is studied by *quantitative genetics*. Heritability of a characteristic can be estimated by comparing correlations between groups of known genetic similarity. Since the heredity of animals can be controlled, they can be used for experimental work in heredity. In working with humans, investigators have to use groups that vary in known degrees, from identical twins to unrelated persons. Results of many studies on inheritance of intelligence and personality indicate that there are indeed significant hereditary components in both [61].

Intelligence. Figure 5-6 shows median (average) sizes of correlations between measured intelligence of persons of different degrees of genetic similarity [20]. Unrelated persons living apart show no correlation (−.01). Identical twins

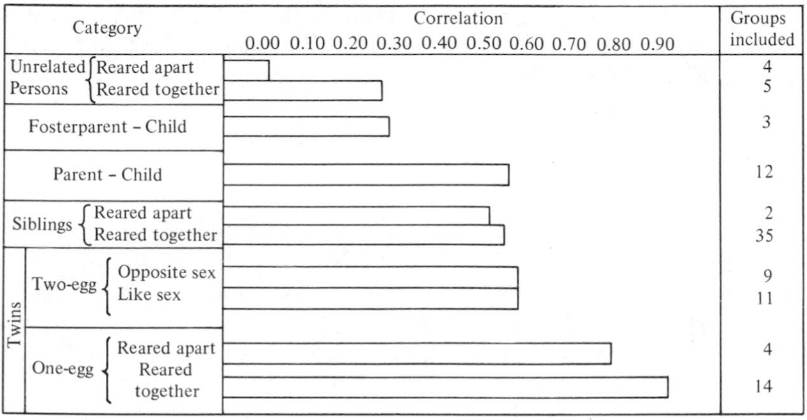

Category	Correlation 0.00 0.10 0.20 0.30 0.40 0.50 0.60 0.70 0.80 0.90	Groups included
Unrelated Persons — Reared apart		4
Unrelated Persons — Reared together		5
Fosterparent – Child		3
Parent – Child		12
Siblings — Reared apart		2
Siblings — Reared together		35
Two-egg Twins — Opposite sex		9
Two-egg Twins — Like sex		11
One-egg Twins — Reared apart		4
One-egg Twins — Reared together		14

Figure 5-6. Median correlation coefficients for intelligence test scores showing degree of similarity between performances of people of varying degrees of relatedness under different and similar environmental conditions.

SOURCE: Data from L. Erlenmeyer-Kimling and L. F. Jervik. *Science*, 1964, **142**, 1477–79.

reared together are very similar (.87). Identical twins reared apart are more closely correlated than those in any other relationship group (.75). Intelligence of parents and children correlates significantly (.50). Heredity components have been found in the following intellectual abilities, listed in order of weight of influence by heredity: word fluency, verbal ability (including spelling and grammar), spatial ability, clerical speed and accuracy, reasoning, number ability, and memory [61]. Sensorimotor intelligence scores were found to be more highly correlated in identical twins than in fraternals [41].

Personality. There is evidence for heritability of several dimensions of personality, the main ones of which are usual activity level; expression of emotions frankly in interpersonal relationships; degree of planning ahead rather than behaving impulsively [61]; extraversion–introversion [54].

Age Trends. Correlations between intelligence of children and parents are low negative in early infancy, zero at around a year, low positive at the end of the second year, and moderate (.5) in early childhood and thereafter [17a]. This pattern is true of children and parents living apart, as well as of those living together. Correlations between stature of parents and children also increase throughout the early preschool years [25].

Sex Differences in Heritability. There is evidence that girls are controlled by heredity more than boys are, most likely because the X chromosome, of which girls have two and boys one, carries more hereditary material than does the Y chromosome. After age 13, measurements of stature correlate more highly for father–daughter than for father–son and for mother–daughter than for mother–son

[25]. Data from the Berkeley Growth Study indicated that girls' intellectual functioning is more genetically determined than is boys, and that the impact of the environment is greater upon boys than it is upon girls [5]. High school boys and girls, studied by a twin control method, showed stronger heritability for girls than for boys on a battery of tests of achievements and aptitudes [34].

Summary

A baby, like all organisms, interacts continuously with the environment. She and her parents influence each other and change each other. Child development is described from different theoretical viewpoints, offering different ways of interpreting and understanding. Six types of interaction are described briefly in this chapter.

Equilibration is a process of regulation that the organism carries on in physical and intellectual modes. Homeostasis is the maintaining of the organism within certain physical limits such as those of chemical content and temperature. Psychological equilibrium involves regulating stimulation to an optimal level and also progressing toward more complex levels of mental organization. Piaget's notion of equilibration includes two complementary processes, accommodation and assimilation. Assimilation is the taking in and using of material from the environment; accommodation is changing the schemas to adjust to reality as it is experienced. Equilibration is enjoyable, as shown by children's curiosity and exploration, looking for problems and incongruities to be solved.

Growth and development, terms that can be used interchangeably, refer to increasing size and complexity of structure and function. The following principles or generalizations hold for many kinds of growth and development: variation in rates between individuals, between sexes, within the organism and of the organism in time; individuals differ in time of reaching maturity; measures of growth are interrelated; organisms behave as though they were seeking to achieve maximum potential, searching for substitute sources of nurture when the usual ones are not available; specific patterns of behavior are differentiated out of larger, global patterns, and then specific patterns are integrated into larger, complex patterns; certain sequences of physical and motor development take place in directions (cephalo-caudal and proximo-distal) in relation to the body; certain behavior patterns mature in orderly sequences; growth is based on a foundation, the organism interacting with the environment to transform itself; critical periods are specific times when the organism will interact with the environment in specific ways that may be harmful or beneficial.

Stage theories, including Erikson's and Piaget's, explain development as proceeding epigenetically, being transformed or reorganized on more and more complex levels that occur in an orderly sequence. Erikson's psychosocial theory uses Freud's psychosexual stages as a base and develops a theory of the healthy personality. The eight stages of man's development involve the development of basic trust versus basic mistrust; autonomy versus doubt and shame; initiative versus guilt; industry versus inferiority; identity versus role diffusion; intimacy versus isolation; generativity versus self-absorption; ego integrity versus despair. Piaget shows how children develop intelligence in the process of dealing with the world and coming to know it. His sensorimotor period, spanning infancy, is subdivided into six stages. The preoperational period, from around 2 to 7, includes the stages of preconceptual and intuitive thought. The period of concrete operations comprises the school years, and the period of formal operations (logical thought) comprises the years of adolescence.

Memory means the storing of experience in such ways that it can be retrieved and used. The process includes perception, attention, coding, and enriching with meaning. Memory performance varies with age, input, and various environmental aspects. Learning is an active process, not something that is done to a person. When academic learning is measured in terms of time, focused aid can help slow learners to achieve more and to increase their self-esteem and motivation. Human beings learn easily from observing one another and hearing or reading of the experiences of others. Through socialization, children and, to some extent, others learn to think, feel, and behave as members of social groups. Selecting among what she sees, hears, and reads, an individual imitates behavior that she expects will be rewarding to her. The components of modeling are attention, symbolic representations in memory, new integrations of motor acts, and control of selection through incentive or motivational processes. Classical conditioning involves linking a new response with an old one, operant conditioning involves strengthening a response when it occurs. Positive reinforcements increase the likelihood of recurrence of an event, negative reinforcements decrease it. Individuals can use reinforcement systematically to change their own behavior. Manipulation of reinforcements is complicated and often does not bring the desired results because not all variables are understood.

Maturation is the growth toward maturity of the body, its structures, and functions—growth that is relatively independent of experience. Most developmental processes involve both maturation and learning.

Evolutionary adaptation accounts for certain behavior patterns that mature quickly into a complex and relatively fixed form. The environment to which a species is adapted is the one in which it emerged in its present form. Attachment behavior in the human infant is most easily understood in terms of evolutionary adaptation. Behavioral systems have also evolved. They are not always in harmony with each other.

Hereditary characteristics in human beings are sometimes the result of single pairs of genes, but often of numbers of genes working together. Most human beings carry several dangerous recessive genes, which will do no harm unless they are matched with the same dangerous genes from the partner in reproduction. Birth defects can be predicted on a chance basis, and some can be predicted with certainty. An ovum contains an X chromosome, a sperm either an X or a Y chromosome. The source of sex differences is in the X and Y chromosomes, including differences in heritability, females being more influenced by heredity. These functions include intelligence and many of its components and also certain personality dimensions. Correlations between physical and mental measurements of parents and children increase during the preschool period.

References

1. Abernathy, E. M. Relationships between physical and mental growth. *Monographs of the Society for Research in Child Development,* 1936, **1**:7.
2. Ainsworth, M. D. S. The development of infant-mother attachment. In B. M. Caldwell and H. N. Ricciuti (eds.). *Review of child development research,* vol. 3. Chicago: University of Chicago Press, 1973.
3. Bandura, A. Influence of models' reinforcement contingencies on the acquisition of imitative responses. *Journal of Personality & Social Psychology,* 1965, **1,** 589–595.
4. Bandura, A. Behavior theory and the models of man. *American Psychologist,* 1974, **29,** 859–869.
5. Bayley, N., and E. S. Schaefer. Correlations of maternal and child behaviors with the development of mental abilities: Data from the Berkeley growth study. *Monographs of the Society for Research in Child Development,* 1964, **29**:6.
6. Bloom, B. S. Time and learning. *American Psychologist,* 1974, **29,** 682–688.
7. Bower, T. G. R. *Development in infancy.* San Francisco: W. H. Freeman & Co., Publishers, 1974.
8. Bowlby, J. *Attachment and loss.* vol. I: *Attachment.* London: Hogarth, 1969.
9. Brenner, A. and L. H. Stott. *School readiness factor analyzed.* Detroit: Merrill-Palmer Institute (undated).
10. Bronfenbrenner, U. *Two worlds of childhood.* New York: Russell Sage Foundation, 1970.
11. Brucefors, A., I. Johannesson, P. Karlberg, I. Klackenberg-Larsson, H. Lichtenstein, and I. Svenberg. Trends in development of abilities related to somatic growth. *Human Development,* 1974, **17,** 152–159.
12. Bühler, C. *The first year of life.* New York: Day, 1930.
13. Craik, F. I. M., and R. S. Lockhart. Levels of processing: A framework for memory research. *Journal of Verbal Learning and Behavior,* 1972, **11,** 671–684.
14. Davis, C. M. Self-selection of diet by newly weaned infants. *American Journal of Diseases of Children,* 1928, **36,** 651–679.
15. Dember, W. N. Motivation and the cognitive revolution. *American Psychologist,* 1974, **29,** 161–168.
16. Dennis, W. *Children of the crèche.* New York: Meredith Corporation, 1973.
17. Eibl-Eibesfeldt, I. Concepts of ethology and their significance in the study of human behavior. In H. W. Stevenson, E. H. Hess, and H. L. Rheingold (eds.). *Early behavior.* New York: John Wiley & Sons, Inc., 1967, pp. 127–146.
17a. Eichorn, D. H. Developmental parallels in the growth of parents and their children. *Newsletter of the Division on Developmental Psychology of the American Psychological Association,* Spring, 1970.
18. Erikson, E. H. *Childhood and society.* New York: W. W. Norton & Company, 1963.
19. Erikson, E. H. *Identity, youth and crisis.* New York: W. W. Norton & Company, 1968.
20. Erlenmeyer-Kimling, L. K., and L. F. Jarvik. Genetics and intelligence: A review. *Science,* 1964, **142,** 1477–1479.
21. Fantz, R. L. The origin of form perception. *Scientific American,* 1961, **204,** 66–72.
22. Fouts, G., and P. Liikanen. The effects of age and developmental level on imitation in children. *Child Development,* 1975, **46,** 555–558.
23. Freud, S. *The ego and the id,* New York: W. W. Norton & Company, 1962.
24. Garn, S. M. Fat thickness and developmental status in childhood and adolescence. *Journal of the American Medical Association,* 1960, **99,** 746–751.

25. Garn, S. M. Body size and its implications. In L. W. Hoffman and M. L. Hoffman (eds.). *Review of child development research.* vol. 2, New York: Russell Sage Foundation, 1966, pp. 529–561.
26. Gesell, A. *The embryology of behavior.* New York: Harper, 1945.
27. Gesell, A. and H. Thompson. *The psychology of early growth.* New York: Macmillan Publishing Co., Inc., 1938.
28. Halverson, H. M. An experimental study of prehension in infants by means of systematic cinema records. *Genetic Psychology Monographs,* 1931, **10,** 107–286.
29. Hartup, W. W., and B. Coates. Imitation of a peer as a function of reinforcement from the peer group and rewardingness of the model. *Child Development,* 1967, **38,** 1003–1016.
30. Havighurst, R. J. Minority subcultures and the law of effect. *American Psychologist,* 1970, **25,** 313–322.
31. Hunt, J. V., and N. Bayley. Explorations into patterns of mental development and prediction from the Bayley scales of infant development. *Minnesota Symposium on Child Psychology,* 1971, **5,** 52–71.
32. Jones, M. C., and P. H. Mussen. Self-conception, motivations, and interpersonal attitudes of early- and late-maturing girls. *Child Development,* 1958, **29,** 492–501.
33. Ketcham, W. A. Relationship of physical and mental traits in intellectually gifted and mentally retarded boys. *Merrill-Palmer Quarterly,* 1960, **6,** 171–177.
34. Klinger, R. Sex differences in heritability assessed by the Washington precollege test battery of achievement/aptitude measures. Paper presented at the meeting of the Society for Research in Child Development, Santa Monica, 1969.
35. Lane, I. M., and R. C. Coon. Reward allocation in preschool children. *Child Development,* 1972, **43,** 1382–1389.
36. Lewis, M. The meaning of a response, or why researchers in infant behavior should be Oriental metaphysicians. *Merrill-Palmer Quarterly,* 1967, **13,** 7–18.
37. Lipsitt, L. P. Learning in the human infant. In H. W. Stevenson, E. H. Hess, and H. L. Rheingold (eds.). *Early behavior,* New York: John Wiley & Sons, Inc., 1967, pp. 225–247.
38. Lorenz, K. *King Solomon's ring.* New York: Thomas Y. Crowell Company, 1952.
39. Masters, J. C., and M. D. Christy. Achievement standards for contingent self-reinforcement: Effects of task length and task difficulty. *Child Development,* 1974, **45,** 6–13.
40. Masters, J. C., and P. A. Pisarowicz. Self-reinforcement and generosity following two types of altruistic behavior. *Child Development,* 1975, **46,** 313–318.
41. Matheny, A. P. Twins: Concordance for Piagetian-equivalent items derived from the Bayley Mental Test. *Developmental Psychology,* 1975, **11,** 224–227.
42. McClearn, G. E. Behavioral genetics: An overview. *Merrill-Palmer Quarterly,* 1968, **14,** 9–24.
43. McGraw, M. B. Major challenges for students of infancy and early childhood. *American Psychologist,* 1970, **25,** 754–756.
44. Milner, B. Memory and the medial regions of the brain. In K. H. Pribram and D. E. Broadbent. *Biology of memory.* New York: Academic Press, Inc., 1970, pp. 29–50.
45. Mussen, P. H., and M. C. Jones. The behavior-inferred motivations of late- and early-maturing boys. *Child Development,* 1958, **29,** 61–67.
46. Notz, W. W. Work motivation and the negative effects of intrinsic rewards: A review with implications for theory and practice. *American Psychologist,* 1975, **30,** 884–891.
47. Papoušek, H. Experimental studies of appetitional behavior in human newborns

and infants. In H. W. Stevenson, E. H. Hess, and H. L. Rheingold (eds.). *Early behavior.* New York: John Wiley & Sons, Inc., 1967, pp. 249–277.

48. Parke, R. D. Some effects of punishment on children's behavior. *Young Children,* 1969, **24,** 225–240.

49. Piaget, J. *Play, dreams and imitation in childhood.* New York: W. W. Norton & Company, 1962.

50. Piaget, J. *Six psychological studies.* New York: Random House, Inc., 1967.

51. Piaget, J., and B. Inhelder. *The psychology of the child.* New York: Basic Books, Inc., 1969.

52. Pines, M. *The brain changers.* New York: Harcourt Brace Jovanovich, Inc., 1973.

53. Reese, H. W. Models of memory and models of development. *Human Development,* 1973, **16,** 397–416.

54. Scarr, S. Social introversion-extraversion as a heritable response. *Child Development,* 1969, **40,** 823–832.

55. Scott, J. P. *Early experience and the organization of behavior.* Belmont, Calif.: Brooks/Cole Publishing Co., 1968.

56. Shuttleworth, F. K. The physical and mental growth of girls and boys age six to 19 in relation to age at maximum growth. *Monographs of the Society for Research in Child Development,* 1939, **4:**3.

57. Stone, C. P., and R. G. Barker. Aspects of personality and intelligence in post-menarcheal and premenarcheal girls of the same chronological age. *Journal of Comparative Psychology,* 1937, **23,** 439–455.

58. Sullivan, W. If we master the gene. *New York Times,* June 14, 1970.

59. Tanner, J. M. *Education and physical growth.* London: University of London Press, 1961.

60. Tanner, J. M. Relation of body size, intelligence test scores and social circumstances. In P. Mussen, J. Langer, and M. Covington (eds.). *Trends and issues in developmental psychology.* New York: Holt, Rinehart and Winston, Inc., 1969.

61. Vandenberg, S. G. Human behavior genetics: Present status and suggestions for future research. *Merrill-Palmer Quarterly,* 1969, **15,** 121–154.

62. Walter, G. Comments. In J. M. Tanner and B. Inhelder (eds.). *Discussions on child development.* vol. I. New York: International Universities Press, 1953.

63. Watson, J. S., and C. T. Ramey. Reactions to response-contingent stimulation in early infancy. *Merrill-Palmer Quarterly,* 1972, **18,** 219–227.

64. Wolff, P. Autonomous systems in human behavior and development. *Human Development,* 1974, **17,** 281–291.

65. Zern, D. S. An interpretation of the effects of stimulation on development: Its role as a resolvable disequilibrator. *Genetic Psychology Monographs,* 1974, **90,** 532–547.

Readings in
An Overview of Human Life and Growth

In an earlier, and possibly in some ways happier, time, man was considered the final and triumphant item of creation, the master and user of other living things. Even the early evolutionary biologists considered that man stood at the apex of evolution; they did not seem aware of the possibility that the process of evolution might continue, resulting in the appearance of new species. They seemed even less aware of the possibility that the evolutionary process of man resulted in a creature who had within him the seeds of his own destruction, like the sabre-toothed tiger, whose overdeveloped canine teeth prevented him from ingesting his prey.

Ecology is the branch of biology that studies the relationship of living things to their environment, including other living things. Recently ecologists have included man as the subject of their study. In general, the results of their investigations have been frightening. Especially in North America man is seen as a fouler of his environment—air, water, and soil—to such an extent that ecologists say that if present trends go unchecked, man may make his continued existence impossible.

In the first article in this chapter, William W. Ballard, a biologist, describes some of the facts about man's evolutionary development and speculates about the future. He makes the important distinction between man as a species and men as individuals who together make up the species. Each individual has characteristics of the species that have arisen during the course of evolution, but each individual has his own personal history, during which he has learned some ways of behaving that may be, in the long run, maladaptive for the species. Ballard's article has been very useful to us in teaching child development courses. We found ourselves referring frequently to his notion of the two computers when we discussed opposing processes or ideas in all sorts of contexts.

Lawrence K. Frank, the author of the second article, gave form, direction, and impetus to the field of child development. Frank's genius provided a flow of ideas for research, education, and theory. He was responsible for establishing child development centers, the parent education movement, and interdisciplinary research. In the article presented here, Frank demonstrates his characteristic warmth and wonder while analyzing the growth processes at work in infants. He describes how the child elaborates his individuality through interaction. In the terms used by Ballard in the first article, Frank shows how the "second computer" begins, based on the beginnings of the "first computer."

Erikson and Piaget, the authors of the third and fourth selections, are also primarily concerned with the development of the "second computer." But both are explicit in their statement that their theories are based on biology. Although both are dealing with psychological material, they start from biological characteristics of man.

The epigenetic theory of Erik H. Erikson is represented by the next essay, taken from his book Identity, Youth and Crisis. An artist, teacher, and philosopher thoroughly trained in Freudian psychoanalysis, Erikson has made enormous contributions to the field of child development. His theory is built upon Freudian theory, which he extends and develops into a way of understanding and describing the healthy personality throughout life. Erikson describes stages of personality growth, showing for each one a relation of personality to bodily development and to interaction with the culture. Each stage is derived from and built upon the one preceding it. The organization of this book is shaped by Erikson's stages in childhood and adolescence. The content is influenced by his thinking.

Jean Piaget, the world-famous Swiss psychologist, is the author of the fourth piece in this section. Piaget is primarily a genetic epistemologist, a scientist-philosopher who investigates the production of knowledge. He has developed a comprehensive theory of the mental structures through which human beings build their concept of reality and deal with it. Piaget has stimulated psychological research all over the world. Americans have produced hundreds of studies in response to his theories and findings. Like Erikson's theory of personality development, Piaget's account of the growth of intelligence is epigenetic and interactional. Piaget's theory is very compatible with a child development point of view, because the child's mind is seen as resulting from biologically given beginnings actively engaged with the environment.

The Rise and Fall of Humanity

William W. Ballard

The reading that follows is the last part of a lecture titled " The Rise and Fall of Humanity." In the first part Ballard summarizes the development of living things during the course of four billion years of earth history, the accelerating growth of knowledge in the last few thousand years, and the serious threats to man's continued existence that have stemmed from this knowledge. Basically, Ballard says, the present crisis has arisen because there are too many people on the earth and they are demanding more than the earth can provide. These events have occurred because man as a species of animal is composed of men and women as individuals.

To maximize the amount of life that can be supported in a given ecosystem, a large number of species of plants, animals, and decomposers are brought into balance, each occupying its own niche and following its own instructions to make the best of the things available to it while contributing to the flow of energy and the recycling of materials. If one species in the ecosystem gets out of balance the whole community develops an instability that may either result in an irreversible change in its character, or in the control or rejection of the destabilizing element.

From *Dartmouth Alumni Magazine*, 1970, **62** (6), 60–64. Reprinted by permission of the author, the Dartmouth Alumni College, and the *Dartmouth Alumni Magazine*.

The human species has been manipulating its environment since the invention of agriculture, favoring the plants and animals that serve it for food, repressing or even exterminating others. Where this was overdone—e.g., Mesopotamia, the Near East, Yucatan—ghost cities and records of dead cultures remain to show how powerfully nature can strike back. Quite recently we have begun to use the treasure trove of fossil fuels to grow the food to satisfy the multiplying demands of our own population, and we congratulate ourselves on having temporarily freed ourselves from the normal restrictions of the natural world. It is a dangerous game we are playing.

No good asking why the human *species* takes these risks. A species is an invention of the mind, a generalization. Only human *individuals* actually walk and breathe and make decisions and it is the collection of individuals who have been doing what I say the species has been doing. What went wrong with human individuals, that they have gotten their species and their environment into such a mess? The other face of this question is, what is an indvidual supposed to be doing, and within what limits is he supposed to be held?

THE PRIMARY COMPUTER   To simplify, I shall restrict the latter question to animals rather than plants or decomposers. I shall pick animals that are not on a rampage, animals that have (so far as we can tell) no conscious reasoning ability, no thoughts, loyalties, hopes, or faiths. Some kind of earthworm or some frog will do. I assume that whatever one of these animals does, any choice that it makes, is determined by its inherited computer system. It receives from its ancestors a scanning mechanism which reports what all the circumstances around and inside it are at the moment. This information is checked against an inherited memory encoded in its central nervous system. The computer then not only orders up the strategy and tactics that had met that sort of situation successfully before, but directs what every cell, what every organ, what the whole earthworm or frog must be doing to contribute to that response. (Directions for unsuccessful responses are not encoded in this primary computer, because they simply are not inherited.)

To see what this genetic computer requires the individual worm or frog to do, let us follow his life history, watching him obey and reconstructing from what he does the nature of the commands.

1. As a member of a bisexual species he (or she) starts as a fertilized egg, a single diploid individual with unique heterozygous genic individuality. First, *he develops*. Since the fertilized egg is insulated to a degree from the outside world, his computer works at first mostly on internal information. It refers to the inherited memory in the chromosomes and brings out instructions of various intricate sorts to the ultrastructures of the cell, programmed so that the cell divides into two, then four, then eight cells . . . until the word gets back to the multiplied computers in the multiplied cells that it is time to activate their inherited instructions for differentiation. Tissues and organs are formed, in such sorts and such patterns as have enabled the species to survive so far. The new individual acquires the sensory and neural apparatus for bringing in more and more information from the outside, and this is referred to the more and more specialized computer developing out of the inherited instructions, in a central nervous system (in the case of a frog, a brain and spinal cord). He begins

to move about, respire, feed, excrete, defend himself, in directions and at rates calculated to be appropriate to the sensed state of affairs from moment to moment. This is quite a trick for a self-built computer to bring off, and as an embryologist I wish I understood more of how it is done.

2. The young earthworm or pollywog, having broken loose from its protective envelopes and used up its dowry of yolk, is next under orders to *reach adulthood*. He recognizes dangers and opportunities by continually referring the information flowing in from his sensory apparatus to his inherited memory. He certainly has not learned his behavioral responses from his parents, never having met them. It is the inherited computer which tells him what to do from one millisecond to the next. He survives or not, partly by luck but also partly according to whether his own inherited variant of the species-specific computer will deliver the right answers to the problems of his own day and place. (The *species* survives by offering up enough varieties so that some individuals will have what the new situations demand, the wastage of the other individuals being a necessary part of the cost. No other way has yet been discovered for meeting the demands of an unpredictable future, i.e. winning a game the rules for which have not yet been written.)

3. Our earthworm or frog, if lucky, finds himself a sexually mature individual, with his instructions to reproduce now turned on. These instructions, activated by seasonal or other environmental signals, operate upon particular genes, particular cells, particular organs, and particular behavioral mechanisms set off through the nervous system. Without knowing it, much less knowing why, the animals seeks out a mate, copulates, and shares in the production of fertilized eggs that bring us again to phase 1 of the cycle.

4. Having blindly and without thought followed his instructions to (1) develop, (2) make do, survive, gain strength, and (3) reproduce, our earthworm or frog subsequently (4) *dies*. It is the ancient law. So far as the interests of the individual are concerned, it is absurd.

But now how about man? How unique is he? Does he not learn by experience and education, manage his own life, consciously determine what jobs he shall tackle, what ends he shall serve? My argument that he too is run by an inherited computer program rests partly on the observed fact that (1) he develops, (2) he makes every effort to reach maturity, (3) if lucky enough he sets the cycle going again, and (4) he dies. There is nothing unique about that. Experience, learning, individual preferences serve only for minor embellishments.

I select one case to illustrate that an animal's program is mostly inherited. Four to six weeks after fertilization (depending on temperature) a salamander embryo will have used up its yolk and must by then have acquired an elaborate repertoire of locomotor, hunting-sensory, food-grabbing, and swallowing behavior to keep itself fed and growing. Does the individual learn this behavior by trial and error? No. Starting a day before any of his muscles were mature enough to contract, you can rear him in a dilute anesthetic solution until he has reached the feeding stage. Put him back into pond water, and in twenty minutes the anesthetic will have worn off and he is swimming, hunting, grabbing, and swallowing like a normal tadpole. One is seeing here the computer-controlled maturation of a computer-controlled behavior. No practice, no learning.

The individual within which this remarkable apparatus matures is an expendable pawn, and the apparatus is not for his enjoyment of life, it is to keep the species going.

THE SECONDARY COMPUTER   There is such an inherited program in the human individual, but there is much more. The baby does not so much learn to walk as to develop the inherited capacity to walk; but then he can learn a dance that no man has ever danced before, he can paint a picture with a brush clasped between his toes. During late fetal life and his first six or eight years he gradually matures a second computer system superimposed on, controlling and almost completely masking the ancient frog-type computer. The evolutionary history of this new device is traceable back to, and in some respects beyond, the time of origin of the modern mammals 70 million or more years ago. It has progressed farthest in particular mammalian orders—the carnivores, hoofed animals, bats, whales and primates, and least in the egg-laying mammals and marsupials.

The new trend has worked certain real advantages, and has been kept under reasonable control, in the higher mammals, but it is my strong suspicion that its over-development in man is the root of our trouble. Like the dinosaurs, we contain in our own structure the reason why we will have to go. Robinson Jeffers[1] said it: "We have minds like the fangs of those forgotten tigers, hypertropied and terrible."

Up to a point, the development of brain and spinal cord follows the same course in frog and man. Sense organs, cranial and spinal nerves, principal subdivisions of the brain, basic fiber tract systems, all form in strictly comparable fashion in both. But the adult human brain is a far different thing from the adult frog brain. It continues the multiplication and interconnection of neurons during a far longer growth period, and adds to the elementary or frog-type apparatus two principal complicating tissues that far overshadow the earlier developments. One is often called reticular substance, the other is the cerebral cortex.

The reticular substance is so called because it is an interweaving of small centers of gray substance with short bundles and interspersed mats of axons (the white substance), quite different from the simple contrast between gray and white substance seen in primitive animals and in early embryos. The frog brain is not without this sort of tissue, but in the brains of advanced vertebrates like the teleost fishes, the reptiles, and the birds, it becomes indescribably complex. The modern mammals push this development to still higher orders of magnitude.

Although neurological science is not yet ready with answers to most specific questions about what happens where in the central nervous system, the new techniques of exploration within the brain suggest that in and through the reticular substance the connections for integrating sensory information with the devices for evaluation and for making decisions and coordinated responses are multiplied exponentially.

Thus, an electrode planted within a single neuron in the reticular substance of the hindbrain can give startling evidence that this one cell is receiving and

[1] R. Jeffers, "Passenger Pigeons," in *The Beginning and the End.*

reacting to sensations reported from widely scattered parts of the body, and sending out coded pulses as a calculated response. Your own brain contains hundreds of millions, probably billions of such cells, every one individually a computer.

The neurologists can now stimulate chosen localized areas through implanted electrodes, either hooked up to wires dangling from the cage ceiling or activated through miniaturized transmitters healed in under the scalp and controlled by radio transmission. In such experiments, stimuli delivered to many parts of the reticular substance cause the animal to react as though he were flooded with agreeable sensation. If the cat or rat or monkey learns how to deliver the stimulus to himself by pressing a pedal, he will do so repeatedly and rapidly, until he falls asleep exhausted. As soon as he wakes up, he goes to pounding the pedal again.

There are other reticular areas which have the reverse effect. If the stimulus comes at rhythmical intervals and the animal discovers that he can forestall it by pressing the pedal, he quickly learns to regulate his life so as to be there and step on it just in time. What kind of sensation such a stimulus produces in him can only be guessed by the experimenter. One might suppose that these areas of reticular substance which have such opposite effects are there to add into the computer's analysis of the situation at the moment a go signal or a stop signal for particular alternative choices, or a sense of goodness or badness, satisfaction or distress, urgency or caution, danger or relaxation. A value judgment, in other words.

It is not difficult to see the survival value of such a device. No doubt the basic mechanism exists in the brains of fishes and frogs, though I am not aware that experiments have been done to locate it. In the reticular substance of mammals, however, we see it hugely developed. The result of overdoing this might produce an awareness of the good and bad features of so very many facets of a situation as to delay and perplex the individual in calculating his single coordinated response.

Mammals are also conspicuously good at remembering experiences from their own lives as individuals, and these memories are loaded with value judgments. There is still no clear answer as to where or in what coded form these new personal memories are stored. But an animal with all this added to the ancestral memory, enhanced with perhaps casually acquired and unwisely generalized connotations of goodness and badness, might predictably be endowed with excessive individuality, prone to unnecessarily variable behavior, chosen more often for self-satisfaction than in the interest of species survival.

The other evolutionary development, the formation of the cerebral cortex, is almost unknown in vertebrates other than mammals, and is feeble in some of these. Cerebral cortex is a tissue of awesome complexity, and our techniques for analyzing what happens in it are still highly inadequate. Stimulation of willing human subjects, in chosen spots exposed surgically, or radio stimulation of these areas through permanently installed electrodes operated by healed-in transistor devices, evoke feelings referred to a particular part of the body, or cause normal-appearing localized movements, e.g. the flexion of an arm or a finger, time and again, upon repetition of the signal. Other areas produce more generalized sensory or motor or emotional or physiologic effects. The patient, his brain exposed under local anesthesia, does not know when the stimulus is applied. When the electrode touches a particular spot of his cortex he may report that he is suddenly remembering a scene identifiable as to time and place, but the memory blacks out when the current is cut off. Stimulation of other areas may elicit emotions of sexual attraction or anxiety or rage graded according to the intensity of the signal.

More wide-ranging experiments with cats, monkeys, or barnyard stock, singly or in groups, free to move in large caged areas, show the possibility of turning on and off a great range of complex emotions, behavior, and even personality traits, by local stimulation.[2] The effect produced through a permanently planted electrode is area specific. Though not predictable before the first stimulus is given, the response is repeated with each stimulus, many times a day or over periods of months or years.

In subjective comparison of mammals with greater or less personal individuality one gets the impression that the degrees of freedom of choice, of imaginative recognition of possible ways to react to situations, of storage capacity and retentiveness of memory, and the richness of association, are correlated with the intricacy and amount of the cerebral cortex and reticular substance. Animals highest on both scales include porpoises, elephants, cats and dogs, apes, and people.

One cannot underestimate the effects on the human species of other evolutionary trends that came to a climax in us, for instance the development of upright posture that frees the hands, the reshaping of the fingers for grasping and manipulating, the perfection of binocular vision that can bring into focus either the hands or the far distance at will. Far more significant than these was the development of speech, made possible by and controlled in a particular small area of the new cerebral cortex. This expanded the powers of the human secondary computer by orders of magnitude, even in comparison with that of close relatives like apes.

We no longer communicate with each other by baring teeth, raising hackles and flaunting rumps, but in symbolic language. We can make abstractions and generalizations, and artificial associations. Through speech we can feed into the recording apparatus of each others' secondary computers not only the vast and rather accidental store of individually acquired and long-lasting memories of our own experience, but also the loads of approval or disapproval which we deliberately or unwittingly put upon them. We increasingly remove ourselves into created worlds of our own, calculating our choices by reference to a memory bank of second-hand ghosts of other people's experiences and feelings, prettied up or uglified with value judgments picked up who knows where, by whom, for what reason.

Language gave a fourth dimension to the powers of the secondary computer, and writing a fifth dimension. We can now convince each other that things are good or bad, acceptable or intolerable, merely by agreeing with each other, or by reciting catechisms. With writing we can color the judgments of people unborn, just as our judgments are tailored to the whim of influential teachers in the past.

[2] J. M. R. Delgado, 1969, *Physical Control of the Mind.*

Symbols have given us the means to attach a value judgment to some abstract noun, some shibboleth, and transfer this by association to any person or situation at will. We invent, we practice, we delight in tricks for saying things indirectly by poetry and figures of speech, that might sound false or trite or slanderous or nonsensical if we said them directly. A more normally constructed animal, a porpoise or an elephant, mercifully spared such subtleties, might well look at human beings and see that each one of us has become to some degree insane, out of touch with the actual world, pursuing a mad course of options in the imagined interest of self rather than of species.

The primary computer is still there, programmed in the interest of species survival. With his new powers, man should do better than any other animal at understanding the present crisis and generating an appropriate strategy and tactics. Instead, the effort is drowned out in the noise, the flicker-bicker, the chattering flood of directives from the personalized secondary computer. In pursuit of his own comfort and his own pleasure, man wars against his fellows and against the good earth.

The frame of each person is like a racing shell with two oarsmen in it, back to back, rowing in opposite directions. The one represents the ancient computer system, comparing the personal situation of the moment with an inherited value system and driving the person to perform in such a way that the species will survive, irrespective of how absurd his own expendable life may be. The other represents the secondary computer system, probably located in reticular substance and cerebral cortex, surveying chiefly the memories of childhood and adult life, and deciding how to act according to the value-loaded store of personal experience.

It is this runaway evolutionary development of our superimposed second computer that has produced our inventors, our artists, our saints and heroes, our poets, our thinkers. Our love and hate, ecstasy and despair. The infinite variety of human personalities. It has also atomized the species into a cloud of ungovernable individuals. We split our elections 48 to 52, make laws to break them, and either ignore community priorities or establish them by political blind-man's-buff in frivolous disregard of real emergencies. Six experts will come violently to six different decisions on how to meet a crisis because their personal histories lead them to weigh the same data differently. Each of us can see bad logic and conflicts of interest affecting the judgment of most of our associates; it is more difficult to detect them in ourselves. Our individually acquired prejudices have been built into our secondary computers.

Yet it is a glorious thing to feel the uniqueness, the power of decision, the freedom of being human. Who would prefer to be even so wonderful a creature as a dog, an elephant, a horse, a porpoise? I believe nevertheless that just this ungovernable power of the human individual, the essence of our humanity, is the root of the trouble.

The California biologist Garrett Hardin, in a famous essay called "The Tragedy of the Commons," showed that this accounts for practically all the facets of our apocalyptic crisis, from the population explosion to runaway technology.[3] He is referring to the community pasture where anyone may feed

[3] G. Hardin, 1968, *Science* **162**: 1243. "The Tragedy of the Commons."

his animals. Overgrazing will bring erosion and irreversible deterioration in it. Each herdsman, calculating the advantage and disadvantage to himself of putting out one more animal to graze, balancing his small share of the possible damage against his sole ownership of the extra income, adds another animal in his own interest, and another, and another. All do, and all lose together. The tragedy is the inescapable disaster when each herdsman pursues his own advantage without limit, in a limited commons. This is the tragedy that leaves us with too many human mouths to feed, soil impoverished and washed or blown away, forests skinned off, lakes ruined, plastic bottles and aluminium cans scattered over the countryside, rivers clogged with dead fish, bilge oil spreading on public waters, streets and highways made obscene with advertisements. It is what gives us choking smog, the stink and corruption below paper mills and slaughter houses, the draining of one well by another in a falling water table, the sneaking of radioactive wastes into the air and the oceans.

All these, Hardin makes clear, are problems with *no technological solution.* To be sure, the technology stands ready, but the trouble starts with some individual, you, me, whose response to a situation is to give highest priority to his personal chance of profit, or his family's, or his country's. He has a vivid sense of the value to himself of his own freedom, but the total effects of all such freedoms on the species and on the natural world which supports it is invisible or far out of focus. The technology might just as well not exist.

Some of these problems that will not be solved by technology alone can indeed be brought under control by compacts, treaties, and other agreements between willing groups, or by laws imposed by the majority upon a minority in the common interest. Hardin, however, puts the finger on the population problem as the worst example of the worst class of problems, in which all of us must restrict the freedom of all of us, when none of us want to. He is properly skeptical of conscience or altruism as forces for uniting the community when nearly all of us are still daring to gamble on the continued capacity of the commons to withstand collapse. What is needed, he says, is a fundamental extension of morality.

My way of agreeing with him is to say that human nature is our chief enemy because the species-preserving function of our primary computer has not yet been built into the secondary computer which generates our human nature. It is by now clear that our nature as individuals is not so much inherited as learned by babies as they grow into people, in and from their individual, accidental, and culture-bound experiences. We need to incorporate into the decision-making apparatus that will really control them a new survival morality, a system of values the principal axiom of which is that anything which threatens the welfare of the species is bad, anything that serves to bring the species into harmony with its environment is good. We must, each of us, because of this inner drive, regulate our numbers and our selfish wants as rigorously as the forces of natural selection would have done had we not learned how to set them aside.

Do we know how to create a human nature that can keep the species going without undue sacrifice of the privilege and joy of being human? How much freedom must we give up? Do we want to? Is there time?

Basic Processes in Organisms

Lawrence K. Frank

If we are to understand the infant as a persistent, but ever changing, organism, we need to think in terms that are dynamic, which calls for a recognition of the ongoing processes by which the infant grows, develops, matures, and ages while continually functioning and behaving. As a young mammalian organism, the human infant lives by much the same basic physiological processes as other mammals.

The recognition of process has come with the acceptance of such recently formulated conceptions as that of self-organization, self-stabilization, self-repair, and self-direction which are characteristic not only of organisms but of various man-made machines such as computers and systems designed to operate a planned sequence of activities with the use of positive and negative feedbacks (Wiener 1961; Von Foerster and Zopf 1962). The organism may be said to be "programmed" by its heredity but capable of flexible functioning through the life cycle.

Moreover, it must be re-emphasized that each infant differs to a greater or lesser extent from all other infants, exhibiting not only individual variation but also displaying a considerable range of intra-individual variability, or continually changing functioning and physiological states, especially during the early months of life when the infant is not yet fully organized or capable of adequate self-stabilization.

Since most of our knowledge of infancy and childhood is derived from observations and measurements of selected variables, responses to stimuli, at a given time or a succession of times, we do not gain an adequate conception of the continuous, dynamic processes of living organisms, especially since we tend to focus upon the outcomes, without recognizing the processes which produce them. Accordingly, some account of these basic processes and how they operate may provide a conceptual model for understanding the multidimensional development of infants during the first year of life. Whatever is done to and for the infant, what privations, frustrations and deprivations he may suffer, what demands and coercions he must accept, what spontaneous activity and learning he displays, may be viewed as expressions of his basic functioning processes.

Every experience in the life of an infant evokes some alteration in these organic processes whereby he manages not only to survive but to grow and develop, to learn while carrying on his incessant intercourse with the surrounding world. Thus, by focusing on the organic processes we may discover what is taking place when we speak of adjustment, learning, adaptation, and the transitions encountered at critical stages in his development.

The concept of mechanism indicates or implies a deterministic relationship between antecedent and consequent, usually as a *linear* relationship in which the consequent is proportional to the antecedent. The concept of *process* involves a dynamic, *non-linear* operation, whereby the same process, depending upon where, what, how, and in what quantities or intensities it operates, may produce different products which may be all out of proportion to that which initiates or touches off the process. For example the process of fertilization and gestation operates in all mammals to produce the immense variety of mammalian young. But different processes may produce similar or equivalent products, an operation which has been called "equifinality" by Bertalanffy (1950).

A brief discussion of the six basic processes operating in organisms will indicate how the infant organism is able to persist and survive by continually changing and is thereby able to cope with the particular version of infant care and rearing to which he is subjected.

These six processes are: The Growth Process, The Organizing Process, The Communicating Process, The Stabilizing Process, The Directive or Purposive Process, and The Creative Process. (Frank, 1963).

THE GROWTH PROCESS   The infant who has been growing since conception continues, with a brief interruption and often some loss of weight, to grow incrementally, adding gradually to his size and weight. His growth may be slowed down by inadequate or inappropriate feeding, by some difficulties in digesting and assimilating whatever foodstuff he be given, or by a variety of disturbances and dysfunctions. A continuing upward trend in weight is expected as an expression of normal development, although recent cautions have been expressed on the undesirability of too rapid increase in weight and the vulnerability of a fat, waterlogged infant.

This incremental growth in size and weight indicates that the infant is maintaining an excess of growth over the daily losses through elimination of urine and feces, through skin and lungs, and also in the replacement of many cells that are discarded. Thus, millions of blood corpuscles are destroyed and replaced each day, the iron of those destroyed being salvaged and reused. Likewise, cells of the skin and lining of the gastrointestinal tract, of the lungs, kidneys, liver, indeed of almost all organ systems, except the central nervous system and brain, are continually being replaced at different rates.

Probably more vitally significant but less clearly recognized is the continual replacement of the chemical constituents of cells, tissues, and bony structures, like the skeleton and the teeth in which different chemicals are discarded and new materials are selected out of the blood stream to replace them. Here we see a dramatic illustration of the statement that an organism is a configuration which must continually change in order to survive, a conception which is wholly congruous with the recently formulated assumption of the world as an aggregate of highly organized complexes of energy transformations.

Growth, incremental and replacement, is a major functioning process, gradually producing an enlarging infant as the growing cells differentiate, specialize and organize to give rise to the varied tissues and organ systems in the developing embryo and fetus. In this prenatal development the creative process is also operating to produce the unique, unduplicated human infant along with the operation of the organizing process.

THE ORGANIZING PROCESS   Only recently has the process of self-organization been recognized in scientific thinking as basic to all organisms which start with some kind of genetic inheritance and undergo multiplication and duplication of cells with differentation and specialization of components that become organized into a living organism. (Von Foerster and Zopf, 1962). Thus the initial development of an infant takes place through the operation of the growth and the organizing processes which continue to operate throughout its life, maintaining the organism as it undergoes various transitions and transformations and copes with the many discontinuities encountered in its life cycle.

Since the normal infant arrives fully equipped with all the essential bodily components and organ systems, the growth process and the organizing process operate to incorporate the intakes of food, water, and air into its ever changing structure-functioning. Most of the highly organized foodstuffs, proteins, fats, and carbohydrates, are progressively broken down, disorganized, and random-ized, and the products of these digestive operations are then circulated through the blood stream from which the constituent cells, tissues, and fluids select out what they need for metabolism and organize these into their specialized structure-functioning components. The recent dramatic findings in molecular biology show how this organizing process operates within the cell as the DNA (the carrier of the genetic information) of the genes directs the production of the various proteins and the utilization of the minerals and vitamins for the growth and multiplication of cells and the maintenance of their functioning.

Also of large significance for the understanding of organic processes are the sequential steps in the utilization of food stuffs for metabolism involving many steps and numerous specialized enzymes and catalysts. Unfortunately some infants suffer from so-called metabolic errors when one or more of these steps in the metabolic sequence is missing or inadequate and therefore his growth and development and healthy functioning are jeopardized.

In the self-organizing organism we encounter circular and reciprocal operations in which every component of the organism by its specialized function-ing, gives rise to, and maintains, the total organism of which it is a participant; concurrently, the total organism reciprocally governs when, what, and how each of these components must function and operate to maintain the organized whole. This capacity for self-organizing arises from the autonomy of each component of an organism which over millions of years of evolution has developed its own highly individualized and specialized functioning within the total organic complex but functions according to the requirements of the organ-ism in which it operates.

COMMUNICATION PROCESS   Obviously, these autonomous components which give rise to growth and organization must continually communicate, internally and with the external "surround." The infant has an inherited communication network in his nervous system, his circulatory system, and his lymphatic system. Through these several channels every constituent of an organism continually communicates with all others, directly or indirectly, and with different degrees of speed in communication. Each component continually sends and receives messages whereby its functioning operations are regulated, synchronized, articulated, and related to all others, with greater or less immediacy. The infant is born with most of these internal communications already functioning, having been in operation for varying periods of its prenatal development but with the central nervous system still immature. The infant also has the sensory apparatus for various inputs, of light, of sound, touch, taste and smell, also for pain, heat and cold, and for gravity and for atmospheric pressure changes. But the infant is also initially prepared for dealing with the varying intensities and durations of these intakes and impacts, gradually increasing his capacity for filtering, buffering, mingling, and transducing these inputs whereby he may monitor these sensory communications according to his ever changing internal, physiological states and the kinesthetic and proprioceptive messages by which he continually orients himself and gradually achieves an equilibrium in space.

The infant must carry on this incessant intercourse with the world more or less protected by adults from too severe or hazardous impacts and provided with the food and care required by his helpless dependency. But the infant often must try to defend himself from what his caretakers try to impose on him or compel him to accept, as in feeding, toilet training, etc. Under this treatment much of the infant's energies may be expended in these efforts to maintain his stability and integrity against unwelcomed and uncongenial treatment which may interfere with his normal functioning and compromise his growth and development and learning as a unique organism. Thus we may say that the growth and organizing processes contribute to and are dependent upon the communication process, which operates through the inherited receptors of the infant which may become progressively altered, refined, and increasingly sensitized through learning. Quite early the infant may become receptive to nonverbal communications such as tones of voice, smiling, tactile comforting, or painful treatment.

STABILIZING PROCESS   Since the world presents so many different and continually varying messages and impacts, organisms must be able to cope with the ever changing flux of experience and maintain their integrity and functional capacities by monitoring all their organic functions. While all other organisms have evolved with their species-specific range of sensory awareness and capacity for perception and for living in their ancestral life zones, the human infant, and a few other mammals are able to live in a wide variety of climates and habitations and maintain their internal world within fairly close limitations upon intraorganic variability. This becomes possible through the operation of the stabilizing process.

The stabilizing process operates through a network of physiological feedbacks, both negative and positive, to maintain a dynamic equilibrium and is not limited to the concept of homeostasis which Cannon used to describe the maintenance of the fluid internal environment. The stabilizing process maintains continually changing physiological states. At birth it is not fully developed or operationally effective and hence the infant needs continual care, protection, and appropriate nutrition. But as he grows and develops he increasingly regulates his internal functioning by responding appropriately to the various inputs and outputs, intakes, and outlets. Obviously an infant who must grow, both incrementally and by replacement, cannot tolerate too stable an internal environment which might prevent or limit such growth and adaptive functioning. With his increasing exposure to the world the infant learns to calibrate all his sensory inputs and increasingly to "equalize his thresholds," as Kurt Goldstein (1939) has pointed out.

Not the least significant and often stressful experience under which an infant must maintain his internal stability are the varying practices of child care and feeding, the efforts of parents to regularize his functioning and compel him to conform to whatever regimen of living they wish to establish. Clearly the stabilizing process is essential to the infant's survival and to his continuing growth and development and the variety of learning which he must master. Happily, most infants achieve a progressive enlargement of their capacity for living and for self-regulation and self-stabilization to assume an autonomy expressing their integrity in the face of often uncongenial treatment and surroundings.

THE DIRECTIVE OR PURPOSIVE PROCESS   With the achievement of motor coordination and locomotion, by creeping and crawling, and then assuming an erect posture and learning to walk, the infant enlarges the purposive or goal seeking process which involves continual scanning, probing, and exploring the world and developing his selective awareness and patterned perception, and especially the ability to ignore or to reject what may interfere or distract him in his endeavour to attain remote or deferred goals. Obviously, the purposive process cannot operate effectively until the infant has achieved a considerable degree of internal stabilization and of neuro-muscular coordination, and the ability to cope with a three dimensional, spatial world.

Since the child initially is attracted or impelled by whatever he may become aware of or has an impulse to seek, to handle, to put into his mouth, or otherwise to manipulate, the purposive process is frequently blocked and the child may be severely punished in his attempts to develop his autonomous mastery of his small world. Thus the purposive process operates differentially in each infant who is likely to be attracted by and responsive to different dimensions of his environment at different times; these early explorations provide an endless sequence of learning experiences which involve, not only the actual world of nature, but the wide range of artifacts and of highly individuated personalities with whom he is in contact. With language the infant learns to deal with people and verbal symbols of language for goal seeking.

THE CREATIVE PROCESS   As noted earlier, the creative process begins to operate early in gestation to produce a unique infant as a human organism with the same basic organic functions and similar or equivalent components which, however, are different in each infant. From birth on, therefore, each infant is engaged in creating a highly selective environment or a "life space" that is as congenial and appropriate for his individualized organism, with its peculiar needs and capacities, as is possible under the constraints and coercions imposed by others upon his growth, development, functioning, and learning. In infancy and childhood the individual is more creative than in any other period in his life cycle, but this creativity may be either ignored or discouraged by those who are intent upon making the child conform as nearly as possible to their image or ideal of attainment.

Within recent years the purposive and creative processes have become major foci in the studies of early child growth, development, and education, but it must be remembered that the purposive and creative processes cannot operate independently because they are inextricably related to and dependent upon the other four basic processes which reciprocally contribute to the operation of these two processes.

Most of the training and education of the infant and young child involves curbing, regulating, focusing, and patterning, and also evoking the communicating and stabilizing and directive processes which are more amenable to intervention and control by others. Through supervision and regulation of these processes the child is largely molded, patterned, and oriented into the kind of organism-personality favored by his parents and appropriately prepared for living in his cultural and social order. As he grows older the infant is expected to learn the required conduct for group living and to master the various symbol systems by which he can relate cognitively to the world and negotiate with other people. It appears that learning as an expression of the purposive and the creative processes may be compromised and sometimes severely distorted or blocked when the child is expected or compelled to alter the organizing, communicating, and stabilizing processes, as required by his parents and other more experienced persons.

In the discussion of humanization we will see how the young mammalian organism is transformed into a personality for living in a symbolic cultural world and for participating in a social order, through the various practices of infant care and rearing that are focused upon, and directly intervene in, the operation of these six basic organic processes. But each infant is a highly individualized organism who develops his own idiosyncratic personality through the development and utilization of his basic organic processes.

References

BERTALANFFY, L. VON, "Theory of Open Systems in Physics and Biology," *Science*, CXI, 1950, pp. 27–29. See also Yearbooks of Society for General Systems Research.

FRANK, L. K., "Human Development—An Emerging Discipline," in *Modern Perspectives in Child Development*, In honor of Milton J. E. Senn, Eds. Albert J. Solnit and Sally Provence, New York: International Universities Press, 1963.

———. "Potentiality: Its Definition and Development," in *Insights and the Curriculum*, Yearbook, Association for Supervision and Curriculum Development, Washington, D.C.: National Education Association, 1963.

GOLDSTEIN, KURT, *The Organism*, New York: American Book Company, 1939.

VON FOERSTER, HEINZ, and ZOPF, JR., GEORGE W., Eds., *Principles of Self Organizing Systems*, London: Pergamon Press, 1962.

WIENER, NORBERT, *Cybernetics*, Cambridge and New York: M.I.T. Press and John Wiley and Sons, Inc., 1961.

The Life Cycle : Epigenesis of Identity

Erik H. Erikson
HARVARD UNIVERSITY

Whenever we try to understand growth, it is well to remember the *epigenetic principle* which is derived from the growth of organisms *in utero*. Somewhat generalized, this principle states that anything that grows has a ground plan, and that out of this ground plan, the parts arise, each part having its time of special ascendancy, until all parts have arisen to form a functioning whole. This, obviously, is true for fetal development where each part of the organism has its critical time of ascendance or danger of defect. At birth the baby leaves the chemical exchange of the womb for the social exchange system of his society, where his gradually increasing capacities meet the opportunities and limitations of his culture. How the maturing organism continues to unfold, not by developing new organs but by means of a prescribed sequence of locomotor, sensory, and social capacities, is described in the child-development literature. As pointed out, psychoanalysis has given us an understanding of the more idiosyncratic experiences, and especially the inner conflicts, which constitute the manner in which an individual becomes a distinct personality. But here, too, it is important to realize that in the sequence of his most personal experiences the healthy child, given a reasonable amount of proper guidance, can be trusted to obey inner laws of development, laws which create a succession of potentialities for significant interaction with those persons who tend and respond to him and those institutions which are ready for him. While such interaction varies from culture to culture, it must remain within "the proper rate and the proper sequence" which governs all epigenesis. Personality, therefore, can be said to develop according to steps predetermined in the human organism's readiness to be driven toward, to be aware of, and to interact with a widening radius of significant individuals and institutions.

It is for this reason that, in the presentation of stages in the development of the personality, we employ an epigenetic diagram analogous to the one employed in *Childhood and Society* for an analysis of Freud's psychosexual stages.[1] It is, in fact, an implicit purpose of this presentation to bridge the theory of infantile sexuality (without repeating it here in detail) and our knowledge of the child's physical and social growth.

In Diagram 1 the double-lined squares signify both a sequence of stages and a gradual development of component parts. In other words, the diagram formalizes a progression through time of a differentiation of parts. This indicates (1) that each item of the vital personality to be discussed is systematically related to all others, and that they all depend on the proper development in

From *Identity, Youth and Crisis*, Copyright © 1968 by W. W. Norton & Company, Inc., pp. 92–96. Reprinted by permission of W. W. Norton & Company and Faber and Faber Ltd.

[1] See Erik H. Erikson, *Childhood and Society*, 2nd ed., New York: W. W. Norton & Company, Inc., 1963, Part I.

282

DIAGRAM 1

	1	2	3	4	5	6	7	8
VIII								INTEGRITY vs. DESPAIR
VII							GENERATIVITY vs. STAGNATION	
VI						INTIMACY vs. ISOLATION		
V	Temporal Perspective vs. Time Confusion	Self-Certainty vs. Self-Consciousness	Role Experimentation vs. Role Fixation	Apprenticeship vs. Work Paralysis	IDENTITY vs. IDENTITY CONFUSION	Sexual Polarization vs. Bisexual Confusion	Leader- and Followership vs. Authority Confusion	Ideological Commitment vs. Confusion of Values
IV				INDUSTRY vs. INFERIORITY	Task Identification vs. Sense of Futility			
III			INITIATIVE vs. GUILT		Anticipation of Roles vs. Role Inhibition			
II		AUTONOMY vs. SHAME, DOUBT			Will to Be Oneself vs. Self-Doubt			
I	TRUST vs. MISTRUST				Mutual Recognition vs. Autistic Isolation			

the proper sequence of each item; and (2) that each item exists in some form before "its" decisive and critical time normally arrives.

If I say, for example, that a sense of basic trust is the first component of mental vitality to develop in life, a sense of autonomous will the second, and a sense of initiative the third, the diagram expresses a number of fundamental relations that exist among the three components, as well as a few fundamental facts for each.

Each comes to ascendance, meets its crisis, and finds its lasting solution in ways to be described here, toward the end of the stages mentioned. All of them exist in the beginning in some form, although we do not make a point of this fact, and we shall not confuse things by calling these components different names at earlier or later stages. A baby may show something like "autonomy" from the beginning, for example, in the particular way in which he angrily tries to wriggle his hand free when tightly held. However, under normal conditions, it is not until the second year that he begins to experience the whole critical alternative between being an autonomous creature and being a dependent one, and it is not until then that he is ready for a specifically new encounter with his environment. The environment, in turn, now feels called upon to convey to him its particular ideas and concepts of autonomy in ways decisively contributing to his personal character, his relative efficiency, and the strength of his vitality.

It is this encounter, together with the resulting crisis, which is to be described for each stage. Each stage becomes a crisis because incipient growth and awareness in a new part function go together with a shift in instinctual energy and yet also cause a specific vulnerability in that part. One of the most difficult questions to decide, therefore, is whether or not a child at a given stage is weak or strong. Perhaps it would be best to say that he is always vulnerable in some respects and completely oblivious and insensitive in others, but that at the same time he is unbelievably persistent in the same respects in which he is vulnerable. It must be added that the baby's weakness gives him power; out of his very dependence and weakness he makes signs to which his environment, if it is guided well by a responsiveness combining "instinctive" and traditional patterns, is peculiarly sensitive. A baby's presence exerts a consistent and persistent domination over the outer and inner lives of every member of a household. Because these members must reorient themselves to accommodate his presence, they must also grow as individuals and as a group. It is as true to say that babies control and bring up their families as it is to say the converse. A family can bring up a baby only by being brought up by him. His growth consists of a series of challenges to them to serve his newly developing potentialities for social interaction.

Each successive step, then, is a potential crisis because of a radical change in perspective. Crisis is used here in a developmental sense to connote not a threat of catastrophe, but a turning point, a crucial period of increased vulnerability and heightened potential, and therefore, the ontogenetic source of generational strength and maladjustment. The most radical change of all, from intrauterine to extrauterine life, comes at the very beginning of life. But in postnatal existence, too, such radical adjustments of perspective as lying relaxed, sitting firmly, and running fast must all be accomplished in their own good time.

With them, the interpersonal perspective also changes rapidly and often radically, as is testified by the proximity in time of such opposites as "not letting mother out of sight" and "wanting to be independent." Thus, different capacities use different opportunities to become full-grown components of the ever-new configuration that is the growing personality.

Equilibrium

Jean Piaget
UNIVERSITY OF GENEVA

The psychological development that starts at birth and terminates in adulthood is comparable to organic growth. Like the latter, it consists essentially of activity directed toward equilibrium. Just as the body evolves toward a relatively stable level characterized by the completion of the growth process and by organ maturity, so mental life can be conceived as evolving toward a final form of equilibrium represented by the adult mind. In a sense, development is a progressive equilibration from a lesser to a higher state of equilibrium. From the point of view of intelligence, it is easy to contrast the relative instability and incoherence of childhood ideas with the systematization of adult reason. With respect to the affective life, it has frequently been noted how extensively emotional equilibrium increases with age. Social relations also obey the same law of gradual stabilization.

An essential difference between the life of the body and that of the mind must nonetheless be stressed if the dynamism inherent in the reality of the mind is to be respected. The final form of equilibrium reached through organic growth is more static and, above all, more unstable than the equilibrium toward which mental development strives, so that no sooner has ascending evolution terminated than a regressive evolution automatically starts, leading to old age. Certain psychological functions that depend closely on the physical condition of the body follow an analogous curve. Visual acuity, for example, is at a maximum toward the end of childhood, only to diminish subsequently; and many other perceptual processes are regulated by the same law. By contrast, the higher functions of intelligence and affectivity tend toward a "mobile equilibrium." The more mobile it is, the more stable it is, so that the termination of growth, in healthy minds, by no means marks the beginning of decline but rather permits progress that in no sense contradicts inner equilibrium.

It is thus in terms of equilibrium that we shall try to describe the evolution of the child and the adolescent. From this point of view, mental development is a continuous construction comparable to the erection of a vast building that becomes more solid with each addition. Alternatively, and perhaps more appropriately, it may be likened to the assembly of a subtle mechanism that goes through gradual phases of adjustment in which the individual pieces become more supple and mobile as the equilibrium of the mechanism as a whole becomes more stable. We must, however, introduce an important distinction between two complementary aspects of the process of equilibration. This is the distinction between the variable structures that define the successive states of equilibrium and a certain constant functioning that assures the transition from any one state to the following one.

There is sometimes a striking similarity between the reactions of the child and the adult, as, for example, when the child is sure of what he wants and acts as adults do with respect to their own special interests. At other times there is a world of difference—in games, for example, or in the manner of reasoning. From a functional point of view, i.e., if we take into consideration the general motives of behavior and thought, there are constant functions common to all ages. At all levels of development, action presupposes a precipitating factor: a physiological, affective, or intellectual need. (In the latter case, the need appears in the guise of a question or a problem.) At all levels, intelligence seeks to understand or explain, etc. However, while the functions of interest, explanation, etc., are common to all developmental stages, that is to say, are "invariable" as far as the functions themselves are concerned, it is nonetheless true that "interests" (as opposed to "interest") vary considerably from one mental level to another, and that the particular explanations (as opposed to the function of explaining) are of a very different nature, depending on the degree of intellectual development. In addition to the constant functions, there are the variable structures. An analysis of these progressive forms of successive equilibrium highlights the differences from one behavioral level to another, all the way from the elementary behavior of the neonate through adolescence.

The variable structures—motor or intellectual on the one hand and affective on the other—are the organizational forms of mental activity. They are organized along two dimensions—intrapersonal and social (interpersonal). For greater clarity we shall distinguish six stages or periods of development which mark the appearance of these successively constructed structures:

1. The reflex or hereditary stage, at which the first instinctual nutritional drives and the first emotions appear.

2. The stage of the first motor habits and of the first organized percepts, as well as of the first differentiated emotions.

3. The stage of sensorimotor or practical intelligence (prior to language), of elementary affective organization, and of the first external affective fixations. These first three stages constitute the infancy period—from birth till the age of one and a half to two years—i.e., the period prior to the development of language and thought as such.

4. The stage of intuitive intelligence, of spontaneous interpersonal feelings, and of social relationships in which the child is subordinate to the adult (ages two to seven years, or "early childhood").

5. The stage of concrete intellectual operations (the beginning of logic) and of moral and social feelings of cooperation (ages seven to eleven or twelve, or "middle childhood").

6. The stage of abstract intellectual operations, of the formation of the personality, and of affective and intellectual entry into the society of adults (adolescence).

Each of these stages is characterized by the appearance of original structures whose construction distinguishes it from previous stages. The essentials of these successive constructions exist at subsequent stages in the form of substructures onto which new characteristics have been built. It follows that in the adult each stage through which he has passed corresponds to a given level in the total hierarchy of behavior. But at each stage there are also temporary and secondary characteristics that are modified by subsequent development as a function of the need for better organization. Each stage thus constitutes a particular form of equilibrium as a function of its characteristic structures, and mental evolution is effectuated in the direction of an ever-increasing equilibrium.

We know which functional mechanisms are common to all stages. In an absolutely general way (not only in comparing one stage with the following but also in comparing each item of behavior that is part of that stage with ensuing behavior), one can say that all action—that is to say, all movement, all thought, or all emotion—responds to a need. Neither the child nor the adult executes any external or even entirely internal act unless impelled by a motive; this motive can always be translated into a need (an elementary need, an interest, a question, etc.).

As Claparède (1951) has shown, a need is always a manifestation of disequilibrium: there is need when something either outside ourselves or within us (physically or mentally) is changed and behavior has to be adjusted as a function of this change. For example, hunger or fatigue will provoke a search for nourishment or rest; encountering an external object will lead to a need to play, which in turn has practical ends, or it leads to a question or a theoretical problem. A casual word will excite the need to imitate, to sympathize, or will engender reserve or opposition if it conflicts with some interest of our own. Conversely, action terminates when a need is satisfied, that is to say, when equilibrium is re-established between the new factor that has provoked the need and the mental organization that existed prior to the introduction of this factor. Eating or sleeping, playing or reaching a goal, replying to a question or resolving a problem, imitating successfully, establishing an affective tie, or maintaining one's point of view are all satisfactions that, in the preceding examples, will put an end to the particular behavior aroused by the need. At any given moment, one can thus say, action is disequilibrated by the transformations that arise in the external or internal world, and each new behavior consists not only in re-establishing equilibrium but also in moving toward a more stable equilibrium than that which preceded the disturbance.

Human action consists of a continuous and perpetual mechanism of readjustment or equilibration. For this reason, in these initial phases of construction, the successive mental structures that engender development can be considered as so many progressive forms of equilibrium, each of which is an advance upon its predecessor. It must be understood, however, that this functional mechanism, general though it may be, does not explain the content or the structure of the various needs, since each of them is related to the organization of the particular stage that is being considered. For example, the sight of the same object will occasion very different questions in the small child who is still incapable of classification from those of the older child whose ideas are more extensive and systematic. The interests of a child at any given moment depend on the system of ideas he has acquired plus his affective inclinations, and he tends to fulfill his interests in the direction of greater equilibrium.

Before examining the details of development we must try to find that which is common to the needs and interests present at all ages. One can say, in regard to this, that all needs tend first of all to incorporate things and people into the subject's own activity, i.e., to "assimilate" the external world into the structures that have already been constructed, and secondly to readjust these structures as a function of subtle transformations, i.e., to "accommodate" them to external objects. From this point of view, all mental life, as indeed all organic life, tends progressively to assimilate the surrounding environment. This incorporation is effected thanks to the structures of psychic organs whose scope of action becomes more and more extended. Initially, perception and elementary movement (prehension, etc.) are concerned with objects that are close and viewed statically; then later, memory and practical intelligence permit the representation of earlier states of the object as well as the anticipation of their future states resulting from as yet unrealized transformations. Still later intuitive thought reinforces these two abilities. Logical intelligence in the guise of concrete operations and ultimately of abstract deduction terminates this evolution by making the subject master of events that are far distant in space and time. At each of these levels the mind fulfills the same function, which is to incorporate the universe to itself, but the nature of assimilation varies, i.e., the successive modes of incorporation evolve from those of perception and movement to those of the higher mental operations.

In assimilating objects, action and thought must accommodate to these objects; they must adjust to external variation. The balancing of the processes of assimilation and accommodation may be called "adaptation." Such is the general form of psychological equilibrium, and the progressive organization of mental development appears to be simply an ever more precise adaptation to reality.

Reference

CLAPARÈDE, E. *Le développement mental*. Neuchâtel: Delachaux et Niestlé, 1951.

Appendix A
Recommended Daily Nutrients

1. For Canadians

						Water-Soluble Vitamins						
Age (years)	Sex	Weight (kg)	Height (cm)	Energy[a] (kcal)	Protein (g)	Thiamin (mg)	Niacin[e] (mg)	Riboflavin (mg)	Vitamin B$_6$[f] (mg)	Folate[g] (μg)	Vitamin B$_{12}$ (μg)	Ascorbic Acid (mg)
0–6 mos.	Both	6	—	kg × 117	kg × 2.2 (2.0)[d]	0.3	5	0.4	0.3	40	0.3	20[h]
7–11 mos.	Both	9	—	kg × 108	kg × 1.4	0.5	6	0.6	0.4	60	0.3	20
1–3	Both	13	90	1400	22	0.7	9	0.8	0.8	100	0.9	20
4–6	Both	19	110	1800	27	0.9	12	1.1	1.3	100	1.5	20
7–9	M	27	129	2200	33	1.1	14	1.3	1.6	100	1.5	30
	F	27	128	2000	33	1.0	13	1.2	1.4	100	1.5	30
10–12	M	36	144	2500	41	1.2	17	1.5	1.8	100	3.0	30
	F	38	145	2300	40	1.1	15	1.4	1.5	100	3.0	30
13–15	M	51	162	2800	52	1.4	19	1.7	2.0	200	3.0	30
	F	49	159	2200	43	1.1	15	1.4	1.5	200	3.0	30
16–18	M	64	172	3200	54	1.6	21	2.0	2.0	200	3.0	30
	F	54	161	2100	43	1.1	14	1.3	1.5	200	3.0	30
19–35	M	70	176	3000	56	1.5	20	1.8	2.0	200	3.0	30
	F	56	161	2100	41	1.1	14	1.3	1.5	200	3.0	30
36–50	M	70	176	2700	56	1.4	18	1.7	2.0	200	3.0	30
	F	56	161	1900	41	1.0	13	1.2	1.5	200	3.0	30
51	M	70	176	2300[b]	56	1.4	18	1.7	2.0	200	3.0	30
	F	56	161	1800[b]	41	1.0	13	1.2	1.5	200	3.0	30
Pregnant				+300[c]	+20	+0.2	+2	+0.3	+0.5	+50	+1.0	+20
Lactating				+500	+24	+0.4	+7	+0.6	+0.6	+50	+0.5	+30

[a] Recommendations assume characteristic activity pattern for each age group.
[b] Recommended energy allowance for age 66½ years reduced to 2,000 for men and 1,500 for women.
[c] Increased energy allowance recommended during second and third trimesters. An increase of 100 kcal per day is recommended during the first trimester.
[d] Recommended protein allowance of 2.2 g per kg body weight for infants age 0–2 mos. and 2.0 g per kg body weight for those age 3–5 mos. Protein recommendation for infants, 0–11 mos., assumes consumption of breast milk or protein of equivalent quality.
[e] Approximately 1 mg of niacin is derived from each 60 mg of dietary tryptophan.
[f] Recommendations are based on the estimated average daily protein intake of Canadians.
[g] Recommendation given in terms of free folate.

		Fat-Soluble Vitamins			Minerals					
Age (years)	Sex	Vitamin A (µg RE)[i]	Vitamin D (µg cholcalciferol)[j]	Vitamin E (mg α-tocopherol)	Calcium (mg)	Phosphorus (mg)	Magnesium (mg)	Iodine (µg)	Iron (mg)	Zinc (mg)
0–6 mos.	Both	400	10	3	500[l]	250[l]	50[l]	35[l]	7[l]	4[l]
7–11 mos.	Both	400	10	3	500	400	50	50	7	5
1–3	Both	400	10	4	500	500	75	70	8	5
4–6	Both	500	5	5	500	500	100	90	9	6
7–9	M	700	2.5[k]	6	700	700	150	110	10	7
	F	700	2.5[k]	6	700	700	150	100	10	7
10–12	M	800	2.5[k]	7	900	900	175	130	11	8
	F	800	2.5[k]	7	1000	1000	200	120	11	9
13–15	M	1000	2.5[k]	9	1200	1200	250	140	13	10
	F	800	2.5[k]	7	800	800	250	110	14	10
16–18	M	1000	2.5[k]	10	1000	1000	300	160	14	12
	F	800	2.5[k]	6	700	700	250	110	14	11
19–35	M	1000	2.5[k]	9	800	800	300	150	10	10
	F	800	2.5[k]	6	700	700	250	110	14	9
36–50	M	1000	2.5[k]	8	800	800	300	140	10	10
	F	800	2.5[k]	6	700	700	250	100	14	9
51	M	1000	2.5[k]	8	800	800	300	140	10	10
	F	800	2.5[k]	6	700	700	250	100	9	9
Pregnant		+100	+2.5[k]	+1	+500	+500	+25	+15	+1[m]	+3
Lactating		+400	+2.5[k]	+2	+500	+500	+75	+25	+1[m]	+7

[h] Considerably higher levels may be prudent for infants during the first week of life to guard against neonatal tyrosinemia.

[i] One µg retinol equivalent (1 µg RE) corresponds to a biological activity in humans equal to 1 µg retinol (3.33 IU) and 6 µg β-carotene (10 IU).

[j] One µg cholecalciferol is equivalent to 40 IU vitamin D activity.

[k] Most older children and adults receive enough vitamin D from irradiation but 2.5 µg daily is recommended. This recommended allowance increases to 5.0 µg daily for pregnant and lactating women and for those who are confined indoors or otherwise deprived of sunlight for extended periods.

[l] The intake of breast-fed infants may be less than the recommendation but is considered to be adequate.

[m] A recommended total intake of 15 mg daily during pregnancy and lactation assumes the presence of adequate stores of iron. If stores are suspected of being inadequate, additional iron as a supplement is recommended.

SOURCE: Committee for Revision of the Canadian Dietary Standard. Recommended daily nutrients. Bureau of Nutritional Sciences, Health and Welfare, Canada, 1974.

2. For Americans[a]

	Age (years)	Weight (kg)	Weight (lbs)	Height (cm)	Height (in)	Energy (kcal)[b]	Protein (g)	Fat-Soluble Vitamins Vitamin A Activity (RE)[c]	Fat-Soluble Vitamins Vitamin A Activity (IU)	Fat-Soluble Vitamins Vitamin D (IU)	Fat-Soluble Vitamins Vitamin E Activity[e] (IU)
Infants	0.0–0.5	6	14	60	24	kg × 117	kg × 2.2	420[d]	1,400	400	4
	0.5–1.0	9	20	71	28	kg × 108	kg × 2.0	400	2,000	400	5
Children	1–3	13	28	86	34	1,300	23	400	2,000	400	7
	4–6	20	44	110	44	1,800	30	500	2,500	400	9
	7–10	30	66	135	54	2,400	36	700	3,300	400	10
Males	11–14	44	97	158	63	2,800	44	1,000	5,000	400	12
	15–18	61	134	172	69	3,000	54	1,000	5,000	400	15
	19–22	67	147	172	69	3,000	54	1,000	5,000	400	15
	23–50	70	154	172	69	2,700	56	1,000	5,000		15
	51+	70	154	172	69	2,400	56	1,000	5,000		15
Females	11–14	44	97	155	62	2,400	44	800	4,000	400	12
	15–18	54	119	162	65	2,100	48	800	4,000	400	12
	19–22	58	128	162	65	2,100	46	800	4,000	400	12
	23–50	58	128	162	65	2,000	46	800	4,000		12
	51+	58	128	162	65	1,800	46	800	4,000		12
Pregnant						+300	+30	1,000	5,000	400	15
Lactating						+500	+20	1,200	6,000	400	15

[a] The allowances are intended to provide for individual variations among most normal persons as they live in the United States under usual environmental stresses. Diets should be based on a variety of common foods in order to provide other nutrients for which human requirements have been less well defined.

[b] Kilojoules (kJ) = 4.2 × kcal.

[c] Retinol equivalents.

[d] Assumed to be all as retinol in milk during the first six months of life. All subsequent intakes are assumed to be half as retinol and half as β-carotene when calculated from international units. As retinol equivalents, three fourths are as retinol and one fourth as β-carotene.

		Water-Soluble Vitamins							Minerals						
	Age (years)	Ascorbic Acid (mg)	Folacin[f] (µg)	Niacin[g] (mg)	Riboflavin (mg)	Thiamin (mg)	Vitamin B$_6$ (mg)	Vitamin B$_{12}$ (µg)	Calcium (mg)	Phosphorus (mg)	Iodine (µg)	Iron (mg)	Magnesium (mg)	Zinc (mg)
Infants	0.0–0.5	35	50	5	0.4	0.3	0.3	0.3	360	240	35	10	60	3
	0.5–1.0	35	50	8	0.6	0.5	0.4	0.3	540	400	45	15	70	5
Children	1–3	40	100	9	0.8	0.7	0.6	1.0	800	800	60	15	150	10
	4–6	40	200	12	1.1	0.9	0.9	1.5	800	800	80	10	200	10
	7–10	40	300	16	1.2	1.2	1.2	2.0	800	800	110	10	250	10
Males	11–14	45	400	18	1.5	1.4	1.6	3.0	1,200	1,200	130	18	350	15
	15–18	45	400	20	1.8	1.5	2.0	3.0	1,200	1,200	150	18	400	15
	19–22	45	400	20	1.8	1.5	2.0	3.0	800	800	140	10	350	15
	23–50	45	400	18	1.6	1.4	2.0	3.0	800	800	130	10	350	15
	51+	45	400	16	1.5	1.2	2.0	3.0	800	800	110	10	350	15
Females	11–14	45	400	16	1.3	1.2	1.6	3.0	1,200	1,200	115	18	300	15
	15–18	45	400	14	1.4	1.1	2.0	3.0	1,200	1,200	115	18	300	15
	19–22	45	400	14	1.4	1.1	2.0	3.0	800	800	100	18	300	15
	23–50	45	400	13	1.2	1.0	2.0	3.0	800	800	100	18	300	15
	51+	45	400	12	1.1	1.0	2.0	3.0	800	800	80	10	300	15
Pregnant		60	800	+2	+0.3	+0.3	2.5	4.0	1,200	1,200	125	18+[h]	450	20
Lactating		80	600	+4	+0.5	+0.3	2.5	4.0	1,200	1,200	150	18	450	25

[e] Total vitamin E activity, estimated to be 80 per cent as α-tocopherol and 20 per cent other tocopherols. See text for variation in allowances.

[f] The folacin allowances refer to dietary sources as determined by *Lactobacillus casei* assay. Pure forms of folacin may be effective in doses less than one fourth of the recommended dietary allowance.

[g] Although allowances are expressed as niacin, it is recognized that on the average 1 mg of niacin is derived from each 60 mg of dietary tryptophan.

[h] This increased requirement cannot be met by ordinary diets; therefore, the use of supplemental iron is recommended.

SOURCE: Food and Nutrition Board, National Research Council. Recommended dietary allowances. Eighth rev. ed., 1974. Washington, D.C.: National Academy of Sciences, 1974.

Appendix B
Height and Weight Interpretation Charts

These charts make it possible to show graphically a child's *status* as to height and weight for any one measurement of size. If two or more measurements are made, separated by a time interval, the child's *progress* will also be shown graphically.

How to Measure Weight and Height Accurately

Use a beam-type platform scale. Weigh the child without shoes, barefoot, or in stockings, wearing minimal clothing, underwear or gym clothes. For children under 24 months, recumbent length is measured between the crown of the head and the bottom of the heel, with the back flat, the knees extended, and the soles of the feet at right angles with the ankles. For children above two, stature is measured as standing height. Without shoes, the feet should be together. Have the child stand normally erect, chin tucked in, eyes looking straight ahead. Stature is the distance between the floor and a horizontal board or bar firmly touching the crown of the head. Up to 36 months, record weight to the nearest quarter kilo (250 grams) and height to the nearest centimeter. At older ages, the nearest kilogram and the nearest centimeter are close enough.

GRAPHING HEIGHT AND WEIGHT STATUS

On the day he was measured, Carl was 7 years and 4 months old. His stature was 122 centimeters and his weight 22 kilograms. To plot his growth status, first find on the age scale of the weight graph a point one third of the way between 7 and 8 years. Imagine a line drawn vertically upward to the point where it intersects with another imaginary horizontal line drawn through a point on the weight scale at 22. Put a dot on the graph at this point. Similarly, find the imaginary vertical line at the bottom of the height scale. Put a dot at the point where that line intersects with an imaginary horizontal line through 122 centimeters. Each of these dots falls just below the 50th percentile line on the graph. These show that Carl is slightly below the average child of 7 years and 4 months, slightly lighter and slightly shorter; he is neither heavy nor light for his height.

GRAPHING HEIGHT AND WEIGHT PROGRESS

On his eighth birthday Carl weighs 25 kilograms and is 126 centimeters tall. As in the earlier measurement, put a pencil dot on the eight-year vertical line where it intersects with the imaginary line through 25 kilograms on the weight graph, and the imaginary line through 126 centimeters on the height graph. Lines connecting the two pairs of dots are roughly parallel with the printed 50th percentile lines. In the eight months between measurements Carl grew proportionately in height and weight.

EVALUATION OF WEIGHT AND HEIGHT MEASUREMENTS

If the points representing a child's height and weight are not about the same distance above or below the same percentile curve, the difference may indicate that the child is normally slender or normally stocky. If the difference between the stature and weight percentile is more than 25 percentiles, a further check on his or her health should be made.

Normal progress in height and weight gives lines for such a child that stay roughly the same distance from adjacent printed lines on the graph. When the lines go steeply up, or if one goes up and the other is nearly horizontal, a medical investigation of the child's health or nutritional condition is called for. Around the age of 11, a child's lines may cross the printed percentile lines, because there are individual differences in the timing and strength of the puberal growth spurt. A child's lines may go up more steeply for a period of time, or be more horizontal than the printed lines.

Girls' Stature and Weight by Age Percentiles: Ages 2 to 18 Years

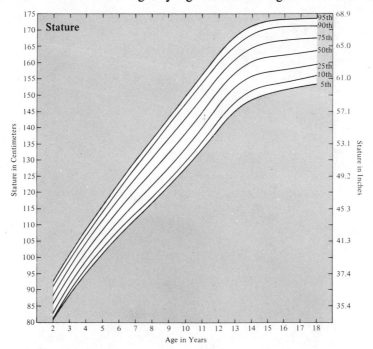

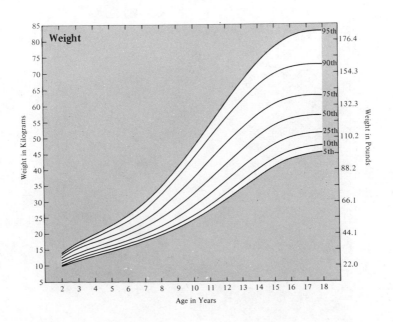

Boys' Stature and Weight by Age Percentiles: Ages 2 to 18 Years

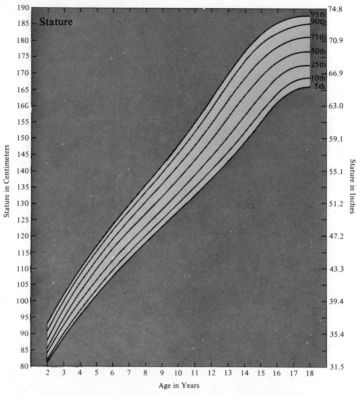

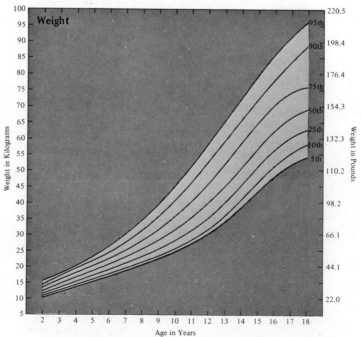

Appendix C
Communicable Diseases of Childhood

	Chickenpox	Diphtheria	Measles	Mumps	Polio
Cause	A virus: Present in secretions from nose, throat and mouth of infected people.	Diphtheria bacillus: Present in secretions from nose and throat of infected people and carriers.	A virus: Present in secretions from nose and throat of infected people.	A virus: Present in saliva of infected people.	3 strains of polio virus have been identified: Present in discharges from nose, throat, bowels of infected people.
How spread	Contact with infected people or articles used by them. Very contagious.	Contact with infected people and carriers or articles used by them.	Contact with infected people or articles used by them. Very contagious.	Contact with infected people or articles used by them.	Primarily, contact with infected people.
Incubation period (from date of exposure to first signs)	13 to 17 days. Sometimes 3 weeks.	2 to 5 days. Sometimes longer.	About 10 to 12 days.	12 to 26 (commonly 18) days.	Usually 7 to 12 days.
Period of communicability (time when disease is contagious)	From 5 days before, to 6 days after first appearance of skin blisters.	From about 2 to 4 weeks after onset of disease.	From 4 days before until about 5 days after rash appears.	From about 6 days before symptoms to 9 days after. Principally at about time swelling starts.	Apparently greatest in late incubation and first few days of illness.
Most susceptible ages	Under 15 years.	Under 15 years.	Common at any age during childhood.	Children and young people.	Most common in children 1 to 16 years.
Seasons of prevalence	Winter.	Fall, winter and spring.	Mainly spring. Also fall and winter.	Winter and spring.	June through September.
Prevention	No prevention.	Vaccination with diphtheria toxoid (in triple vaccine for babies).	Measles vaccine.	Mumps vaccine.	Polio vaccine.
Control	Exclusion from school for 1 week after eruption appears. Avoid contact with susceptibles. Immune globulin may lessen severity. (Cut child's fingernails.) Immunity usual after one attack.	Booster doses (see Appendix D). Antitoxin and antibiotics used in treatment and for protection after exposure. One attack does not necessarily give immunity.	Isolation until 7 days after appearance of rash. Immune globulin between 3 and 6 days after exposure can lighten attack. Antibiotics for complications. Immunity usual after one attack.	Isolation for 9 days from onset of swelling. Immunity usual after one attack but second attacks can occur.	Booster doses (see Appendix D). Isolation for about one week from onset. Immunity to infecting strain of virus usual after one attack.

	Rheumatic Fever	Rubella	Smallpox	Strep Infections	Tetanus	Whooping Cough
Cause	Direct cause unknown. Precipitated by a strep infection.	A virus: Present in secretions from nose and mouth of infected people.	A virus: Present in skin pocks and discharges from mouth, nose and throat of infected people. Rare in U.S.	Streptococci of several strains cause scarlet fever and strep sore throats: Present in secretions from mouth, nose and ears of infected people.	Tetanus bacillus: Present in a wound so infected.	Pertussis bacillus: Present in secretions from mouth and nose of infected people.
How spread	Unknown. But the preceding strep infection is contagious.	Contact with infected people or articles used by them. Very contagious.	Contact with infected people or articles used by them.	Contact with infected people; rarely from contaminated articles.	Through soil, contact with horses, street dust, or articles contaminated with the bacillus.	Contact with infected people and articles used by them.
Incubation period (from date of exposure to first signs)	Symptoms appear about 2 to 3 weeks after a strep infection.	14 to 21 (usually 18) days.	From 8 to 17 (usually 12) days.	1 to 3 days.	4 days to 3 weeks. Sometimes longer. Average about 10 days.	From 7 to 10 days.
Period of communicability (time when disease is contagious)	Not communicable. Preceding strep infection is communicable.	From 7 days before to 5 days after onset of rash.	From 2 to 3 days before rash, until disappearance of all pock crusts.	Greatest during acute illness (about 10 days).	Not communicable from person to person.	From onset of first symptoms to about 3rd week of the disease.
Most susceptible ages	All ages; most common from 6 to 12 years.	Young children, but also common in young adults.	All ages.	All ages.	All ages.	Under 7 years.
Seasons of prevalence	Mainly winter and spring.	Winter and spring.	Usually winter, but anytime.	Late winter and spring.	All seasons, but more common in warm weather.	Late winter and early spring.
Prevention	No prevention, except proper treatment of strep infections. (See Strep Infections.)	Rubella (German measles) vaccine.	Vaccination (no longer given routinely in U.S.).	No prevention. Antibiotic treatment for those who have had rheumatic fever.	Immunization with tetanus toxoid (in triple vaccine for babies).	Immunization with whooping cough vaccine (in triple vaccine for babies).

	Rheumatic Fever	Rubella	Smallpox	Strep Infections	Tetanus	Whooping Cough
Control	Use of antibiotics. One attack does not give immunity.	Isolation when necessary, for 5 days after onset. Immunity usual after one attack.	Vaccinia immune globulin may prevent or modify smallpox if given within 24 hours after exposure. Isolation until all pock crusts are gone. Immunity usual after one attack.	Isolation for about 1 day after start of treatment with antibiotics—used for about 10 days. One attack does not necessarily give immunity.	Booster dose of tetanus toxoid for protection given on day of injury. Antitoxin used in treatment and for temporary protection for child not immunized. One attack does not give immunity.	Booster doses (see Appendix D). Special antibiotics may help to lighten attack for child not immunized. Isolation from susceptible infants for about 3 weeks from onset or until cough stops. Immunity usual after one attack.

SOURCE: *The Control of Communicable Diseases*, American Public Health Association, 1975, and *Report of Committee on Control of Infectious Diseases*, American Academy of Pediatrics, 1974. Courtesy of Metropolitan Life.

Appendix D
Vaccination Schedule

This schedule for first vaccinations is based on recommendations of the American Medical Association and the American Academy of Pediatrics. A first test for TB (tuberculosis) may be recommended at one year. Your physician may suggest a slightly different schedule suitable for your individual child. And recommendations change from time to time as science gains new knowledge.

Disease	No. of Doses	Age for First Series	Booster
Diphtheria Tetanus Whooping Cough	4 doses	2 months 4 months 6 months 18 months	At 4 to 6 years— before entering school. As recommended by physician.
Polio (Oral vaccine)	4 doses	2 months 4 months 6 months 18 months	At 4 to 6 years— before entering school. As recommended by physician.
Rubella (German measles)	1 vaccination	After 1 year	None
Measles	1 vaccination	1 to 12 years	None
Mumps	1 vaccination	1 to 12 years	None

Courtesy of Metropolitan Life.

Author Index

Entries in *italics* refer to pages on which bibliographic references are given. Entries in **boldface** refer to selections by the authors cited.

Subject Index